Review of
Agricultural Policies in

MEXICO

ORGANISATION FOR ECONOMIC CO-OPERATION AND DEVELOPMENT

ORGANISATION FOR ECONOMIC CO-OPERATION AND DEVELOPMENT

Pursuant to Article 1 of the Convention signed in Paris on 14th December 1960, and which came into force on 30th September 1961, the Organisation for Economic Co-operation and Development (OECD) shall promote policies designed:

- to achieve the highest sustainable economic growth and employment and a rising standard of living in Member countries, while maintaining financial stability, and thus to contribute to the development of the world economy;
- to contribute to sound economic expansion in Member as well as non-member countries in the process of economic development; and
- to contribute to the expansion of world trade on a multilateral, non-discriminatory basis in accordance with international obligations.

The original Member countries of the OECD are Austria, Belgium, Canada, Denmark, France, Germany, Greece, Iceland, Ireland, Italy, Luxembourg, the Netherlands, Norway, Portugal, Spain, Sweden, Switzerland, Turkey, the United Kingdom and the United States. The following countries became Members subsequently through accession at the dates indicated hereafter: Japan (28th April 1964), Finland (28th January 1969), Australia (7th June 1971), New Zealand (29th May 1973), Mexico (18th May 1994), the Czech Republic (21st December 1995), Hungary (7th May 1996), Poland (22nd November 1996) and the Republic of Korea (12th December 1996). The Commission of the European Communities takes part in the work of the OECD (Article 13 of the OECD Convention).

Publié en français sous le titre :

EXAMEN DES POLITIQUES AGRICOLES
DU MEXIQUE

FOREWORD

This study of Mexico's agricultural policy was undertaken as part of the OECD's continuing work on Member countries' policies and agricultural trade. The Mexican study evaluates the development and the effects of policies, particularly on agricultural trade, against the principles for agricultural policy reform laid down in the OECD Ministerial Communiqué of 1987, and further developed at the meeting of Agricultural Ministers in 1992.

The study gives detailed explanations of the methods applied to calculate the Producer and Consumer Subsidy Equivalents (PSE and CSE) and the other indicators used to measure the support provided to agriculture. The quantitative analysis covers the period 1979-95. It includes an annex presenting the PSE and CSE calculations by product as well as a statistical annex presenting the background material referred to in the study. The analysis of agricultural policy developments in Mexico, in 1996, and the results of PSE/CSE calculations for 1996 are presented in the OECD publication, *Agricultural Policies in OECD Countries: Monitoring and Evaluation*, 1997.

The study was written by Gérard Bonnis and Rafael Patrón Sarti. The authors have received helpful comments from other colleagues in the Directorate for Food, Agriculture and Fisheries, in particular by Wilfrid Legg and Luis Portugal. Statistical assistance was provided by Véronique de Saint-Martin.

The Committee for Agriculture and the Trade Committee approved this Report on 21 March 1997. On 9 May 1997, the OECD Council agreed to its derestriction.

TABLE OF CONTENTS

Chapter 1

THE ECONOMIC AND AGRICULTURAL SITUATION

List of Figures

Chapter 2
AGRICULTURAL POLICIES

Chapter 3

ANALYSIS OF SUPPORT TO AGRICULTURE

Annex I. BACKGROUND TABLES

List of Tables

Annex II. ASSISTANCE TO MEXICAN AGRICULTURE

List of Figures

List of Tables

Notes to Tables

ACRONYMS

AGROASEMEX	Mexican Agricultural Insurance Company (since 1990)
ALBAMEX	Mexican Compound Feed Company (until 1993)
ALGODONERA	Mexican Commercial Cotton Trader (until 1989)
ANAGSA	National Agricultural Insurance Company (until 1992)
ANDSA	National Stores
ASERCA	Support Services for Agricultural Marketing (since 1991)
AZUCAR SA	Mexican Sugar Company (until 1994)
BANCOMEXT	National Bank for Foreign Trade (since 1937)
BANRURAL	National Rural Credit Bank (since 1975)
BANXICO	Bank of Mexico (since 1925)
BORUCONSA	CONASUPO Rural Warehouses (since 1965)
CECONC	CONASUPO Extension Centres (since 1965)
CFE	Federal Commission for Electricity
CICOPLAFEST	Commission for the Control of Processing and Use of Pesticides, Fertilisers and Toxic Substances (since 1988)
CIMMYT	International Wheat and Maize Improvement Centre
CNA	National Water Commission (since 1989)
CNG	National Livestock Confederation
CNR	National Irrigation Commission
COAAZUCAR	Sugar Industry Committee (since 1991)
COFEMEX	Mexican Coffee Council (since 1993)
CONADECA	National Cocoa Commission (until 1990)
CONAFRUT	National Fruit Commission (until 1993)
CONASUPO	National Basic Foods Company (since 1965)
CONAZA	National Commission for Arid Zones (since 1970)
DICONSA	CONASUPO Commercial Distribution and Promotion (since 1965)
DIF	National Scheme for the Integrated Development of the Family (since 1972)
DDR	Rural Development District (since 1991)
DR	Irrigation District (until 1991)
DT	Rainfed District (until 1991)
FEFA	Special Agricultural Trust Fund (since 1965)
FEGA	Technical Assistance and Loan Guarantee Trust Fund (since 1972)
FERRONALES	National Railway Company (in process of privatisation)
FERTIMEX	Mexican Fertiliser Company (until 1992)
FICART	Trust Fund for Credit in Irrigated and Rainfed Areas (until 1994)
FIDAZUCAR	Trust Fund for Sugar (until 1993)
FIDEC	Trust Fund for Commercial Development
FIDELIST	Trust Fund for the Liquidation of the Tortilla Subsidy (since 1990)
FIDELIQ	Trust Fund for the Liquidation of Auxiliary Institutions and Organisations
FIMAIA	Fund for the Creation and Development of Machinery and Equipment Centres for the Sugar Industry (until 1993)
FINA	National Sugar Finance Company (since 1943)
FIRA	Trust Fund for Agriculture (since 1954)

FIRCAVEN	Trust Fund to Restructure the Overdue Portfolio of BANRURAL
FIRCO	Trust Fund for Shared Risk (since 1981)
FMIA	Mexican Foundation for Agricultural Research
FOCIR	Rural Sector Capitalisation and Investment Fund (since 1993)
FOGAN	Livestock Fund (until 1993)
FONAES	National Solidarity Fund to Support Enterprises (since 1991)
FONDO	Trust Fund for Agriculture, Livestock and Poultry Development (since 1954)
FORMA	Trust Fund for the Organisation of the Sugar Market (since 1994)
GATT	General Agreement on Tariffs and Trade (since 1947)
IDA	Meat Processing Industry (until 1992)
ICONSA	CONASUPO Industries (until 1992)
IMPA	Institute for Sugar Cane Improvement
IMPECSA	Promotion of Retail Distribution (in process of liquidation)
IMTA	Mexican Institute of Water Technology
INCARURAL	National Institute of Training in Rural Areas (since 1981)
INDA	National Institute for Agrarian Development (since 1996)
INE	National Institute of Ecology (since 1992)
INI	National Institute for Indigenous Communities
INIFAP	National Institute for Forestry, Agricultural and Livestock Research (since 1985)
INMECAFE	Mexican Coffee Institute (until 1993)
LICONSA	CONASUPO Industrial Milk (since 1965)
MICONSA	CONASUPO Industrialised Maize (until 1992)
NAFIN	National Development Bank (since 1934)
NAFTA	North American Free Trade Agreement (since 1994)
NDP	National Development Plan (1995-2000)
OUA	Water User Association (since 1992)
PACE	Programme to Support the Marketing in Ejidos (since 1980)
PEMEX	Mexican Petroleum
PROCAMPO	Programme of Direct Payments to the Countryside (since 1994)
PROCEDE	Programme for the Certification of Ejido Property Rights (since 1993)
PROFEPA	Office of the Federal Attorney for the Protection of the Environment (since 1992)
PRONABIVE	National Company of Veterinary Products
PRONASE	National Seed Production Company (privatised in 1992)
PRONASOL	National Solidarity Programme (since 1989)
RAN	National Agrarian Registry (since 1992)
SAGAR	Secretariat of Agriculture and Rural Development (since 1995)
SARH	Secretariat of Agriculture and Water Resources (until 1994)
SECOFI	Secretariat of Commerce and Industrial Development
SEDESOL	Secretariat of Social Development (since 1992)
SEDUE	Secretariat of Urban Development and the Environment (until 1991)
SEMARNAP	Secretariat of Environment, Natural Resources and Fisheries (since 1995)
SEMIP	Secretariat of Energy, Mines and State-owned Industries (until 1995)
SESA	Ejido Services (until 1993)
SHCP	Secretariat of Finance and Public Credit
SIRECA	System for the Restructuring of Agricultural Overdue Portfolio (since 1994)
SNICS	National Seed Inspection Service
SPP	Secretariat of Budget and Planning (until 1991)
SRA	Secretariat of Agrarian Reform
TABAMEX	Mexican Tobacco Company (until 1992)
TIF	Slaughterhouse meeting Federally approved standards for inspection
TRICONSA	CONASUPO Industrialised Wheat (until 1992)

SUMMARY AND CONCLUSIONS

The opening up of the Mexican economy to international competition, deregulation and privatisation have been the most significant macroeconomic policy developments in recent years. These developments, and in particular joining NAFTA, have strongly influenced the evolution of the agricultural sector. In agricultural policy Mexico has made substantial efforts to reduce support and move away from the most distorting and consumer-financed forms of market price support and trade barriers. Mexico is moving towards more market-oriented farm income support measures, based on acreage but not directly related to output. These policy changes have been broadly in line with the principles for agricultural policy reform agreed by OECD Ministers in 1987. However, the poor provision of basic infrastructure and efficient marketing channels, and the limited development of research, training and extension services, are still major impediments to structural adjustment and economic diversification of rural areas, hampering the ability of many farmers to respond efficiently and effectively to market signals. Moreover, the variability experienced in the overall economy in Mexico has also been a constraint on agricultural structural adjustment. Mexico needs to continue on the present path of significant agricultural policy reform with better targeted agricultural policy measures to enhance agricultural sector productivity, structural adjustment, rural development, protection of the environment, and increase sustainable employment opportunities. It is essential that the progress already made in agricultural policy reform should be consolidated, within the framework of macro-economic developments and the development of an open economy. But due consideration needs to be given by policy-makers to the structural impediments in agriculture, rural development and the environment.

ECONOMIC AND DEMOGRAPHIC DEVELOPMENTS

Since the mid-1980s, the Mexican economy has been progressively opened to international markets, in sharp contrast to a long period in which economic policy was based on import substitution that Mexico pursued until the early 1980s. A greater reliance on markets, a more liberalised trading regime, privatisation of state-owned enterprises, efforts to deregulate the agro-food sector and to reduce structural impediments in the economy, have been particularly evident since the late 1980s. These developments coincided with Mexico's accession to the GATT in 1986, the entry into force of the North American Free Trade Agreement (NAFTA) in 1994, and the implementation of the GATT Uruguay Round agreement as from 1995. However, the Mexican economy has experienced a number of economic crises over the review period, and the orientation of economic policy has undergone a number of changes over time, which has impacted on the agricultural sector. The combination of domestic economic reform, trade liberalisation, and the shift to more market oriented agricultural policies, have been major forces for adjustment in the Mexican agricultural sector.

Its Gross Domestic Product (GDP) of around US$235 billion in 1995 ranks Mexico as the fourteenth largest economy in the OECD area. Economic growth in the Mexican economy during the last 15 years has roughly matched the OECD rate, averaging around 2 per cent annually, but with significant annual variations. Although there has been a structural shift in the economy, with a small decrease in the share of agriculture in the overall economy over the last 10 years, the shift appears to have been less marked than in other OECD economies.

With around 91 million people in 1995, Mexico has the third largest population among OECD countries. The growth of population in Mexico, at nearly 2 per cent annually, is about three times the growth rates experienced in the OECD as a whole, resulting in a relatively high proportion of young people in the society and in the labour force. Population growth in Mexico in recent years has added to the demand for jobs, including in rural areas, and has been a major source of labour to the economy. An important demographic characteristic has been the high rates of both permanent and seasonal migration from rural to urban areas in Mexico, and to a lesser extent to other countries, particularly the United States.

The relatively high growth rate of population, combined with a modest growth of GDP, has led to very little growth in real incomes per head during the review period. In 1995, measured GDP per head was on average around US$6 800 at purchasing power parity exchange rates. The average income is among the lowest in the OECD area, and there is great income disparity throughout the economy, especially between urban and rural areas.

Despite the rapid growth in the population of working age, measured unemployment rates in 1995 of around 6 per cent of the urban labour force are among the lowest in the OECD area, although there is some evidence of a high rate of employment in the informal economy. However, there is a relatively high level of under-employment in rural areas. Moreover, relatively slow economic growth and the average low levels of education and training, and the poor access to information have impeded the smooth functioning of the labour market.

In contrast with most other OECD countries, a notable aspect in Mexico over the last decade and a half has been the generally high rates of inflation and low rates of domestic saving (although inflation was relatively low in 1993 and 1994). Inflation was particularly severe in 1995, associated with the steep devaluation of the Mexican peso at the end of 1994, which was aggravated by the large outflow of capital and high level of foreign debt.

The developments in the overall economy, the wide disparity in incomes levels, and the large share of the population living in rural areas have been important influences on the pattern and trend in food consumption in Mexico. Overall, the share of food consumption in expenditure is relatively high compared with other OECD countries, reflecting the average low level of household incomes. Maize, wheat and beans are the main sources of food, and while there has been a long run shift towards livestock products, falling real wages have hampered this trend.

It is against this broad economic and demographic background that Mexican agriculture and its agricultural policies have evolved. In many respects the developments in the agricultural sector, and the marked shift in agricultural policies to encourage the sector to more fully respond to market signals, mirror developments in the overall economy. The importance of the agricultural sector and the rural economy means that the influence of macroeconomic developments on agriculture, and *vice versa*, are particularly significant in Mexico compared with most other OECD countries.

THE AGRICULTURAL SITUATION

Agriculture is a significant sector in the Mexican economy, in terms of output, employment and trade compared with most other OECD countries. Agriculture currently accounts for around 7 per cent of total GDP, and a quarter of total employment. It is the major activity in rural areas in terms of employment and income generation. Many of those employed in Mexican agriculture are seasonal or part time workers, complementing their agricultural incomes with work in urban areas.

The geographical position of Mexico favours the production of a great variety of commodities, ranging from temperate to tropical crops. Around two thirds of the value of agricultural output in Mexico is from crop production. Maize (principally for human consumption) is the main agricultural commodity, by value and in terms of crop area, followed by sugar, beans, wheat, and sorghum. Coffee, citrus, and other fruits and vegetables are also important. Beef and veal are the major livestock products, followed by dairy products.

Overall, the volume of agricultural output has grown on average by around 2 per cent annually since 1980, mainly achieved through increased yields, with little change in agricultural land area. The yield increases have been due to improved farming techniques and better seed varieties, benefiting from higher levels of purchased inputs, especially fertilisers, and irrigation in some areas. However, there is a very high variation in yields across Mexican farms. While yields of wheat on the larger commercially oriented farms in northern Mexico are relatively high by OECD standards (irrigation being a major factor), maize yields on the smaller farms in the rainfed areas are very low. Milk yields tend to be relatively low compared to other OECD countries.

The structure of agriculture in Mexico has been strongly influenced by the post-revolutionary system of land re-distribution. The present situation can be characterised as an agricultural structure composed of "commercial" farms, "traditional" farms (poor, but with commercial potential) and "subsistence" farms (very poor with virtually no commercial potential). The average size of farm holding is about 25 hectares overall, but a small number of large scale, commercial farm holdings, (more than 50 hectares) account for a large proportion of agricultural output, while a large number of small scale farm holdings produce only enough for own consumption. Some farm households even need to supplement their production through purchases of maize. The commercial farms located in the northern part of the country tend to be capital intensive, relying heavily on irrigation and purchased inputs, such as machinery, seed and fertilisers.

Agricultural labour productivity has increased over the review period, as shown by an increase in agricultural GDP while the level of agricultural employment has remained largely unchanged. In general, labour productivity and incomes from farming reflect the structural characteristics of Mexican agriculture, being highest on the commercial large-scale northern located farms. Overall, however, (bearing in mind the lack of firm data on many of the smaller and subsistence farms) farm incomes are low, possibly less than 20 per cent when compared with incomes in the rest of the economy.

From 1989 to 1994, agricultural imports grew faster than exports, resulting in an agricultural trade balance deficit. In 1995, the share of agricultural products in total trade represented about 4 per cent of imports and 5 per cent of exports. Agricultural exports increased substantially and the agricultural trade balance became positive, mainly as a result of the devaluation of the peso, which gave a competitive edge to Mexican production. Despite the contraction of imports due to currency devaluation, the share of both exports and imports in agricultural GDP increased, reflecting in particular the opening of the economy to NAFTA partners.

LAND REFORM

The system of land tenure is governed by the Agrarian Law. Two major types of property rights exist: ejido and private. The ejido is a form of land tenure where the beneficiaries as a group, but not as individuals, have the right to use the land. Ejido land belonged to the state and could not be sold or rented until 1992. The size of cultivated areas in private properties is limited, according to the type of agricultural activity (e.g. maximum of 100 hectares for irrigated crop land).

The intention of land re-distribution introduced after the Revolution in 1917 was to increase equity in land distribution, compared to the situation which prevailed during the pre-revolutionary period, characterised by a large proportion of large-scale "latifundios". The number of farm holdings reached 3.8 million in 1991, mainly as a result of population growth and land re-distribution. However, the ejido system had poorly defined property rights and imposed excessive restrictions on land mobility, and on farmers entering into contractual arrangements.

In 1992, the reform of land tenure established a new legal framework for property rights, authorising ejido farmers to sell (if authorised by the ejido assembly), rent or mortgage their plots of land. The aim is to provide incentives to farmers to improve their productivity through the establishment of property rights, and thus the encouragement of investment in agricultural and forestry activities. By allowing farmers better access to credit, the land reform also contributes to the consolidation of small plots into viable farms. Provisions on the maximum size of agricultural area in use in private properties remain unchanged for individuals, although corporations can now farm up to 25 times the limits for individuals.

AGRICULTURAL TRADE MEASURES

In 1986, Mexico's accession to the GATT was aimed at increasing trade in all sectors of the economy. In 1987, Mexico went beyond its GATT commitments and unilaterally reduced the maximum tariff rate to 20 per cent. In 1989, import permit requirements were removed for most agricultural commodities. Entering into force in 1994, NAFTA is the first free trade agreement signed between advanced industrial nations and a developing nation in which all agricultural and agro-food trade was included. In 1994, all remaining import permits for agricultural commodities were converted to tariffs or tariff quotas, which will be totally phased out between the NAFTA members, according to various tariff reduction schedules, by 2008 at the latest. By 2004, only imports of maize, milk powder, and sugar will remain protected. The tariff reduction schedules are based on the tariffs actually applied prior to the implementation of the NAFTA. The signing of NAFTA by Mexico, the US and Canada has had a major impact on trade and domestic agricultural policy in Mexico. However, NAFTA does not require specific reduction commitments in domestic support and export subsidies. Moreover, provisions on sanitary and phytosanitary measures, and quality standards, constitute general rather than specific guidelines for trade between the NAFTA partners.

Compared with Mexico's obligations under NAFTA, the commitments made by Mexico under the Uruguay Round Agreement during the implementation period through to 2004 are rather modest. However, they are important in having "locked in" ceiling levels of support and border protection. This observation reflects the high levels at which the new tariffs have been bound – on the basis of Mexico's GATT commitments in 1986 – under the Agreement and the flexibility allowed under the provisions on domestic support, notwithstanding the more constraining commitments on export subsidies. The reduction in the AMS commitment from US$9.5 billion to US$8.3 billion between 1995 to 2004 will be made easier given that the domestic-import price gap has since narrowed, or has been eliminated completely. Within the overall evolution of a less protected trade regime in Mexico, the impact on trade and diversion of trade flows also depends on the greater liberalisation of trade with the NAFTA partners. While the growth of trade between Mexico and NAFTA is evident, the effects on trade with the rest of the world is less clear, although negotiations are in process to sign bilateral agreements with other trade partners, including the European Union and Latin American countries. Mexico is also a member of the APEC (Asia Pacific Economic Cooperation).

FOOD AND AGRICULTURAL POLICY DEVELOPMENTS

As part of the overall economic policy based on import substitution and trade protection, the main agricultural policy objective until the mid-1960s was to improve Mexico's agricultural productive capacity, while contributing to employment creation and the inflow of foreign currency. Domestic food supplies largely met demand from the 1940s to the mid-1960s. From the mid-1960s to 1980, when demand exceeded food supply, the main objective of agricultural policy was to provide abundant and inexpensive food supplies to help poor consumers – through the creation of CONASUPO – and to support urbanisation and industrialisation. The latter objective was helped by the discovery of new oil reserves in Mexico and the oil boom of 1973.

The Mexican Food System (SAM) was established in 1980 with the aim of re-attaining self-sufficiency in beans, cereals and oilseeds by 1985, and improving the diet of a target population of 19 million, through the distribution of a "basic-food basket" at subsidised prices. The SAM also entailed the provision of subsidies to producers through higher output and lower input prices. The debt crisis triggered by weakening oil prices in 1982 forced the government to streamline its agricultural policy objectives and reduce the increasing share of foreign exchange going to food imports. The cost of the SAM could no longer be sustained, and the programme was terminated at the end of 1982. From 1983 to 1988, the main agricultural policy objective was to improve the productivity of the sector as a way to economise on scarce foreign exchange, mainly through the reduction of the cost of credit to farmers and lower prices for farm inputs. This policy stance was given extra emphasis when oil prices further fell sharply in 1986.

Throughout most of the 1980s, consumer and producer prices for major agricultural products were set (or strongly influenced) by the government through consumer subsidies and maximum retail food prices, government purchase from producers at guaranteed prices for basic commodities, export and import controls, including import licensing, and direct subsidies to private and public sector food processors.

A sharp change in direction was signalled in 1989 when Mexico embarked on an ambitious programme of reform of agricultural policy, aimed at modernising agriculture and enhancing the role of markets. The main objectives were to increase efficiency in resource use, while allowing cheaper imports to restrain price increases and increase the welfare of the rural population. The reforms involved a process of fundamental structural changes, including the privatisation of state-owned agricultural marketing and processing enterprises, and the shift from production linked price support to direct payments to farmers, in particular PROCAMPO. The reforms, which are still under way, have been underpinned through Mexico's increasing integration into the global economy and trade liberalisation, especially through NAFTA, and the GATT Uruguay Round Agreement.

In the 1990s, state intervention in the agricultural sector has been reduced and important steps have been taken to deregulate the agro-food sector. The number of state-owned agencies* involved in the implementation of agricultural policy has been considerably reduced. Some have been downsized and restructured (CONASUPO, BANRURAL), others liquidated (TABAMEX, CONAFRUT, ANAGSA, ALBAMEX), others dismantled (AZUCAR, INMECAFE, CONADECA), and others privatised (FERTIMEX, PRONASE). The only notable exception was the creation of ASERCA in 1991 to assist in the formation of private markets.

The objectives of agricultural policy reform have been reaffirmed in the Alliance for Agriculture programme ("Alianza para el Campo") for the period 1995-2000. This programme consists of a set of specific measures primarily aimed at improving farmers' skills and stimulating technological development to increase the productivity and competitiveness of the Mexican farm sector in the context of NAFTA. A key feature of the Alliance is the decentralisation of decision-making from federal to the State level through State Agricultural Councils, involving State governments and agricultural producers. The Councils are responsible for assessing and approving technological packages and their financing by State Trust Funds. This decentralised approach to decision making is essential for improving efficiency in resource use in a country where large regional differences exist.

PROCAMPO

A major element of reform was the introduction in 1994 of a 15 year programme of direct payments to farmers (PROCAMPO), which accompanied a reduction of market price support and transfers from consumers. This coincided with the entry into force of NAFTA, which resulted in the immediate liberalisation of imports of sorghum and beef and veal from the United States and Canada. While some border measures, minimum producer prices for maize and beans and consumer subsidies still remain as part of the package of agricultural policy instruments, PROCAMPO payments are progressively replacing price support policies for grains and oilseeds. Together with the gradual liberalising of import measures according to NAFTA and the Uruguay Round agreements, this represents a major shift in policy direction, which is broadly in line with the 1987 OECD Ministerial principles concerning improvement of market orientation. In 1994, parallel to the introduction of PROCAMPO payments, the levels of administered producer prices were decreased by 13 per cent for maize, 14 per cent for beans, 9 per cent for soyabeans, and 6 per cent for wheat.

PROCAMPO payments are based on historical acreage. In 1995, they were of M$ 440 (US$69) per hectare. PROCAMPO payments are fixed in real terms as from 1996. These payments, as they are based on historical acreage and not related to the level of current output, allow for a greater role for markets in determining production decisions, while promoting the efficient use of available land, water, labour and capital. Larger farmers will continue to receive the greatest share of support. However, these payments will also benefit subsistence farmers who previously did not receive any price support and were often taxed by having to pay higher supported prices for the maize they purchased for their own consumption.

---

* See the list of acronyms for the full titles of state-owned agencies.

In 1994, the PROCAMPO programme of area payments to producers of grains, beans and oilseeds, led to a sharp rise in public expenditure on direct payments to farmers. The share of PROCAMPO payments in total budgetary expenditures on agricultural policies increased from 21 per cent in 1994 to 27 per cent in 1995.

The "transfer efficiency" (the increase in farm household income as a ratio of the increase in transfers from taxpayers and consumers) of direct payments to farmers is greater than the support provided to farmers through market price policies. PROCAMPO payments are not linked to the production of a particular-commodity, nor to the scale of current output. Producers' decisions on how much and what to produce, and the allocation of resources, will not depend on the payments but only on price developments. PROCAMPO payments impose no burden on consumers, and production and trade distortions are also smaller.

FARM INPUT POLICY MEASURES

Encouraging structural adjustment and improving animal production and crop yields have been important policy objectives in Mexico. Over the review period, measures have been implemented to reduce farm input costs, in particular through interest concessions, and to provide general services to the agricultural sector as a whole. Among the various subsidised farm inputs those for fertilisers were significant in the 1980s. In the 1980s, the share of measures to reduce input costs in total agricultural support was high, often higher than the share of market price support. However, in the 1990s this share decreased to under one-fifth following the abolition (or sharp reduction) in several input subsidies, in particular fertilisers and insurance. In 1995 new subsidies to modernise farm equipment and improve productivity were announced under the Alliance for Agriculture, in particular under PRODUCE.

Mexican farmers have experienced considerable difficulty in obtaining credit and have been exposed to high and volatile interest rates associated with high rates of inflation. In the 1980s, interest concessions on loans and crop insurance programmes mainly benefited producers of maize and beans, and included some farmers considered to have no (or limited) commercial potential. Subsidised credit has been granted in recent years mainly in the form of investment loans to improve farm physical assets, especially for land under irrigation. Given the budgetary constraints and the need to improve farm structures and productivity, credit and debt rescheduling have been re-oriented toward farms with potential for most profitable investments. The coverage of loans by development banks has been reduced to a small share of the cultivated area, and interest concessions have been tightened.

Commercial banks have considered Mexican farmers to be a high risk group in general, and the guarantees the banks require could not be afforded by many farmers. The benefits of land title on credit flows have not yet been as forthcoming as expected after the reform of the land tenure legislation in 1992. Many commercial banks remained hesitant to lend to individual ejido farmers with meagre plots of rainfed land, given the high transaction costs and substantial risks associated with small loan sizes, and the already high levels of outstanding ejido debt. The introduction of PROCAMPO payments in 1994, which can also serve as collateral for loans, could help to overcome this situation. The expected increase in the size of farms – although there is a maximum limit on cultivated area in private properties – through the rental of land or formation of farmers' associations will allow resources for credit and equipment purchases to be pooled.

AGRICULTURAL SECTOR-WIDE POLICY MEASURES

A wide range of sector-wide policies are intended to improve the productive base of Mexican agriculture. In the 1980s, the share of measures to provide general services in total agricultural support was 10-25 per cent. However, in the 1990s, this share decreased to around 6-8 per cent. Over the review period, expenditure has mainly been for infrastructure improvement and, to a lesser extent, research, training, and extension.

Agricultural research has been largely production oriented with an emphasis on increasing yields and little regard to cost. Research has focused mainly on irrigated land, rather than rainfed and tropical areas, although the latter areas account for about three-quarters of the total farmland. Agricultural research institutions have been under the responsibility of the Secretariat of Agriculture and Rural Development, which co-ordinates research efforts and is responsible for the allocation of research funds. The existing research institutions have only a limited capability in economic analysis and their research priorities have been focused on increasing output, rather than ways that can help farmers and the government in meeting the current agricultural policy objectives, including sustainable agricultural farm practices to meet environmental objectives. However, efforts are being made to gather the information needed to assist farmers in managing their resources effectively to improve productivity and environmental performance. The recent decentralisation of research and technical assistance functions from the federal to State governments, as well as including producers in the setting of research priorities, could contribute to improving productivity of agriculture.

As is the case for agricultural research, most of the training and extension programmes have been designed for output maximisation. Moreover, agricultural extension institutions were very fragmented, with a lack of effective co-ordination. Since the establishment of the National Extension Scheme in 1989, efforts have been made to regroup and decentralise extension services, increase the number of private advisers, and introduce cost-sharing between producers and the government. However, information flows between extension workers and researchers were not efficient in feeding information back to the research effort, and researchers did not always address ways in which research results can be put in practice at the farm level. The technical transfer programme, linked to applied research activities through the PRODUCE foundations, gives more consideration to these aspects, including a larger role for the participation of producers.

A specific problem in Mexico is the need to improve the statistical information on agricultural policy and its dissemination to facilitate policy analysis and assessment. The recent creation of the Centre of Agricultural Statistics within SAGAR could contribute to improve the current situation.

Since 1994, the Government has started to revise the legal framework and agreements on sanitary and phytosanitary measures to make them compatible with its main trading partners. The aim of these measures is to rationalise sanitary standards and meat processing technology across the country, and to simplify the issue of phytosanitary certificates. There is still a large number of different state organisations supervising quality and sanitary control services under the responsibility of different Secretariats. An autonomous National Phytosanitary and Sanitary Commission was created in 1996. However, the transfer of quality and sanitary control functions to the private sector, including through laboratory accreditation, has to date been very limited.

The main basic agricultural infrastructure investments in Mexico essentially cover irrigation. About 25 per cent of grains and oilseeds are produced under irrigation. However, the potential for further expansion of irrigation networks is limited and plans relating to new investment are mainly to complete and improve existing irrigation systems. Until 1992, most of the installation work was undertaken with government assistance. Since then the regulatory framework has been revised, with increasing responsibility given to organised users operating and maintaining irrigation infrastructure. An increasing share of the operation and maintenance cost has been recovered through user fees, although water users are not yet fully covering these costs.

Since 1989, steps have been taken to privatise state-owned agricultural marketing and processing industries, and to introduce competition into agricultural markets, with the main objective of improving efficiency. The state-provided marketing structure, servicing the production of the main staple crops, has been maintained only in remote rural areas. Marketing and promotion have benefited from improved information and transparency in commodity markets. However, private commercial channels need to be further developed, particularly at the wholesale and regional level.

SUPPORT TO AGRICULTURE

The evolution of support to Mexican agriculture, as measured by the PSE, has reflected the changes in agricultural policies, in the context of movements in key macroeconomic variables, especially high inflation and exchange rate volatility. The PSE measured as a percentage of the value of production decreased on average from 34 per cent in 1979-1982 to 3 per cent in 1983-88. It increased to an average of 30 per cent in 1989-94, but decreased to 3 per cent in 1995. Except for the 1979-82 period, the percentage PSE has generally been well below the OECD average (41 per cent in 1989-94). The combined effects of changes in domestic producer prices and variations in border prices, including changes in the external value of the Mexican peso, are reflected in the evolution of market price support. The effects of the peso devaluation resulted in a sharp drop in the PSE in 1983, 1986 and 1995. Given the important influence of macroeconomic developments, great care needs to be taken in the interpretation of the evolution of support to agriculture in Mexico.

The breakdown of the PSE shows a decrease in the share of market price support (net of feed adjustment) in the total PSE from 55 per cent in 1979 to 30 per cent in 1988, followed by an increase to 77 per cent in 1991, and a subsequent decrease to 47 per cent in 1994. Market price support measures have been the main source of support for maize, sugar, milk and pigmeat. From 1994, the effects of the shift from price support to direct payments, following the introduction of PROCAMPO and the liberalisation of trade, became evident. The share of direct payments in the total PSE increased from 2 per cent in 1993 to 26 per cent in 1994, and budgetary expenditures on PROCAMPO payments were increased in 1995. As from 1996 they are fixed in real terms.

Agricultural support, as measured by the PSE, has been calculated for around two-thirds of overall agricultural production in Mexico (although for the crops included they only represent two-fifths of total crop production). An estimate of the value of all budgetary and consumer transfers associated with agricultural policies, for the whole agricultural sector suggests that the value of total transfers accounted for around 3 per cent of GDP on average in 1989-94 (around 2 per cent in the OECD on average), but fell steeply in 1995, due to agricultural policy reform, and the sharp fall in market price support. Total transfers per capita and per hectare of farmland are only around one quarter of the OECD average.

CONSUMER SUBSIDIES

From the mid 1960s to the end of the 1980s, consumers were penalised by having to pay high supported prices for grains and oilseeds. This also affected subsistence farmers as that part of their own consumption which they could not cover through their own production had to be purchased at high prices. However, during that period, to achieve its objective of low consumer prices for food, the Government granted substantial consumer subsidies, including to the food processing industry, mainly through transfers to CONASUPO (US$750 million a year in the 1980s on average). Moreover, general consumer price ceilings were in place to regulate the prices of basic foods. In the mid-1980s, a social programme was introduced to supply low-income families in urban areas with free maize tortillas, supplementing the social milk programme established in the mid-1960s and targeted to children in disadvantaged rural areas. Currently about 3 million families and more than 5 million children benefit from these respective programmes.

Since the end of the 1980s, in line with the decreasing role of state-owned agencies in the direct marketing of agricultural commodities, the setting of consumer prices by the government has been progressively eliminated for a wide range of commodities. Since 1995, the role of CONASUPO has been limited to the purchase of maize to cover the needs of the tortilla programme and state-owned retail shops. More than 20 000 state-owned retail shops still provide subsidised food to about 1 million consumers, mainly in rural areas. Moreover, the shift from market price support (financed by consumers) to direct payments to producers (financed by taxpayers) has also benefited consumers.

Overall, the percentage Consumer Subsidy Equivalent (CSE) was negative at around 8 per cent in 1979-82 and 10 per cent in 1989-94, representing an implicit tax on consumption. However, the percentage CSE became positive at around 20 per cent in 1983-88 and 12 per cent in 1995, representing a subsidy on consumption. Over the review period, the percentage CSE has been generally below the OECD average.

RURAL DEVELOPMENT

Agriculture is by far the main employer of people in rural areas. Despite relatively high birth rates in the rural areas, the growth of the population remaining in rural areas has been slower than that of urban areas, due to emigration of rural people. Information on the situation in rural areas is not comprehensive, in terms of infrastructure, employment, incomes, and the overall standard of living. However, available evidence suggests that rural areas in the middle and southern parts of the country tend to be poor. The geophysical characteristics and long distances in Mexico are not conducive to low cost installation of basic infrastructure in many rural areas, where there are few large conurbations nearby, and transportation is often poor and costly.

Economic policy in the 1980s was heavily focused on the development of large industries and urbanisation, to the detriment of the rural economy. In many rural areas, the basic infrastructure (water supply, sewage, electricity and telecommunications) was not developed and farmers had to survive in a largely self-sufficient economy. Agricultural policies were an integral element in the development of the rural economy as a whole, through the control of the purchase and marketing of agricultural products by state-owned agencies.

More financial support to improve the development of rural areas has been given in the 1990s, in particular through the National Solidarity Programme (PRONASOL). Rural households have been participating in the efforts to improve the infrastructure by contributing to the costs of such investments, sometimes through community based initiatives by forming solidarity committees. However, the lack of basic infrastructure, including communications and transportation with urban centres, continues to be a serious impediment to the development of rural areas. Through the decentralisation objective of the Alliance for Agriculture, there is potential for more effective co-operation between the federal and State governments, and the private sector, to help to create other sources of income and reduce regional income disparities.

AGRICULTURE AND THE ENVIRONMENT

During recent decades, soil salinisation and erosion, the depletion of water resources and the loss of biodiversity have been the main environmental impacts of agriculture. It is estimated that about 80 per cent of arable land is sensitive to soil erosion, of which about 20 per cent is highly erodible and not suitable for cultivation. The demand of water for agricultural, urban and industrial uses has expanded rapidly, and maintaining the level of groundwater resources has become critically important. As a result of inappropriate irrigation techniques, soil salinisation has become critical in some areas. Agricultural expansion in the tropical areas has led to deforestation, with negative impacts on biodiversity and wildlife habitats.

However, the development of property rights through a property register for the entitlement to PROCAMPO payments will provide an incentive for farmers to farm in a more environmentally sustainable way, which could reduce "slash and burn" practices that were prevalent in the past in some parts of Mexico. Apart from the registration of pesticides toxicity, no specific agro-environmental measures have been implemented to achieve the objective of agricultural production compatible with environmental sustainability. The shift from price support to PROCAMPO payments contributes to promoting a more efficient use of natural resources by reducing distortions in the supply of agricultural commodities. However, there is a need to incorporate well defined environmental objectives in agricultural policies, with a particular focus on pollution prevention. Well-targeted agri-environmental measures are needed, to address those environmental benefits or harm (in accordance with the polluter pays principle) attributed to farmers.

The process of agricultural policy and land reform will likely induce changes in the size, technique and efficiency of farms. Farms will tend to become larger (although still limited by the maximum size for private properties under the land tenure law), more specialised and mechanised, and will use more purchased inputs, including chemicals. Such structural adjustment is necessary to improve economic efficiency, but it may lead to increased pressures on the environment although experience in the OECD countries shows that economically and environmentally sustainable practices in agriculture can be compatible with modern farming methods, provided that farmers take preventive and site-specific actions.

STRENGTHENING POLICY REFORM

The principles and actions defined by the OECD Ministers in 1987 and subsequently reiterated in OECD Ministerial Councils are the basis of the reform of agricultural policies. In particular, OECD Ministers specified that the long-term objective of reform should be to "allow market signals to influence by way of a progressive and concerted reduction of agricultural support, as well as by all other appropriate means, the orientation of agricultural production". The sharing of the diverse experiences of OECD countries, including Mexico, is valuable in helping each country to design and implement market oriented policies needed to facilitate the improvement of the structure and performance of the agricultural sector.

Mexico has radically altered the direction of its economic and agricultural policies in recent years with greater emphasis on the role of markets, deregulation, and more liberal trade, as Mexico has moved from a relatively closed to an open economy. Mexico has made substantial efforts to move away from the most distorting form of agricultural support measures (market price support), and is shifting to direct income support to farmers, decoupled from the production of specific commodities. However, it is essential to ensure that the momentum of these trends in policies is continued.

The opening up of the Mexican economy to international competition has been one of the most significant events in its macroeconomic policy strategy. Tariff reduction is ongoing under NAFTA and under the Uruguay Round Agreement, which will exert pressure on producers to adapt to the growing influence of international markets, thus contributing to the structural adjustment of agriculture, while reducing the burden on consumers and taxpayers. Trade has greatly expanded, especially with Canada and the United States, Mexico's partners in NAFTA, as well as with other countries in Latin America, with which Mexico has regional trade agreements. Through its commitments to open trade, in particular with NAFTA partners, Mexico has taken important steps in the direction of market orientation.

Since 1983, total support to Mexican agriculture, as measured by the percentage PSE, has been low compared with the OECD average, and its recent evolution shows the increasing importance of direct payments. The move toward a system of direct payments not linked to the production of specific commodities (PROCAMPO) has reduced production and trade distortions, and is of benefit to farms previously not benefiting from the system of market price support. One of the other positive features of PROCAMPO is that it is intended to be implemented over a fixed time period, which will help farmers in their planning decisions.

Given the level of economic development in Mexico, and the importance of food in consumer expenditures, better targeted consumer policies will bring benefits both to consumers and taxpayers. Moreover, subsidies on food consumption would be more cost effective if they were more closely linked to broader development programmes such as health and education, primarily targeted at poor areas. However, the burden on consumers due to agricultural policies has been low compared with many other OECD countries.

The major underlying problems of a large part of the agricultural sector in Mexico are structural: low productivity is associated with a farm structure characterised by numerous small, fragmented and often subsistence farms (ejido and private); many farmers still have a limited capability to tackle the challenges and capitalise on the opportunities provided by a recently opened economy; and marketing and promotion channels are poorly developed, particularly at the regional level. Moreover, the poor provision of basic infrastructure, including roads, is still a major impediment to the development and economic diversification of rural areas, hampering the ability of farmers to market their products. An integrated approach to policies is imperative if balanced socio-economic development in rural areas is to be achieved. Future policy reform needs to give greater emphasis to facilitate the creation of new sources of income in rural areas, to structural adjustment in agriculture, the development of marketing and promotion, the improvement of basic infrastructures as well as research, training and extension services.

The Alliance for Agriculture offers the potential to overcome some of these structural problems, particularly by taking account of regional differences. This is important in a country like Mexico where there exist huge variations in levels of agricultural development and agro-ecological conditions, and where acute structural and social problems are widespread in rural areas. As Mexico is opening its borders to agricultural trade, it has become more evident that there is a need to modernise on and off farm infrastructure, as a way to improve the long-term viability of farms as they adjust to a more market-oriented economy. However, a high priority needs to be given to better targeting, evaluation and monitoring of policy measures to ensure the most cost-effective use of budgetary funds.

In moving towards an open economy in the agricultural sector, the need to streamline the complex decision-making, institutional framework, and implementation of policies is necessary. This has started, with privatisation and decentralisation, which will increase transparency and improve the efficiency by which support is transferred to farmers. Increasing transparency of Mexico's support system will help the operation of agricultural markets, and it will increase the stability of the horizon in which farmers make their decisions.

The developments in macroeconomic policy show how strongly macroeconomic policy and the effect of the sharp devaluation of the peso in 1995 influenced the price signals in the agricultural sector. These macroeconomic developments should, however, be viewed as providing the opportunity for continuing the agricultural policy reform process, and reducing the burden on the economy.

Achieving the agricultural policy objectives in Mexico within the context of the present economic reform will require not only specific, well targeted policy measures, but also an appropriate balance between structural adjustment objectives, alleviating rural poverty, protecting the environment, and providing economically efficient employment opportunities. There is a need to strengthen policies towards education, training, research, and extension, and encourage the development of alternative sources of income and job opportunities in rural areas, so that farmers can respond efficiently and effectively to market signals and the agricultural sector can develop on a sound foundation.

In conclusion, it is essential that the progress already made in agricultural policy reform should be consolidated, within the framework of macroeconomic developments and the development of an open economy. This requires a coherent approach to policy.

THE ECONOMIC AND AGRICULTURAL SITUATION

A. GENERAL ASPECTS

1. Background

Mexico is located in the north part of the American continent, neighbouring the United States to the north and Belize and Guatemala to the south. It is surrounded by the Pacific Ocean in the west and by the Gulf of Mexico and the Caribbean Sea in the east. With a **total area** of over 197 million hectares, it ranks fourth in size among OECD countries. The topography of the country consists mainly of an elevated plateau, flanked by two mountain chains that run north to south on the east and west of the country, sloping down into narrow coastal plains. The Peninsula of Baja California breaks off the western mountain chains while the Yucatan Peninsula is a flat calcareous formation in eastern Mexico. About 31 million hectares in Mexico is **arable land**, representing only 16 per cent of the total land area. Grasslands account for 41 per cent, forests 25 per cent, and bushland nearly 16 per cent. The average agricultural population density of about 0.9 persons per arable hectare is relatively high among OECD countries.

The **climate** in Mexico is largely variable. In general, the north is dry (with extreme seasonal temperature variations), the centre is temperate and the south is hot and humid. Annual rainfall tends to be scarce with around 250 mm in the semiarid north and 450-750 mm in the centre; however parts of south-eastern Mexico receive between 1 000 to 4 000 mm.

Mexico's **population** is the third largest in the OECD area with over 91 million people in 1995 and an average density of 46 persons per square kilometre. The annual population growth of 2 per cent in the ten years to 1995 was the second highest in OECD countries, although it has been declining steadily over the review period. The official language of the country is Spanish. Mexico's **total GDP** ranks as the fourteenth largest in the OECD area. However, the country is at the lower end of OECD countries in terms of per capita output, at around US$6 780 per head at purchasing power parity[1] exchange rates, compared to an OECD average estimate of around US$18 660 in 1995.

2. The government

Mexico (*Estados Unidos Mexicanos*) is a federal republic of 31 states and the Federal District. The President is the head of the executive and is elected by popular vote for a single six-year term. The legislative power is vested in a congress (*Congreso de la Unión*), consisting of an upper house (*Cámara de Senadores*) and a lower house (*Cámara de Diputados*). The upper house has 128 senators who are elected for six years, with 4 senators for each state and the Federal District. The lower house is made up of 500 members elected for 3-year terms: three hundred are elected from districts based on direct votes, and the rest are elected based on a system of proportional representation of the political parties. The judicial power is vested in the supreme court (*Suprema Corte de Justicia*). The chief executive of each state is an elected Governor for a six-year term; the head of the Federal District is appointed by the President. The present government is from the Institutional Revolutionary Party (PRI), which is constituted by different social groups, and has formed the governments in Mexico since 1929.

B. GENERAL ECONOMIC SITUATION

1. Economic growth

After the implementation of structural reform and macroeconomic stabilisation measures in the middle of the 1980s, Mexico's economy grew at an average annual rate of 3 per cent between 1989 and 1994. However, a severe balance of payments crisis in December 1994 made necessary further adjustment efforts, with a large decline in growth in 1995. Strong fiscal and monetary discipline and the continuation of structural reform efforts, are conditions that need to be pursued to achieve sustainable growth in the medium term (OECD, 1995).

With a high level of border protection, Mexico pursued an import substitution policy sustained mainly by an oil boom before 1982.[2] In the aftermath of discovering new sources of oil in the country and rising international oil prices, Mexico increased its foreign debt. However, as oil prices fell in 1982, the country announced a moratoria on its debt repayments and the Mexican peso was heavily devalued, inducing a large increase in inflation (Figure 1).

The debt crisis brought the country into recession, during which growth of GDP fell by over 4 per cent in 1983 (see Table I.1, Annex I). In that year, a new administration began the implementation of structural economic reforms, which aimed to move away from the import substitution policy towards a more open market-orientated policy. This policy became explicit when Mexico joined the GATT in 1986. With the macroeconomic reforms, economic growth resumed in 1984, although inflation was at high levels. In 1985 and 1986, two external shocks complicated the adjustment process; first, an earthquake hit Mexico City requiring emergency expenditure and, second, a halving of oil prices reduced foreign exchange earnings. The latter was a major influence leading the exchange rate to depreciate, which

◆ Figure 1. **Inflation in Mexico and OECD average**

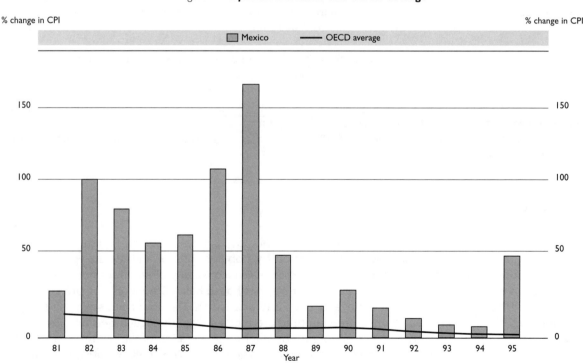

Note: December to December inflation for Mexico; the OECD average excludes the Czech Republic, Hungary, Mexico, Poland and Turkey.
Source: INEGI and OECD Secretariat, 1997.

contributed to even higher inflation. With rapid increases in the domestic price of imports and falling real incomes, output fell by nearly 4 per cent in 1986 (OECD, 1992).

As inflation continued to hinder efforts to stabilise the economy, a new component was added in the overall adjustment process. In December 1987, with cumulative inflation of 159 per cent after one year, representatives of labour and the industrial and agricultural sectors met with the government and agreed to implement a stabilisation programme known as the Pact for Economic Solidarity or *Pacto*. The *Pacto* aimed at stabilising key economic variables, mainly inflation, in order to help economic growth. Under the *Pacto*, controls were set in 1988 on the exchange rate, wages, and the prices of a "basic basket" of essential goods and services. Also, the maximum tariffs on imports were reduced to 20 per cent in order to allow foreign competition to exert downward pressure on domestic prices (although import permits on some key products were maintained). Macroeconomic stabilisation policies, with the support of the *Pacto*, succeeded in reducing inflation to below 20 per cent in 1989, and the economy recorded growth rates of around 2 per cent in 1987 and 1 per cent in 1988 of the GDP.

A continuous problem hindering the investment required to return to a sustainable growth path was the large transfers of capital abroad associated with the foreign debt. In 1989, under the "Brady Plan",[3] Mexico restructured its public foreign debt. Investment by the private sector was also strongly encouraged through a series of measures including: privatisation of major state enterprises, liberalisation of foreign direct investment provisions, and extensive deregulation of the financial system (OECD, 1992). The Mexican economy entered a recovery period in which the economy grew faster than population from 1989 to 1992, and inflation continued to decline, to 8 per cent in 1993. Rising portfolio and direct investments, and capital repatriation, increased the net private capital inflows to almost US$22 billion in 1993. Although economic growth in 1993 fell below 1 per cent before the signing of the North American Free Trade Agreement (NAFTA) between Canada, USA and Mexico, it accelerated to 3.5 per cent in 1994.

In 1994, unprecedented events in Mexico's political life for more than 50 years, including the assassination of the leading candidate in the presidential elections, triggered large outflows of capital from the country. As a depreciation of the peso could have resulted in a crisis of confidence in the Mexican financial system, and meant abandoning the major policy objective of keeping inflation down, reserves were used to maintain the value of the peso in the belief that it was a temporary crisis.[4] However, the combination of a policy setting allowing the rapid expansion of domestic demand and the exchange rate commitment, soon became unsustainable. With a diminished level of foreign reserves, the authorities abandoned their exchange rate commitment in December 1994, and the currency abruptly depreciated bringing about a turmoil in the financial markets.[5] In 1995, with tighter monetary and budgetary policies, inflation rose to around 50 per cent, economic growth fell by near 7 per cent, and the exchange rate was allowed to float freely.

2. Population growth and rural-urban migration

The Mexican population was around 14 million in 1921, following the Mexican revolution of 1910 during which the population decreased. Population grew from 1950 to 1970 at an average annual rate of over 3 per cent. However, in the following two decades both the fertility rate as well as the crude birth rate decreased steadily. From 1980 to 1990, the average annual rate of population growth was 2.3 per cent. The large population increase has led to an age structure of the population in which persons less that 20 years old represent half of the total population. This phenomenon has led to rapid grow of the labour supply, as young people seek to enter the labour market.

As the Mexican population has grown, so has migration from rural to urban areas (Figure 2). At the end of the 1930s, manufacturing output started to grow at a faster pace than agricultural output, such that in 1945 it became a larger sector in the economy.[6] The change in the composition of output created a "pull" factor, creating higher job opportunities in the urban areas. Nevertheless, population continued to grow in the rural areas, but it was partly absorbed through expansion on to new agricultural land (Figure 3). As the expansion started to level off by the late 1960's, it created a "push" factor that helped to propel people out of the rural areas. With scarcer land available for cropping, migration to the cities

◆   Figure 2. **Urban and rural population of Mexico**

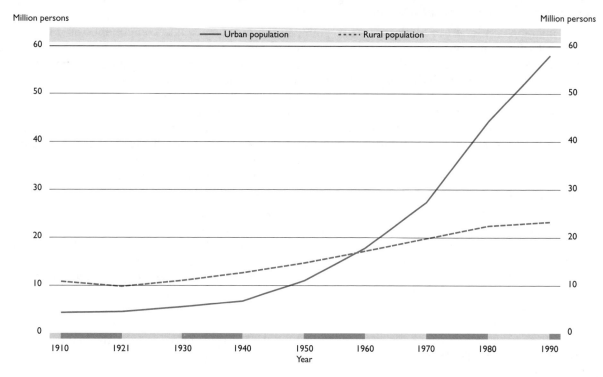

Source: INEGI.

◆   Figure 3. **Agricultural harvested land and population in Mexico**
1940 = 100

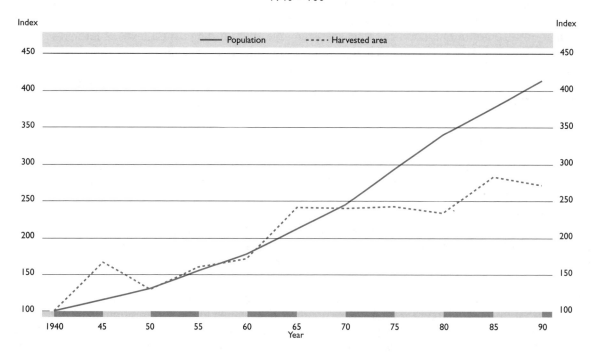

Note: Harvested area is for major food anf feed crops; maize, wheat, beans, rice, sorghum and soyabeans.
Source: INEGI and SAGAR.

became a major phenomenon. From 1965 to 1970, around one million persons moved from rural areas into Mexico City.[7]

Migration to urban areas, plus the indigenous growth of the cities themselves, is one of the major demographic challenges facing Mexico. As the urban population grew more than fivefold from 1950 to 1990, the rural population[8] grew by only one third as much during the same period. This has imposed severe pressures on the expansion of urban infrastructure.

An important demographic feature in Mexico has been international migration. This has been a source of employment for rural labour, but with a seasonal dimension. The harvest season in the United States has traditionally absorbed Mexican labour since the beginning of the century. Nevertheless, it seems that although most migration of Mexican labour to the United States has been towards rural areas in the past (especially in the South West of the United States), most of the migration currently taking place is destined towards urban areas. Differences in living standards have thus been exerting pressure not only on migration from rural to urban areas in Mexico, but also on international migration.

3. Employment

Total employment in Mexico was just under 33 million persons, or 54 per cent of the working-age population (12 years and over) in 1993.[9] The relatively low percentage reflects the large share of young people in the total population, which in turn has contributed to the increase in the labour force by 3.5 per cent each year, or more than 1 million persons. The "open unemployment rate" in urban areas increased from 2.8 per cent in 1990 to 3.7 per cent in 1994.[10] In 1995, in the aftermath of the financial crisis, large job losses led to a rise in the "open unemployment rate" of 5.5 per cent at the end of the year. However, the open unemployment rate is not considered a good indicator of available capacity on the labour market in a country with an informal sector and no unemployment insurance (OECD, 1995).

Mexico's labour market is characterised by a large proportion of "informally employed" people. Typically, people from low income categories cannot afford to be unemployed for a long period. The result is that they move into the "informal employment" sector. This sector, which covers mainly service activities and is made of small and micro-enterprises, has traditionally been growing and is estimated to have reached 35 per cent of the total labour force by 1993 (OECD, 1995). It is not clear as to how many of the rural persons migrating to the urban areas become employed in the "informal" sector, but due to the low level of education in the rural areas of Mexico, it is considered to be high.[11]

4. External trade and the balance of payments

Before 1982, Mexico's trade balance was negative as the real value of the currency appreciated (OECD, 1992). Total merchandise imports exceeded exports by US$4.9 billion in 1981 (excluding trade by in-bond industries[12]). The situation was aggravated mainly as a result of a large public foreign debt. In that year, the current account registered a deficit of US$16.5 billion. Following the currency devaluation in 1982, a slowdown in domestic demand together with a more favourable exchange rate, helped to maintain a positive trade balance until 1989.

As Mexico started to move towards a more open economy in the mid-1980's, both total merchandise exports and imports started to increase. Mexican industry was successful in increasing its exports by 68 per cent from 1988 to 1994. However, imports grew by 190 per cent during the same period, with a large share of capital goods and intermediate inputs. These imports reflected to a large extent the modernisation process by Mexican firms which faced greater foreign competition. In 1994, Mexico registered a negative trade balance of US$24.3 billion (excluding trade by in-bond industries), which was the main component of the deficit registered in the current account that reached US$28.8 billion at the end of that year. As capital financing this deficit moved out of the country, the Mexican peso suffered an abrupt depreciation at the end of 1994. Improved international competitiveness as a result of the depreciation of the peso, and the fall in domestic spending entailed by tight economic policies, brought the current account close to balance in 1995.

5. Government budget

Since the beginning of the 1990s, Mexico has maintained a public budget close to balance. In 1982, the public sector deficit had reached nearly 16 per cent of GDP, so the Mexican government embarked on an adjustment process, which included cuts in public expenditure, while improved revenues helping to lower the deficit to around 7 per cent of GDP in 1984. However, payment of the foreign debt was difficult as Mexico remained very heavily indebted.

The burden of servicing the foreign debt was indeed one of the major constraints on the growth of the Mexican economy in the 1980s. This was particularly manifest in 1986-87 when the devaluation of the currency increased the net transfer of Mexican resources abroad. This contributed to the increase of the public budget deficit in 1987 to the level of 1982 in terms of share of GDP. In 1989, Mexico restructured its debt with the international banking community, which reduced outflows abroad.

Both the reduction of servicing the foreign debt and stricter public finances contributed to a further reduction of the public budget deficit from over 9 per cent of GDP in 1988 to nearly zero by the end of 1991. The following two years Mexico achieved a budget surplus and the budget was balanced in 1994 and 1995.

C. AGRICULTURAL SECTOR SITUATION

1. Agriculture in the economy

Mexican agricultural GDP (excluding forestry and fisheries), is among the five largest in the OECD area. While experiencing a moderate downward trend over time, the agricultural sector in Mexico contributed 7.6 per cent to GDP in 1995. However, in the early 1990's, agriculture employment represented about 25 per cent of total employment. The large difference between the share of agriculture in total GDP and total employment reflects a relatively low overall level of agricultural labour productivity (see Table I.1, Annex I). However, these estimates tend to be downward biased as they do not consider part-time farming and under-employment in agriculture (Schmitt, 1988), and may conceal a wide range of levels of productivity across different farms and regions. A low agricultural labour productivity may also be linked to education levels. Only about one third of the rural population completes primary education, while the corresponding figure for the urban population is almost two thirds.[13]

Agricultural value added grew at an annual average of 1.2 per cent between 1980 and 1994, with large variations following not only developments in the overall economy, but also climatic fluctuations. Crops account for nearly two thirds, and livestock one third of value added in agriculture. Including the food industry, the contribution of the agro-food sector was around 13 per cent of total GDP in 1994.

While Mexico had been a net importer of agricultural and food products since 1989, it became a net exporter in 1995, partly as a result of the peso devaluation, but also as the US and Canadian markets expanded through NAFTA. While the share of agricultural and food exports to total exports was around 14 per cent in 1993, the share of agricultural and food imports to total imports was over 12 per cent.

Since the devaluation of the peso in 1982, increases in agricultural and food prices were lower than increases in overall consumer prices, except for a sharp rise in agricultural prices in 1990, when the government increased administered prices for major agricultural commodities (Figure 4). This can partly be explained by price controls set by the government on basic food products, but may also reflect gains in agricultural productivity. The share of food in total private consumption is relatively high at around 37 per cent in 1992, reflecting low incomes in Mexico as compared to other OECD countries.

2. Agricultural employment and wages

Agricultural wages[14] have tended to lag behind wages in other sectors of the Mexican economy. In 1992, it is estimated that an average agricultural worker received about 15 per cent of the average wage of all employees in Mexico. This gap has been widening since 1986 when the wage differential was estimated to have been 25 per cent (see Table I.1, Annex I). However, agricultural wages data may be underestimated as they include farmers at the subsistence level. Moreover, there is a great variation of

◆ Figure 4. **Change in agricultural and food prices relative to overall consumer prices (CPI)**
1980 = 100

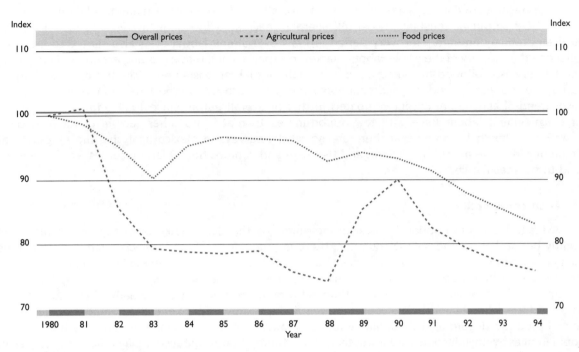

Source: Banco de México and OECD Secretariat.

◆ Figure 5. **Unit labour costs and GDP in Mexico**
1980 = 100

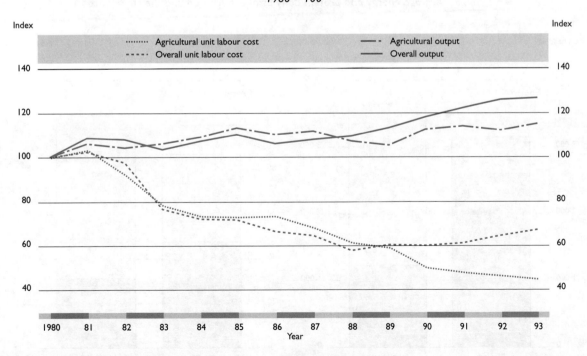

Note: Output is the change in GDP; unit labour cost is the ratio of labour cost to GDP at constant prices.
Source: Table I.1, Annex I.

relative wages among the agricultural sector, and farm income from non-agricultural activities is ignored in the data.

With the adjustment measures in the 1980s, overall unit labour costs (defined as labour costs per unit of GDP output at constant prices) fell sharply, reaching a low point in 1988 (Figure 5). As the Mexican economy entered a recovery period in 1989, overall unit labour costs also started to increase, reflecting the capacity of the whole labour market to expand along with a growing economy. Agricultural unit labour costs followed the same trend as overall unit labour costs until 1989, but did not increase during the recovery period, instead continuing the downward trend. The latter may reflect both the lower trend of agricultural output compared to that of overall output since 1989, and also because a large agricultural labour force with few opportunities to move into other sectors of the economy. However, it should be noted that there are no official surveys in Mexico analysing the employment situation within the agricultural sector, and the level and composition of farm incomes, so the reasons tend to be speculative.

3. Food consumption

Average food consumption in Mexico, measured by the daily intake of energy and proteins, is slightly below that in other OECD countries. However, the source of food reflects a larger use of crops than animal products (FAO, 1995). Whereas about 83 per cent of the daily energy intake of the average Mexican comes from crop products (of which maize, wheat and beans are important), the equivalent for the United States is only 33 per cent. In terms of protein, 60 per cent of the daily intake comes from crop products, whereas for the US consumer, the figure is only 35 per cent, the reminder coming from animal products (Figure 6). This primarily reflect a lower demand for animal products by the Mexican population as average incomes are lower than in the United States, but also it may reflect differences in consumer preferences (maize is mainly used for food and consumed as "tortillas" in Mexico, whereas it is used for feed in the United States).

◆ Figure 6. **Average energy and protein daily intake in Mexico and the United States**
1992

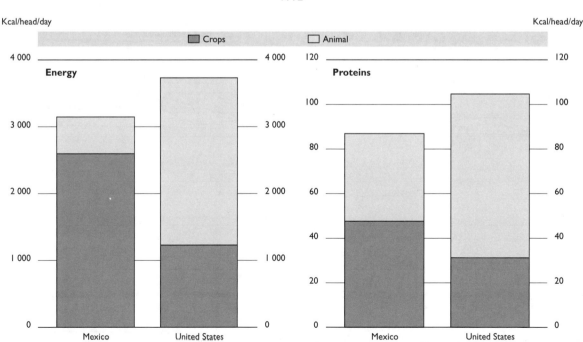

Source: FAO, *Production Yearbook*, 1994.

◆ Figure 7. **Crops and livestock products in agricultural production**
Share of value in 1994

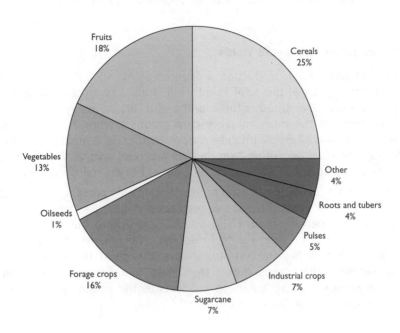

Crop production in Mexico
(M$ 58.7 billion)

Fruits 18%
Cereals 25%
Vegetables 13%
Oilseeds 1%
Other 4%
Roots and tubers 4%
Forage crops 16%
Pulses 5%
Sugarcane 7%
Industrial crops 7%

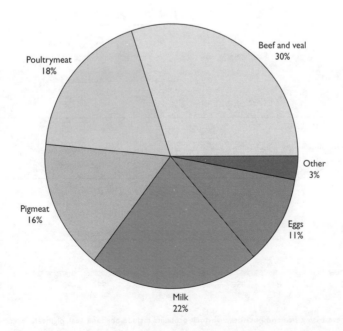

Animal production in Mexico
(M$ 36.8 billion)

Poultrymeat 18%
Beef and veal 30%
Pigmeat 16%
Other 3%
Eggs 11%
Milk 22%

Source: SAGAR.

In most OECD countries per capita consumption of energy and protein has increased over time. However, in Mexico a slight decrease was registered from 1980 to 1992. While in 1980 energy intake was 3 180 kcal/head/day and protein intake was 85 grams/head/day, the corresponding figures for 1992 were 3 146 kcal/head/day and 79 grams/head/day respectively. Also, the share of food in total private expenditure increased slightly from 36 per cent in 1980 to 37 per cent in 1992 (see Annex I; Table I.1). This could be seen as one of the consequences of declining real earnings in Mexico during the same period.

4. Agricultural production, areas and yields

The total **value** of agricultural production amounted to M$ 95.5 (US$28) billion in 1994.[15] Crops accounted for about three fifths of the total value while animal products accounted for the remaining two fifths. Crop production is diversified in the country, with cereals (mainly maize, wheat and sorghum) and fruits and vegetables as the most valuable crop groups (Figure 7). Other important groups are forage, sugarcane and industrial crops (mainly coffee). The main animal products which provide an important contribution to total agricultural production are beef and veal, milk, poultry and pigmeat. However, poultry and eggs together account for 29 per cent of animal production.

There were peaks in the evolution of crop production (mainly cereals) in 1981, 1985 and 1990, after which a steady and significant upward trend was registered (Figure 8). The peaks were essentially due to both favourable prices (specially maize) and weather conditions, but they also reflected growth in the overall economy exerting an effect through demand. The troughs in 1982 and 1988 were due to droughts and unfavourable economic conditions after the peso devaluations. Animal production increased at a slower pace than crops during the 1980s, but started to trend higher in the 1990s, reflecting growing consumer demand for these products as the economy grew, and given the higher income elasticities of demand for livestock products.

◆ Figure 8. **Trends in the value of agricultural production in Mexico**
1980 = 100

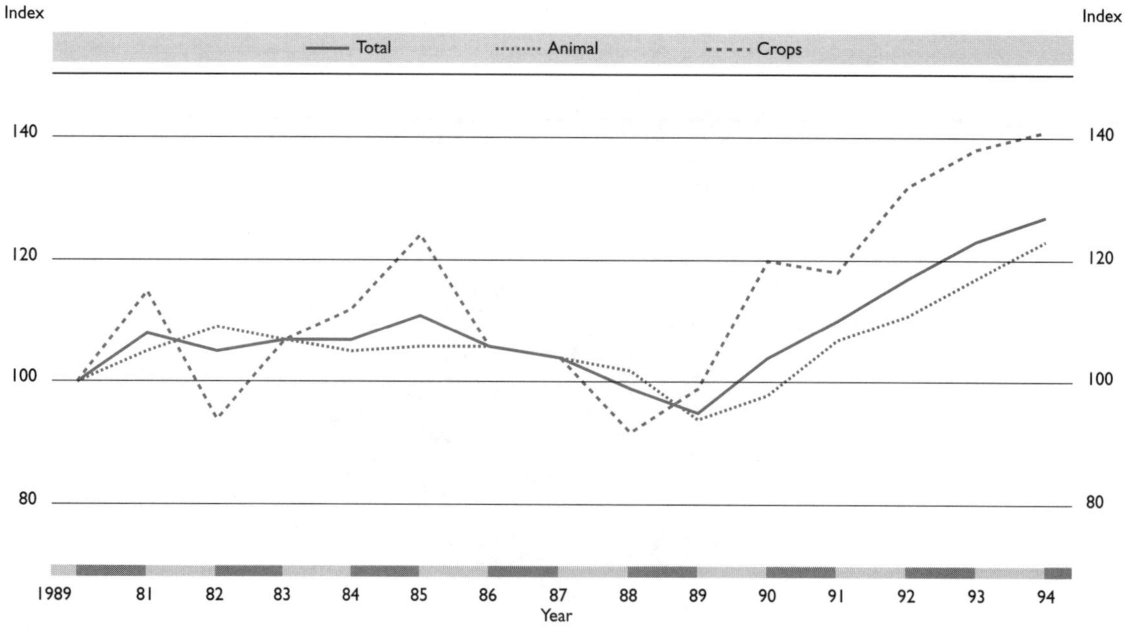

Note: Crops include maize, wheat, barley, rice and potatoes; livestock products include beef and veal, pigmeat, sheepmeat, poultrymeat, eggs and milk.
Source: SAGAR.

◆ Figure 9. ***Share of crops in the cultivated area of Mexico***
1994

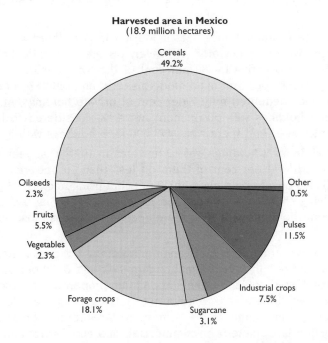

Harvested area in Mexico
(18.9 million hectares)

Cereals
49.2%

Oilseeds
2.3%

Other
0.5%

Fruits
5.5%

Pulses
11.5%

Vegetables
2.3%

Forage crops
18.1%

Industrial crops
7.5%

Sugarcane
3.1%

Source: SAGAR.

The **agricultural area** under cultivation is mainly devoted to maize. In 1994, 18.9 million hectares were cultivated with annual and perennial crops. Maize accounted for over 43 per cent of the area, followed by beans with around 11 per cent and sorghum with nearly 7 per cent. In turn, fruits and vegetables covered nearly 8 per cent of the area (Figure 9). The area devoted to crops has, however, changed over time. The sorghum area expanded rapidly in the 1960s, reflecting its increasing use as feed. During the 1970s and 1980s some of the maize area was converted to sorghum. However, this tendency was reversed in the 1990s as a result of a more favourable profit ratio for maize relative to sorghum.

Since 1980, average **yields** of maize tended to increase whereas those for wheat remained stable after a rise at the beginning of the 1980s (see Table I.2, Annex I). In 1995, a drought and higher costs of production decreased overall yields, with a major effect on wheat. However, regional variations of yields, especially for maize, tend to be high, depending on climate, input use, management and farm structures. While farmers attained average maize yields of 7.2 tonnes per hectare in the irrigated areas of the north-western state of Sinaloa in 1994, yields obtained by farmers in rain-fed areas in other states varied from 0.4 to 3 tonnes per hectare during the same crop year. Wheat yields are higher than the average for OECD countries, reflecting primarily the use of modern technology by commercial farmers.

5. Agricultural structures

Land tenure in Mexico takes two major forms: ejido and private. The ejidos are communal owner-ship systems created for the peasantry in the Agrarian Law of 1915 (see Section D). In 1991, there were around 30 000 ejidos with a total surface of 103.3 million hectares, or more than half of the area of the country. However, ejido land in farm holdings (units of production under the same administration devoted to agricultural or forestry production in rural Mexico) amounted to only 31.1 million hectares, whereas that in private farm holdings was 57.2 million hectares. The total number of farm holdings in

Mexico was 3.8 million in 1991, with 2.7 million in ejidos, 1 million on private land and 0.1 million sharing both types of land tenure. The average size of a farm holding in Mexico was 25 hectares in 1991 (INEGI, 1994). Private and ejido farm holdings have similar proportions of arable and irrigated land (see Table I.3, Annex I).

There is a wide diversity of farm holdings sizes in Mexico. In 1991, there were 1 million **private farm holdings** with an average size of 55 hectares. However, private and ejido holdings of 20 or fewer hectares were predominant, accounting for 80 per cent of the total (Figure 10). Only 35 per cent of private holdings used tractors, 31 per cent used modern seeds, and only 57 per cent applied chemical fertiliser. Technical assistance benefited only 7 per cent of private holdings. At the upper end, there were 117 000 private farm holdings with 50 or more hectares, considered to be largely commercial enterprises, whereas at the lower end there were 453 000 farm holdings with 2 or fewer hectares.

The average size of **ejido farm holdings** was 12 hectares in 1991. That year, there were 2.7 million ejido holdings in Mexico, with 90 per cent of them on less than 20 hectares. Average technological characteristics were similar to private holdings with 39 per cent using tractors, 33 per cent using modern seeds, 54 per cent applying chemical fertilisers and 9 per cent receiving technical assistance. There were only 31 000 ejido farms holdings with 50 or more hectares, whereas those with 2 or fewer hectares amounted to 823 000.

A major feature of the size structure of Mexican farm holdings is the existence of a large proportion of small holdings or "minifundios". In 1991, 1.3 million farm holdings or 34 per cent of the total had 2 or less hectares regardless of the type of land ownership. A large proportion of these holdings are likely to be farmed for **subsistence**, with little access to modern technology, especially fertilisers, modern seeds and machinery. On the other hand, farms with 5 or more hectares tend to be **semi-commercial** (only a proportion of the production is marketed) or **commercial**, and account for almost 41 per cent of the total. These farm holdings tend to make more use of modern technology and account for the largest proportion of marketed output.

◆ Figure 10. *Size structure of private and ejido farm holdings in Mexico*
1991

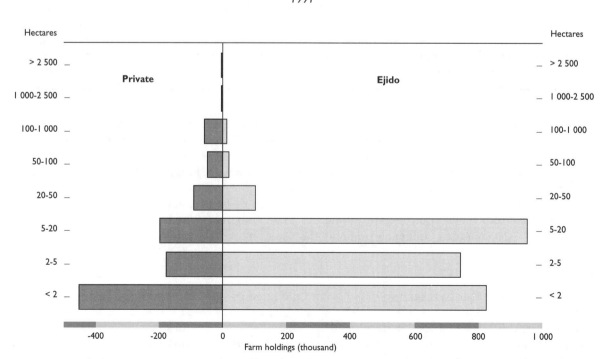

Source: INEGI, VII Agricultural-Livestock Census, 1991.

6. Structure of the agro-food industry

a) Downstream sector

Until 1989, Mexico's public marketing board CONASUPO, purchased part of the domestic production of 12 crops (maize, beans, wheat, barley, rice, sorghum, soyabeans, safflower, cottonseed, copra, sunflower, and sesame). It also acted as one of the importers of these commodities, as well as the sole importer of powdered milk. CONASUPO activities involved the purchase, storage, transportation, processing and retailing of these commodities. Table I.4 (Annex I) summarises CONASUPO's affiliates, and their functions during their period of activity. In 1990, CONASUPO reduced its market intervention to only maize, beans and powdered milk (but remains the sole importer of the latter). The marketing of other crops is now undertaken by the private sector. However, structural problems became evident as CONASUPO withdrew from markets. An outdated rail and road transportation infrastructure, together with high interest rates paid for storing crops, resulted in large marketing costs for some producers. As a result, the government created ASERCA (Support Services for Agricultural Marketing), aimed at helping the development of private markets (further details are given in Chapter II). To modernise the marketing infrastructure, the government started the process of privatising ANDSA (National Stores) and FERRONALES (National Railway Company), which stores and transports respectively a large part of the commercial production and imports of agricultural commodities. Also, CONASUPO has been gradually transferring its rural warehouses (BORUCONSA) to producers.

Among other state agencies that in the past were involved in the marketing of agricultural commodities are: AZUCAR, S.A., which was responsible for processing and marketing all the sugar produced in Mexico; INMECAFE which purchased and marketed between 30 and 40 per cent of the production of coffee beans; CONADECA with a market share of around 55 per cent of cocoa production; ALGODONERA MEXICANA, S.A. that marketed between 5 to 15 per cent of domestic cotton fibre, and TABAMEX which had the monopoly of the purchase of tobacco. All these agencies were disbanded in the early 1990s.

b) Upstream sector

Agricultural input industries in the past were largely owned by the government, but since 1990 there has been a large process of restructuring and privatisation. The production and marketing of most fertilisers was in charge of the state agency FERTIMEX, whose main aim was to keep fertiliser costs low to farmers.[16] Processed feeds were manufactured and marketed by ALBAMEX with a market share of around 10 per cent, and SESA provided machinery and technical services to the ejidos and small farmers. In 1992, FERTIMEX was privatised, and ALBAMEX and SESA dismantled. The state company PRONASE is responsible for the production, certification and marketing of improved seeds, specially basic food seeds (maize, beans, rice and wheat). Nevertheless, since 1991 the private seed companies were allowed to patent and verify[17] their seed varieties, thus encouraging its market participation (for further details see Chapter II).

7. Agriculture and the environment

In Mexico, environmental problems that are related to agricultural activities include soil erosion, deforestation, and water pollution and depletion. But, agriculture has also suffered from pollution emanating from urban and industrial activities, mainly in the central plateau. Around 80 per cent of the arable soils are affected by different **erosion** processes, of which 20 per cent are severely eroded. Farmland in the northern arid regions of Mexico is mainly exposed to wind erosion while that in the humid tropics is affected by water erosion as a result of the loss of vegetation and heavy rainfall on fragile soils. In the southern tropical states of Mexico, **deforestation** is related to soil erosion, as tropical forests have been cut down to clear land for livestock and crop production, oil extraction or urbanisation. Although there are no accurate statistics, it is estimated that an average of around 0.5 million hectares of tropical forests were cleared annually between 1985 and 1992. The associated loss of biodiversity could be a major problem.[18] In the southern state of Oaxaca, it is estimated that 4.6 million hectares suffer from severe erosion,[19] exerting pressure on the rural population (most of whom are in a state of poverty) to migrate. While Mexican agriculture uses around 8 times less inorganic fertilisers per unit of agricultural land than most other OECD countries, fertiliser and pesticide use is heavily skewed towards commercial farms, the residuals of which in water supplies carry environmental risks.

Water pollution is a major problem in Mexico as a large proportion of urban development is at high altitudes with limited sewage treatment plants. As rivers run down toward coastal zones, the water reaching the dams or the sea is often already polluted by human and industrial waste. An index of water quality has been developed by the National Water Commission (CNA), taking into account chemical and biological agents (with 100 representing water of highest purity and zero fully polluted water). In 1994, it was found that in 29 out of the 37 main water regions of Mexico the index was 54, classifying the average water status as polluted. Soil salinisation is also a major problem for some areas of north-western Mexico mainly as a result of deficient irrigation procedures. It is estimated that between 0.6 and 0.8 million hectares have salinisation problems. Although most irrigation water comes from water stored in dams, the use of groundwater is common in the arid north, where the water table is being depleted. The **water depletion** problem is exacerbated as rain that could replenish water tables is scarce in these areas.

8. Agricultural trade

Agricultural trade in Mexico has greatly increased since the mid-1980s. In the ten years to 1995, exports of agro-food products increased 2.7 times while imports expanded 2.5 times, resulting in a total trade flow of over US$11 billion dollars (Figure 11). Mexico has registered an agricultural trade deficit since 1989, mainly because of the appreciation of the peso, but also as it lowered trade barriers on relatively highly protected agricultural products, allowing imports to climb from a low US$1.4 billion in 1986 to a peak US$7.3 billion in 1994. In 1995, with exports amounting to a record US$5.9 billion, the

◆ Figure 11. *Evolution of agro-food trade in Mexico*

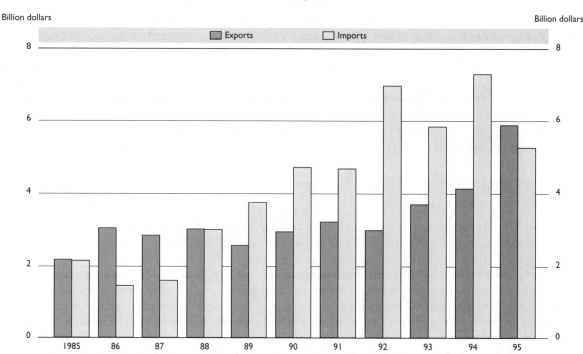

Source: Banco de México.

◆ Figure 12. **Mexico agro-food exports and imports**
Share of value in 1995

Agro-food exports
(US$5.86 billion)

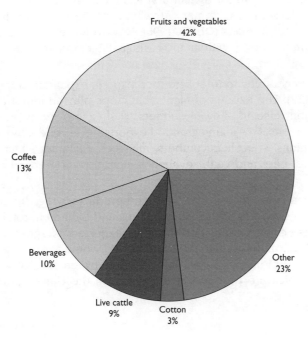

Fruits and vegetables
42%

Coffee
13%

Beverages
10%

Live cattle
9%

Cotton
3%

Other
23%

Agro-food imports
(US$5.22 billion)

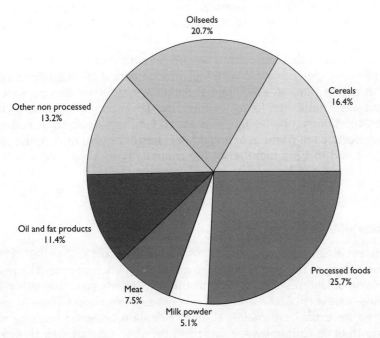

Oilseeds
20.7%

Cereals
16.4%

Other non processed
13.2%

Oil and fat products
11.4%

Meat
7.5%

Milk powder
5.1%

Processed foods
25.7%

Source: Banco de México.

agro-food trade balance was in surplus, partly aided by the devaluation of the peso, but also as a result of greater market access to countries with whom preferential trade agreements were signed. With the implementation of the NAFTA in 1994, Mexico opened the possibility to expand its market for products where it is competitive in the United States and Canada (and vice versa).

Although Mexico is among the largest agricultural producers in the OECD, the output of cereals, oilseeds and milk have been insufficient to meet growing consumption, so it is becoming an increasingly large net importer of these products (OECD, 1996). However, Mexico is among the largest exporters of fruits and vegetables in the world, with an increasingly larger market share, and the fourth largest exporter of coffee.

The share of fruits and vegetables to total agro-food exports expanded from 31 per cent in 1989 to 42 per cent in 1995 (Figure 12). The exports of high value crops play an important role not only in the agricultural trade balance, but also in allowing farmers to shift into more profitable crops, as trade barriers are removed. In 1995, Mexico's main agro-food exports were: coffee, live cattle, tomatoes, beer, tequila, peppers, cotton, onions, squash, cucumbers, mangoes, bananas, sugar and orange juice. The main agro-food imports were: beef and veal, soyabeans, maize, powdered milk, sorghum, cottonseed and wheat.

The main traditional destination for Mexican agro-food products is the United States (see Table I.5, Annex I). The share of Mexico's exports to the United States and Canada in total agro-food exports was 89 per cent in 1993-94. These countries are also the main exporters of agro-food products to Mexico, with a 76 per cent share of Mexican imports in the same period. Some agro-industries, such as beef and veal, have become highly complementary and integrated between Mexico and the United States. Mexico exports live cattle, which are then fed at lower cost in the United States, and subsequently imports beef and veal.

D. LAND REFORM

1. The post-revolutionary agrarian situation

At the end of Spanish colonisation land ownership in Mexico was concentrated among few people in the "latifundios" or large land holdings, leaving little land to most of the people in the rural communities. The 1910 Mexican revolution eventually brought about the Agrarian Law of 1915, which later became a part of Article 27 of the Mexican Constitution of 1917. The Agrarian Law established the redistribution of the land to the peasantry.

Within the Agrarian Law two other major land tenure features were added: the establishment of maximum limits to land use under private ownership, which banned the latifundio system, and the official establishment of the "ejido" as a communal agrarian system for the peasantry. For private owners, a maximum limit was established for agricultural use. This was 100 hectares under irrigation, or larger in case of rain-fed conditions (one hectare of irrigated land was deemed as equivalent to two of rain-fed arable land, four hectares of pasture, and eight hectares of brush). Also, in the 1920s, under the "ejido" system, a peasant had to be a member of the community to have access to the use of land. Individual parcels of land could not be sold or rented, keeping the land tied to the community. The land could be inherited but remained the property of the nation.

2. The current agrarian situation

Land redistribution resulting from the Agrarian Laws had reached more than half of the total surface area of Mexico by the beginning of the 1990s, involving about 3.5 million people. The result has been a more equitable distribution of land resulting from redistribution efforts since the 1920s. The conditions at that time involved large amounts of land and a relatively small rural population. Moreover, the rural and agricultural infrastructure expanded (mainly through irrigation projects) bringing about a 7.6 per cent average annual growth of agricultural value added in the 1946-1956 period. However, by the late 1960s arable land became increasingly scarce while the pressure on more agricultural land continued (see Section B.2). The rural population doubled from nearly 10 million in 1921 to 20 million in 1970 (see Figure 2).

Population pressure on agricultural land favoured "minifundios" or small farms of 2 hectares or less, both in the private and the communal systems. The productivity of the majority of these farms is poor given that much of the land has agro-ecological constraints. The land tends to be in hilly areas highly susceptible to soil erosion, and rainfall is usually uneven. Also, they are often far from modern means of transportation, making the access to inputs such as fertilisers and seeds more difficult. Most of them are associated with a subsistence economy, where farmers have to temporally migrate in search of work either within the agricultural or the industrial sectors. This situation has hindered efforts to increase the agricultural productivity of these lands, and poverty is the prevailing condition among farmers and their families.

The post-revolution agrarian laws discouraged the growth of large scale farms in Mexico. The laws inhibited the association of small farmers given that their land could be subject to expropriation if the combined size surpassed the legally established limits. The laws also introduced some insecurity of ownership. Private producers were afraid of investing in infrastructure since the possibility of expropriation of their land was always present. For instance, if 300 hectares were farmed under rain-fed conditions, and the owner wanted to invest in irrigation infrastructure, the maximum amount of land allowed for farming would decrease to 100 hectares, a situation which would permit the legal expropriation of the remaining 200 hectares.

As the ejido land could not be rented, transferred, sharecropped, or used within commercial associations, the flow of capital into the ejido was limited. With ejido land transactions forbidden, farmers could not acquire more land and therefore could not expand their scale of production. Also, credit institutions would distance themselves from the ejidos, since the land was not accepted as a guarantee for collateral. Nevertheless, large areas of the ejido land were rented illegally, outside any legal framework, creating disadvantages for both the land owners and the renters.

3.   The current agrarian laws

These developments and insecurities prompted the Mexican government to modify the agrarian reform laws to better meet the needs of the rural population facing the prospect of increasingly open markets. In 1992, Article 27 of the Mexican Constitution, and the Agrarian Law, were reformed. Land redistribution was declared to have ended, individuals within the ejidos were awarded increased rights to their lands, and commercial associations of farmers were permitted.

The new legislation establishes a flexible regime of land tenure within the ejidos. The agricultural ejido land is divided into two categories: for common use and parcelled plots. Common land cannot be transferred to other individuals, but it can be used in productive associations of farmers or rented for up to 30 years. The decision on what to do with the common land is made by the local ejido assembly. The parcelled land is also property of the ejido, but the individual ejidatario has the permanent right to use his parcel of land. Although the parcel belongs to the ejido, the individual can rent his land for up to 30 years. He can also sell the land to other members of the ejido.

The ejido assembly is allowed to authorise the separation of parcelled land from the ejido, and with it individuals can become private property owners. If the ejido parcel is converted into private property, the former ejido member can sell or rent it to other persons outside the ejido, obtain a mortgage or use it as if it were any other type of private property.

The reforms to the Agrarian Law created the Agrarian Procurement Office (*Procuradoría Agraria*), coordinated by the Secretariat of Agrarian Reform, with the main function of providing legal advice to ejido members. In order to establish the limits of individual parcels, and award property titles, the government created the Programme for Certification of Ejido Rights (PROCEDE: *Programa de Certificación de Derechos Ejidales y Titulación de Solares Urbanos*).[20] Also, Agrarian Courts were created to settle disputes over land tenure, giving security to land ownership.

Recent agrarian reforms have established that the former size limits on land ownership should remain the same. However, the law now permits the formation of larger plots through productive associations of farmers. Also, joint stock associations are allowed to own land, with maximum limits up to 25 times the size of individual private land areas, with foreign investment permitted. These established limits are designed to avoid the emergence of disguised latifundios, thus recognising the need of land for the peasantry.

NOTES AND REFERENCES

1. Purchasing power parities (PPPs) are the rates of currency conversion that eliminate the differences in price levels between countries. *Source:* OECD (1997), *Main Economic Indicators*, Paris.

2. An historical account of economic growth policies is given in: OECD (1992), OECD *Economic Surveys: Mexico*, Paris.

3. A plan designed to provide partial debt relief from private foreign lenders bearing the name of former US Secretary of Treasury.

4. Before the devaluation of the peso in December 1994, the exchange rate regime consisted of a fluctuating band, which was widened daily to allow for a certain degree of peso depreciation. An historical account of the exchange rate regime can be found in the *OECD Economic Surveys of Mexico* of 1992, 1995 and 1996.

5. The *OECD Economic Survey of Mexico* 1995, details the origins and evolution of the 1994-1995 Mexican crisis.

6. At the end of the world depression in 1934, manufacturing output expanded 161 per cent, reaching 18 per cent of the GDP in 1945, while the share of agriculture to total output decreased to 16 per cent. *Source:* INEGI (1994), *Estadísticas Históricas de México*, Mexico.

7. Data from CONAPO (National Council on Population) based on the 9th General Population Census 1970. Mexico City comprises the Federal District and the surrounding municipalities from the State of Mexico.

8. Rural population is that living in communities of less than 2 500 people. *Source:* INEGI.

9. *Source:* INEGI (1993), *Encuesta Nacional de Empleo*, Mexico.

10. Employment statistics are based on the National Survey of Employment, INEGI. The "open unemployment rate" refers to people aged twelve and over, who were not employed in the reference week, and had been searching for work in the two months prior to the survey, without any success.

11. Schools in rural areas have deficiencies in terms of completion as well as enrolment rates. In 1990-91, between 40 and 50 per cent of schools in rural areas did not offer the six grades required to finish the primary basic education, as compared to 10 per cent or less in urban areas. In recent years, specific government programmes have aimed to increase the enrolment rate through the use of school meals, student grants and medical care.

12. The in-bond or "maquila" industry refers to the use of Mexican labour to assemble foreign goods that are re-exported to the countries of origin. It is mainly located along the US-Mexico border.

13. *Source:* INEGI, *11th General Population Census 1990*. Based on individuals aged 15 years or older who finished six years of primary school or higher degrees.

14. Wages are estimates from national account data reported by INEGI. The term "wage" is used rather than "compensation" since most farmers are self-employed and are outside social security or other schemes.

15. *Source:* SAGAR (1995), *Anuario Estadístico de la Producción Agrícola de los Estados Unidos Mexicanos, 1994,* and Dirección General de Información Agropecuaria, Forestal y de la Fauna Silvestre, SAGAR.

16. Mexico is an oil producing country, and the ammonia required for nitrogen fertiliser was provided by PEMEX (*Petróleos Mexicanos*) at a low cost.

17. Under the 1991 Seed Law, the new category "verified" can be used by private seed companies to indicate the viability of the seed. Also, under the 1991 Law on Development and Protection of Intellectual Property, plant varieties are patentable.

18. According to the World Bank, Mexico ranks fourth in diversity of biological varieties after Brazil, Colombia and China.

19. 2.8 million hectares are totally eroded and 1.8 suffer "accelerated" erosion. *Source:* SEDESOL, 1991.

20. The individual parcels within the ejidos were not properly delineated, such that land rights awarded under the new Agrarian Law could be a matter of dispute among ejido members.

BIBLIOGRAPHY

FAO (1995), *Production Yearbook, 1994*, Vol. 48, Rome.

INEGI (1994), *VII Censo Agrícola-Ganadero*, Mexico.

OECD (1992), *OECD Economic Surveys: Mexico*, Paris.

OECD (1995), *OECD Economic Surveys: Mexico*, Paris.

OECD (1996), *The Agricultural Outlook, Trends and Issues to 2000*, Paris.

OECD (1996), *OECD Economic Surveys: Mexico*, Paris.

SCHMITT, G.H. (1988), "What do Agricultural Income and Productivity Measurements Really Mean?" *Journal of Agricultural Economics*, Vol. 2, pp.139-157.

2

AGRICULTURAL POLICIES

A. AGRICULTURAL POLICY FRAMEWORK

1. Agricultural policy making

During the first year of the 6-year Presidency in Mexico, the executive branch of the federal government (*Poder Ejecutivo Federal*) prepares a National Development Plan (NDP) and send it to Congress for comments and advice. The NDP covers the six years of the administration, and is the result of a nation-wide public consultation. The NPD for the period 1995-2000 was published in May 1995.

In July 1995, as part of the preparation of the agenda for agricultural policies for the period 1995-2000, the President established the Intersecretarial Commission of the Agricultural Cabinet (CIGA) (see the composition of CIGA in Figure 1). The themes discussed by CIGA were: certification of land titles; final modalities of operation of the Programme of Direct Payments to the Countryside (PRO-CAMPO); productivity and competitiveness enhancement; rural credit; marketing of agricultural products; extension and organisational support for technological development; federalisation of SAGAR. The consensus reached between farmers' associations and the various Secretariats during the working sessions of CIGA resulted in the "Alliance for Agriculture", which was presented by the Secretary of Agriculture to the President in October 1995.

More generally, agricultural policy making stems from the President's Agricultural Cabinet (see Figure 1). This Cabinet deals with major agricultural policy decisions, including the setting of administered prices, direct payments, and the size of any import and export quotas in accordance with NAFTA and GATT commitments. It is also in charge of approving consumer prices submitted by SECOFI for certain foods.

In practice, proposals for the approval of the Agricultural Cabinet are submitted by SAGAR after close consultation with the two state-owned agencies CONASUPO (National Basic Foods Company) and ASERCA (Support Services for Agricultural Marketing), and farmers' associations. The decisions of the Agricultural Cabinet are also guided by the recommendations of ad hoc working groups which include representatives from various Secretariats and government agencies. Since 1988, the setting of producer prices of maize and beans by the Agricultural Cabinet has to be ratified by the *Pacto* (Pact for Economic Solidarity) which is a consultation process between the government and all the main components of the private and social sectors, aimed at lowering inflation (see Chapter I, Section B.1.). In 1995, the Pacto has continued to operate, but under the name of "Alliance to Restore the Economy".

The Congress is directly responsible for approving the national budget, including the allocation of budgetary resources between the Secretariats, among the main programmes and state-owned agencies involved in agricultural matters. The budget of PROCAMPO has to be approved by the Congress each year.

2. Objectives of agricultural policy

Agricultural policy objectives have evolved over time, reflecting the changes in the broader economic policy objectives in Mexico. Over the review period, the goals of agricultural policy have included: domestic food self-sufficiency, lowering food prices to help poor consumers; the improvement of farm incomes; the reduction of income disparities within agriculture; and the development of exports to generate foreign currency.

◆ Figure 1. **Government bodies involved in agricultural policy making**

Government bodies	Composition	Main activity
Agricultural Cabinet	Président SAGAR (Agriculture) SHCP (Finance) SECOFI (Trade) SRA (Agrarian Reform) SEDESOL (Social Development) SEMARNAP (Environment) CONASUPO (National Basic Foods) BANRURAL (Rural credit) FIRA (Rural credit) AGROASEMEX (Insurance) ASERCA (Marketing support, PROCAMPO)	Major agricultural policy decisions
Intersecretarial Commission of the Agricultural Cabinet (CIGA)	SAGAR (Agriculture) SHCP (Finance) SECOFI (Trade) SRA (Agrarian Reform) SEDESOL (Social Development) SEMARNAP (Environment) STPS (Labour) SEP (Education) Governors Senators Deputies Farmers' associations	Preparation of the 1995-2000 national development programme for the agricultural sector
Congress	Deputies Senators	Approval of budget

(1) shown between first two rows.

Note: (See list of acronyms at the end of Chapter II for full title of Secretariat/agencies.)
1. In lits extended sessions.
Source: OECD Secretariat, 1997.

From the mid-1960s to 1980, as part of the overall economic objective of encouraging urbanisation and industrialisation through import substitution, the main objective of agricultural policy was to provide abundant and inexpensive food supplies to consumers. Following the discovery of new oil reserves in Mexico and the oil boom of 1973, the Government established the Mexican Food System (SAM) in 1980, with the aim of re-attaining[1] self-sufficiency in beans, cereals and oilseeds by 1985. The debt crisis triggered by weakening oil prices in 1982 forced the government to reduce expenditure on the agricultural sector. The cost of the SAM could no longer be sustained, and the programme was terminated at the end of 1982. From 1983 to 1988, the main agricultural policy objective was to improve the productivity of the sector as a way to economise on scarce resources. This change in direction was given extra emphasis when oil prices crashed in 1986.

During the period 1989-1994, Mexico embarked on an ambitious and radical programme to reform agricultural policy, aimed at more market orientation, less domestic regulation and more trade liberalisation, and better policy targeting. This originated from the overall process of stabilising the economy, liberalising foreign trade (especially through NAFTA), and privatising public enterprises which started with the "debt" crisis brought by the world oil glut and price fall in 1982 (see Chapter I, Section B.1.). Within this broad context, in May 1990, the **National Programme for the Modernisation of Agriculture** was formulated for the period 1990-1994. This programme was aimed primarily at increasing the welfare of the rural population and the efficiency in resource use, and improving the agricultural trade balance, in particular through more market orientation, less regulation and better policy targeting.

For the period 1995-2000, these objectives have been reaffirmed in the **Alliance for Agriculture Programme** (see Box II.1). More specifically, the programme defines the aims of agricultural policy:

- to raise producers' income;
- to increase agricultural production at a higher rate than population growth;
- to reach a balance in agricultural trade;
- to obtain self-sufficiency in basic foodstuffs;
- to reduce regional differences in productivity, employment and income; and,
- to contribute to rural poverty alleviation, natural resources conservation and better occupation of the territory by the population.

3. Agricultural policy measures

In order to achieve the objectives stated above, the Government has implemented a combination of general and sector-specific measures, with an increasing emphasis in recent years on direct payments not based on current specific commodity production. The creation of a competitive environment for

---

Box II.1   **The Alliance for Agriculture Programme**

The Alliance for Agriculture (*Alianza para el campo*) programme was announced at the end of 1995 to be implemented from 1996-2000. It consists of a set of specific programmes primarily aimed at improving farmers' skills and stimulating technological development with a view to increasing the productivity and competitiveness of the Mexican farm sector in an open economy. The global budget of Alliance is shared between the federal government – around M$1.2 billion (US$158 million) in 1996 – and state governments – around M$0.7 billion (US$92 million) in 1996. The federal budget is allocated among the various States by the Intersecretarial Commission of the Agricultural Cabinet (CIGA). The State Agricultural Councils (*Consejo Estatal Agropecuario*) are responsible for approving project proposals to receive funds from the Alliance programmes submitted by farmers' associations, and for evaluating the implementation of these projects once approved.

PRODUCE programmes

	Ferti-irrigation	Prairies	Rural equipment	Mechanisation	Farm studies and projects
Principal aim	to increase productivity in irrigated areas through an efficient use of water and fertilisers	to improve livestock production through the efficient use of pastureland	to promote the use of intermediate technology by small farms with commercial potential	to increase and renew the country's machinery stock	to support studies to develop projects which promote sustainable agriculture
1996 targets	110 000 hectares of cropland	200 000 hectares of pastureland		11 450 tractors (new and repaired vehicles)	
Upper limit of support	M$2 450 (US$322) per hectare	M$70 000 (US$9 210) per farm		M$20 000 (US$2 631) per new tractor M$5 000 (US$658) per repaired tractor	M$20 000 (US$2 631) per farm

(continued on next page)

(continued)

The Programme PRODUCE is the main programme within the Alliance for Agriculture. Its main objectives are to improve the production base of farms and to promote the introduction of technologies in order to increase farm productivity. Under PRODUCE, payments are granted directly to farmers once and for all during the 1996-2000 period for the purchase of capital goods, and for the provision of technical support by private foundations. Farmers can benefit from several measures of support at the same time, although there is a maximum support limit per project component. PRODUCE includes five sub-programmes: ferti-irrigation, prairies, rural equipment, mechanisation, and farm studies and projects.

Other programmes associated with the production of specific commodities

	Milk production	Genetic improvement	Seed exchange	Coffee	Oilseeds production	Rubber
Principal aims	to increase milk production and reduce the share of imports through genetic improvement of livestock	to renew the cattle population	to increase the productivity of maize and beans through the use of certified seed	to increase productivity of coffee plantations	to increase the production of oilseeds by expanding the cultivated area	to increase the production of rubber by expanding the cultivated area
1996 targets	10% increase in domestic milk production	import of genetic material to breed 140 500 head of cattle	use of certified seed for 230 000 ha maize, 55 000 ha beans, and 4 500 ha of rice and chickpeas	increase in productivity on 337 000 ha	additional area of 350 000 ha soya, 450 000 ha cotton, 150 000 ha palm oil, 57 000 ha coconut, and 5 350 African palm	additional area of 40 000 ha
Upper limit of support	M$4 000 (US$526)/bull M$1 500 (US$197)/ heifer, 100% of the cost of training farmers		Certified seed sold to farms at the lowest price of seed from harvest	50% of the cost of planting	M$3 500 (US$460) per hectare of African palm	

Other programmes are also part of the Alliance for Agriculture programme. Some of them are associated with the production of specific commodities while others are more general, and intended to benefit agriculture as a whole (animal health, plant health, rural training and extension, rural employment, women in rural development, marketing and promotion). They are all intended to improve productivity.

One of the key features of Alliance for Agriculture is the decentralisation of its implementation at the rural development district (DDR)[2] level, which supervision has been transferred to the State governments. In each State, Trust Funds (*Fideicomisos*) have been created to provide a single channel for all payments to eligible farmers to support farm equipment purchase, and PRODUCE foundations (*Fundaciones* PRODUCE) have been established to provide farmers with technical assistance, in co-ordination with the National Institute for Forestry, Agricultural and Livestock Research (INIFAP). With the Foundations, there will be a greater participation of producers in deciding the kind of research that should be carried out to solve the main problems hindering economic efficiency.

agriculture is being addressed through general reforms of the economic system in Mexico, including trade liberalisation, privatisation of state-owned agencies, and land tenure reform (see Chapter I, Section D). Trade liberalisation is being underpinned by Mexico's accession to the GATT in 1986 and was reinforced with the entry into force of NAFTA in January 1994 and the Uruguay Round Agreement in 1995.

In the 1980s, the main agricultural policy measures to assist **producers** in Mexico were those that directly or indirectly supported farm prices and incomes, and those that sought to improve the production base (see Chart 1). Price and income support policies have included measures to support domestic prices, generally complemented with trade measures. Measures to improve the agricultural production base have consisted of credit subsidies; tax concessions; reduction of farm input costs; research, education and extension; inspection, pest and disease control; development of agricultural structures and infrastructures; rural development; and marketing and promotion.

Since the end of the 1980s, there has been a marked shift from price support and trade measures, to direct payments to farmers, especially through PROCAMPO (see Chart 2). The system of property rights for land and water was fundamentally changed to allow the development of a land market and a market for water concession rights. To accompany this change in the policy mix while helping producers to adapt to the influence of international markets, additional measures were taken to improve the production base of farms, to help farmers diversify into more competitive agricultural activities, and apply resource conservation practices, in particular through the Alliance for Agriculture Programme (see Box II.1).

The following sections provide a detailed description of these various agricultural policy measures. On the **consumer side,** specific measures relating to food consumption are an important part of Mexican agri-food policy. They are described in Section L. The transfers from consumers or taxpayers resulting from these support measures, and the trends since 1979, are discussed in Chapter III. Market transfers which are borne by consumers as a result of agricultural policies are also detailed in Chapter III.

4. Agricultural policy implementation

The structure for implementing agricultural policy in Mexico is complex, with a large number of Secretariats and state-owned agencies involved, and the evolution over time of the number of agencies and their supervision by Secretariats (see Figures 2 and 3).

a) Secretariats

The Secretariat of Agriculture and Hydraulic Resources (SARH) was created in 1976 through the merger of two Secretariats (Hydraulic Resources and Agriculture). The budget and personnel of SARH increased substantially during the implementation of the Mexican Food System (SAM) from 1980 to 1982. In 1983, SARH employed more than 133 000 people within 46 General Directorates and supervised 89 state-owned agencies. In 1995, SARH became the **Secretariat of Agriculture and Rural Development (SAGAR).** This decision reflected the new priority given to the link between agriculture and rural development, and the transfer of responsibilities for implementing water and forestry policies to the **Secretariat of Environment, Natural Resources and Fisheries (SEMARNAP).** SAGAR is currently structured into three Under-secretariats: agriculture and livestock (policy implementation and sanitary and phytosanitary control); planning (economic studies, diffusion of information, and international affairs for the agricultural sector); and rural development. The number of SAGAR employees is currently about 35 000, within 11 General Directorates, and about 85 per cent of the staff are employed in the states and Rural Development Districts (DDRs).

Since their creation in 1991, greater impetus has been given to the participation of the DDRs in agricultural policy implementation as well as in the preparation and creation of agricultural and regional development plans and programmes. Since 1993, 193 DDRs are in place in the 32 States, including 708 Rural Development Service Centers (CADER) acting as focal points to farmers for the provision of basic services (extension, research, access to credit, inputs). As part of the decentralisation process, the DDRs have been placed under the supervision of the state governments. The role of state governments

Chart 1. **Main agricultural policy measures in Mexico in the mid-1980s**

Commodity	Price and income support measures			Consumer measures			Measures (non-commodity specific) to improve the production base
	Support prices		Border measures [1]	Consumer subsidy		Retail price ceilings	
	Guaranteed price CONASUPO	Concerted price		Social programme	Other [2]		
Maize	x		P		x	x	
Beans	x		P		x	x	
Wheat	x		P		x	x	
Barley	x		P		x	x	
Sorghum	x		P		x		
Rice	x		T		x	x	
Soyabeans	x		P		x	x	
Sugarcane		x	P		x	x	
Cotton		x	P				
Coffee		x	P		x	x	
Tobacco		x	P			x	
Fruits and veg.			P				
Milk			P	x		x	
Beef and veal			T			x	
Pigmeat			T				
Poultrymeat			P				
Eggs			P			x	

Measures (non-commodity specific) to improve the production base:

input subsidies:
interest concessions
fertiliser
fuel tax concessions
insurance
electric water pumping
feed
improved seed
cultivation services
breeding material
general services:
research
training
extension
pest and disease control
structures/infrastructures
marketing and promotion

1. (P) = import permits, (T) = import tariffs.
2. Government transfers to the first buyer of agricultural production.
See list of acronyms for full title of Secretariats/agencies.
Source: OECD Secretariat, 1997.

Chart 2. **Main agricultural policy measures in Mexico in 1995**

Commodity	*Price and income support measures*							*Consumer measures*			*Measures (non-commodity specific) to improve the production base*
	Market price support			Direct payments		Border measures[2]		Consumer subsidy		Retail price ceilings	
	CONASUPO minimum price	Concerted price	PACE marketing subsidy	ASERCA marketing support	PROCAMPO area payments[1]	NAFTA	GATT Uruguay Round[3]	Social programmes	Other[4]		
Maize	x		x		x	Q	TQ	x	x	x	*input subsidies:*
Beans	x		x		x	Q	TQ		x		interest concessions
Wheat					x	T	TQ		x	x[5]	fuel tax concessions
Barley					x	Q	TQ				insurance
Sorghum					x	Free	T				electric water pumping
Rice				x	x	T	T				feed
Soyabeans					x	Free	T				*general services:*
Sugarcane		x				Q	TQ			x[5]	research
Cotton					x	T	T				training
Coffee						T	TQ				extension
Tobacco						T	T				pest and disease control
Fruits and veg.						Q/T/Free	T				structures/infrastructures
Milk						Q	Q	x		x	marketing and
											promotion
Beef and veal						Free	T				*land tenure reform:*
Pigmeat						T	T				development of a land
Poultrymeat						Q	TQ				market
Eggs						Q	T				

1. In 1995, payments were granted for the production of the crops listed below plus safflower. Since the Autumn/Winter 1995/96 crop season, farmers under PROCAMPO may devote their land to any crop, livestock, or forestry production, or place it in an approved environmental programme.
2. (Q) = duty-free import quotas, (TQ) = 50 per cent tariff quotas, (T) = import tariffs, (Free) = duty-free imports.
3. The Uruguay Round commitments are not necessarily applied.
4. Government transfers to the first buyer of agricultural production.
5. The consumer price ceilings for wheat products and sugar were abolished in the course of 1995.

See list of acronyms for full title of Secretariats/agencies.

Source: OECD Secretariat, 1997.

◆ Figure 2. **Government agencies involved in the implementation of agricultural policies in the mid-1980s**

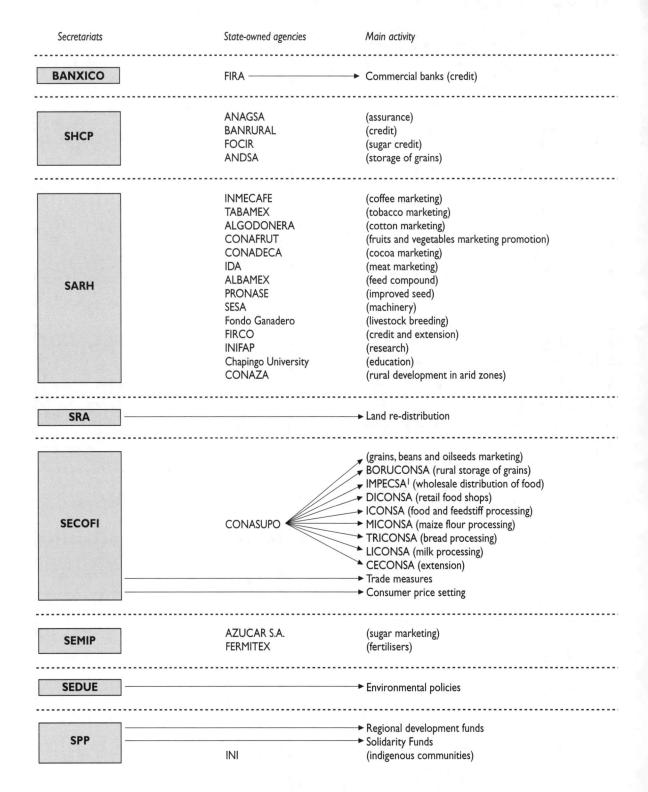

Secretariats	State-owned agencies	Main activity
BANXICO	FIRA ──────────▶	Commercial banks (credit)
SHCP	ANAGSA BANRURAL FOCIR ANDSA	(assurance) (credit) (sugar credit) (storage of grains)
SARH	INMECAFE TABAMEX ALGODONERA CONAFRUT CONADECA IDA ALBAMEX PRONASE SESA Fondo Ganadero FIRCO INIFAP Chapingo University CONAZA	(coffee marketing) (tobacco marketing) (cotton marketing) (fruits and vegetables marketing promotion) (cocoa marketing) (meat marketing) (feed compound) (improved seed) (machinery) (livestock breeding) (credit and extension) (research) (education) (rural development in arid zones)
SRA	───────────────▶	Land re-distribution
SECOFI	CONASUPO	(grains, beans and oilseeds marketing) BORUCONSA (rural storage of grains) IMPECSA[1] (wholesale distribution of food) DICONSA (retail food shops) ICONSA (food and feedstiff processing) MICONSA (maize flour processing) TRICONSA (bread processing) LICONSA (milk processing) CECONSA (extension) Trade measures Consumer price setting
SEMIP	AZUCAR S.A. FERMITEX	(sugar marketing) (fertilisers)
SEDUE	───────────────▶	Environmental policies
SPP	 INI	Regional development funds Solidarity Funds (indigenous communities)

Note: See list of acronyms at the end of Chapter II for full title of Secretariat/Agencies.
1.   In process in privatisation.
Source: OECD Secretariat, 1997.

in implementing agricultural policies has become more prominent in 1996 with the launching of the Alliance for Agriculture programme (see Box II.1).

In addition, SAGAR supervises various state-owned agencies, although their number has decreased over time. Many of the agencies responsible for crop marketing (see Section A.4.*b*. below) and farm inputs supply disappeared in the early 1990s. In 1995, the main institutions supervised by SAGAR were: the National Basic Foods Company (CONASUPO); Support and Services to Agricultural Marketing (ASERCA); the Trust Fund for Shared Risk (FIRCO); the National Institute for Forestry, Agricultural and Livestock Research (INIFAP); and Chapingo Agricultural University (see Figure 3).

The **Secretariat of Commerce and Industrial Development (SECOFI)** is responsible for trade policy and the implementation of retail and wholesale food price ceilings. Until 1995, it also supervised the activities of CONASUPO and its affiliates (see Box II.2). In 1995, two of the affiliates of CONASUPO

◆   Figure 3.   ***Government agencies involved in the implementation of agricultural policies in 1995***

Secretariats		State-owned agencies	Main activity
		FIRA	Commercial banks (credit)
SHCP	NAFIN →	AGROASEMEX	(insurance)
		BANRURAL	(credit)
		FOCIR	(marketing and promotion)
		ANDSA[1]	(storage of grains)
SAGAR		CONASUPO	→ (maize and beans consumer subsidies)
			→ BORUCONSA[1] (rural storage of grains)
		ASERCA	→ PROCAMPO (direct payments)
			→ (marketing and promotion)
		COAAZUCAR	(sugar marketing)
		FIRCO	(credit and extension)
		INIFAP	(research)
		Chapingo University	(education)
		INCARURAL	(extension)
SRA		INDA	(extension)
		RAN	(land registration)
		PROCEDE	(land certification)
SECOFI			→ Trade measures
			→ Consumer price setting
SEMARNAP		INE	(ecology)
		CNA	(irrigation)
		PROFEPA	(environmental regulations)
SEDESOL		DICONSA	(retail shops)
		LICONSA	(milk distribution)
		FIDELIST	(maize tortilla coupons)
		CONAZA	(rural development in arid zones)
		INI	(indigenous communities)
			→ Poverty alleviation funds

Note: See list of acronyms at the end of Chapter II for full title of Secretariats/agencies.
1. In process of privatisation.
Source: OECD Secretariat, 1997.

Box II.2. **CONASUPO and its affiliates**

Since its creation in 1965, the **National Basic Foods Company (CONASUPO)** has been primarily responsible for lowering food prices in remote urban and rural areas, while helping small and medium-sized food retailers. CONASUPO has intervened in the market for staple foods, from the purchase of agricultural commodities to processing, wholesaling, and retailing. Until 1990, CONASUPO purchased part of the domestic production and imported maize, beans, wheat, sorghum, malt barley, rice, soyabeans and other oilseeds. CONASUPO sold its domestic purchases and imports to its affiliates and private millers and retailers at a price equivalent or below the purchase price, thus without charging them its own storage, financial, and transportation costs. However, since 1991, only maize and beans (which are very important commodities in the Mexican diet) have been domestically purchased by CONASUPO. In 1995, the share of CONASUPO in the purchasing of domestic production of maize and beans has declined. Since its inception in 1965, CONASUPO is also charged with milk powder imports.

CONASUPO has had a number of affiliates dealing with storage (BORUCONSA); food processing (MICONSA, ICONSA, TRICONSA, and LICONSA); extension (CECONCA); wholesale food distribution (IMPECSA); retail distribution (DICONSA), and financing (FIA). However, these affiliates have been either privatised (FIA in 1991, ICONSA in 1992, MICONSA in 1994); dismantled (TRICONSA in 1986, CECONCA in 1987); put into liquidation (IMPECSA in 1995); restructured (closure of about 600 Conasuper shops of DICONSA in urban areas in 1990, privatisation of nine plants of LICONSA in 1991-93); or transferred to SEDESOL (LICONSA and DICONSA in 1995). In the case of BORUCONSA, a process of transfer to ejido producers has been put in place.

Until 1992, **ICONSA (CONASUPO Industries SA)** produced food (vegetable oil, wheat and maize flour, and paste) and feedstuffs (oil cake, concentrate, by-products of wheat and maize). In 1987, the 19 mills of ICONSA employed 5 600 persons. In 1990, 10 mills of ICONSA were sold at M$ 430 (US$151) million. Until 1994, **MICONSA (CONASUPO Industrialised Maize SA)** specialised in maize flour production. In 1987, the 5 mills of MICONSA employed 1 500 persons, producing 412 000 tonnes of maize flour, being the second-largest maize flour producer in Mexico The private company MINSA which has purchased MICONSA in 1994 currently supplies 27 per cent of the domestic market. Until 1986, **TRICONSA (CONASUPO Industrialised Wheat SA)** produced bread from the wheat flour produced by ICONSA. In 1986, TRICONSA employed 500 persons, producing 137 million loaves of bread.

Since 1965, **LICONSA (Industrialised Milk CONASUPO)** produces and supplies milk (at subsidised price) to low-income families in disadvantaged areas. Until 1990, its 17 plants produced between 1 and 1.5 billion litres of liquid milk (reconstituted from imported skimmed milk powder), and employed 7 500 persons. From 1991 to 1993, nine plants were sold at M$ 230 (US$74) million. Since 1994, LICONSA produces about 1 billion litres of rehydrated milk a year. In 1995, LICONSA owned 9 plants of liquid milk and one of powder milk and employed 4 680 people.

CECONCA (CONASUPO Extension Centres) specialised in technical training in marginal rural areas. **FIA (Fund for Associate Industry)** was created in 1980 to provide financial support to small and medium enterprises suppliers of CONASUPO commercial affiliates. **BORUCONSA (CONASUPO Rural Warehouses)** was created to supply DICONSA and IMPECSA distribution network in rural areas. In 1995, BORUCONSA owned 1 377 warehouses with a storage capacity of around 4 million tonnes.

DICONSA (CONASUPO Commercial Distribution and Promotion SA), (an affiliate of CONASUPO since its inception) function is to supply basic products to people living in marginal urban and rural areas at subsidised prices; to regulate consumer prices at retail level; and to assist farmers and small and medium processors in selling their surplus production. In 1980, DICONSA operated 6 400 rural stores (CONASUPER C), 2 000 urban stores (CONASUPER B), 120 supermarkets (CONASUPER A), and 9 hypermarkets. In 1995, the number of DICONSA stores had risen to 19 800 in rural areas, but had fallen to 1 000 in urban areas. In 1994, the sales value of basic products distributed by DICONSA accounted for M$ 2.8 (US$0.8) billion.

The opening of CONASUPER stores led to a significant fall in small retailers' profit margins. This situation led CONASUPO to purchase IMPECSA in 1979. The main objectives of **IMPECSA (Promotion of Retail Distribution SA)** was to assure a constant supply of basic products to marginal areas at accessible prices; to improve the efficiency of distribution systems in Mexico; and to protect consumers' interests through wholesale price regulation. IMPECSA bought either from producers or CONASUPO food processing affiliates, and sold to public and private small and medium size traders or processors, including to its own distribution network. The selling price was fixed so that it did not exceed the average wholesale price

(continued on next page)

(continued)

for these products in Mexico, while authorising a margin for retailers. IMPECSA ceased operating in 1995 and its capital assets are in the process of liquidation.

ANDSA (National Stores SA) is not an affiliate of CONASUPO, but provides storage services at commercial rates to CONASUPO, especially in urban and commercial production areas. ANDSA currently owns 965 storage facilities with a storage capacity which rose from 5.3 million tonnes in 1980 to 5.8 million tonnes in 1994. BORUCONSA and ANDSA storage facilities currently account for over 50 per cent of Mexico's basic food storage capacity. ANDSA is in process of privatisation. In 1993, 3 frigorific units of ANDSA were sold for M$ 13 (US$4) million.

(LICONSA and DICONSA) were transferred to the **Secretariat of Social Development (SEDESOL),** as well as the Trust Fund for the Liquidation of the Tortilla Subsidy (FIDELIST) (see Figure 3). Since its creation in 1992, SEDESOL is also responsible for implementing the National Solidarity Programme, which is now known as the Poverty Alleviation Programme (see Box II.3).

Box II.3. **The Poverty Alleviation Programme**

In 1989, **the National Solidarity Programme (PRONASOL)** was established by the Secretariat of Budget and Planning (SPP), which was in charge of regional development issues, to carry out projects designed to overcome poverty in Mexico. Projects are oriented mainly toward rural areas, as they have the highest concentration of poor households. In 1992, PRONASOL was attached to the newly created Secretariat for Social Development (SEDESOL) and its main objectives were to promote community initiatives and decisions through a bottom-up approach, and to create new relationships between low-income communities and the government in carrying out policies for poverty alleviation.

PRONASOL was implemented along three general lines: supply of basic infrastructure (housing, electrification, roads); social welfare (health, education, nutrition); and support to productive activities, including agricultural production. Until 1994, health and education centres, assistance to women, electrification and drinking water supply, rural roads, and agricultural production were among the main activities carried out by PRONASOL. The global budget of PRONASOL has increased continuously since its creation in 1989. It rose from M$ 1.64 (US$0.66) billion in 1989 to M$ 9.27 (US$2.74) billion in 1994. About 60 per cent of these resources were allocated to rural areas, and approximately 10 per cent to agricultural activities (see also Sections D and J).

Indigenous groups, peasant communities, and poor urban neighbourhoods have participated directly in PRONASOL programmes through the formation of Solidarity Committees which determine the projects to be carried out and the modalities of their implementation, in consultation with the public authorities. The second level of decision is constituted by the Municipal Council, chaired by the President of the Municipality and composed of representatives of the urban or rural communities. The Municipal Council is responsible for gathering the proposals of all the Solidarity Committees and selecting priorities according to the level of poverty among the communities and the nature of the projects. At the federal level, the Secretariat for Social Development establishes standards and general procedures for the implementation of PRONASOL programmes, and co-ordinates the participation of the different institutions and states in order to allocate federal and state resources.

In 1995, PRONASOL has continued to operate, but under the name of ''**Poverty Alleviation Programme**''. Greater emphasis has been given to the better targeting of financial assistance, in particular through the regrouping of number of former PRONASOL activities within three Funds: the Fund for social development at municipal level; the Fund for state priorities; and the Fund for employment and education promotion. In addition, the social programmes implemented by LICONSA (milk), the Trust Fund for Tortilla Subsidy Payments (maize tortilla) and DICONSA (retail shops) were transferred from the Secretariat of Commerce and Industrial Development (SECOFI) and placed under the supervision of the Secretariat for Social Development.

The **Secretariat of Agrarian Reform (SRA)** is in charge of implementing land tenure reform (see Chapter I, Section D), including land registration, dispute settlements for property rights, land allocation among "ejido" members, and legal assistance to ejidos for the selling or renting of their land to the private sector. This Secretariat currently employs about 12 000 persons. The **Secretariat of Finance and Public Credit (SHCP)** implements budgetary transfers to the public sector, including the various Secretariats, the National Rural Credit Bank (BANRURAL), the Mexican Agricultural Insurance Company (AGROASEMEX), and the Rural Sector Capitalisation and Investment Fund (FOCIR) through the National Development Bank (NAFIN) (see Figure 3). Until 1994, the Trust Fund for Agriculture (FIRA) depended from the **Bank of Mexico (BANXICO)**. In 1995, FIRA became independent.

b) State-owned agencies

As in all other sectors of the economy, the number of state-owned agencies involved in the marketing of agricultural products has been considerably reduced, especially since 1989. Some have been completely disbanded, and others privatised. The only notable exception was the creation of ASERCA in 1991, though with a different type of mandate. The privatisation process is still ongoing, as part of current economic policy objectives. The most important state-owned agencies involved in agricultural price and income support policies over the period under review are described in Box II.4.

B. PRICE AND INCOME SUPPORT POLICIES

1. Price support policies

a) Grains, beans and oilseeds

From the creation of CONASUPO in 1965 until 1988, **producer prices** were determined by the Mexican authorities for the twelve major food and feed grains, beans and oilseeds (maize, beans, wheat, barley, sorghum, rice, soyabeans and other oilseeds – sunflower (since 1971), safflower, cottonseed, sesame, and copra). This was achieved through the direct purchase from producers by CONASUPO at guaranteed prices, import controls (permits), and government transfers to absorb CONASUPO losses. The thrust of the policy was to support producers with higher prices than on world markets, keep prices to consumers at a lower level than producer prices, and to provide a market in which producers from different regions and with different costs of production were able to sell their products. However, during the 1980s, guaranteed prices were sometimes below international prices, as a result of lags in adjustment to changing macroeconomic conditions and anti-inflationary policies.

Until 1988, the Agricultural Cabinet set *guaranteed prices* (*precio de garantia*) for these 12 crops for each crop season (see Annex I, Table II.1). Before farmers' planting decisions were made, the Agricultural Cabinet decided the commodities for which guaranteed prices would be announced. Guaranteed prices were the prices CONASUPO would pay for the crops at harvest time and, when appropriate, were adjusted at the discretion of the government or for any nominal increases in prices of farm inputs between the time of announcement and harvest time. Guaranteed prices were applied at the same level in all parts of the country and were intended to cover a weighted average of production costs for a variety of representative technologies and areas, with international prices serving only as a guide. Production costs vary widely in Mexico, however, and the setting of guaranteed prices was essentially a compromise between producer and consumer interests, within the budget available to support low consumer and higher producer prices.

The quantity of production eligible to receive guaranteed prices was unlimited: CONASUPO acted as the buyer of last resort for all those producers who could not find markets for their production. However, the discretionary way of announcing guaranteed prices and adjusting them with inflation created uncertainty among producers. The share of domestic production purchased by CONASUPO varied greatly depending on crop and year, but generally ranged between 15 and 35 per cent for grains and beans, and between 5 and 10 per cent for oilseeds (see Annex I, Table II.2). When excluding the part of domestic production which was consumed by producers themselves, CONASUPO's share of marketed production ranged between 20 to 60 per cent for maize and beans over the period between 1965 to 1988.

Box II.4. **State-owned agencies involved in agricultural price
and income support**[3]

The number of staff employed by the **National Basic Foods Company (CONASUPO)** and its affiliates decreased from 53 000 in 1989 to 3 400 persons in 1995. Its overall budget (including the affiliates) increased from M$ 2 (US$160) million in 1965 to around M$ 9 (US$1.4) billion in 1995, around half of which were transfers from the government (see detailed description of CONASUPO and its affiliates in Box II.2).

Since its creation in 1991, **ASERCA (Support and Services to Agricultural Marketing)** is responsible for promoting the marketing of wheat, sorghum, rice, soyabeans and other oilseeds, as well as the export of cotton and fruits and vegetables. ASERCA does not purchase agricultural commodities, but provides market information, and helps producers to find distribution channels. Until 1995, ASERCA granted payments to private millers who bought the domestic production of wheat, sorghum, and oilseeds in areas distant from the main consumption centres as a way to provide support to producers. In the case of rice, payments are granted directly to producers for each tonne produced. ASERCA also assists cotton producers through a hedging programme, and grants them payments for the purchase of improved seed and pesticides. In the period 1992-94, ASERCA payments amounted to more than M$ 1.4 (between US$0.4 and US$0.5) billion a year. In 1995, the amount of ASERCA payments decreased to M$ 297 (US$46) million. Since 1994, ASERCA has been responsible for implementing the PROCAMPO direct payments programme (see Section B.2.a) through its 16 regional branches. In 1995, the amount spent by PROCAMPO to support farmers' income accounted for M$ 5.9 (US$0.9) billion.

In 1982, the **Mexican Sugar Company(AZUCAR SA)** was created by merging the National Commission of Sugar Producers and the Sugar Factories Executive Committee. Until 1992, AZUCAR SA was responsible for processing most, and marketing all of the sugar produced in Mexico. Its sugar factories produced about three-quarter of total domestic production and AZUCAR SA had the sole purchasing and selling rights on all sugar and by-products produced in Mexico, including from private mills. It was first supervised by the Secretariat of Energy, Mines and State-owned Industries (SEMIP). AZUCAR SA employed 800 persons in 1988. Its overall budget reached a maximum of M$ 3.3 (US$1.4) billion in 1988. From 1988 to 1992, all the sugar factories were privatised and AZUCAR SA was progressively dismantled. From 1990 to 1992, 21 sugar factories were sold at M$ 1.4 (US$0.5) billion. In 1991, the **Sugar Agroindustry Committee (COAAZUCAR)** was created to facilitate transactions and monitor agreements between the sugar factories (*ingenios*) and the sugarcane producers (*cañeros*, and to publish statistical information and provide technical assistance to the sugar industry. In 1995, its budget was M$ 5 (US$0.8) million, with a staff of 27 persons.

INMECAFE (Mexican Coffee Institute) was created in 1958, purchasing and marketing part of the domestic coffee production. It was supervised by SAGAR. Its global budget reached a maximum of M$ 300 (US$212) million in 1987. In 1993, INMECAFE was dismantled and the **Mexican Coffee Council (COFEMEX)** was established to co-ordinate the modernisation of the coffee industry through the search of sources of financing and marketing promotion. In 1995, the budget of COFEMEX was M$ 5 (US$0.8) million.

TABAMEX (Mexican Tobacco Company) was created in 1972 and placed under the supervision of SAGAR. It had the sole right for the purchase and processing of Mexican tobacco. It was a profitable enterprise and did not receive government transfers. In 1990, TABAMEX affiliates were sold for M$ 46 (US$16) million, and TABAMEX headquarters were restructured into the Tobacco Regulating Committee and the Tobacco Research Institute, the objectives of which are respectively to serve as mediator between producers and buyers, and provide technical assistance to tobacco growers. TABAMEX was liquidated in 1992.

The private firm **ALGODONERA (Mexican Commercial Cotton Trader)** was acquired by the Government in 1969 during a period of low world prices of cotton. It was supervised by SAGAR and its primary activity was the purchase of domestic cotton fibre and its subsequent sale to domestic or external textile manufacturers. ALGODONERA was a profitable enterprise and did not receive government transfers. In 1989, its six plants were sold for M$ 7 (US$3) million.

CONAFRUT (National Fruit Commission) was created in 1961 to help fruit growers in the processing and marketing of fruits, to assist in the propagation of reproductive material, and to provide research and technical assistance. Supervised by SAGAR, the overall budget of CONAFRUT reached a maximum of M$ 32 (US$13) million in 1989. That year, its processing plant Benefrut Guerrero was sold for M$ 1.6 (US$0.6) million. CONAFRUT was liquidated in 1993.

(continued on next page)

(continued)

From 1973 to 1989, **CONADECA (National Cocoa Commission)** was responsible for controlling the domestic supply of cocoa. In 1990, CONADECA was dismantled and the National Union of Cocoa producers (UNPC) was formed to assist producers in the marketing and export of respectively 55 and 45 per cent of the domestic production of cocoa.

IDA (Meat Processing Industry) was created in 1989 to regulate the supply of beef and veal, pigmeat and poultrymeat in Mexico City. Since 1990, the slaughtering and packaging activities of IDA have decreased, and its assets were transferred to livestock producers in 1992.

In 1989, as part of the overall process of reforming agricultural policy, the government decided to progressively remove guaranteed prices, as well as import barriers and consumer prices ceilings for all grains, beans and oilseeds. This decision was based on the grounds that guaranteed prices set at the same level in all parts of the country prevented the development of regional markets and private distribution channels; created an impediment to the diversification of production and its orientation by the market; and did not encourage the production of high quality products. Moreover, the price support policy involved a high level of Government transfers to cover the deficit of CONASUPO and its affiliates.

In 1989, guaranteed prices were removed for wheat, malt barley, sorghum, rice, soyabeans and other oilseeds and CONASUPO stopped purchasing them. This created serious difficulties for the marketing of these crops, due to poor private distribution networks; lack of marketing infrastructure; limited experience of producers in negotiating selling prices directly with buyers; international price volatility; and lack of knowledge of export markets. For these commodities (except barley), as a transitional step, **concerted prices** *(precio de concertación)* were fixed by the Federal government, in agreement with buyers and producers. For barley, the concerted prices were negociated between producers and the industry (brewers), with the government acting as an arbitrator. For wheat, rice, and oilseeds, concerted prices were set (at the same level) for all parts of the country. For sorghum, they were established for Tamaulipas State only (this State is located close to the US border and distant from the main consumption zones), and the crop from the rest of the country was sold at market prices.

In 1991, following the removal of imports permits and trade liberalisation for sorghum, soyabeans and other oilseeds in 1989 and 1990, ASERCA (Support and Services to Agricultural Marketing) was created with the main objective of promoting the development of private agricultural markets in order to facilitate direct transactions between producers and buyers. ASERCA has provided budgetary support to wheat millers, compound feed processors, and the vegetable oil processing industry to help them purchase the domestic production of wheat, sorghum, soyabeans and other oilseeds at concerted prices, as a way to provide support to producers. For these commodities, the support granted by ASERCA to buyers *(apoyo a la comercialización)* covered the difference between the concerted price and an **indifference price** – an implicit price at which first buyers are "indifferent" between buying domestic or imported crops or, in other words, the price producers would receive in the absence of concerted prices. The indifference price is calculated by the Government for each consumption area in Mexico as the border price, cif, plus the import tariff, plus the cost incurred in delivering the commodity from the border to the major consumption area, less the domestic handling costs between the different production areas and the consumption areas (see Graph 1). In the case of rice, ASERCA has granted per-tonne payments to producers for all domestic production (including the part which is self-consumed). Payments to rice producers are fixed at the same level across the country. From 1992 to 1994, wheat was the main commodity for which marketing was supported by ASERCA (see Annex I, Table II.3).

Given the importance of maize and beans in Mexican agriculture and in the diet, the removal of guaranteed prices, as well as import barriers, was deferred for both commodities. On the contrary, in 1990, the level of guaranteed prices was substantially increased. This resulted in a major shift from traditional crops to maize and beans, mainly in the north-western and north-eastern regions. In addition, particularly good weather conditions led to a significant increase in maize production, while

♦   Graph 1. **The Indifference Price Scheme**

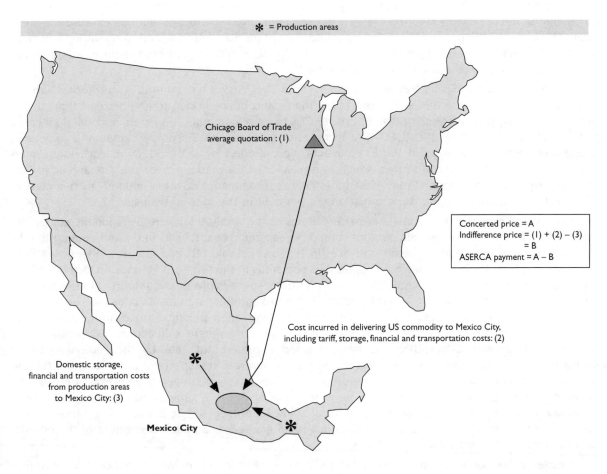

* = Production areas

Chicago Board of Trade
average quotation : (1)

Concerted price = A
Indifference price = (1) + (2) − (3)
= B
ASERCA payment = A − B

Cost incurred in delivering US commodity to Mexico City,
including tariff, storage, financial and transportation costs: (2)

Domestic storage,
financial and transportation costs
from production areas
to Mexico City: (3)

Mexico City

Source: OECD Secretariat, 1997.

imports increased for the other grains and oilseeds. Since 1993, it became clear that the distortions in production created by different price support schemes for grains, beans and oilseeds had to be corrected.

In 1994, the Programme of Direct Payments to the Countryside (PROCAMPO) was established with the main objective of market liberalisation and shifting from commodity price to farm income support (see Section B.2.*a*). It was foreseen that the guaranteed prices for maize and beans would be progressively aligned with international prices, while producers would be provided assistance through PROCAMPO **area payments** for estimated income losses. Moreover, PROCAMPO payments are also granted to producers of other grains, beans, and most oilseeds, to eliminate distortions in the choice of crop planted by farmers. In 1994, the level of administered prices for grains, beans and oilseeds and the level of per-tonne budgetary payments for rice were reduced with the introduction of PROCAMPO payments. In 1995, malt barley was included in PROCAMPO and concerted prices for that commodity were replaced by an indifference price, which the brewery industry has committed itself to pay to buy barley domestic production (see Section 1.*a.iv*. below).

In 1995, to protect producer interests while encouraging the development of a private marketing sector, **minimum prices** (*precio mínimo*) were set for maize and beans at a level lower than international prices. For the Spring/Summer 1995 crop season, due to the scarcity of domestic supply resulting from drought conditions and the sharp increase in market prices, the minimum price was lower than the market price. CONASUPO was then authorised to purchase maize at the domestic market price to cover its needs. In 1995, concerted prices for wheat, sorghum, rice, soyabeans and other oilseeds were abolished and ASERCA payments were not granted, except for rice. ASERCA started providing advice to maize, wheat, sorghum and soyabeans producers to promote exports and help them to adapt to the influence of international markets (see Section K).

Since 1980, for the Spring/Summer crop seasons, CONASUPO has granted a **marketing subsidy** (*apoyo a la comercialización*) to ejidatarios producing maize and beans in non irrigated areas, through the Programme to Support the Marketing in Ejidos (PACE), to help them pack, transport, and sell their crops to CONASUPO's rural stores (BORUCONSA) (see Annex I, Table II.4). Since 1991, small and communal properties were also included in PACE. Payments are provided by CONASUPO for each tonne marketed, up to 50 tonnes per producer, which is equivalent to a mark-up over the guaranteed prices received by those producers. From 1980 to 1995, this programme covered around 40 per cent of CONASUPO purchases of domestic production (34 per cent in the case of beans).

Concerning **consumption**, consumer price ceilings at the retail level were traditionally set by the government for maize tortillas, maize flour, bread, wheat flour, beans, rice, beer, and vegetable oils. This practice was abolished for beans and rice (in 1989), vegetable oils and fats (in 1991), wheat flour and bread (in June 1995), and maize flour sold in urban areas in the form of 1 kg bags (in October 1995). Since its inception in 1965, CONASUPO has sold its domestic purchases and imports of grains, beans and oilseeds (but only until 1990 for crops other than maize and beans) to its affiliates (see Box II.2) and private millers and retailers at a price equivalent to or below their purchase price (which is a general consumer subsidy). The resulting deficit was covered by government transfers to CONASUPO (see Section L). Moreover, CONASUPO has been granted a preferential rate by the National Railway Company[4] (FERRONALES) – which has the monopoly on train transportation in Mexico – for the transport of its grains from producing or import areas to processing or storage places. From 1991 to 1994 (when price ceilings for bread and wheat flour were in place), ASERCA subsidised wheat millers to help them keep the price of bread and wheat flour at a low level (see Annex I, Table II.3). Since 1984, a subsidy for the consumption of maize tortillas has been granted to a targeted segment of the population (which is a targeted consumer subsidy).

Border measures have complemented domestic measures in determining producer and consumer prices. Mexico has always been a net importer of grains and oilseeds, in both raw and processed forms. Imports of maize, beans, wheat, barley (without husks) – until 1993 –, and sorghum, soyabeans and other oilseeds – until 1988 – were duty-free, but subject to import permits. Imports of barley (with husks) and malt required permits and tariffs. For all these commodities, import quotas were set twice a year by estimating the size of the next domestic harvest, and the amount of imports that would be necessary to satisfy domestic demand. Imports of rice did not require permits, but were subject to tariffs. In 1989, import permits were removed for sorghum, soyabeans and other oilseeds, and imports were duty-free until 1990, although seasonal tariffs were introduced in 1991. From 1979 to 1990, CONASUPO was the main importer of grains, beans and oilseeds, its share of imports ranging between 50 and 100 per cent. Since 1991, CONASUPO has ceased importing grains and oilseeds (see Annex I, Table II.5).

With the entry into force of NAFTA in 1994, import permits were removed for wheat, maize, beans, and barley of United States and Canadian origin, and replaced by tariffs (wheat) and tariff quotas (maize, beans, and barley). That year, the seasonal import tariff was removed for sorghum. Tariffs and tariff quotas will be gradually phased out by 2003 (wheat, barley, rice, soyabeans) or 2008 (maize, beans).

Under the Uruguay Round Agreement which came into effect in 1995, maize, beans, malt barley, and wheat imports are subject to tariff quotas, with fixed quotas subject to a tariff of 50 per cent. A major share of the quotas has been allocated to the NAFTA partners, the quota levels under NAFTA being accountable for commitments with the United States and Canada in the Uruguay Round Agreement (except for barley). Base tariffs have been set at 50 per cent for the imports of wheat flour, sorghum, milled rice, soyabeans and Soya oil (at 10 per cent for paddy rice), with a tariff reduction schedule of 10 per cent by 2004. However, in 1995 and 1996, the rates actually applied on the import of those commodities were set at lower levels, similar to the NAFTA levels. Although never implemented in the past, provisions for export subsidies have been included for maize, beans, wheat and sorghum for Mexico in the Agreement (see Section C).

The following sections (1.a.i to 1.a.vii) provide complementary information specific to one of the above commodities.

i) Maize

About 95 per cent of domestic maize **production** white maize which is mainly used for human consumption. About 42 per cent of maize producers are subsistence farmers and thus do not market their crops. Overall, producers retain close to one third of maize production for their own consumption, including livestock and feed requirements. They sell to intermediary traders, livestock owners, CONASUPO (at BORUCONSA warehouses where only shelled maize is purchased), and in some instances directly to the agro-food industry (Nixtamal[5] factories, flour companies, livestock feed mills, cereal processors, starch factories). Yellow maize is mainly imported and used for starch production and animal feed, although it has also been used for human consumption. Since 1991, the government has set separate guaranteed prices for white maize and yellow maize, with a 20 per cent premium for white maize (see Annex I, Table II.1). The marketing subsidy granted to ejido farmers (PACE) increased from 1 per cent (until 1989) to around 7 per cent (since 1990) of the guaranteed prices (see Annex I, Table II.4). For the Spring/Summer 1995 crop season, the minimum price for white maize was M$ 815/tonne (US$127/tonne) and the marketing subsidy granted to ejido farmers was on average M$ 56/tonne (US$9/tonne), whereas the average domestic market price was M$ 1 234/tonne (US$192/tonne), due to an increase in world prices. For the Autumn/Winter 1995/96 crop season, the minimum price for white maize was set at M$ 850/tonne (US$112/tonne), whereas the average domestic market price was higher (at around M$ 1 600/tonne (US$211/tonne) between March and August 1996.

Concerning **consumption,** until 1990, CONASUPO sold maize from domestic and imported purchases mainly to Nixtamal factories (*molineros*) (around 55 per cent), the remainder being sold to flour companies (*harineros*) (around 15 per cent), DICONSA retail stores (around 13 per cent), and other public organisations, State governments, or directly to consumers (around 17 per cent) (see Annex I, Table II.6). Since 1985, flour companies have bought maize directly from producers and have received payments from CONASUPO to lower selling prices to the tortilla factories. Payments to the flour companies are provided for maize flour sold to the tortilla factories in the form of 20 kg bags (which are still subject to price controls). From 1991 to 1995, due to the significant increase in domestic production of maize, CONASUPO also sold maize to livestock producers, feed and starch factories. In 1994, the percentage of maize sales to the feed industry reached 55 per cent of total CONASUPO sales of maize. In the course of 1995, CONASUPO has stopped selling maize to starch factories and the feed sector, but payments to the flour companies have remained. CONASUPO has two main clients: the Nixtamal factories (which purchased around 1.9 million tonnes of maize from CONASUPO in 1995) and DICONSA stores (which sold around 650 000 tonnes of maize and 420 000 tonnes of maize flour to about 1 million families in 1995) (see Graph 2).

Selling prices by CONASUPO have varied according to the recipients (see Annex I, Table II.7). Selling prices have been set at a level lower than purchase prices for the Nixtamal factories, especially those located in Mexico City (due to price controls for tortillas), and for the DICONSA shops. Selling prices by the private flour companies to tortilla factories have roughly corresponded to the purchase price of domestic production, CONASUPO payments thus compensating flour companies for storage, financial and transportation costs. Since May 1996, to streamline the efficiency of the flour industry, CONASUPO establishes the level of payments to the flour companies on the basis of a weighted average import price of maize (using a technical coefficient to express it in maize flour equivalent). From 1991 to 1995, sales were set at levels lower than purchase prices for the feed sector and the starch factories. Since 1995, as consumer price ceilings at the retail level are still in place for maize tortillas, CONASUPO and flour companies continue to sell maize and maize flour (20 kg bags) to Nixtamal

◆ Graph 2. **Maize consumption subsidies**
Situation at the end of 1995

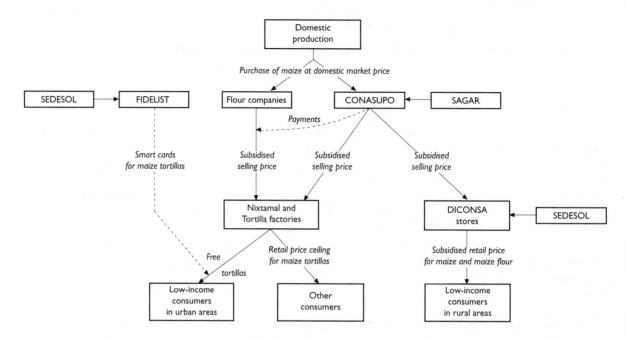

Note: See list of acronyms at the end of Chapter II for full title of Secretariat/agencies.
Source: OECD Secretariat, 1997.

factories at subsidised price (general consumer subsidy). Since its transfer to the Secretariat for Social Development (SEDESOL) in 1995, DICONSA receives government transfers to cover the difference between the price of maize and maize flour purchased from CONASUPO (at the market price) and the selling price to rural (poor) consumers (at the subsidised price).

In 1984, a programme of subsidy for tortilla consumption was established, with a view to progressively substitute for the general consumer subsidy for tortilla. This programme was targeted at low-income families in urban areas (targeted consumer subsidy). Until 1986, tortillas were sold directly by CONASUPO to 2.5 million families in selected areas at prices below the official consumer price ceilings. From 1986 to 1990, CONASUPO distributed coupons (*Tortibonos*) to about 1 million households allowing them to buy maize tortillas at preferential prices (50 per cent lower than the retail price) mainly through DICONSA retail outlets in low-income urban neighbourhoods. In 1991, the Tortibonos programme was replaced by the Programme to Subsidise the Consumption of Tortillas (*Tortilla sin Costo*). One kilogramme of tortillas is provided daily free of charge to low-income families (those earning less than two minimum wages a month) in registered tortilla factories in 202 cities (see Annex I, Table II.8). To facilitate the control of the volumes distributed and the allocation of the subsidies, the programme is implemented through the use of plastic cards with bar codes (smart cards). From 1992 until 1994, CONASUPO received government transfers for the "smart cards programme" through the Trust Fund for Tortilla Subsidy Payments (FIDELIST). FIDELIST was transferred to the Secretariat for Social Development (SEDESOL) in 1995. From 1991 to 1995, the number of families who benefited from the tortilla smart cards programme increased from 2 to 2.8 million. Free tortillas currently represent about 3 per cent of the total annual consumption of maize in Mexico.

Retail price ceilings for tortillas and maize flour in Mexico City have been set at a lower level than in the rest of the country (see Annex I, Table II.7). However, in October 1995, the retail price ceiling for 1kg bags of maize flour in urban areas was removed. In April 1996, a single national retail price ceiling was established for maize tortillas, by increasing retail prices in Mexico City by 27 per cent to M$ 1.40/kg (US$0.18/kg), and selling prices by CONASUPO to the Nixtamal factories in Mexico City and in the rest of the country were also established at the same level, at M$ 425/tonne (US$56/tonne).

Concerning **trade measures**, under NAFTA, Mexico granted duty-free minimum access of 2.5 million tonnes and 1 000 tonnes (to be increased by 3 per cent a year) for maize **imports** from the United States and Canada respectively. In 1994 and 1995, the tariff quota was filled. In 1996, SECOFI authorised a substantial increase of the duty-free quota[6] committed under NAFTA. The quota was allocated via prior assignment (*asignación directa*) to starch factories (40 per cent), the feed sector (33 per cent), flour companies (26 per cent), and cereal traders (1 per cent) in 1994, and via prior assignment (93 per cent) and "first come-first served" basis (7 per cent) in 1995. The base above-quota tariff was set at 215 per cent (or US$206/tonne), to be reduced by 24 per cent by 2000, and then gradually phased out between 2000 and 2008. Under the Uruguay Round Agreement, a 50 per cent import tariff quota was established on a Most Favoured Nation basis, including 2.5 million tonnes for the United States, 1 000 tonnes for Canada, and 10 000 tonnes for other countries (to apply from 2000 in the latter case). To prevent maize flour **exports**, a 200 per cent export tariff was enforced during November and December 1995.

ii) Beans

In 1990, two different guaranteed prices were set for the **production** of beans according to consumer preferences (preferred varieties, other varieties), with a 10 per cent premium for preferred varieties (see Annex I, Table II.1). In 1995, minimum prices were set for three categories of beans, with a 20 per cent premium for highly preferred varieties over preferred varieties. The marketing subsidy granted to ejido farmers (PACE) increased from 1 per cent (until 1989) to 5 per cent (from 1990 to 1995) of the guaranteed prices (see Annex I, Table II.4).

On the **consumer** side, until 1990, CONASUPO sold 40 to 50 per cent of its total beans sales to DICONSA retail shops (40-50 per cent), the remainder being shared between the private sector (traders and the packaging industry), the wholesale distribution sector (IMPECSA), social programmes, and, since 1992, exports, although there are no regular export programmes in place (see Annex I, Table II.9). Since 1991, the share of CONASUPO sales to the private sector increased to more than 50 per cent of total sales, following the removal of retail price ceilings for beans in December 1989. The selling prices of beans by CONASUPO vary according to volume, varieties (27 varieties are commonly consumed), and State. Until 1994, except for the private sector and exports which were sold at the market price, preferred varieties were sold by CONASUPO to DICONSA, IMPECSA, and social programmes at the guaranteed price, and the other varieties at a price lower than the guaranteed price. However, in 1995, selling prices were increased to cover CONASUPO handling costs: they ranged between M$ 1 920/tonne (US$299/tonne) for less preferred varieties (such as B*ayo*) and M$ 2 160/tonne (US$336/tonne) for highly preferred varieties (such as *Flor de M*a*yo*).

Concerning **imports**, under NAFTA, duty-free minimum access was granted to the United States for 50 000 tonnes, and to Canada for 1 500 tonnes (quotas to be increased by 3 per cent a year). The base above-quota tariff was set at 139 per cent (or US$480/tonne), to be reduced by 24 per cent by 2000, and then gradually phased out by 2008. Under the Uruguay Round Agreement, a 50 per cent import tariff quota was established on a Most Favoured Nation basis, consisting of 50 000 tonnes for the United States, 1 500 tonnes for Canada, and 5 000 tonnes for other countries.

iii) Wheat

The domestic **production** of wheat is composed of different qualities of common wheat – hard quality used for the industrial white bread (19 per cent), partly-hard quality used for the manually prepared "bolillo" bread (26 per cent), soft quality for cakes and tortillas (33 per cent), and poor quality used as a mix (6 per cent) –, and durum wheat (16 per cent), used for pasta. A low percentage of wheat is used as feed grains, especially poor quality common wheat. Guaranteed prices have always been the same for all qualities of wheat, except in 1988 when a 15 per cent premium was given to hard and partly-hard qualities of common wheat. Until 1989, guaranteed prices were fixed at a level allowing domestic production to be sold competitively with wheat flour imported under 15 per cent tariffs (see Annex I, Table II.1). Introduced in 1989, the concerted prices for wheat were abolished for the Spring/Summer 1995 crop season.

On the **consumer side**, until 1990, CONASUPO sold its domestic purchases and imports of wheat to millers at a price equivalent to or below the purchase price. From 1992 to 1994, to keep wheat flour and bread prices in line with price ceilings at the retail level while buying the domestic production at concerted prices, payments granted by ASERCA to wheat millers were based on the volume of purchases to producers and the volume of sales to the domestic market (see Annex I, Table II.3). In 1994, the payments granted by ASERCA to wheat millers was based on the volume of domestic production bought at concerted prices from the North Western States of Baja California Norte, Sonora, Chihuahua, and Sinaloa (which are distant from the main consumption areas), which represented around 50 per cent of total domestic production of wheat. In June 1995, those ASERCA payments which were based on the volume of sales ceased, since consumer price ceilings for wheat flour and bread had been removed. For the Spring/Summer 1995 crop season, ASERCA payments to purchasers of the domestic production of wheat were also discontinued, as concerted prices had been abolished.

Concerning **trade measures** under NAFTA, base tariffs for wheat and wheat flour **imports** were set at 15 per cent, and will gradually be removed by 2003. Under the Uruguay Round Agreement, a 50 per cent import tariff was set for wheat flour, although the rate of 15 per cent has continued to apply. A 50 per cent import tariff quota of 604 612 tonnes was established for wheat on a Most Favoured Nation basis, of which around 55 per cent was allocated to the United States and about 29 per cent to Canada. The above-quota tariff for wheat imports was set at 74 per cent or US$100/tonne, to be reduced by 10 per cent by 2004. Wheat **exports** from Mexico to Canada are exempted from the Canadian Wheat Import Act, although part of the Mexican production is prevented from entering both Canada and the United States due to phytosanitary restrictions. To prevent exports of wheat flour (sold at subsidised price in Mexico) to the United States, export permits were necessary until 1989, but have since been removed. Under NAFTA, the tariff applied by the United States on wheat flour imports from Mexico was removed in 1994, Canada had never applied import tariffs on Mexican wheat flour. The tariff applied by the United States on wheat imports from Mexico will be removed over five years for common wheat and over ten years for durum wheat. The tariff applied by Canada on wheat imports from Mexico will be removed over five years.

iv) Barley

About 80 per cent of the domestic **production** of barley is for malt production. In 1958, the private enterprise IASA (Agricultural Promotion SA) was created by brewers to promote the production of high quality malt barley. Through its 12 regional branches and with its own funds, IASA provides free technical assistance to barley growers, and sells them seeds and pesticides to meet the quality standards required by the industry. From 1965 to 1989, CONASUPO purchased a significant part of the domestic production at guaranteed prices set at a level slightly higher than wheat in order to control land substitution between these two crops. Since 1989, IASA has committed itself to purchase all the domestic production, while controlling its quality. Until 1994, IASA purchased barley at prices agreed between brewers and producers with SAGAR acting as a facilitator (testigo). In 1994, malt barley was not included in PROCAMPO, which resulted in a shift from production to other eligible crops, but, since 1995, malt barley has been eligible for PROCAMPO payments. Since 1995, IASA purchases barley at an indifference price calculated by SAGAR. On the **consumer** side, until 1990, CONASUPO has sold its domestic purchases and imports of malt barley to brewers at a price equivalent to or below their purchase price.

Until 1993, imports of barley and malt required permits. They were duty-free (barley without husks), or subject to a tariff of 5 per cent (barley with husks) 10 per cent (malt). Since 1994, under NAFTA, duty-free **import** quotas were set for barley and malt at 120 000 tonnes for the United States, and 30 000 tonnes for Canada (to be increased by 5 per cent a year). The quota is allocated to brewers.

Under the Uruguay Round Agreement, a 50 per cent import tariff quota of 4 742 tonnes was established on a Most Favoured Nation basis, of which around 25 per cent was allocated to the United States and about 49 per cent to Canada. In both agreements, the above-quota tariff was set at 128 per cent (or US$155/tonne for NAFTA; or US$160/tonne for the Uruguay Round Agreement), to be removed by 2003 under NAFTA and decreased by 10 per cent by 2004 under the Uruguay Round Agreement. Under both agreements, a tariff of 175 per cent (or US$212/tonne) was set for imports of malt, although it is to be removed by 2003 under NAFTA and decreased by 10 per cent by 2004 under the Uruguay Round Agreement. The import of beer processed from malt is subject to a 16 per cent tariff to be phased out by 2001 under NAFTA. It is subject to a 40 per cent tariff to be decreased by 10 per cent over ten years under the Uruguay Round Agreement, although a 20 per cent tariff has been applied. Concerning **exports**, under NAFTA, the tariffs applied by the United States on malt and barley imports from Mexico were removed in 1994. The tariffs applied by Canada on malt and barley imports from Mexico will be removed in 1998.

v) Sorghum

Sorghum is used exclusively for animal feed. It represents about 70 per cent of total feed grains consumption, except from 1991 to 1995 due to the increased use of maize for feed (see Annex I, Table II.10). Until 1989, the ratio between guaranteed prices for the **production** of grain sorghum and maize varied between 0.6 to 0.8, intended to control land substitution between these two crops (see Annex I, Table II.1). In 1990, as a result of trade liberalisation, the abolishment of guaranteed prices for sorghum and the maintenance of a guaranteed price for maize, Mexico's sorghum acreage declined significantly. The concerted prices established in 1989 for sorghum produced in Tamaulipas State were abolished for the 1995 crop year.

On the **consumer** side, until 1990, CONASUPO sold its domestic purchases and imports of sorghum to livestock producers and the compound feed industry at a price equivalent to or below the purchase price. From 1991 to 1994, ASERCA granted support to the compound feed factories buying the domestic production of sorghum at the concerted price in the Tamaulipas State, representing between 25 and 40 per cent of total domestic production (see Annex I, Table II.3).

In 1989, the prevailing duty-free **import** permit was removed and imports of sorghum became duty-free. In 1991, a 15 per cent seasonal import tariff was introduced for grain sorghum entering the country between mid-May and mid-December. Within NAFTA, this seasonal import tariff was removed in 1994 for the United States and Canada, but it is still applied on a Most Favoured Nation basis under the Uruguay Round Agreement. Concerning **exports**, under NAFTA, the tariffs applied by the United States and Canada on sorghum imports from Mexico were removed in 1994.

vi) Rice

Until 1989, the guaranteed prices for paddy rice **production** were maintained at a level close to those for maize (see Annex I, Table II.1). The per-tonne bugetary payments granted by ASERCA to rice producers were increased from M$ 60/tonne in 1991 to M$ 120/tonne in 1993, but decreased to M$ 74/tonne in 1994 with the introduction of PROCAMPO payments (see Annex I, Table II.3). In 1995, the concerted prices for rice were abolished, but ASERCA continued to provide payments to rice producers at the same rate as in 1994.

On the **consumer** side, until 1990, CONASUPO sold its domestic purchases and imports of rice to the industry at a price equivalent to or below the purchase price. In 1989, price ceilings for rice at retail level were removed.

Rice **imports** have never required permits but were subject to import tariffs of 10 per cent for paddy rice and 20 per cent for milled rice. Under NAFTA, these tariffs will be removed by 2003. Under the Uruguay Round Agreement, import tariffs were maintained at 10 per cent for paddy rice and were set at 50 per cent for milled rice, although the rate of 20 per cent has continued to apply on milled rice. In 1990, **export** permits were eliminated for rice. Under NAFTA, the tariffs applied by the United States on rice imports from Mexico will be removed by 2003 for paddy rice, and were removed in 1994 for milled rice. Canada has never applied import tariffs on Mexican (paddy or milled) rice.

vii) Soyabeans and other oilseeds

Until 1989 different guaranteed prices were set for the **production** of soyabeans, safflower, cotton-seed, and sesame, copra and sunflower (see Annex I, Table II.1). The concerted prices established in 1989 for soyabeans and other oilseeds were abolished for the 1995 crop year.

On the **consumer** side, until 1990, CONASUPO sold its domestic purchases and imports of soyabeans and other oilseeds to oil crushers at a price equivalent to or below the purchase price. From 1991 to 1994, ASERCA granted payments to oil crushers based on the volume of domestic production of soyabeans bought at concerted prices. In 1993 and 1994, safflower was also included in the ASERCA support scheme (representing 50 per cent of the domestic production of safflower in 1993, and 10 per cent in 1994). In 1991, consumer price ceilings at the retail level were removed for vegetable oils and fats.

In 1989, the prevailing duty-free **import** permit was removed and imports of soyabeans became duty-free. In 1991, a 10 per cent seasonal import tariff was introduced which applies from the beginning of August to the end of January. Within NAFTA, this seasonal tariff will be removed by 2003 for imports from both the United States and Canada. Under the Uruguay Round Agreement, a 50 per cent import tariff was set for soyabeans, although the seasonal tariff of 10 per cent has continued to apply. Under NAFTA, the following tariffs will also be removed by 2003: 10 and 20 per cent tariffs for crude and refined Soya oil respectively; 15 per cent for Soya meal; 10 and 15 per cent import tariffs for cottonseed oil and cottonseed oil cake respectively. Imports of cottonseed and sesame have already been duty-free since 1990. Under the Uruguay Round, imports of crude Soya oil is subject to a 50 per cent tariff, although the rate applied was 10 per cent in 1995. Concerning **exports**, the United States and Canada have never applied import tariffs on Mexican soyabeans. Within NAFTA, the import tariff imposed on Mexican Soya oil was removed by Canada in 1994, and will be removed by the United States by 1998.

Domestic vegetable oil prices are also influenced by the import regime for animal fats and butter. For animal fats, under NAFTA, import permits were replaced by a duty-free quota of 35 000 tonnes for the United States and 1 000 tonnes for Canada. Under the Uruguay Round Agreement, a 50 per cent tariff quota of 39 600 tonnes was established on a Most Favoured Nation basis, of which around 95 per cent was allocated to the United States. The base above-quota tariff was set in both cases at 282 per cent (or US$930/tonne). It will be phased out by 2003 for NAFTA partners, and decreased by 10 per cent for signatories of the Uruguay Round Agreement. The trade regime for butter is described in Section f below.

b) Sugarcane

During the 1960s, a policy of ensuring low consumer prices for sugar reduced the profitability of the sugar industry and many private mills – 75 per cent of the sugar factories (*ingenios*) were in the private sector – were purchased by the government. In the 1970s, the government owned 75 per cent of the 65 sugar factories. The 1979 Sugar Ordinance (*Decreto Cañero*) established that, to determine the producer price for sugarcane, the percentage of sugar in crushed cane would be determined for each factory in relation to the factory actual rate of sugar recovery (adding, as appropriate, 2.64 per cent on factory losses in refined sugar equivalent), with a guaranteed minimum of 83 kilogrammes of sugar per tonne of cane. For more than 30 years until 1992 (through AZUCAR, SA since 1982), the Federal government had the monopoly on purchases and sales of sugar, honey and alcohol domestic **production**, imports and exports. From 1988 to 1992, all state sugar factories were privatised. The 61 sugar factories still in operation can freely sell their production.

Until 1991, **concerted prices** for sugarcane were set by the government in consultation with the sugar industry and cane producers, and linked to a Consumer Price Index made of wholesale prices of the previous crop year (1st October/30th September), as published by BANXICO. The 1991 Sugar

Ordinance established that the concerted prices of sugarcane would be based on an implicit sugar content – calculated per "kg of standard partly-refined sugar that is recovered from each tonne of sugarcane" (KARBE)[7] – and linked to wholesale prices for sugar – using a "kg of standard partly-refined sugar" (KABE). The 1991 Sugar Ordinance and its 1993 amendment provide for an increase in the share of the KARBE price from 54 per cent (until 1994) to 57 per cent (in 1997) of the net wholesale (ex-factory, net of handling costs, packing charges, and VAT) KABE price, as estimated by SECOFI. Since 1991, the Sugar Industry Committee (COAAZUCAR) has been charged with the implementation of the 1991 Sugar Ordinance, in close consultation with SAGAR, SECOFI, the National Chamber of Alcohol and Sugar Industries, and the two National Unions of Sugarcane Producers. Since the 1995/96 crop season (zafra), some sugar millers were authorised to negotiate directly the factory recovery rates to be used in the calculation of KARBE with cane growers. For the 1995/96 crop season the KARBE price for each tonne of sugarcane was M\$ 1 484/kg (US\$195/kg), or 56 per cent of the net wholesale KABE price of M\$ 2 650/kg (US\$349/kg).

On the **consumer** side, from 1982 to 1991, to keep consumer prices at a low level, the operating losses of AZUCAR SA were covered by government transfers which decreased from M\$ 557 (US\$223) million in 1989 to M\$ 140 (US\$49) million in 1990. Until 1994, consumer price ceilings for partly-refined and refined sugar at wholesale and retail levels were set by the government. To encourage the competitiveness of the sugar industry, these consumer price controls were lifted in August 1995.

Until 1990, **imports** of refined sugar were duty-free but subject to permits. A variable import levy (VIL) was introduced in 1991, designed to control domestic prices for refined sugar. As part of NAFTA commitments, the United States and Mexico have agreed to specific provisions to govern trade between them in sugar and syrup goods in view of reaching free trade by 2008 for sugarcane and refined sugar. The VIL was replaced by a duty-free tariff quota set for each marketing year following projections on net surplus production for each country, although a minimum duty-free access of 7 258 tonnes is granted by the United States to Mexico ("minimum boat-load"). Under NAFTA, the net exporter (net importer) status is given when the domestic sugar production exceeds (does not exceed) sugar and HFCS (High Fructose Corn Syrup) consumption – in 1995, 80 per cent of HFCS consumption was imported, but consumption accounted for only 2 per cent of Mexico's total consumption of refined sugar equivalent. When Mexico is a net exporter, it is allowed a maximum duty-free access to the United States of 25 000 tonnes of sugar (raw value) from 1994 to 2000, to raise to 250 000 tonnes from 2000 to 2008. By 2000, above-quota import tariffs will be aligned between Mexico and the United States. They will be phased out by 2008. In 1994, they were of US\$195 and US\$252 per tonne for Mexican imports of raw and refined sugar respectively. Duty-free treatment is granted for re-exports of sugar to the United States after processing in Mexico, and for imports of refined sugar that is of Mexican origin. Tariffs on processed products with high sugar content will be removed by 2003. The "most favoured nation" treatment applies on sugar imports from Canada and on the United States Refined Sugar Re-export Programme, as this sugar is not considered of United States origin.

Under the Uruguay Round Agreement, a 50 per cent tariff quota was established for imports of raw, partly-refined and refined sugar, and processed products with high sugar content on a Most Favoured Nation basis, with a quota of 110 000 tonnes, which will rise to 183 800 tonnes by 2004. The above-quota tariff was set at 173 per cent (or US\$400/tonne) and will be reduced by 10 per cent by 2004. An import tariff of 50 per cent was established for sugarcane, to be reduced by 28 per cent by 2004. Provisions for export subsidies have been included for Mexican sugar in the Agreement (see Section C).

c) Cotton

Until 1990, **concerted prices** for cotton were established by the government in consultation with producers associations and the textile industry. ALGODONERA purchased between 5 and 16 per cent of domestic fibre **production** (mostly from ejidatarios) and sold it to the textile industry or exported it ALGODONERA passed on to producers the price it received from sales, minus a margin to cover its operational costs: it did not operate at a deficit. Since 1990, after the privatisation of ALGODONERA, to promote exports, ASERCA has provided support through direct payments for the purchase of seeds and pesticides (see Section F) and advice (see Section K) to cotton producers, while helping them to adapt to the influence of international markets through a "risk hedging programme". ASERCA plays the role of a private broker: for a fee, producers are guaranteed a minimum price which is fixed using the New-York cotton futures exchange. This risk hedging scheme is proving very successful and will be extended to other crops (see Section K).

Imports of cotton have never been subject to permits. Under NAFTA, the import tariff was decreased from 20 to 10 per cent and will be phased out by 2003. Under the Uruguay Round Agreement, imports of cotton are subject to a 50 per cent tariff, although the rate of 10 per cent has continued to apply.

Until 1983, the government used **export** licensing requirements to restrict exports and thus depress domestic prices of cotton. A tax of 0.5 per cent was applied on exports of cotton lint. Export licences and duties have since been abolished. Under NAFTA, duty-free access was granted by the United States to Mexican cotton for 10 000 tonnes, and imports from Mexico will become duty-free by 2003. As part of the various bilateral agreements which constitute the Multi-Fibre Arrangement (MFA), exports of textile and clothing to the United States are subject to voluntary export restraints.

d) Coffee

Since 1973 and until 1993, INMECAFE supported coffee producers, exporters, and processors in the areas of credit access, storage, processing, and marketing. Over this period, INMECAFE purchased, marketed and exported between 30 and 40 per cent of domestic **production**, mainly from small farmers – owning less than 20 hectares of land, of which less than 5 hectares were under coffee. INMECAFE provided producers with free fumigation services and some research and extension services. Until 1989, Mexican export quotas were established by the International Coffee Organisation (ICO). In Mexico, the Coffee Marketing Committee established production quotas for the domestic and the export markets (90 per cent of the Mexican production is exported to both ICO Member countries and non-ICO Member countries). Until 1993, **concerted prices** were established for coffee beans (*cereza* and *verde*) by SECOFI, in consultation with producers, exporters and processors' associations, based on international quotations of processed coffee. INMECAFE returned any profit from export sales to producers. INMECAFE operational costs were covered by Government transfers which ranged from M$ 0.7 (US$31) million in 1979 to M$ 280 (US$112) million in 1989.

In 1993, INMECAFE was liquidated and the National Solidarity Fund to Support Enterprises (FONAES) provided credit to coffee growers' associations to help them purchase INMECAFE processing facilities (*beneficios*) (see Section J). Since 1994, the Mexican Coffee Council (COFEMEX)[8] has promoted consultations between producers and processors with a view to increase the productivity of the sector and to modernise technology. COFEMEX monitors and evaluates the performance of the Mexican coffee sector through periodic surveys. It maintains an export register and is responsible for issuing certificates of origin to exporters. COFEMEX also represents national interests in international forums. Concerning **consumption**, retail price ceilings on coffee products (roasted beans, coffee extract and coffee powder) were abolished in 1991.

Until 1993, coffee beans and coffee extract were subject to **import** permits and a 20 per cent tariff. In 1994, under NAFTA, these permits were removed and the 20 per cent import tariff will be progressively phased out by 2003. Moreover, as part of NAFTA commitments, neither Canada or Mexico will take actions pursuant to any international coffee agreement and associated measures to restrict trade in coffee between them. However, up to 2003, under a safeguard provision, the 20 per cent tariff for coffee extract may continue to apply on a quota of 200 tonnes for the United States (with a 3 per cent annual increase until 2002), and 30 tonnes for Canada (with a 5 per cent annual increase). For coffee extract, the Uruguay Round Agreement established a 50 per cent import tariff quota of 12 000 tonnes on a Most Favoured Nation basis, which will increase to 20 800 tonnes by 2004, although the rate of 20 per cent has continued to apply. The above-quota tariff was set at 156 per cent (or US$360/tonne) and will be reduced by 10 per cent by 2004. Imports of coffee beans are subject to a 80 per cent tariff, although the rate applied in 1995 was 72 per cent.

Until 1992, coffee **exports** required permits and were subject to taxes of up to 30 per cent, depending on international prices. The export licensing system was abolished in 1993 with the liquidation of INMECAFE. Under NAFTA, the tariff imposed on Mexican coffee extract by the United States was removed in 1994. The United States and Canada have never applied import tariffs on Mexican coffee beans, and, in the case of Canada, on coffee extract. To increase demand of Mexican coffee in the United States and Canada, the "rule of origin" final proviso was strengthened for coffee beans and coffee extract (see Section C).

e) *Other crops*

i) *Tobacco*

From 1972 to 1990, TABAMEX and its affiliate plants Mexican Tobacco Exporters SA, Aztec Tobaccos SA, and Stemmed Tobacco Lazaro Cardenas were the only purchasers of all tobacco grown in Mexico. About 30 per cent of domestic **production** was exported through contracts with international tobacco firms and the rest sold on the domestic market. **Concerted prices** were set by the government in consultation with tobacco growers but they did not include premia for quality. TABAMEX produced improved seed, lowered the cost of inputs to producers through its affiliate INFERMEX (Insecticides and Fertilisers SA), did some experimental work, and provided technical assistance to growers. TABAMEX also operated a crop insurance programme and tried to control tobacco production in relation to domestic and international demand. TABAMEX passed on to producers the price it received from sales, minus a margin to cover its operational costs: it did not operate at a deficit. Since 1990, following the liquidation of TABAMEX and the privatisation of its affiliate plants, private investment has become very significant in the tobacco sector. Producer prices have been set directly between tobacco growers, processors and exporters, with the Tobacco Regulating Committee acting as a mediator. They vary according to the quality of tobacco produced.

Under NAFTA, a 50 per cent tariff was set for **imports** of raw tobacco and cigarettes. These tariffs will be removed by 2003. Under the Uruguay Round, imports of raw tobacco and cigarettes are subject to 50 and 75 per cent tariffs respectively. They will be reduced by 10 per cent by 2004. Concerning **exports**, the tariff applied by the United States on raw tobacco imported from Mexico was removed in 1994. The tariffs imposed on cigarettes produced in Mexico by the United States and Canada will be phased out by 2003. Canada has never applied import tariffs on Mexican raw tobacco.

ii) *Fruits and vegetables*

Mexico is a net exporter of many fruits and vegetables which account for a significant share of both the value of production and the value of exports (see Chapter I, Section C). **Producer and consumer prices** for fruits and vegetables have never been administered by the government, but have been influenced by border measures, although export restrictions have been removed. From 1961 to 1993, CONAFRUT helped fruit producers, processors and exporters, mainly through the dissemination of information on markets and processing technologies. From 1980 to 1985, through the Trust Fund for Citrus and Tropical Fruits (FIDEFRUT), CONAFRUT provided packing, and marketing services, including the control of quality standards. CONAFRUT had some income from the sale of reproductive material and processed fruits, but this covered only a small share of its expenses, the remaining being financed through government budgetary transfers, although these were limited. Since 1991, ASERCA has provided fruit and vegetable producers with marketing and promotion services (see Section K).

Concerning **imports** of fruits, under NAFTA, the 20 per cent import tariffs (15 per cent for pears) governing the trade of all major fruits between Mexico, Canada and the United States were either removed in 1994 (limes, strawberries, bananas, and mangoes), or will be gradually removed by 1998 (oranges, pears) or by 2003 (peaches, grapes, watermelons, apples, avocados) (see Annex I, Table II.11). The import tariff for oranges was removed in 1994 for Canada, and was converted to a seasonal 20 per cent tariff for the United States. The 20 per cent import tariff for orange juice will be progressively phased out by 2008 for both Canada and the United States, but, under a safeguard provision, the tariff in place in 2000 may continue to be applied until 2003. Under a safeguard provision, the 20 per cent import tariff for apples may continue to apply up to 2003, within a quota which was set in 1994 at 55 000 tonnes for the United States and 1 000 tonnes for Canada (with a 3 per cent annual increase). The import tariffs for grapes and watermelons were converted to a seasonal tariff. The import tariff for avocados was removed in 1994 for Canada, and will be removed by 2003 for the United States.

Concerning imports of vegetables, under NAFTA, the 10 per cent import tariffs imposed by Mexico on Canada and the United States for all major vegetables (except potatoes) were either removed in 1994 (eggplants), or will be gradually removed by 1998 (tomatoes) or by 2003 (cucumbers, onions, potatoes) (see Annex I, Table II.11). The import tariff for chillies was removed in 1994 for Canada, and will be removed in 1998 for the United States. The import tariff for onions will be removed in 1998 for Canada, and in 2003 for the United States. The import tariffs for tomatoes and cucumbers were removed in 1994 for Canada, and were converted to a seasonal tariff (cucumbers) and a seasonal tariff quota (tomatoes) for the United States to be removed by 2003. Imports of potatoes are duty-free within a quota of 15 000 tonnes for the United States and 4 000 tonnes for Canada (to be increased annually by 3 per cent), and are subject to a 272 per cent (or US$354/tonne) above-quota tariff which will be removed by 2003.

Under the Uruguay Round Agreement, all the above-mentioned fruits and vegetables (except potatoes) are subject to a 50 per cent tariff, which will decrease by 28 per cent (by 10 per cent for most temperate fruits) by 2004 although the rates of 10 to 20 per cent prevailing in 1992 have continued to apply (except for grapes) (see Annex I, Table II.11). A 50 per cent tariff is applied on imports of potatoes within a quota of 1 000 tonnes on a Most Favoured Nation basis, with an above-quota tariff of 272 per cent (or US$354/tonne) to decrease by 10 per cent by 2004.

Until 1990, **export** restrictions were imposed on fruits and vegetables (including tomatoes, chillies, and watermelons) in the form of sowing permits issued by the National Horticultural Producers Confederation (CNPH) for a fixed volume of production, and through the issuance of origin certificates by producers' associations, as a means of raising quality standards. Since then, agricultural producers may grow fruits and vegetables and export them without restrictions.

Under NAFTA, concerning the export of fruits, the tariffs applied by the United States on all major fruits imported from Mexico were either removed in 1994 (grapes, peaches, pears, strawberries), or will be gradually removed by 1998 (mangoes, oranges) or by 2003 (limes, watermelons, avocados). The United States have never applied import tariffs on Mexican apples and bananas. The tariff applied by the United States on oranges imported from Mexico was converted to a seasonal tariff. Fresh concentrated orange juice is subject to a tariff of US cents 9.25/litre to be phased out by 2008. Frozen concentrated orange juice is subject to a US cents 4.625/litre tariff quota of 151.4 million litres, with an above-quota tariff of US cents 9.25/litre which will decrease in three steps until 2008. However, under a safeguard provision, the tariff in place in 2000 may continue to be applied until 2003. Single-strength orange juice (not concentrated) is subject to a US cents 2.65/litre tariff quota of 15.4 million litres, with an above-quota tariff of US cents 5.3/litre. to be phased out by 2008. Concerning the export of vegetables, the import tariffs applied by the United States on Mexican onions and cucumbers will be gradually removed by 2008. The United States import tariffs imposed on Mexican chillies and eggplants were converted to a seasonal tariff (to be removed by 2003). Mexican exports of tomatoes to the United States are subject to a seasonal duty-free tariff quota (to be removed by 2003) associated with a specific safeguard provision (see description of the snap-back mechanism in Section C 2.a.i). When the duty-free quota volumes are breached, triggering the snap back tariffs, protection remains low, at 10 per cent. The import tariff applied by the United States on Mexican potatoes will be removed by 1998.

Since 1992, the export of various fruits and vegetables (including avocados, chillies, and strawberries) to the United States has been subject to the granting of "marketing orders" by the United States authorities. To ensure that *quality standards* of Mexican fruits and vegetables are in conformity with United States rules, a working group has been created under NAFTA to establish or modify the marketing orders. The working group also reviews field inspection and certification procedures for quality standards. Mexican exports of avocados, chillies, and strawberries to the United States and Canada have been prevented by their non compliance with United States and Canadian *phytosanitary standards*. In accordance with the Canadian quarantine regulations, Mexican peaches and cherries exported to Canada must receive a chemical treatment which limits their use to the agro-food industry. The Canadian quarantine treatment is systematically applied on Mexican potatoes.

f) Milk and dairy products

Around one third of domestic fresh milk production is sold for direct consumption, without pasteurisation. Two-thirds are sold to dairies for pasteurisation, for fresh consumption (56 per cent) and processing into dairy products (44 per cent). About one per cent is sold to LICONSA (CONASUPO Industrial Milk). The dairy sector is highly concentrated: the three largest dairy factories produce 45 per cent of pasteurised liquid milk (of which LICONSA accounts for 11 per cent, mainly produced from dehydrated imported milk powder), one firm produces 70 per cent of powdered milk and another produces all condensed milk. However, there is less concentration in the production of cheese, yoghurt and other dairy products.

Producer prices for fresh milk are supported by import restrictions and import taxes on milk powder. In liquid milk equivalent, the share of milk imports on consumption ranged from 22 per cent in 1980 to 33 per cent in 1990, and was of around 20 per cent over the last five years (Mexico is among the main importing countries of milk powder in the world). Since 1965, CONASUPO has held the monopoly on imports of milk powder. CONASUPO imports milk for LICONSA (55 per cent), the private sector (44 per cent) and the National Scheme for the Integrated Development of the Family (DIF) (1 per cent) (see Section L). Until 1991, CONASUPO imposed a levy on top of the import price to align import prices at the level of domestic prices, so that private buyers and LICONSA were indifferent between buying domestic production or imported milk. In 1991, LICONSA ceased its commercial activities to focus exclusively on social programmes, which led to the privatisation of some of its dairy plants. Since 1991, sales by CONASUPO to the private sector have been realised through auction, with a minimum bid price set initially at a higher level than the import price. Since 1995, the minimum bid price has been set at the import price plus the handling charges incurred by CONASUPO. Until 1991, LICONSA provided milk producers with animal breeding services, feed, and feed storage facilities, although only to a limited extent.

Until 1992, **consumer price** ceilings were set by the federal government for fresh milk at the retail level. Since then, they have been set by State governments. Since 1995, only the retail prices of pasteurised 1 litre milk bottles – which account for 75 per cent of the domestic market for liquid milk – are set by the State governments. In 1995, the average national retail price ceiling for pasteurised fresh milk was M$ 2.75/litre (US$0.43/litre). In March 1996, it was increased by 30 per cent. Since its inception in 1965, LICONSA has implemented the Programme for Social Supply of Milk for children of low-income families and, since 1991, for children less than 12 years old (see Annex I, Table II.8). The number of children covered by this programme increased ten-fold from 425 000 in 1980 to 4.8 million in 1990. Since 1991, the programme has been re-targeted to disadvantaged rural areas, and the number of beneficiaries was increased to 6.8 million in 1993, covering more than 60 per cent of the country's 2403 municipalities. Since 1994, only children in families with income of less than two minimum wages are entitled to participate in the programme. In 1995, 5.4 million people (of which 97 per cent children) were included, representing an annual distribution of 1.1 billion litres of milk (or 11 per cent of total milk consumption in Mexico). Beneficiaries are entitled to buy 4 litres a week per child at subsidised prices (M$ 0.65 (US$0.10) per litre of rehydrated milk in 1995). The milk is distributed in liquid form (80 per cent) and, in remote areas, powder form (20 per cent), through LICONSA agents, DICONSA stores, and private retail shops. It is intended in the future that the selection criteria for beneficiaries will be aligned with those benefiting from the maize tortilla "smart cards" programme (see Section B.1.*a.i*).

Until 1993, **imports** of milk powder were duty-free, but subject to permits which were exclusively granted to CONASUPO. Since 1994, under NAFTA, a duty-free tariff quota of 40 000 tonnes was established for the United States (to be increased by 3 per cent a year). This quota was included under the Uruguay Round Agreement, which also established a duty-free tariff quota of 80 000 tonnes for other countries (without any increase), on a Most Favoured Nation basis. The above-quota tariff was set in both agreements at 139 per cent (or US$1 160/tonne) to be phased out by 2008 under NAFTA, and to decrease by 10 per cent by 2004 under the Uruguay Round Agreement.

For other dairy products, the NAFTA and Uruguay Round Agreement import regimes differ. Under NAFTA, the import permits for cheeses were converted to a 20 per cent tariff (40 per cent tariff for fresh cheese) to be removed by 2003. The 20 per cent tariff on butter imports will be phased out by 2003. Under the Uruguay Round Agreement, a 50 per cent import tariff quota of 9 405 tonnes was established for fresh, processed, and soft cheeses on a Most Favoured Nation basis, of which around 75 per cent was allocated to the United States. The above-quota tariff was set at 139 per cent (or US$1 160/tonne). Other kinds of cheese and butter are subject to a 50 per cent import tariff, although the rate applied in 1995 was 20 per cent.

Concerning **exports**, under NAFTA, the import tariffs established by the United States for Mexican cheese, milk powder, and butter were converted to duty-free tariff quotas of 5 500, 422, and 43 tonnes respectively (with above-quota tariffs of 69.5, 78 and 95.7 per cent respectively). The quotas are to be increased by 3 per cent a year and phased out by 2003. Dairy products were not included in the NAFTA for trade between Mexico and Canada.

g)   Beef and veal

The production of beef and veal generally involves several stages. Private traders (*acopiadores*) buy calves from producers (*criadores*) at the farm gate and re-sell them to farmers specialised in fattening (*engordadores*). After 6 months (grain-fed) to 2 years (grass-fed) fattening, the steers are sold to middle-men (*introductores*) who transport and re-sell them to slaughterhouses. However, an emerging trend in beef production is the vertical integration between producers' associations and slaughterhouses (see Section H). On average, Mexican cattle fed intake is composed of grass and green fodder (two-thirds), and feedgrains (one third).

As with other meat products, no system of purchasing at guaranteed prices has existed for beef and veal. Until 1988, **producer prices** for beef and veal were influenced essentially by border measures, but import permits were removed in 1988 and free trade was initiated with NAFTA partners in 1994. On the **consumer** side, more than 80 per cent of cattle slaughtered and consumed in Mexico is steer (*novillo*). Until 1987, retail price ceilings for low-quality cuts (between one-half and two-thirds of the veal consumed in Mexico) were set by the federal government. In 1989, around 80 per cent of Mexico City's carcasses were supplied by the state-owned Meat Processing Industry (IDA). Until 1992, IDA imported live cattle and controlled beef and veal supply to Mexico City through the country's biggest slaughter facility (*Ferrería*). IDA passed on to middlemen (*introductores*) the price it received from sales. In 1993, IDA was privatised and livestock producers were subsequently provided with investment capital by the Rural Sector Capitalisation and Investment Fund (FOCIR) (see Section K) to built new slaughterhouses.

Until 1988, **imports** of beef and veal were duty-free, but subject to permits to protect domestic producers from foreign supplies of beef. In 1989, these import permits were removed and imports of beef and veal became duty-free. However, due to a surge in beef imports (in particular fresh beef originating from the United States and frozen beef originating from Australia and New Zealand) which in turn led to a rapid accumulation of animals ready for slaughter and thus depressed domestic prices, import tariffs were introduced in 1993, at 15 per cent for live cattle, 20 per cent for fresh beef and 25 per cent for frozen beef. Under NAFTA, these tariffs were removed in 1994 and trade was fully liberalised with both the United States and Canada. Under the Uruguay Round Agreement, imports of live cattle, beef and veal are subject to a 50 per cent tariff, although, since 1994, the rates of 15 per cent for live cattle, 20 per cent for fresh beef and 25 per cent for frozen beef have continued to apply on a Most Favoured Nation basis. For offal, the import tariff of 20 per cent applied under NAFTA will be removed by 2003, and the 25 per cent base import tariff set under the Uruguay Round Agreement will be reduced by 10 per cent by 2004, although the rate of 20 per cent has continued to apply on a Most Favoured Nation basis.

Until 1986, in order to maintain low prices for the domestic beef and veal market, **exports** of feeder cattle were subject to export quotas. In 1987, the government prepared a plan to liberalise trade in feeder cattle over a five-year period. This plan has allowed for the conversion of the 1987 export quota of 1.23 million head to a 20 per cent tax (or M$ 60 (US$42) per head). This export tax was removed in 1992. Under NAFTA, the import tariffs applied by the United States and Canada on Mexican live cattle, and beef and veal were removed in 1994. Meat exports from Mexico are exempted from both the Canadian Meat Import Act and the US Meat Import Law. However, Mexican exports of beef and live cattle have sometimes been prevented by *sanitary standards* (regions contaminated by bovine tuberculosis) for exports to the United States, and *inspection standards* for exports to Canada (see Section H). Exports to the United States and Canada have also been limited to the 12 states free of cattle ticks.

h) Pigmeat

Vertically-integrated firms (controlling the entire process from production to distribution) account for approximately 30 per cent of Mexican pigmeat production. Another 30 per cent of the production is attributed to medium-sized farms and producers' associations. The remaining 40 per cent of production comes from small producers ("backyard production"). **Producer prices** for pigmeat have always been supported by border protection. On the **consumer side**, until 1992, retail price ceilings for pigmeat were fixed and controlled by the government. Until 1992, the state-owned Meat Processing Industry (IDA) controlled the supply of pigmeat to Mexico City.

Until 1987, **imports** of pigmeat were duty-free, but subject to permits. In 1988, the import permits were replaced by a 20 per cent tariff, which led to a surge in pigmeat imports. Under NAFTA, this tariff is to be phased out by 2003. However, under a safeguard provision, the 20 per cent tariff may continue to apply up to 2003 for imports above a quota of 63 400 tonnes (38 per cent fresh, 62 per cent frozen pigmeat) for the United States (with a 3 per cent annual increase), and 6 000 tonnes for Canada (with a 5 per cent annual increase). Under the Uruguay Round Agreement, pigmeat imports are subject to a 50 per cent tariff, although the rate applied since 1994 has been 20 per cent. Under NAFTA, the imports of pigmeat offal are subject to a 10 to 20 per cent tariff, which will be removed by 2003.

Concerning **exports**, the United States and Canadian governments have never imposed import tariffs on Mexican pigmeat. However, pigmeat exports to the United States have been prevented by sanitary restrictions, although the Sonora State has been recognised free of pig fever by the Mexican authorities.

i) Poultrymeat

Highly integrated poultry producers account for only a small share of total production. About 80 per cent of the poultrymeat consumed in Mexico is bought from local markets where poultry is sold whole by small-scale producers. **Producer prices** for poultrymeat have always been supported by import restrictions. Until 1992, the state-owned Meat Processing Industry (IDA) was the main supplier of poultrymeat to Mexico City. IDA had the import monopoly over poultrymeat and purchased the domestic poultry production from middlemen at a price covering its own processing margins.

Until 1993, **imports** of poultrymeat were subject to permits and a 10 per cent tariff. Under NAFTA, a duty-free quota of 95 000 tonnes (with an annual 3 per cent increment) was granted to imports from the United States for poultrymeat (13 000 tonnes), turkeymeat (2 000 tonnes), boneless poultrymeat (27 000 tonnes), and offal of poultry and turkey (53 000 tonnes). The above-quota tariff was set at 260 per cent or US$1 680/tonne – 133 per cent or US$1 850/tonne for turkeymeat – to be phased out by 2003. In 1995, the duty-free quota for turkey offal was allocated via prior assignment to packaging enterprises (80 per cent) and traders located in the border fringe (20 per cent). For boneless poultrymeat, the duty-free quota has been entirely assigned to packaging enterprises. Cities located close to the United States border may import poultrymeat freely but with the obligation to sell it locally and not to the rest of the country. Under the Uruguay Round Agreement, a 50 per cent import tariff quota of

40 500 tonnes was established on a Most Favoured Nation basis, of which around 98 per cent was allocated to the United States.

Concerning **exports,** under NAFTA, the import tariff applied by the United States on Mexican poultrymeat was removed in 1994. However, the presence of Newcastle disease in Mexican poultry have prevented exports to the United States. Poultrymeat products were not included in the NAFTA for trade between Mexico and Canada.

j) Eggs

Producer prices for eggs have always been supported by import restrictions. Until 1992, **consumer price** ceilings of white eggs have been set and controlled by the government at wholesale and retail levels.

Until 1993, the **import** of fresh eggs was subject to permits and a 10 per cent tariff, while imports of other types of eggs was subject to a 20 per cent tariff. Around 57 per cent of imports were allocated to traders located in the United States border fringe with obligation to sell locally, the remainder being shared between breeders (26 per cent) and other traders (18 per cent). Under NAFTA, the imports of fresh eggs from the United States are duty-free within a quota of 6 500 tonnes (to be increased by 3 per cent a year). The above-quota tariff was set at 50 per cent and will be phased out by 2003. In 1995, the duty-free quota was allocated via prior assignment to traders located in the border fringe (70 per cent) and registered traders (15 per cent), and, via public auction, to other traders (15 per cent). The imports of other types of eggs are subject to a 20 per cent tariff, to be removed by 2003. Under the Uruguay Round Agreement, egg imports are subject to a 50 per cent tariff.

Concerning **exports,** under NAFTA, the import tariff applied by the United States on Mexican eggs was removed in 1994. However, the presence of Newcastle disease and salmonella in Mexican eggs sometimes prevents exports to the United States. Eggs were not included in the NAFTA for trade between Mexico and Canada.

2. Direct payments

a) PROCAMPO

i) Main objectives

A major change in Mexican agricultural support policy to producers has been to initiate the shift from the price support scheme for cereals and oilseeds to direct income payments under PROCAMPO (Programme of Direct Payments to the Countryside). The programme, which started in the 1993/1994 Autumn/Winter crop season for a 15 years duration, is intended to guarantee some income support to help farmers with the structural adjustment resulting from agricultural reforms embarked upon by the Mexican government. Through this programme, the government intended to reduce the distortions in allocation of resources created by the scheme of guaranteed prices; encourage farmers to make production decisions based on their expectations; and shift production to crops for which farmers have a comparative advantage.

Direct payments under PROCAMPO are expected to have a significant effect on support distribution among Mexican farmers: a large number of farmers eligible to receive PROCAMPO payments did not benefit from guaranteed prices, especially subsistence farmers, since they did not market most of their production, and yet needed to purchase grains at higher support prices. As PROCAMPO is shifting support from market prices to direct payments, it is also expected to benefit consumers through lower food prices, having an important effect on the welfare of low-income families (urban population, landless rural workers, and net-consuming subsistence farmers). Also the competitiveness of the livestock sector is expected to increase, by accessing formerly high cost feed grains at world prices.

The programme is also intended to encourage a more environmentally sustainable agriculture. Crops that had benefited from relatively high administered prices, expanded into areas with fragile soils, thus promoting soil erosion and the excessive use of fertilisers. The reduction of price distortions should lead to a more efficient use of natural resources. Moreover, PROCAMPO is expected to lead to an expansion in the growth of forests and the conservation of natural resources, since payments are allowed to be used for these purposes.

In summary, the objectives of PROCAMPO, as defined by the Mexican government, are to:

- grant direct income support to about 3 million farmers, including those who did not benefit from administered price schemes;

- promote shift in production towards products that have a comparative advantage;

- support the incomes of producers by giving certainty over time regarding future income support levels;

- compensate for the adverse effect on world markets due to subsidies granted to producers in other countries;

- encourage the organisation of producers in order to achieve greater efficiency in marketing and distribution;

- allow consumers to have access to food at market prices within an open economy; and,

- stop environmental degradation by promoting forest recovery and soil conservation practices, thus moving towards a more environmentally sustainable agriculture.

ii) Description and implementation

To be eligible for PROCAMPO payments, land must have been cultivated with maize, beans, wheat, sorghum, rice, soyabeans, safflower, cotton, or barley in any crop season over the three year period prior to August 1993. Farmers who did not grow these crops at that time but do so currently are thus not eligible to receive support. The payments are granted to farmers who actually cultivate the land, being owners or renters, individuals or corporations. The first payments were made for the Autumn/Winter 1993/1994 crop season (for the Spring/Summer 1995 crop season in the case of barley and safflower). In 1994, eligible farmers could allocate land to any job creation activity. In 1995, payments were restricted to farmers growing one of the nine eligible crops. As from the Autumn/Winter 1995/96 crop season, farmers can devote land to any crop, livestock, or forestry activity, or place it in an approved environmental programme and receive the same area payment rate, but they are not allowed to leave the land idle or use it for any other activity. Any environmental activity (including one year land set aside) must be designed in co-ordination with the Secretariat of Agriculture, Livestock and Rural Development (SAGAR) and the Secretariat of Environment, Natural Resources, and Fisheries (SEMARNAP).

ASERCA, through its 16 regional centres, is in charge of implementing PROCAMPO. In 1993, it started the establishment of a register of eligible land (*catastro*), through a field survey based on individual applications (*cédula de registro*). To be eligible for PROCAMPO payments, farmers must possess documents proving ownership or rights of tenancy on the eligible land; be in conformity with the provisions of the Agrarian Law on maximum cultivated area per farm (see Chapter I, Section D); and voluntarily register with the local municipality each year. In each DDR (Rural Development District), there is a subcommittee of control and monitoring, constituted by farmers and their associations, and public institutions, to validate and improve the registry of eligible producers, and ensure a transparent payment. Payments are made to producers by cheque, payment order, or direct deposit in their bank accounts. Producers may transfer their rights to receive PROCAMPO payments (*cesión de derechos*) to banks, state governments, or other institutions (such as farm input retailers, private marketing companies, state-owned agencies) to allow the use of payments as collateral for participating in development projects. It is estimated that this scheme accounted for around 14 per cent of PROCAMPO payments in the Spring/Summer 1996

Payments are made per hectare for each crop season and, for greater transparency, were fixed at the same level across the country. A transitional period until 1996 was implemented to help farmers to progressively adjust from guaranteed price schemes to direct area payments. From the Autumn/Winter 1993/94 to the the Autumn/Winter 1994/95 crop season, the guaranteed prices have decreased by 20 per cent for maize, and by 24 per cent for beans (see Annex I, Table II.1). Over the same period, PROCAMPO

◆ Figure 4. **Crops cultivated on the land eligible for PROCAMPO payments in the 1995 crop year**
'000 hectares

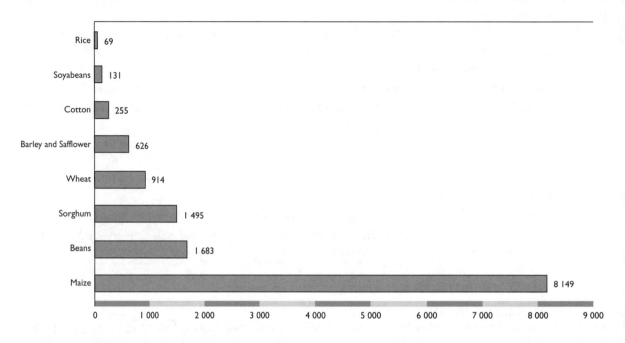

Source: ASERCA.

◆ Figure 5. **PROCAMPO in 1995: shares of eligible producers and payments by area size**
In %

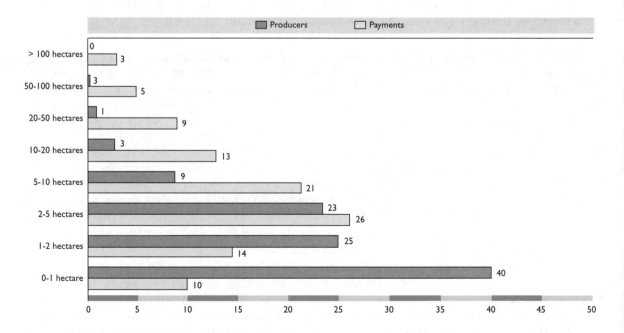

Source: ASERCA.

payments were increased by 20 per cent to M$ 400 (US$62) per hectare. In 1995, as a result of high inflation brought about by the devaluation of the peso at the end of 1994, guaranteed prices for maize and beans were increased in nominal terms (see Annex I, Table II.1) and the government raised PROCAMPO payments to M$ 440 (US$69) per hectare (in the Spring/Summer 1995 crop season). In 1996, it was decided that PROCAMPO payments will be fixed in real terms, to apply from the Spring-Summer 1996 crop season payment of M$ 484 (US$64) per hectare until the end of PROCAMPO implementation.

In 1994, PROCAMPO payments benefited around 3 million farmers on 13.6 million hectares, with a total budgetary cost of around M$ 4.9 (US$1.4) billion. For the 1995 crop year, the coverage was 2.9 million farmers on 13.3 million hectares (as some areas were affected by drought or flood and the land registration process was improved), with an estimated budgetary cost of M$ 5.9 (US$0.9) billion. That year, the land eligible for PROCAMPO payments was mainly cultivated with maize (more than 60 per cent), beans (around 13 per cent), sorghum (about 11 per cent), and wheat (less than 7 per cent) (see Figure 4). Most of this land (80 per cent) was in rainfed areas. Around 88 per cent of the producers benefiting from PROCAMPO payments cultivated less than five hectares and received about half of the total amount of payments (see Figure 5). Subsistence farmers – owner-operators of plots (*predios*) of less than two hectares and producing maize and beans with low yields – accounted for about 65 per cent of eligible producers and received about a quarter of the total amount of payments. It is estimated that PROCAMPO budgetary expenditures reached about M$ 6.8 (US$0.9) billion in 1996.

b) Disaster payments

Since 1972, in co-operation with other federal agencies and State governments, CONASUPO has implemented programmes of civil protection – known as "Presidential Programmes" (see also Section L) – to assist the population affected by natural disasters. One of these programmes provides support in kind (food assistance) to those farmers whose crops have been affected by climatic hazard (mainly drought or frost). The value of this food assistance increased from M$ 1.8 (US$0.8) million in 1988 to M$ 24 (US$3.7) million in 1995, equivalent to a rise from M$ 20 (US$9) per family in 1988 to M$ 66 (US$10) per family in 1995 (see Annex I, Table II.12). The number of families covered increased from 90 000 in 1988 to 360 000 in 1995.

Since 1990, the National Solidarity Programme (PRONASOL) (see Box II.2) has assisted farmers affected by natural disasters, mainly through the Programme of Support to Coffee Growers and the Solidarity Fund for Production (see Section D.3). In co-ordination with the National Institute for Indigenous Communities (INI), the Programme of Support to Coffee Growers has provided emergency credit assistance to poor coffee producers which were not any more contracted by INMECAFE and had been affected by the 1989 frost. As part of its mandate, the Solidarity Fund for Production has authorised debt write-off to low-income (maize and beans) producers affected by events beyond their control, including climatic hazard.

In 1995, about 120 000 tonnes of maize feedgrains were sold at a price reduced by 15 per cent to farmers affected by the five-year drought plaguing northern Mexico (Chihuahua, Coahuila, Durango, Nuevo Leon, Tamaulipas), where 67 000 heads of cattle have died, 100 000 have been sold below market value, and another 250 000 are at risk. The cost for the Trust Fund for Shared Risk (FIRCO) of this support was M$ 19.5 (US$3) million. In 1995, ASERCA transferred M$ 33.6 (US$11) million to the States of Chihuahua and San Luis Potosi to help them assist areas affected by drought.

C. TRADE POLICY

1. Background

Until the mid-1980s, trade policy was essentially based on import-substitution policies. In 1979, about 60 per cent of the value of all **imports** was subject to permits. In 1982, the balance-of-payments crisis led to a tightening of import restrictions and this percentage increased to 100 per cent. In 1984, the first signs of liberalising the trade regime began with the reduction of permit requirements to 83 per cent of the value of all imports.

Since the mid-1980s, Mexico has embarked on a large programme of trade liberalisation, as part of an overall policy for economic growth. Two events hastened the liberalisation of trade. In 1986, Mexico's accession to the GATT was aimed at increasing trade flows in all sectors of the economy, with a view to shift production towards products that have a comparative advantage. Accelerated trade liberalisation was also a key component of the *Pacto* (Pact for Economic Solidarity) initiated in 1987 (see Chapter I, Section B.1). The *Pacto* was based on the assumption that competition from cheaper imports would put a ceiling on inflation for traded goods. In 1986, as part of GATT commitments, Mexico reduced import permits to cover 28 per cent of the value of all imports, down from 35 per cent in 1985. In 1987, Mexico went beyond its GATT commitments – which set overall tariff ceilings at 50 per cent – and unilaterally reduced the maximum tariff rate to 20 per cent, down from 100 per cent in 1986. In 1987, Mexico also reduced the number of tariff positions to five (0, 5, 10, 15, and 20 per cent), down from eleven in 1986. The overall trade weighted average tariff was more than halved from 13 per cent in 1986 to less than 6 per cent in 1987.

By the end of 1988, under the new *Pacto* (Economic Growth and Stability Pact), to avoid disparities between the different sectors of the economy, tariffs were raised for all goods for which imports were duty-free or subject to a 5 per cent tariff. As a result, the overall trade weighted average tariff increased to 10 per cent in 1990. However, the reduction of the share of the value of imports subject to permits initiated in 1984 continued over the period 1987-93. In 1993, only 9 per cent of the value of imports were still subject to import permits, although the share was higher for agricultural products. The pursuit of trade liberalisation reached a milestone in 1994 with the entry into force of NAFTA and was reinforced in 1995 with the implementation of the Uruguay Round Agreement on Agriculture (see Section C.2. below).

Mexico's **export** policy has tended to be less restrictive than its import policy, as shown by the number of goods subject to export taxes which is half of that for import tariffs. Since the mid 1980s, export taxes have been reduced along with tariffs, and the number of goods on which export restrictions was applied has been reduced considerably. The value of all exports subject to licensing decreased from 10 per cent of the total value of exports in 1983 to 2 per cent in 1994, after reaching a peak of 23 per cent in 1986. Most of the export licensing requirements were imposed on agricultural commodities, endangered species and petroleum derivatives (see Section H).

2. Agricultural trade measures

During the 1980s, import of most agricultural products was duty-free, but subject to **import permits**. Permits were issued on a discretional basis by the Secretariat of Commerce (SECOFI), for quantities calculated as the difference between consumption and domestic production. In 1988, about 85 per cent of the value of crop production and 20 per cent of the value of livestock production required import permits. In 1989 and 1990, import permit requirements were removed for sorghum, oats, rice, oilseeds, sugar, live cattle, and beef and veal. The number of agricultural commodities requiring an import permit fell from 320 in 1985 to 57 in 1990. During the same period, the share of the value of agricultural imports subject to permits decreased from 79 per cent to 12 per cent. In 1990, about 20 per cent of the total value of agricultural imports entered the country duty free, while the remaining 80 per cent were subject to **import tariffs** of between 5 and 20 per cent. All remaining import permits were converted into tariffs or tariff quotas in 1994 for NAFTA partners, and in 1995 for the other Most Favoured Nations (see 2.*a.i* and 2.*a.iii* below).

During the 1980s, more than two-third of the value of exports required licenses aimed at controlling exports (coffee, cocoa, tobacco, fruits and vegetables), or supply of the domestic market for products of the basic food basket, for which retail prices were fixed (wheat, live cattle). In 1988, 62 per cent of the value of crop production and 60 per cent of the value of livestock production were still subject to an **export license** regime. Export licensing requirements have been removed for cotton (1984), live cattle (1987), wheat (1990), rice (1990), fruits and vegetables (1990), cocoa (1992), tobacco (1992), and coffee (1993). With the entry into force of NAFTA in 1994, all remaining export licenses have been removed.

a) Agricultural trade agreements

i) The North American Free Trade Agreement (NAFTA)

Entered into force on 1 January 1994, NAFTA is the first regional integration agreement to be signed between advanced industrial nations and a developing nation.[9] In sectors traditionally highly protected in international trade, such as agriculture, the agreement states that all agricultural and agro-food trade between the United States and Mexico will be duty-free by 2008. NAFTA has particular relevance for Mexican agriculture: nearly 90 per cent of the value of Mexican agricultural exports is destined to its North American neighbours, and over 75 per cent of its agricultural imports originate there (see Chapter I, Section C.8). Some products such as sugar, dairy products, poultrymeat, and eggs, were excluded from the Mexico-Canada sub-treaty.

Concerning agriculture, NAFTA includes provisions on market access, domestic support, export subsidies, and sanitary and phytosanitary measures. In the area of **market access**, NAFTA partners have converted all non-tariff barriers to agricultural trade (including import permits) into tariffs or tariff quotas (referred to as tariffication) in 1994. Furthermore, all tariffs will have to be phased out over a maximum 15-year transitional period to 2008. For those products which were still subject to tariffs in 1993, the pace of tariff elimination can be either immediate (in 1994), or within 5, 10 or 15 years, thus recognising that time is needed for farmers to adjust to the new trade environment (see Annex I, Table II.13). NAFTA also provides for reduction in trade measures throughout agro-food production chains. All the products of a production chain are subject to the same tariff reduction schedule. This applies to the wheat/wheat flour/bread, soyabeans/oil/oil cake, and feedgrains/livestock/meat agro-food chains.

A general **safeguard provision** can be temporarily imposed if increased imports constitute a "substantial cause of threat" or "serious injury" to the industry concerned. Actions that can be taken include the suspension of tariff reduction or the re-establishment of the base tariff provided for in NAFTA ("snap-back mechanism"). Compensation must be given to the trading partner in the form of trade concession equal in value to the loss resulting from the implementation of the safeguard. A specific safeguard provision applies on imports of some sensitive products (such as apples, coffee extract, and pigmeat) in the form of specific tariff quotas: the base tariff can be re-imposed on imports above the quota while the tariff reduction continues to apply within the quota. However, the snap back provision has only been applied on a little share of Mexican imports from the United States and Canada. The **rule of origin** restricts the trade within NAFTA partners of merchandise which was not produced in NAFTA countries. According to the "de minimis" proviso, NAFTA only applies to goods for which less than 7 per cent of the production cost is of foreign origin.

Provisions on **domestic support** establish that each NAFTA country should endeavour to move toward domestic support policies that have minimal or no effect on agricultural trade and production. A working group has been established to work towards the elimination of all agricultural **export subsidies** between the NAFTA countries. If Mexico (or another NAFTA country) considers that a non-NAFTA country is exporting an agricultural product into the territory of a NAFTA partner with export subsidies, Mexico (or another NAFTA country) may request consultations with the NAFTA partner to agree on measures to counter the effect of such subsidised imports. However, this scheme has not yet been implemented by any of the NAFTA partners.

NAFTA requires that all **sanitary and phytosanitary measures** adopted should be based on scientific principles using international standards whenever possible, although stricter standards can be imposed. The agreement states that such measures cannot be used to discriminate between domestic and foreign products, where identical or similar conditions prevail, and that they should not be used to create disguised restrictions to trade between the partners.

With the entry into force of NAFTA, duty-free market access has been granted to a significant share of the volume of agro-food **imports** from the United States (36 per cent) and Canada (41 per cent) (see Figure 6). For most agricultural products previously requiring import permits, duty-free import quotas were established on the basis of trade flows over the period 1989-91 (see Annex I, Table II.13). The quotas will be increased each year by 3 per cent (5 per cent for some products). Quotas have been allocated by a Committee composed of SECOFI, SAGAR, producers, and consumers. Efforts are being made to allocate quotas through public auction, although, in 1995, for most products, they have been allocated through prior assignment. For maize, beans, barley and milk, during the first six years of NAFTA, an aggregate 24 per cent of the above-quota tariff will be removed, and the remaining 76 per cent will be gradually phased out over the next 2 to 9 years depending on the commodities. Tariffs on products that accounted for 57 per cent of the total value of imports between Mexico and the United States in 1993 were eliminated in 1994. This included sorghum, coffee, live cattle, and beef and veal. On the basis of 1994 weights, tariffs on products that made up a further 6 per cent of the value of imports will be gradually removed by 1998, an additional 32 per cent by 2003, and the final 5 per cent by 2008 (which includes maize, beans, sugar, and milk powder) (see Annex I, Table II.13). However, tariff preferences available to the United States and Canada for a number of products have provided a comparative advantage to imports of these products originating from these countries relative to some other non-NAFTA countries.

In 1994, NAFTA granted duty-free market access to a high share of agro-food **exports** from Mexico to the United States (61 per cent) and Canada (89 per cent) (see Figure 6). Duty-free import quotas have been established by the United States for most Mexican agricultural products previously requiring import permits, with quotas set at levels far above the levels of trade flows between the two countries over the period 1989-91. Mexico's **sanitary and phytosanitary measures** applied to imports and exports underwent a substantial overhaul in 1994, with the introduction of a new regulatory framework (see Section H).

ii) Other regional trade agreements

The Mexico-Chile Economic Complementary Accord (ACE) came into force in January 1992. Under the ACE, the maximum tariff allowed on most trade between the two countries is 10 per cent. Tariffs will be phased out over a period of 4 to 6 years, although important agricultural commodities are excluded from tariff reductions such as: maize, beans, wheat, barley, sugar, vegetable oils, apples, grapes (seasonal tariff), processed tobacco, and powdered milk. In 1994, Mexico signed free trade agreements with Costa Rica, Colombia, Venezuela, and Bolivia. All the agreements contain special provisions on agriculture, although within the context of continuing trade liberalisation. Within the Latin American Integration Assosciation (ALADI), other bilateral trade agreements are being negotiated with Panama, Nicaragua, Guatemala, Honduras and El Salvador. Negotiations are also in process with the Common Market of the South (MERCOSUR)[10] and the European Union, and Mexico is an active member of APEC.[11]

iii) The Uruguay Round Agreement on Agriculture

The Agreement on Agriculture of the Uruguay Round (UR), which was signed in 1994, began to be implemented as from 1 January 1995 according to detailed country schedules and applies to signatories ("Most Favoured Nations"), including the United States and Canada. As with NAFTA, this Agreement includes provisions in the areas of market access, domestic support and export subsidies, and there is a separate Agreement on the Application of Sanitary and Phytosanitary Measures. While the NAFTA commitment is to totally eliminate tariffs by 2008, the UR Agricultural Agreement commitment for Mexico is to reduce tariffs on average by 24 per cent by 2004. The UR Agricultural Agreement does require specific reduction commitments in domestic support and export subsidies.

In the area of **market access**, all non-tariff measures have been converted into tariffs or tariff quotas. On the basis of Mexico's bound tariff at the time of its accession to the GATT in 1986, the base tariff under the UR Agricultural Agreement has been set at 50 per cent for most agricultural products, although the rates actually applied in 1995 were generally lower, except in the case of tariff quotas (see Annex I, Table II.13). The commitments in tariff reductions for Mexico are more relaxed than for developed nations (24 per cent over a period of 10 years instead of 36 per cent over a period of 6 years), reflecting Mexico's eligibility for Special and Differential Treatment. Tariff quotas were set at levels ensuring market access levels in line with previous import levels. Import concessions already

◆ Figure 6. **Tariff reduction schedules applied on agricultural trade under NAFTA**
Share of volume, based on 1989-91 trade flows

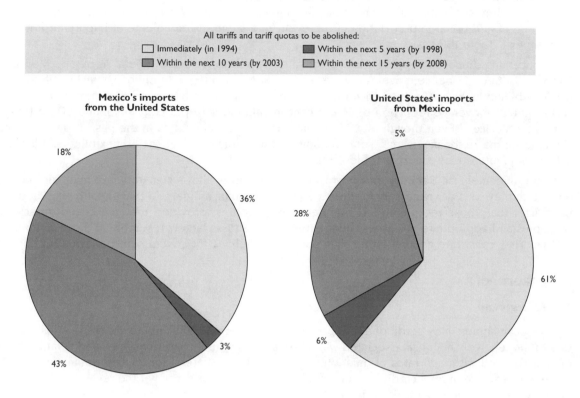

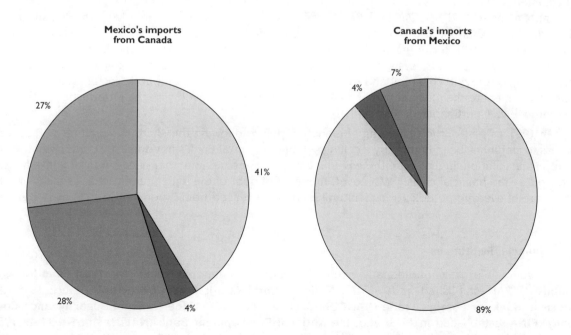

granted under NAFTA have been included in the UR minimum access commitment, and Mexico has granted increased access for milk powder on a Most Favoured Nation basis (see Annex I, Table II.13). The import of most agricultural commodities are subject to a **safeguard provision** which allows for the imposition of additional import duties in the event of a surge in the volume of imports at low prices (see Annex I, Table II.13).

Concerning **domestic support**, Mexico committed itself to reduce the Total Aggregate Measure of Support (AMS) by 13 per cent over ten years, from 1991 M$ 28.6 (US$9.5) billion in 1995 to 1991 M$ 25.2 (US$8.3) billion in 2004. The UR Agricultural Agreement imposes a freeze on all **export subsidy** levels, and requires an average reduction of 24 per cent in value and 16 per cent in volume over a ten-year period for Mexico.[12] Even though Mexico did not grant export subsidies in the past, it declared some amounts for maize, beans, wheat, sorghum, and sugar, in order to retain the flexibility to grant such subsidies in future (see Annex I, Table II.14).

The Agreement on **Sanitary and Phytosanitary Measures** allows signatories to maintain the standards that they consider necessary for the protection of human, animal and plant health. Standards may be stricter than those recommended by international bodies, provided they are based on scientific principles and appropriate risk assessment criteria. These rules largely resemble to those contained in NAFTA. They constitute general rather than specific guidelines for government behaviour in this area.

D. CREDIT POLICY

1. Background

Mexican farmers have traditionally experienced considerable difficulty to get credit. This has been due to the relatively high risk associated with Mexican agricultural conditions, high and volatile interest rates associated with high rates of inflation, and the lack of collateral for loans for many farmers. The share of agriculture in total credit has remained at around 6-7 per cent over the review period, broadly in line with the share of agriculture in GDP.

In 1988, the financial system underwent a radical transformation which led to the re-privatisation[13] of commercial banks in 1992. During that period, development banks and trust funds were reduced in size and number, and re-organised (total staff was cut by 25 per cent in 1990). This resulted in a decrease in the share of development banks in total lending to around 20 per cent in 1994 (down from 50 per cent in 1988), including in the agricultural sector. Until 1992, rural credit markets were also affected by the land tenure system because ejido farmers could not sell or mortgage their land. Thus, they could not provide collateral and were consequently dependent on public sector credit. However, this impediment to the efficient use of credit has since been removed with the introduction of the land reform in 1992 (see Chapter I, Section D).

In 1995, as part of the tightening of monetary policy following the sharp devaluation of the peso, access to credit has been limited by a ceiling set on the Central Bank's net domestic credit, with the aim of reducing inflation. In that year, the government had to rescue a number of commercial banks heavily affected by the financial crisis.[14] Moreover, the level of debt of the agricultural sector, as measured by the share of overdue portfolio in agricultural lending, increased from 2 per cent in 1988 to 15 per cent in 1995.

2. Financial institutions

Development banks traditionally involved in agricultural lending include the **Trust Fund for Agriculture (FIRA)** established in 1954; the **National Rural Credit Bank (BANRURAL)** since 1975; the **Mexican Bank for Foreign Trade (BANCOMEXT)** created in 1934; the **National Sugar Finance Company (FINA)** established in 1943; and, the **National Development Bank (NAFIN)** since 1934. In 1980, agricultural lending was shared among BANRURAL (38 per cent), FINA (35 per cent), FIRA (24 per cent), and BANCOMEXT (3 per cent). The respective share of each of these institutions in total agricultural lending has varied widely over time. In 1993, FIRA, accounted for 40 per cent of total agricultural lending, followed by BANCOMEXT (26 per cent), BANRURAL (17 per cent), FINA (13 per cent), and

NAFIN (4 per cent). The **Solidarity Fund for Production** is not considered by its structure as a development bank, but since its creation in 1990 and until 1995, it has provided M$ 3.5 (US$1.2) billion of agricultural loans, which is equivalent to 15 per cent of the aggregate value of BANRURAL loans over this period. The **Trust Fund for Shared Risk (FIRCO)** was created by Presidential decree in 1981 to provide credit and technical assistance linked to the implementation of integral development projects (see also Section G).

The **Trust Fund for Agriculture (FIRA)** is a second-stage bank which provides credit through commercial banks and BANRURAL field networks. FIRA includes:

- the Trust Fund for Agriculture, Livestock and Poultry Development (FONDO) established in 1954, which provides short-term loans for crops, livestock, and agro-industry;
- the Special Agricultural Trust Fund (FEFA) established in 1965 which channels external funds toward medium and long term loans for crops, livestock, and agro-industry;
- the Technical Assistance and Loan Guarantee Trust Fund (FEGA) created in 1972 which reimburses commercial banks for the cost of credit assessment and technical assistance to low-income producers and provides partial guarantees against borrower defaults; and
- the Trust Fund for Fishery Development (FOPESCA) created in 1988.

Until 1994, FIRA received funds directly from the Bank of Mexico (BANXICO), acting as trustee of the Federal government. Since 1995, FIRA is an autonomous agency. Its four Trust Funds are governed by Technical Committees constituted by representatives from several government agencies, participating banks and producers' organisations. FIRA has its Headquarters in Morelia (Michoacan State), a representation office in Mexico City, 5 regional offices, 32 state offices, 137 agencies which cover all the country, and a total of 1 750 employees. In addition to its own resources and transfers from BANXICO, FIRA channelled financial resources from borrowings from the World Bank, the Interamerican Development Bank (IDB) and BANCOMEXT. In 1989, external funding from IDB and the World Bank ceased. In 1994, FIRA loan programmes were funded by its own resources (59 per cent), BANXICO (37 per cent), and BANCOMEXT (4 per cent).

The origin of **BANRURAL** dates back from 1926, although it was formally created in 1975 by merging three public sector agricultural credit institutions. BANRURAL is the sole first stage development bank essentially aimed at providing credit and banking services to agricultural, fishery, and related activities. Its main objectives are to promote technological change, provide technical assistance, increase agricultural production and productivity, and contribute to producers well-being. From 1976 (1982 for rainfed areas) to 1994, the **Trust Fund for Credit in Irrigated and Rainfed Areas (FICART)** played an important role in channelling external funds to BANRURAL, mainly for investment credit. In the 1980s, BANRURAL lending activities relied extensively on transfers from the government budget. Over that period, BANRURAL had the most extensive network of branches of any bank nation-wide, but many of its loans were not repaid by farmers and were absorbed by the National Agricultural Insurance Company (ANAGSA) (see Section F.3). The closure of ANAGSA in 1990 provoked a radical change in BANRURAL's way to operate. Among other changes, BANRURAL reclassified its target clients and ceased providing credit for unsustainable farming activities. Besides considerable reductions in personnel and other administrative costs, these changes caused a cleaning up of its portfolio and a reduced participation of BANRURAL in agricultural financing. BANRURAL has currently 224 field branches, 12 regional offices, and its Headquarters in Mexico City.

BANCOMEXT provides short, medium and long-term credit to producers, associations, and private enterprises for activities oriented toward exports. From 1989 to 1994, 18 per cent of its loans were allocated to the agro-food sector (11 per cent) and for agricultural activities (7 per cent).

FINA provides credit for sugar production. The sugar industry also benefited from loans through the Trust Fund for Sugar (FIDAZUCAR), until 1993, and the Fund for the Creation and Development of Machinery and Equipment Centres for the Sugar Industry (FIMAIA), until 1993.

NAFIN's main objective is to facilitate access by private enterprises to domestic and international financial markets, buying and selling shares on commission (factorage). NAFIN also provides credit to small and medium agro-food enterprises through other financial institutions. In 1993, NAFIN created the **Rural Sector Capitalisation and Investment Fund (FOCIR)** with a view to promote vertical integration, through associations of producers with investors and entrepreneurs in the fields of agriculture, livestock, forestry, and aquaculture (see Section K).

The **Solidarity Fund for Production** was created as part of the National Solidarity Programme (see Box II.3) with the objective of stimulating farmers' productive activities in rainfed areas of low productivity. The reimbursement of loans is used either to create Solidarity Saving Accounts (created in 1992), or to carry out productive projects, community work, or Municipal Solidarity Fund activities.

The **Trust Fund for Shared Risk (FIRCO)** was created to enhance agricultural productivity of low-income farmers in areas with commercial potential. FIRCO provides credit to farmers to encourage them to adopt new technologies for crop and livestock production. State committees including SAGAR, BANRURAL, and the Mexican Agricultural Insurance Company (AGROASEMEX) representatives evaluate the projects of producers and producers' associations who wish to participate in FIRCO.

3. Interest concessions

Interest concessions are measured as the difference between preferential (lower) interest rates granted to farmers and the (higher) commercial market interest rate (*tasa de interes activa de mercado*). In Mexico, interest rates for commercial activities are often calculated on the basis of a reference rate, such as the interest rate for average cost of term deposits for banks (CPP) or 28 days treasury bills (CETES), plus some percentage points depending on the type of activity or loan term.

During the 1980s, the government provided agricultural loans to crop and livestock producers at interest rates below reference rates (CPP or CETES) through BANRURAL. BANRURAL lent different proportions of working capital (*crédito de avío*) and investment credit (*crédito refaccionario*) to low-income producers. BANRURAL loans were mainly targeted at producers of grains, beans and oilseeds in rainfed areas, which accounted for more than 75 per cent of the 4 to 6 million hectares covered by its loans during the 1980s.

During the same period, FIRA provided short, medium and long term credit via commercial banks to all agricultural producers. Rates and ceilings varied according to producers' income level and the type of production: low-income producers or other (wealthier) producers; production of basic products (grains, beans, oilseeds, milk, meat, poultry, eggs, processed products derived from the previous commodities or inputs required for their production) or other products. The interest rates were below, equivalent or above the reference rate (CPP), and the commercial banks were allowed to add a 5 or 6 percentage points intermediation margin for "counter services" (*servicio de ventanilla*) and to incur the risk of loan defaulting. Interest rates were set at lower levels for the production of basic products and for low-income producers. The maximum amount of credit per producer varied, depending on the type of producer, the type of production and the term of the loan. To facilitate the marketing of the crop of producers able to provide collateral, FIRA also granted an optional (up to 6-month term) secured credit, with a ceiling of 70 per cent of the value of production. Beneficiaries of loans had to contribute a minimum percentage of total investment (5 per cent for low-income producers; 20 per cent for other producers). FIRA credit programmes benefited 750 000 farmers and around 3 million hectares.

Since the end of the 1980s, substantial reforms have been introduced in rural credit policy. BANRURAL has been re-organised and downsized: ANAGSA, which was absorbing a substantial part of BANRURAL loan defaults (see Section F.4) was closed in 1990, and FICART was dismantled in 1993. This has resulted in the reduction of BANRURAL staff to less than 10 000 persons (down from 20 000 employees in 1988). BANRURAL and FIRA interest rates have been progressively aligned to or set above reference rates to cover the administrative costs of these development banks (see Annex I, Table II.15a). In 1995, BANRURAL and FIRA loan rates were set at the CETES rate for "development producers level I" (formerly called low-income producers), with a limit of M$ 150 000 (US$23 360) per producer, and at higher rates for other producers, and above this limit. Over the review period, interest concessions by BANRURAL have decreased dramatically while those by FIRA have remained at a low level (see Figure 7).

◆ Figure 7. **Interest concessions by BANRURAL and FIRA**
US$ million

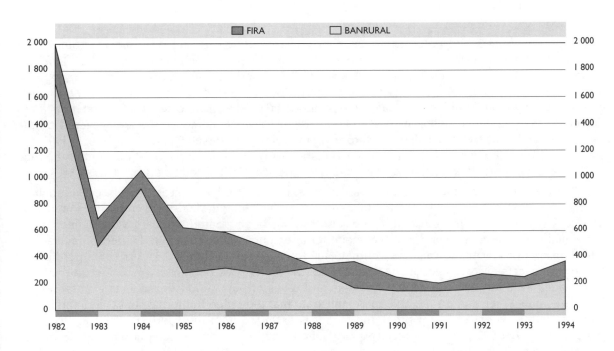

Source: Table II.15b.

◆ Figure 8. **Agricultural lending by FIRA and BANRURAL**
US$ million

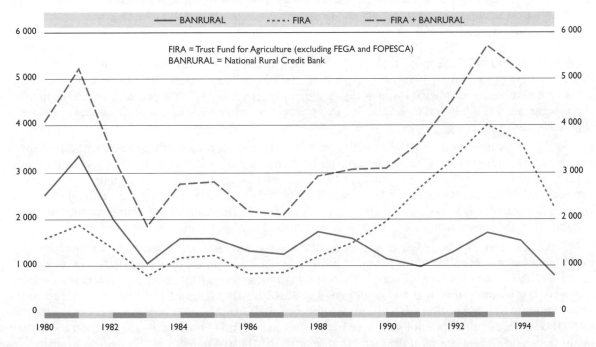

Source: Table II.15b.

Since 1990, the share of investment credit in total agricultural lending has increased significantly for both FIRA and BANRURAL, and the value of agricultural lending by FIRA overtook that of BANRURAL (see Figure 8). However, in 1995, the total value of agricultural lending by both FIRA and BANRURAL has decreased (see Figure 8).

The coverage of BANRURAL credit programmes decreased from 1.7 million farmers (accounting for more than 7 million hectares) in 1988 to about 500 000 farmers (accounting for more than 1 million hectares) in 1995 (see Figures 9 and 10). The share of irrigated land in areas covered by BANRURAL loans has increased to more than 60 per cent, representing an increase from one third (in 1990) to three quarters of the total value of the loans. The number of producers who received credit from FIRA decreased from around 1 million in 1988 to about 700 000 in 1995, although the area covered by the loans increased from 2.3 to 2.6 million hectares over the same period (see Figures 9 and 10). In 1995, the area covered by FIRA and BANRURAL loans was respectively 15.6 per cent and 7.3 per cent of the total cultivated area, while AGROASEMEX insured only 5.5 per cent of the total cultivated area.

The Solidarity Fund for Production was established in 1990 to assist producers excluded from coverage by BANRURAL to benefit from interest-free loans for growing basic crops in rainfed low-productivity areas. "Credit on trust" (*crédito a la palabra*) has been granted interest-free to farmers on an individual basis, without insurance or collateral requirements. These loans are limited on average to 3 hectares per producer and cannot exceed M$ 400 (US$133) per hectare M$ 350 (US$117) per hectare for new producers. On average, only 47 per cent of the loans have been recovered. The other 53 per cent mainly included cases of natural disasters and cases of poor production due to events beyond farmers control. When farmers are able to demonstrate that they tried to produce but failed, the loan is forgiven (in the absence of such proof, the farmer is excluded from the Fund). During the 1990-1994 period, about 720 000 producers received credit from the Fund, representing an area of 1.8 million hectares, mainly cultivated with maize and beans.

Following the frost of 1989, under PRONASOL (see Box II.3) and in co-ordination with the National Institute for Indigenous Communities (INI), the Programme of Support to Coffee Producers was launched to provide credit and technical assistance to producers owning less than five hectares of land for coffee production, and which were not any more attended by INMECAFE. As for the Solidarity Fund for Production, interest-free loans were provided "on trust" for a maximum of two hectares – with yields of less than 1.1 tonnes per hectare – to restore coffee plantations, and, if necessary, to help coffee producers grow alternative crops. In 1995, the programme was implemented by BANRURAL and interest rates on loans charged in US$, at 10 points above a reference 90 days savings rate (LIBOR) with a maximum loan of M$ 1 000 (US$156) per hectare – with yields between 1.1 and 1.7 tonnes per hectare. Producers able to produce more than 1.7 tonnes per hectare could receive credit from FIRA, but at higher interest rates. During 1989-1993, more than 200 000 coffee growers and 246 producers' associations received credit assistance through this programme, covering 347 000 hectares of coffee. In 1995, the programme was extended to around 300 000 producers and 480 000 hectares, or about two-thirds of total coffee area.

FIRCO provides credit to farmers willing to participate in development projects to help them to buy inputs and improve rural infrastructure (see Section I). Once in FIRCO, producers also benefit from a guaranteed minimum revenue equivalent to their previous agricultural income, plus a premium for productivity. Because of the nature of its responsibility, only a small share of FIRCO's budget (10-15 per cent) is financed by loan recoveries, the remainder being in the form of government transfers. From 1989 to 1994, the areas insured by FIRCO covered a total of about 1 million hectares.

Since the end of the 1980s, debt restructuring programmes have been implemented for non-performing loans – loans for which payment has been missed for more than one year – by BANRURAL and BANCOMEXT (for coffee producers). These programmes were mainly based on loans rescheduling with very favourable terms. In 1991, 40 per cent of BANRURAL's loan portfolio were transferred to the Trust Fund to Restructure the Overdue Portfolio of BANRURAL (FIRCAVEN). In 1992, additional BANRURAL overdue investment loans were transferred to the Trust Fund for the Liquidation of Auxiliary Institutions and Organisations (FIDELIQ). That year, BANRURAL's transfer of the overdue portfolio to FIRCAVEN was M$ 4.2 (US$1.3) billion. In 1994, M$ 7 (US$2.1) billion of overdue portfolio by commercial

◆ Figure 9. **Producers receiving credit from FIRA and BANRURAL**
'000

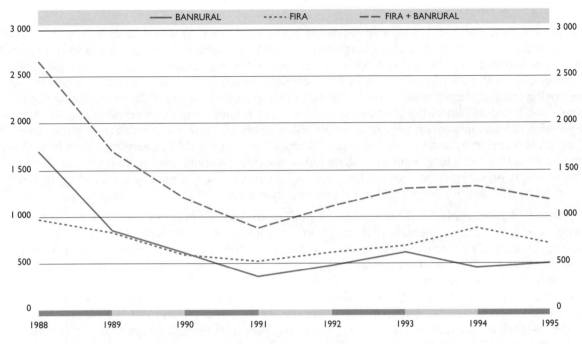

Source: FIRA and BANRURAL.

◆ Figure 10. **Area covered by loans of FIRA and BANRURAL**
Million hectares

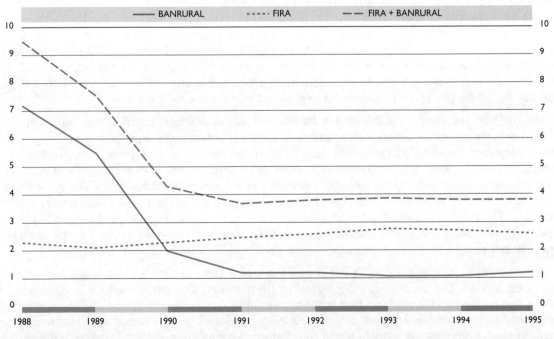

Source: FIRA and BANRURAL.

banks and BANRURAL were transferred to the System for the Restructuring of Agricultural Overdue Portfolio (SIRECA) supervised by FIRA. Producers covered by SIRECA are given a 3 to 7 years grace period on the repayment of the principle, to restructure farming activities, including technological and marketing improvements.

In 1994, excluding overdue interest payments, agricultural loans represented about 51 per cent and 13 per cent of total overdue portfolio (*cartera vencida*) held in Mexico by development and commercial banks respectively. In 1994, approximately 14 per cent of the agriculture portfolio (development and commercial banks) was estimated to be in the overdue portfolio. In 1995, to help banks cope with non-performing loans and make new loans, including in the agricultural sector, debt restructuring schemes were established as part of the Programme for Economic Adjustment.[15] One scheme is based on the conversion of loans into Investment Units (UDI) where debts are indexed to inflation. Another scheme offers direct support to small debtors through Debtors' Agreements (ADE) providing for an immediate interest reduction and a lengthening of the period of maturity. To stimulate the repayment of debt, new loan restructuring schemes have been designed, including in the agricultural sector, in which discounts and debt forgiveness are conditional to on-time reimbursements of the restructured loan.

The debt restructuring and the reforms of rural credit policy implemented since the end of the 1980s have led to the segmentation of rural borrowers into three categories, dealt with by different agencies: the Solidarity Fund for Production for the very poor with little or no commercial potential; BANRURAL and FIRCO for the poor with some commercial potential; and FIRA for all the others. Government transfers to banking institutions are included in Table II.17 in Annex I. They globally increased from M$ 24 million (US$1.1 billion) in 1979 to M$ 2.6 (US$0.8) billion in 1993, and then decreased to M$ 1.6 (US$0.2) billion in 1995. Over the review period, BANRURAL has always accounted for the major share of these transfers (92 per cent from 1979 to 1989; 46 per cent since 1990), followed, since 1990, by PRONASOL (25 per cent), FINA (9 per cent), FIRCO (8 per cent) and FIRA (7 per cent). Transfers to PRONASOL originated from Federal (80 per cent) and State government (20 per cent) budgetary resources.

E. TAXATION OF AGRICULTURE

Before the tax reform of 1988-89, farmers were almost entirely exempt from **income tax.** They were subject to a very preferential (low) income tax treatment known as the "Special Basis for Taxation". This privilege was shared with other sectors, most notably the transport sector. However, a tax concession of 40 per cent was applied on farmers exclusively engaged in agricultural activities. To some extent, this special treatment was considered necessary for tax administration reasons. Because of the small scale and lack of development in many farming activities, it was too costly and almost impossible to bring these activities into the general income tax regime on a conventional basis.

The 1988-89 tax reform established a "simplified regime" which includes the agricultural and transport sectors, as well as other small businesses. It is applied on individual farmers and corporations and is calculated on the difference between farm revenue and farm expenditures, including the purchase of capital goods, thus encouraging farmers to use capital intensive techniques of production. To contribute to the land tenure reform process (see Chapter I, Section D) while avoiding land speculation, proceeds from the sale are exempted from income tax the first time a land parcel is sold by ejidatarios. Full-time farmers are granted a 50 per cent income tax reduction. The reduction falls to 25 per cent if farmers are partly engaged in industrial or commercial activities – which should not exceed 50 per cent of their gross revenues.

The tax reform also introduced a **gross asset tax** of 2 per cent for all individual and corporate businesses. In 1995, the tax rate was decreased to 1.8 per cent. The gross asset tax is applied to the value of real estate (land, buildings) that is subject to property tax (see below), but excluding all other farm assets such as machinery and other equipment. Ejidatarios are exempt and full-time farmers benefit from a 50 per cent tax reduction and can deduct 15 times the minimum wage from the tax base. The reduction falls to 25 per cent if farmers are partly engaged in industrial or commercial activities.

The **Value Added Tax** (VAT) is refunded to all primary crop and livestock producers for the purchase of farm inputs (such as tractors, fertilisers, fungicides, and herbicides), and the payment of services (such as irrigation works, the digging of wells, construction of electric grids for water pumping, fumigation, and land preparation). The tax is refunded in exchange of receipts for the amount paid on farm inputs and services. Low-income farmers can opt for a different (special) status. In this case, they are entirely freed from filing requirements for VAT (though, of course, they forego their rights to receive any refunds). Most basic food stuffs are also free of VAT to consumers.

There is no federal tax on real estate property other than the gross asset tax. However, there are several municipal and state taxes falling on the ownership of agricultural property. The most important is the **property tax** (*impuesto predial*). In most cases, the property tax relates to both buildings and land. Its amount vary according to land values, which often differ according to the type of land use (agriculture or forestry). The tax rates differ across and within states, and between urban and rural land. Until 1992, ejidos were exempt from property taxes. After the 1992 land tenure reform (see Chapter I, Section D), however, ejidos are no longer exempted, but are taxed at a very low rate. In the absence of data, tax concessions were not included in the PSE calculations for Mexico.

F. FARM INPUT SUBSIDIES

In the context of the overall trade policy reform initiated in 1985 (see Section C.1), to offset the increases in farm input prices resulting from the privatisation or the liquidation of state-owned agencies previously involved in providing subsidised inputs to agricultural producers, import barriers have been progressively reduced for most of these inputs. At the beginning of 1993, import licenses for major farm inputs were eliminated. In 1994, under NAFTA, import tariffs for new and used tractors and their implements, other machinery, seeds, fertilisers, agricultural chemicals, and veterinary drugs were removed. No tariff is currently applied on imports of farm inputs from countries subject to the "most favoured nation" treatment. Through the Alliance for Agriculture programme, it is intended to help producers improve the production base of farms and to promote the introduction of technologies in order to increase farm productivity (see Box II.1).

1. Fertilisers

The **Mexican Fertiliser Company (FERTIMEX)** was created in 1943 by Presidential decree to increase production and distribution of organic fertilisers, including guano. The first private producers of fertilisers appeared later, in 1958. In 1965, most private factories were merged with FERTIMEX to concentrate fertiliser production. Except for small quantities of ammonium sulphate, all fertiliser production in Mexico was in the public domain, with the aim of reducing its cost to farmers. FERTIMEX was the main agency responsible for the production, import, marketing and distribution of nitrogen, phosphate and compound fertilisers. FERTIMEX production capacity for these fertilisers was of 5.4 million tonnes for processed, and 5.6 million tonnes for semi-processed fertilisers, shared among 53 plants located throughout the country. FERTIMEX also had the monopoly on imports of potassium fertilisers. FERTIMEX was supervised by the Secretary of Energy, Mines and State-owned Industries (SEMIP) and its number of employees increased from 4 000 in the early 1970s, to 13 000 in the late 1980s. Its global budget increased from M$ 2 (US$160) million in 1973 to more than M$ 3 (US$1) billion in 1991. FERTIMEX was privatised in 1992. Its twelve plants were sold in 1991-92 for around M$ 1 (US$0.3) billion.

During the period of operation of FERTIMEX, prices of fertilisers were fixed by the Finance Secretariat (SHCP) with the approval of the Economic Cabinet. The price of fertilisers was set at the same level, whether ex-factory or delivered to the farm. For this reason, virtually no fertilisers were sold at the factory. Fertiliser was distributed directly by FERTIMEX, or through consignment sales by using BANRURAL, co-operatives or other state-owned agencies retail channels. Fertiliser prices were kept at low levels compared with border prices. High transportation costs and a large number of storage and marketing outlets, coupled with a high per unit subsidy, led the government to support FERTIMEX through budgetary transfers. These transfers increased from M$ 2 (US$101) million in 1979 to M$ 872

(US$382) million in 1988. In 1989, the Government began implementing a plan to cut costs and improve efficiency: the private sector was allowed to import potassium fertilisers, fertilisers subsidies to farmers were decreased, and FERTIMEX withdrew from retail distribution. Government transfers to FERTIMEX increased from M$ 592 (US$237) million in 1989 and M$ 889 (US$294) million in 1991 (see Annex I, Table II.17). Direct subsidies on fertilisers were eliminated with the privatisation of FERTIMEX in 1992.

Domestic production and distribution of ammonia that is used to produce fertilisers is entirely controlled by the state oil firm Mexican Petroleum (PEMEX). Until 1992, FERTIMEX received indirect subsidies from PEMEX in the form of low ammonia prices. Since then, the ammonia produced by PEMEX that is used to produce agricultural fertilisers is sold at preferential rates to private factories: in 1994, the price reduction applied by PEMEX was of 18 per cent. This price reduction is then passed on to farmers by factories and distributors of nitrogen fertilisers, except in some areas due to inefficient distribution channels and local monopoly conditions. In 1995, ASERCA supported the purchase of fertilisers by some producers for a total amount of M$ 68 (US$11) million.

2. Fuel

As for some other sectors of the economy, diesel fuel prices have traditionally been subsidised in agriculture, with the aim of improving competitiveness of the agricultural sector. Since 1994, the fuel tax concession granted to agriculture has been of the order of 35 per cent compared with the market price for diesel. In 1994, the price of diesel for farmers was M$ 0.65 (US$0.19) per litre, against a commercial price of M$ 0.95 (US$0.28) per litre. However, this tax concession is not specific to agriculture.

3. Insurance

Since 1963 and until 1990, the **National Agricultural Insurance Company (ANAGSA)** operated three different insurance programmes for crops, livestock, and machinery. It also administered a life insurance programme for farmers and farm workers. ANAGSA insured all the agricultural loans of BANRURAL, on a compulsory basis. Crops were insured against virtually all risks from weather, disease, fire, low germination, or other causes "not attributable to the producer". ANAGSA reimbursed farmers for the value of all expenditures made up to the time of the disaster (including labour costs) minus the value of salvageable crops. The livestock insurance reimbursed producers for the value of the livestock killed or injured, or the value of lost services, plus any veterinary costs. The insurance for agricultural and agro-industrial machinery covered tractors, trucks, irrigation pumps, and various factory machinery and storage equipment. The area insured by ANAGSA increased from 1.5 million hectares (40 per cent rainfed) in 1979 to 4.7 million hectares (70 per cent rainfed) in 1989, with a peak of 7.7 million hectares in 1982.

ANAGSA subsidised insurance premia at 50 per cent for grains, beans, oilseeds, and livestock production – for other crops such as fruits and vegetables, producers had to pay the insurance premium in its entirety. Moreover, ANAGSA insurance payoffs absorbed a major share of BANRURAL bad loans: from 1987 to 1989, indemnity claims represented 75 per cent of the area insured. Government transfers to ANAGSA increased from M$ 1.1 (US$48) million in 1979 to M$ 1.6 (US$0.6) billion in 1990, mainly to absorb the high level of insurance payoffs (see Annex I, Table II.17).

In 1990, ANAGSA ceased its activities (it was liquidated in 1992) and the Government set up a new agricultural insurance institution, the **Mexican Agricultural Insurance Company (AGROASEMEX),** as a subsidiary of the Mexican public insurance company ASEMEX – the fourth largest Mexican insurance company. Although ASEMEX was privatised, AGROASEMEX has remained state-owned. Contrary to ANAGSA, participation in AGROASEMEX insurance scheme is not linked to participation in BANRURAL, but the selection of beneficiaries is very strict and based on commercial potential. In 1991, according to the crop season, farmers were subsidised by 16 to 18 per cent of insurance premia through government transfers to AGROASEMEX. Since 1992, insurance premia concessions have been increased to 30 per cent. They may be channelled by private insurers who must in turn purchase AGROASEMEX re-insurance policies. The area insured by AGROASEMEX increased from more than 600 000 hectares in 1991 to more than 900 000 hectares in 1995, mostly in irrigated areas. Over the same period, the number of heads of cattle insured by AGROASEMEX increased from around 600 000 to more than 900 000. To improve the monitoring of AGROASEMEX insurance payoffs, insurance premia are based on registered cultivated areas (*predios*). Government transfers to AGROASEMEX increased from M$ 2 (US$0.7) million in 1991 to M$ 196 (US$31) million in 1995 – around half of which via private insurers since 1992 (see Annex I, Table II.17).

4. Irrigation (see also Section I)

In Mexico, around a quarter of the main crops are cultivated under irrigation (around 70 per cent for wheat). Since 1984, in some States and in areas irrigated by groundwater, subsidised rates have been provided to farmers for electric water pumping, through a specific tariff line of the **Federal Commission for Electricity (CFE)**. Since 1991, to improve water use efficiency, it was decided to apply a 3 per cent monthly increase to the electricity consumption rate. The rate increased from M$ 0.68/kWh (US$0.22/kWh) in 1991 to M$ 1.39/kWh (US$0.45/kWh) in 1993. Subsidies for electric pumping increased from M$ 33 (US$174) million in 1984 to M$ 1.1 (US$178) billion in 1995 (see Annex I, Table II.17).

The Mexican government has also traditionally contributed to the cost of operating and maintaining small irrigation schemes in cultivated areas (see Section I). It is estimated that the government transfers for these activities increased from M$ 3 (US$127) million in 1979 to M$ 338 (US$112) million in 1991. With the entry into force of the 1992 Water Law, the progressive transfer of the operation and maintenance responsibility.to organised producers has resulted in a decrease of government transfers to support on-farm irrigation from M$ 316 (US$102) million in 1992 to M$ 230 (US$36) million in 1995 (see Annex I, Table II.17).

5. Feed

Mexican cattle are mainly grass-fed. Only about 5 per cent of calves are fattened with compound feed – composed of feedgrains (62 per cent), oil cake (15 per cent), and other by-products of the agro-food industry (23 per cent) – during 6 months before slaughtering. The main feedgrains consumed in Mexico are sorghum (90 per cent) and (mainly imported) yellow maize (10 per cent) (see Annex I, Table II.10). Over the period 1990-93, compound feed sold by commercial enterprises to livestock producers was used for the production of poultrymeat (36 per cent), pigmeat (26 per cent), milk (23 per cent), eggs (10 per cent), and beef and veal (5 per cent).

Until 1990, **CONASUPO** sold sorghum, and to a lesser extent soyabeans, to livestock producers and animal feed millers at a price equivalent to or below the purchase price, without charging the handling and transportation costs incurred (see Section B.1.1). Since 1991 and until 1995, CONASUPO stopped purchasing sorghum, but sold maize feedgrains at a price below the purchase price (see Annex I, Table II.7). Feed subsidies provided by CONASUPO increased from M$ 2 (US$88) million in 1979 to M$ 2.2 (US$0.8) billion in 1990. Since then, they increased from M$ 350 (US$116) million in 1991 to M$ 1.8 (US$0.5) billion in 1994, and decreased to M$ 1.2 (US$0.2) billion in 1995 (see Annex I, Table II.17). Feed subsidies ceased by the end of 1995, when CONASUPO stopped selling maize for feed.

Since its creation in 1969, the **Mexican Compound Feed Company (ALBAMEX)** manufactured and sold compound feed to livestock producers at subsidised prices. ALBAMEX accounted for about 10 per cent of the domestic compound feed production. It competed with the private feed industry (40 per cent of domestic production) and livestock producers who accounted for 50 per cent of total national feed production. Because of falling demand for its products and internal financial problems, ALBAMEX activity was first re-oriented toward ejidos and small landholders, and then ceased in 1992. Its nine plants were sold in 1990-92 at M$ 70 (US$23) million and ALBAMEX was liquidated in 1993. Since 1992, compound feed has been produced by livestock producers (80 per cent) and commercial enterprises (20 per cent). Government transfers to ALBAMEX increased from M$ 0.6 (US$26) million in 1979 to M$ 28 (US$20) million in 1987, and then decreased to M$ 5(US$2) million in 1991 (see Annex I, Table II.17).

6. Seeds

The **National Seed Production Company (PRONASE)** was created in the 1970s to provide Mexican farmers with certified seed of maize, beans, rice and oilseeds. With 41 processing plants, PRONASE accounts for about 40 per cent of total seed production in Mexico. The private companies are dominant in sorghum (mostly hybrids) and cotton seed production. For wheat, producers' associations produce the major share of seed for the members. The private sector is present in irrigated areas and areas with reliable rainfall, while PRONASE activity is mainly oriented toward rainfed areas (maize and beans).

The marketing of certified seed is done through BANRURAL (60 per cent), authorised private distributors (25 per cent), and PRONASE (15 per cent). The National Institute for Forestry, Agriculture and Livestock Research (INIFAP) provides basic strains of new varieties to PRONASE (and to some producers' associations) for breeding and multiplication, mainly through contracts with farmers. The control of seed quality is done by the National Seed Inspection Service (SNICS). Variety evaluation and registration, which are prerequisites to seed certification, are the functions of the SNICS Plant Varieties Classification Committee (CCPV).

Until 1991, the cost of seeds to producers was kept low through government transfers to PRONASE. These transfers increased from M$ 0.3 (US$13) million in 1979 to M$ 109 (US$36) million in 1991 (see Annex I, Table II.17). The 1991 Law on the Production, Certification and Marketing of Seeds has abolished PRONASE's preferential access to INIFAP breeding materials and, in 1992, government transfers to PRONASE ceased. Since then, PRONASE certifies and sales improved seeds in direct competition with the private sector. To facilitate the development of private firms in the seed sector, a new category of "verified seeds" (seeds for which the viability has been verified) was created, with less stringent requirements than for the production of certified seed. Private investment has become very significant in the seed sector, especially for vegetables. INIFAP started to sell improved seeds, and its share of the market has become significant for maize and beans. In 1992, ASERCA provided seed subsidies to cotton producers for a value of M$ 6 (US$2) million.

7. Pesticides

Over the period 1993-95, ASERCA provided pesticide subsidies (in the form of payments) to cotton producers. These transfers increased from M$ 40 (US$13) million in 1993 to M$ 130 (US$20) million in 1995 (see Annex I, Table II.17). In 1996, these payments were discontinued.

8. Machinery

Ejido Services SA (SESA) was created in 1974 to provide (ejidos and small landholders) clients of BANRURAL with extension and cultivation services. SESA helped low-income farmers through the rent of agricultural machinery at subsidised rates, including tractors, implements, stores, and small-scale agro-industrial plants. SESA also prepared land for new plantations, and provided technical assistance. Government transfers to SESA decreased from M$ 12 (US$35) million in 1985 to M$ 6 (US$2) million in 1991, and SESA was liquidated in 1993 (see Annex I, Table II.17).

9. Improvement of breeding stock

The **Livestock Fund (FOGAN)** was created in the 1970s to improve the genetic quality of cattle for ejidos and small-scale livestock producers. The Livestock Fund provided artificial insemination services for existing cattle, or imported high-quality breeding stock. Government transfers to FOGAN increased from M$ 0.1 (US$3) million in 1979 to M$ 9 (US$3) million in 1992. The Livestock Fund ceased to operate in 1993 (see Annex I, Table II.17).

G. RESEARCH, EDUCATION AND EXTENSION

Given the wide diversity of economic and environmental variables affecting farming in Mexico, and the generally low level of knowledge and literacy of communities living in rural areas, research, training and extension are very important factors for improving the agricultural productivity of many Mexican farmers.

The **National Institute for Forestry, Agricultural and Livestock Research (INIFAP)** was created by SAGAR in 1985, through the merger of the National Research Institutes for Agriculture (INIA), Livestock (INIP), and Forestry (INIF). **Research** is implemented by 20 research centres (12 for crops, 8 dealing with specialised topics), and 85 experiment stations. INIFAP work has focused mainly on crop production in irrigated areas and areas with good rainfall (which account for about 40 per cent of the harvested area, 67 per cent of the value of agricultural production, and 33 per cent of the farming population). For maize and wheat, research and breeding efforts are undertaken in consultation with the International Wheat and Maize Improvement Centre (CIMMYT). The Mexican Institute of Water Technology (IMTA) is also involved in agricultural research.

The share of agriculture in public spending on science and technology deceased from 16 per cent in 1987 to 7 per cent in 1994. However, reforms are under way to encourage private investment in agricultural research, and the development of research in rainfed and tropical areas. Following the privatisation or dismantling of INMECAFE, CONAFRUT, the Institute for Sugar Cane Improvement (IMPA), and the National Cocoa Development Council (CONADECA) in the early 1990s and the transfer of their assets to producers' associations, research on coffee, fruits and vegetables, sugar cane and cocoa has been directly organised by producers' associations themselves, and the cost of research has been recovered through voluntary fees paid by members. A private trust fund, the Mexican Foundation for Agricultural Research (FMIA), was recently created to increase farmers awareness of the benefits of research, and to identify sources of private funding. Efforts are also being made to develop and improve the functioning of private foundations (*patronatos*). These foundations already support INIFAP research activities for crops that are of high interest to agricultural producers (such as vegetables).

As part of the Alliance for Agriculture programme, applied research activities have been decentralised at the regional and State levels through the PRODUCE Foundations (see Box II.1), while the basic research activities remain the responsibility of INIFAP. The National Council of Research, Extension and Technology Transfer (CONIETT) has been established to co-ordinate research and technological development activities between public centres, universities, and the private sector. In 1995, total investment in agricultural research amounted to around 1 per cent of agricultural GDP. Government transfers to INIFAP increased from M$ 0.4 (US$18) million in 1979 to M$ 310 (US$48) million in 1995. Since its creation, government transfers to IMTA increased from M$ 10 (US$7) million in 1987 to M$ 85 (US$13) million in 1995 (see Annex I, Table II.17).

Formal public education in agriculture is mainly done in the Chapingo Autonomous University, the Antonio Narro Agricultural University and the Post Graduate College. The number of registered students at master and doctorate levels in these two universities increased from 134 in 1980 to 453 in 1995. From 1979 to 1994, the number of agricultural technical institutes (higher education level) and the number of enrolled students increased from 10 to 24, and from 1 300 to 2 300 respectively. During the same period, the number of vocational agricultural schools (secondary school level) and the number of enrolled students increased from 100 to 200, and from 35 000 to 71 000 respectively. Over the period under review, government transfers to formal education in agriculture globally increased from M$ 0.9 (US$40) million in 1979 to M$ 1.4 (US$0.2) billion in 1995 (see Annex I, Table II.17). The vocational technical institutes have generally accounted for the major share of these transfers (42 per cent), followed by Chapingo University (22 per cent), the agricultural technical institutes (16 per cent), and the Agricultural University A. Narro and the Post-graduate College (around 10 per cent each).

Agricultural **extension** and technical assistance have been provided by a number of government institutions, including BANRURAL (until 1989), FIRA, through the Technical Assistance and Loan Guarantee Trust Fund (FEGA) and the Trust Fund for Shared Risk (FIRCO). Since their creation, FIRA and FIRCO have associated technical assistance with the provision of credit (see Section D). In 1970, in co-operation with farmers, private firms, and research institutions, FIRA started to establish technology transfer centres and farm demonstration units. Since 1989, there are 15 FIRA technology transfer centres and 2 200 farm demonstration units operating throughout the country, dealing with crop (77 per cent), animal (17 per cent), and fishery and agro-food production (6 per cent).

Since 1989, extension in agriculture has been thoroughly reformed. The National Extension Scheme was established to increase decentralisation, privatisation and cost-sharing of advisory services. *Decentralisation* was achieved through the establishment of decentralised Inter-Institutional Committees for Technology Transfer to ensure that research results are effectively transferred to farmers. By the end of 1995, extension services for crop and livestock production were unified through the National Rural Extension Scheme (SINDER). The National Scheme for Training in Rural Areas will complement the role of SINDER in promoting technological change, in particular for the strategic projects of the Alliance for Agriculture. Both schemes will be developed by the private sector and involve government transfers to be progressively reduced within the next five years.

Privatisation was fostered by FIRA and NAFIN which provided credit for the creation of private advisory firms. In 1990, BANRURAL ceased its direct technical assistance services which were sub-contracted to private advisers. The number of private agricultural extension specialists – which have to be registered by SAGAR since 1991 – reached 3 300 in 1994, 20 per cent of which received support from FIRA. In 1995, around 200 experienced agricultural extension specialists ("second-stage advisers") were contracted by SAGAR in 1995 to provide occasional training to these private advisers nation-wide.

In 1990, the government established the Programme of Private Technical Assistance to encourage *cost-sharing* of extension services, and direct contracts between producers and private advisers. Since 1984, through its Technical Assistance Refund Programme, FIRA has been providing cost sharing to low-income producers contracting private advisers. This programme reimburses part of fellowships and training expenditures to producers and private advisory firms. Since 1990, the part paid by producers has been increased and must cover from 20 per cent of the costs the first year to 100 per cent after 5 years. The same type of cost-sharing scheme was developed recently by FIRCO for its own technical assistance programmes. Producers covered by FIRCO (see Section D) have to pay a progressively higher share of the cost of extension services (from 0 to 100 per cent within 5 years). Government transfers to FEGA increased from M$ 0.3 (US$13) million in 1979 to M$ 449 (US$70) million in 1995. Transfers to FIRCO increased from M$ 0.3 (US$12) million in 1981 to M$ 200 (US$65) million in 1992, and then decreased to M$ 88 (US$14) million in 1995 (see Annex I, Table II.17).

Under PRONASOL (see Box II.2), low-income farmers without commercial potential receive free technical advice from the Solidarity Fund for Production (see Section D). Since 1989, with the financial assistance of the World Bank, SAGAR has provided free advice to low-income producers with commercial potential through the Agricultural Training, Technical Assistance and Research Project (PROCATI) with a total budget of US$20 million. PROCATI covered 25 DDRs, except in wet tropical areas which were already included in the Programme for the Development of the Humid Tropics (PRODERITH) (see Section J). In 1992, the Agricultural and Forestry Research and Extension Project (PIEX) replaced PROCATI. PIEX was designed to operate until 1999 with a total budget of US$300 million, to be financed by half by the Mexican government. PIEX objective is to cover 40 DDRs, including tropical areas, mainly in the centre and the south of the country. Until 1993, PIEX was supervised by two institutions: INIFAP on the research side, and SAGAR on the extension side. In 1994 and 1995, PIEX was directly supervised by SAGAR. However, the low delivery of the project provoked its closure in May 1996. In 1995, PIEX benefited to 43 000 crop producers on 147 000 hectares, and to 13 000 livestock producers with 105 000 heads of cattle. From 1989 to 1992, US$20 million were spent for the implementation of PROCATI. By the end of 1995, US$24 million of external assistance were spent on PIEX.

The **National Institute for Training in Rural Areas (INCA RURAL)** was created in 1981 to promote the development of commercial farming through training and advice in farm economics. In 1992, around 30 000 farmers were trained in the 12 extension centres of INCA RURAL. Government transfers to INCA RURAL ranged from M$ 0.2 (US$8) million in 1981 to M$ 32 (US$10) million in 1992, and decreased to M$ 11 (US$2) million in 1995 (see Annex I, Table II.17). In 1996, the **National Institute of Agrarian Development (INDA)** was created to strengthen the legal, economic and social organisation of farmers and farmers' associations, mainly through the setting and implementation of extension programmes.

H. INSPECTION, PEST AND DISEASE CONTROL

The government has a long-standing policy of controlling plant and animal pests and diseases. In the 1990s, SAGAR implemented a number of phytosanitary programmes, including campaigns against the Mediterranean fly (in co-operation with Guatemala), the production and distribution of beneficial insects, sterile fleas and pesticides, and sanitation campaigns to eradicate boring worm, bovine tuberculosis, aphtous fever (in co-operation with the United States), pig fever, ticks, and African bee. Various States have been declared free of pest by the Mexican authorities (see Annex I, Table II.16). Government transfers to plant health programmes increased from M$ 1.2 (US$53) million in 1979 to M$ 78 (US$25) million in 1992, and then decreased to M$ 33 (US$5) million in 1995. Government transfers to sanitary programmes increased from M$ 0.6 (US$26) million in 1979 to M$ 76 (US$23) million in 1994, and decreased to M$ 46 (US$7) million in 1995 (see Annex I, Table II.17).

Until 1986, imports and exports of all agricultural products required phytosanitary certificates. Since then, the issuance of these certificates has been greatly simplified, and only exports or imports of agricultural products presenting high quarantine risks require them. The 1994 Federal Phytosanitary Law provides that phytosanitary certificates must be delivered within a maximum of three days for both imports and exports. The law led to the creation within SAGAR of the Directorate for Phytosanitary Inspection, in charge of controlling the conformity of agricultural products with international sanitary standards, in particular at the border. Bilateral protocols have been established between Mexico and various countries to facilitate phytosanitary inspection for the exports of specified agricultural products. The National Horticultural Producers Confederation (CNPH) and SAGAR have co-operated to inform vegetable producers on authorised levels of pesticide residues for exports.

In the field of animal production, all slaughterhouses are subject to health inspections, a programme governed by the Secretariat of Health (SSA). Slaughterhouses meeting federally approved standards for inspection (TIFs) have high sanitary standards and advanced technological processing levels. SAGAR has accredited more than 100 TIF slaughter plants, accounting for less than half of the beef and around 23 per cent of the pigmeat slaughtered, and less than 10 per cent of all slaughterhouses in Mexico. A quarter of the TIF slaughter plants deal exclusively with pigmeat, the other plants dealing mainly with beef and poultrymeat, although some slaughter both beef and pigmeat. In 1991, the government began the privatisation of TIF plants and about 80 per cent of these plants are currently owned and operated by regional livestock producers' associations. Technical and sanitary levels in municipal (for beef) or private (for pigmeat) non-accredited slaughter plants tend to be poor, although the larger plants tend to be more technically advanced with better sanitary conditions.[16] Under the 1994 Law on Animal Health, all slaughter and meat processing plants built in Mexico are now required to be TIF plants. Since 1980, the National Company of Veterinary Products (PRONABIVE) has been controlling the provision of drugs to livestock producers, including the supply of Bovine Somatotropine (BST) to milk producers. In 1996, the General Directorates for Plant and Animal Health were merged into the National Phytosanitary and Sanitary Commission.

I. AGRICULTURAL STRUCTURES AND INFRASTRUCTURES

The 1992 land tenure reform (see Chapter I, Section D.) provides for the registering of titles to all ejido land. In 1993, the Programme for the Certification of Ejido Property Rights (PROCEDE) was launched by the Secretariat of Agrarian Reform (SRA) to grant individual titles of property rights to ejidatarios. SAGAR has a general co-ordinating and monitoring role. The National Institute for Statistics, Geography and Information (INEGI) is responsible for the field survey of ejido land and the preparation of a register to be kept by the National Agrarian Registry (RAN). The decision to receive a title, the titling process itself, and the decision to open-up land sales to outsiders each require at least a majority vote in the ejido assembly. The Agrarian Attorney General's Office (PA) is responsible for assisting ejidos to carry out the **land titling** programme. It also arbitrates on ejido land disputes, relying, as appropriate, on Agrarian Courts. In 1993, the budget of PROCEDE was M$ 1 (US$0.3) million, shared between INEGI (86 per cent), RAN and PA. By April 1994, only 38 of the 30 000 ejidos had asked for full titling of land plots, far less behind the government's objectives.

Mexico's 1917 Constitution made all water resources public property, to be controlled by the federal government. **Irrigation** is necessary for the production of agricultural commodities in many regions and has tended to generally absorb a significant share of all public investment in agriculture. New areas brought annually into irrigation markedly dropped from around 200 000 hectares in 1979 to 10 000 hectares in 1995. Since 1989, the Trust Fund for Shared Risk (FIRCO) has provided investment credit at low rates to farmers for the irrigation of between 5 000 to 10 000 hectares of land each year.

The National Irrigation Commission (CNR) was created in 1926. In 1947, CNR became the Secretariat for Hydraulic Resources (SRH), while the Irrigation Districts (DRs) were supervised by the Agricultural and Livestock Secretariat (SAG). In 1977, the two Secretariats were merged to form the Secretariat for Agriculture and Hydraulic Resources (SARH). In 1989, the National Water Commission (CNA) was created and placed under the direct supervision of SARH (SEMARNAP since 1995) to co-ordinate water policy in consultation with other Secretariats, including Finance (SHCP), Social Development (SEDESOL), Mines (SEMIP), Health (SSA), and the Comptroller General. This included the pricing of water; promoting and supporting the development of drinking water, sewage, sanitation, irrigation and drainage systems; the construction, operation and maintenance of government hydraulic works; and the settlement of disputes among water users. Since its creation in 1989, total government transfers to CNA have grown rapidly to reach almost M$ 3 (US$0.5) billion in 1995.

Around 60 per cent of the irrigated area is contained within Irrigation Districts (DRs). These include irrigation systems of more than 3 000 hectares. Smaller-scale irrigation schemes, called Irrigation Units (URs), account for 30 per cent of the irrigated area, and the remaining 10 per cent is under small-scale schemes developed by the private sector.[17] In the past, DRs were a part of the national land re-distribution programme (see Chapter I, Section D.1). In many instances, landless peasants were brought in to populate an area the Government had bought or expropriated. In these DRs, the government constructed dams and canals for irrigation without charge to the farmers. These facilities remained the property of the Federal Government and were managed by CNA. Farmers had little influence over the management of the DRs. In contrast to DRs, farmers in URs had to contribute about 40 per cent of the construction cost, mainly in the form of labour. Upon completion, farmers became owners of these facilities and were responsible for their operation and maintenance. Farmers in DRs and URs were allowed to supplement their allocation of surface water with groundwater, at no charge. They have further benefited from subsidised prices for electricity used for water pumping (see Section F.4). In the 1960s, water users were asked to contribute to about 80 per cent of the operation and maintenance costs of irrigation infrastructure in DRs, through fees depending on the features of DRs. This rate decreased to 20 per cent in the late 1980s. The drop in the recovery rate was due to the expansion of main and secondary water distribution networks, the cost of which farmers were reluctant to contribute.

Since 1989, Mexico has undergone a major change in water policy. Confronted with a situation of limited supply and increasing demand for water, the government established a new regulatory framework to increase water use efficiency. One of the main features of the 1992 Water Law is the creation of a National Water Rights Register and the promotion of a market for water concession rights (*derecho de aguas*). According to the law, CNA may grant 50-year tradable concession rights for water (in volumetric terms) to individuals, groups of individuals (Water User Associations, DRs, etc..), federal, state and municipal departments or agencies. Most requests have been accepted by CNA on the basis of historical uses, and the overall water supply and demand situation of the Irrigation District (DR). The sale of water concession rights to users outside the DR must be approved by two-thirds of users within the DR and CNA, and sale revenues must be returned to the DR and not to the individual holders of rights.

Another key provision of the Water Law is to allow the transfer of responsibility to operate and maintain irrigation works to producers' associations. Within DRs, agricultural producers may form Water User Associations (OUAs) and operate the irrigation systems. The effect of the change on recovery of operation and maintenance costs by DRs has been dramatic. In 1994, the rate of recovery increased to around 80 per cent. However, because most DRs required substantial rehabilitation and modernisation prior to being turned over to OUAs, government budgetary transfers to DRs have continued.

The government transfers to various agencies and programmes involved in rural infrastructure development increased from M$ 16 (US$696) million in 1979 to M$ 3.0 (US$0.9) billion in 1994, and decreased to M$ 2.0 (US$0.3) billion in 1995. These transfers were mainly for irrigation works (54 per cent), rural roads (22 per cent), crop production infrastructure (8 per cent), development of rainfed areas (7 per cent), protection of federal river beds (6 per cent), and livestock production infrastructure (3 per cent) (see Annex I, Table II.17).

J. RURAL DEVELOPMENT

Although the share of population living in rural areas decreased significantly since the 1940s, the rural population has continued to grow (see Chapter I, Section B.2). In recent years, about one third of the population was living in rural areas where agriculture remains the main source of income. Many institutions and programmes are involved in rural development: the Secretariat of Transport and Communications (SCT) is responsible for building roads in rural areas; the Federal Commission for Electricity (CFE) supervises rural electrification; the National Water Commission (CNA) contributes to water resources development, sewage and sanitation; the National Institute for Indigenous Communities (INI) is promoting the welfare of the 10 million Indians, of which half are settled in rural areas; and the Secretariat of Social Development (SEDESOL) is heavily involved in rural development activities through the National Solidarity Programme PRONASOL (see Box II.3). Various trust funds and commissions are also active in the development of rural areas and communities. Among the agencies and activities concerned with rural development, only some are important in influencing farming conditions.

Since the mid 1980s, with the World Bank financial assistance, the National Water Commission (CNA) has implemented the Programme for the Development of the Humid Tropics (PRODERITH). During its second phase (1992-1995), PRODERITH II contributed to the construction of roads and the rehabilitation (drainage, roads) of land in rural areas. Since 1992, the World Bank has also financed a Rural Development Programme for the State of Chiapas, one of the poorest areas in Mexico. It is expected that 320 000 hectares of land will be rehabilitated by CNA in Chiapas by 1999. The total budget allocated to this programme is US$150 million.

In the 1970s, three river commissions were established to develop the Papaloapan, Grijalva and Fuerte river basins. The transfers associated with these three commissions ranged from M$ 1 (US$44) million in 1979 to M$ 16 (US$11) million in 1987. Since 1970, as part of its mandate to promote the development of arid and semi-arid areas (17 States until 1992, 10 States until now), the **National Commission for Arid Zones (CONAZA)** has promoted social welfare (drinking water, housing), erosion control (tree planting, soil conservation), diversification of agricultural production, and the development of producers' associations. By the end of 1992, CONAZA was transferred from SAGAR to SEDESOL. Government transfers to CONAZA increased from M$ 0.3 (US$13) million in 1979 to M$ 66 (US$20) million in 1994, and decreased to M$ 45 (US$7) million in 1995 (see Annex I, Table II.17).

Since 1990, under PRONASOL, several funds and programmes have been created to address poverty issues and promote social development (see Box II.3). Some of them include agricultural activities or are specific to segments of the agricultural population. The **National Fund to Support Enterprises in Solidarity (FONAES)** was established in 1991 to stimulate the economy in the poorer regions of the country, through financial support to develop productive enterprises, which are both economically viable, and have a social function. Priority was given to poor farmers, indigenous groups and inhabitants of low income neighbourhoods in urban areas. The activities carried out have covered agriculture, forestry, rural industry, extractive and small manufacturing businesses. In the first two years of implementation, about 20 000 enterprises received temporary support from FONAES in the form of participation in capital investment and low-interest loans from Guarantee and Financing Funds. Over that period, the Mexican authorities have estimated that 42 000 permanent jobs were created, notably for farmers and indigenous communities living in rural areas. Government transfers to FONAES decreased from M$ 407 (US$131) million in 1992 to M$ 213 (US$63) million in 1994, and increased to M$ 335 (US$52) million in 1995 (see Annex I, Table II.17).

Until 1991, the government assisted the indigenous communities of the Mezquital valley and the Hidalgo region to preserve their cultural heritage. The transfers associated with this programme ranged from M$ 1 (US$41) million in 1981 to M$ 14 (US$5) million in 1991. In 1990, under PRONASOL, the **Regional Solidarity Fund for the Development of the Indigenous Communities** was created to finance productive projects, generate employment, and foster the organisation of indigenous communities. The use of the fund is decided according to the priorities established by the communities themselves. Until 1995, three-quarters of the productive projects (or more than 2 700 projects) were undertaken in agricultural and livestock production. The Mexican authorities have estimated that over that period the overall programme generated more than one million jobs, mostly of a temporary nature. Government transfers to the fund for agricultural activities increased from M$ 34 (US$11) million in 1992 to M$ 106 (US$31) million in 1994, and decreased to M$ 83 (US$13) million in 1995 (see Annex I, Table II.17). The Solidarity Programme for Agricultural Labourers was established in 1990 to help seasonal farm workers to carry out integral projects designed to satisfy their basic needs, such as house improvement, nutrition, health, education and recreation. Government transfers to the programme increased from M$ 1 (US$0.4) million in 1990 to M$ 27 (US$4) million in 1995.

K. MARKETING AND PROMOTION

During the 1980s, the marketing and promotion of agricultural commodities was mainly undertaken by state-owned agencies, which purchased part or the entire domestic production and controlled the imports and exports (see Section A.4.*b*). This was notably the case for grains, beans, and oilseeds (CONASUPO), sugar (AZUCAR SA), coffee (INMECAFE), tobacco (TABAMEX), cotton (ALGODONERA), and cocoa (CONADECA). In the case of fruits, the government assisted producers in the marketing of their crop through the dissemination of information by the National Fruit Commission (CONAFRUT). Government transfers to CONAFRUT ranged between M$ 0.2 (US$9) million in 1979 and M$ 32 (US$13) million in 1990 (see Annex I, Table II.17). Until 1990, the government also promoted the marketing of coconut (IMGUCO), oil seeds (IGO SA), food grains (PRONAPROGA), "maguey" agaves and "nopal" cactuses (PROMANO), as well as the industrial development of the domestic production of coffee (DEINCAMEX) and fruits (Industrial Fruit Complex of Papaloapan Region). In the 1990s, the above state-owned agencies were liquidated, privatised, or their role in the marketing was decreased (CONASUPO), and the government fostered private initiatives through a number of institutions and trust funds which are described below.

Since its creation in 1991, **ASERCA** has promoted the development of regional markets and facilitated exports through budgetary support to buyers of domestic production (wheat, sorghum, soyabeans) (see Section B.1*a*) and the diffusion of market information for various crops and livestock products. Price and other market information are transmitted via television to subscribers through the Integral System of Communication with the Agricultural Sector (SICSA). In 1995, based on the successful experience with the marketing of cotton (see Section B.1*c*), ASERCA started a similar "risk hedging programme" for wheat, sorghum, and soyabeans production, using the Chicago Board of Trade futures quotations. Government transfers to ASERCA's marketing and promotion activities decreased from M$ 301 (US$97) million in 1992 to M$ 145 (US$23) million in 1995 (see Annex I, Table II.17).

In 1993, the **Rural Sector Capitalisation and Investment Fund (FOCIR)** was created to identify promising projects and promote their implementation through joint-ventures between small producers, ejidatarios, national and foreign investors, with the aim of combining production, processing and marketing activities. FOCIR participation in financial investment is limited to 25 per cent of the joint-venture capital shares, with a 5 to 7 year term (this term may be longer for forestry projects) at the end of which private shareholders must purchase FOCIR shares at the market rate. All fields of agricultural activity are covered: half of the on-going projects deal with crop and horticultural production, a third with animal husbandry, and the remaining with forestry and aquaculture. In 1994, FOCIR support benefited more than 4 000 agricultural producers, for a total investment of M$ 450 million. Government transfers to FOCIR decreased from M$ 200 (US$64) million in 1993 to M$ 40 (US$6) million in 1995 (see Annex I, Table II.17).

In 1994, the **Trust Fund for the Organisation of the Sugar Market (FORMA)** was created with the main objective of improving transparency in the sugar market. All sales by sugar factories must be declared to FORMA which is responsible for the diffusion of information on supply, demand, negotiated agreements, volumes, prices, and types of contracts, at national level. FORMA is also charged with trade dispute settlements between buyers and sellers. However, FORMA did not develop as expected as the main priority of the sugar processing industry has been to get access to credit in order to be able to wait for the most opportune period for selling sugar products.

To reduce price uncertainty, agricultural producers may wish to defer the sale of their crop after a period of storage in rural warehouses. ANDSA (National Stores SA) is allowed to issue warehouse certificates (*certificados de depósito*). However, these certificates are not widely acceptable in Mexico, as the quality of the product stored in state warehouses, particularly those of CONASUPO Rural Stores SA (BORUCONSA), often cannot be guaranteed. Most rural storage facilities are open and inadequate due to a lack of appropriate technology, particularly for sorting and grading. To improve this situation, the government established credit programmes through the **Trust Fund for Commercial Development (FIDEC)** to develop a private marketing infrastructure in rural areas. A new regulatory framework is also being established to enhance the credibility of warehouse certificates to become a generally accepted instrument of credit and trade.

L. CONSUMER MEASURES

Consumer measures are extremely important in Mexico, given the great disparities of income and the high level of poverty among the population. General **consumer price ceilings** were put in place in 1950 to regulate the prices of key inputs to the Mexican industry, basic foods and certain other goods. A list of inputs, foodstuff and products of wide consumption subject to price ceiling was published in 1982. Since the end of the 1980s, parallel to the decreasing role of state-owned agencies in the marketing of agricultural commodities (see Section K), the setting of prices at the retail level has been progressively eliminated for a wide range of commodities, including beans, wheat flour, rice, soyabeans, coffee, beef and veal, pigmeat, eggs, and, since 1995, bread, 1 kg bags of maize flour, and sugar. Price ceilings are still in place for maize tortilla, maize flour sold in 20 kgs bags, and pasteurised fresh milk sold in 1 litre bottles (see Section B).

Adherence to official retail price ceilings is monitored by the inspectors of the Secretariat of Commerce and Industrial development (SECOFI), while the Consumer Attorney's Office (CAO) operates largely on referrals from consumers. For goods under "strict control", no change in retail prices is permitted without SECOFI's approval. In 1985, the legislation on consumer price control established the "registered control" and "free registration" categories. In the first case, consumer prices are controlled by SECOFI, but retailers are allowed to raise them every two months by 90 to 95 per cent of the increase in the consumer price index (CPI). Greater increases must be justified by cost analyses and are subject to prior authorisation by SECOFI. Under the "free registration" system, prices must be registered and publicly announced by SECOFI, but further adjustments do not require SECOFI's approval. Until 1989, although price controls covered a wide set of consumer goods, food prices were generally the most strictly controlled. In 1987, consumer prices were strictly controlled for 53 per cent of crop and 37 per cent of livestock products, while less than 1 per cent of food products were under registered control and free registration. Since 1990, with the progressive elimination of official price ceilings, the percentage of food products subject to price control has been greatly reduced, and, in 1996, only the retail price of packed tortillas was still strictly controlled.

Since 1965, to achieve its objective of low prices for food, the Government has granted general **consumer subsidies** to the food processing industries through budgetary transfers to CONASUPO to cover the difference between high purchasing prices to producers and low selling prices to millers and retailers (see Section B.1*a*). Since 1965, milk consumption was subsidised through the LICONSA's Programme for Social Supply of Milk (see Section B.1.*f*). Since 1984, consumer prices for maize were maintained at low levels through CONASUPO's Programme to Subsidise the Consumption of Tortilla (see Section B.1.*a.i*). It is intended to regroup these two targeted consumer subsidy programmes for milk and tortilla and provide families in extreme poverty with a new electronic card so that they can purchase food after complying with certain requirements, including children attendance at school, and periodic medical checks. The electronic card would be charged about M$ 70 (US$9) per month, depending on family size and need. Government transfers to CONASUPO for general consumer subsidies increased from M$ 7 (US$308) million in 1979 to M$ 2.2 (US$0.3) billion in 1995. Concerning targeted consumer subsidies, government transfers to the milk social programme increased from M$ 2 (US$79) million in 1980 to M$ 1.7 (US$0.3) billion in 1995, while transfers to the tortilla consumption programme increased from M$ 8 (US$13) million in 1986 to M$ 468 (US$73) million in 1995 (see Annex I, Table II.8). The value of subsidies increased from M$ 5 (US$218) per child in 1980 to M$ 308 (US$48) per child in 1995 for the milk programme, and from M$ 81 (US$127) per family in 1986 to M$ 167 (US$26) per family in 1995 for the tortilla programme. Consumer subsidies granted by ASERCA to wheat millers to help them sell wheat flour to retailers at controlled prices (see Section B.1.*a.iii*) increased from M$ 392 (US$127) million in 1992 to M$ 786 (US$252) million in 1993, but then decreased to M$ 497 (US$147) million in 1994 and were discontinued in 1995 (see Annex I, Table II.17).

CONASUPO Commercial Distribution and Promotion SA(DICONSA) was created in 1965 to alleviate nutritional deficits in poor areas. Since 1990, DICONSA's retail network (more than 20 000 stores) has been expanded in rural areas where it provides the local population with basic commodities (including maize, wheat flour, beans, sugar, and rice) at subsidised prices. A maximum selling price is fixed by DICONSA that is at least 10 per cent below the average market price. In 1981, average selling prices by DICONSA were lower than private retail prices by 25 per cent in urban areas, and 35 per cent in rural areas. More recently, DICONSA retail prices were on average 18 per cent below prices for similar products in private retail outlets (respectively 19 per cent lower in rural areas, and 13 per cent lower in urban areas). In 1995, the number of consumers buying DICONSA products was around than 1 million, mainly located in rural areas.

CONASUPO and LICONSA also implement social programmes known as "Presidential Programmes" which include **food assistance.** Since 1972, the **National Scheme for the Integrated Development of the Family (DIF)** has provided food rations free of charge to children in schools located in poor districts of the four largest cities, and to elderly, destitute and handicapped people in social assistance centres. In 1987, the composition of the rations was changed from milk powder to maize tortilla and beans. The number of beneficiaries increased from 300 000 in 1979 to 7.3 million in 1994, half of whom were children.

M. SOCIAL MEASURES

Mexico's social policy is implemented through a combination of general and targeted measures. Policy measures for the general population are primarily aimed at improving the quality and coverage of health and education services, and at guaranteeing access to adequate housing. These broad policies are complemented by specific measures targeted at the extremely poor people,[18] to help them enter the labour market or improve their incomes.

The Law on Social Security establishes the possibility of coverage for ejidatarios, and farmers associated in Solidarity groups (see Box II.3) or credit groups. But, de facto, very few farmers and farm workers benefit from the national social security scheme (around 213 000 in 1994). Overall, wages are significantly lower in agriculture than in other sectors (see Chapter I Section C.2.), despite the lack of social security contributions by employers of farm workers. There are no public pension schemes for farmers, and subsistence farmers and landless labourers are the most affected by low wages and the lack of social coverage. They have to rely increasingly on other sources of income and employment opportunities, including seasonal migratory work, in the country and abroad (United States).

N. ENVIRONMENTAL MEASURES

Environmental issues related to agricultural activities are important and multifaceted in Mexico (see Chapter I, Section C.7) and Mexico has a long history of policies related to environmental protection (for example, the first legislation on forest protection dates from 1838). The General Law for

Ecological Balance and Environmental Protection of 1988 promotes joint efforts between the Federal government, States and Municipalities to address environmental issues. The law provides for systematic zoning of the natural resource base at national and state levels (*ordenamiento ecológico*). The National Programme for Environmental Protection of 1990-94 stressed that all governmental policies should take natural resources into account, with the fundamental premise that they are a strategic asset for national autonomy and a basic reserve for future generations (sustainable development).

Environmental policies were successively implemented by a variety of different agencies and Secretariats during the last two decades, reflecting changes in the main environmental issues:

- the Vice-Secretariat for Environmental Improvement under the Secretariat of Health from 1972 to 1981;
- the Vice-Secretariat of Ecology under the Secretariat of Urban Development and Ecology from 1982 to 1991;
- the National Ecology Commission (including the National Institute of Ecology and the Federal Attorney for the Protection of the Environment) under the Secretariat of Social Development (SEDESOL) from 1992 to 1994; and,
- the Secretariat of Environment, Natural Resources and Fisheries (SEMARNAP) since 1995.

SEMARNAP is structured into the three Vice-Secretariats of planning, natural resources (including forestry), and fisheries. It also supervises the activities of three satellite agencies: the National Institute of Ecology (INE), the Office of the Federal Attorney for the Protection of the Environment (PROFEPA), and the National Water Commission (CNA), which was transferred from SAGAR in 1995. INE is responsible for establishing Mexico's environmental protection standards, undertaking environmental impact evaluation, and implementing environmental protection programmes. PROFEPA is responsible for the enforcement of environmental regulations through prosecution for non-compliance, and dispute settlement in the case of environmental pollution. PROFEPA is increasingly focusing its activities on pollution prevention in close consultation with States and municipalities. Field inspections for water quality are carried out by CNA.

However, agriculture is a relatively new area to be addressed by environmental policy in Mexico, which has traditionally focused on industrial and urban pollution. In 1995, to address soil erosion issues, a 5-year Forestry and Soil Conservation Programme was established. The Programme's main objectives are: to promote soil conservation techniques through experimental pilot areas; to restore eroded soils in agricultural and forest areas through tree planting and conservation works; to gather information on soil types through detailed soil maps; and to educate people on the sustainable management of soil resources. Since 1996, farmers eligible for PROCAMPO payments may undertake forestry activities or leave their land set aside for one year to restore fertility (see Section B.2.*i*).

Under the 1988 Environmental Law, various Secretariats organised an Inter-sectoral Commission for the Control of Processing and Use of Pesticides, Fertilisers and Toxic Substances (CICOPLAFEST), in charge of establishing procedures for the approval of pesticides. A catalogue of approved pesticides was published in 1994. In 1995, Mexico began to participate in the OECD programme for the harmonised review of pesticides, with the intention that this will soon lead to the revision of the existing regulatory framework for pesticides.

O. OVERALL BUDGETARY OUTLAYS ON AGRICULTURAL POLICIES

Total budgetary expenditures associated with agricultural policies are presented in Figure 11, with the detail for the main policy measures for the periods 1979-82, 1983-88, 1989-94, and 1995. In 1995, the largest share of budgetary expenditures on agricultural policies was ***direct payments*** with 28 per cent, mainly due to PROCAMPO payments (see Section B.2.*a*). In 1995, expenditure on the ***reduction of input costs general services and formal education***, and ***consumer subsidies*** each accounted for a share of about 20 per cent of total expenditure. In the periods 1979-82 and 1983-88, the reduction of input costs represented the largest share of total budgetary expenditures associated with agricultural policies, with 43 per cent and 51 per cent respectively, mainly in the form of interest concessions on loans (more than

◆ Figure 11. **Total budgetary expenditure associated with agricultural policies**

☐ Direct payments ☐ General services and formal education
☐ Sub-national and rural development ☐ Consumer subsidies
☐ Reduction of input cost ☐ Price support measures

A. Average 1979-82

B. Average 1983-88

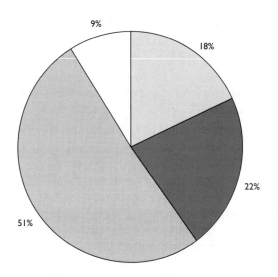

C. Average 1989-94

D. 1995

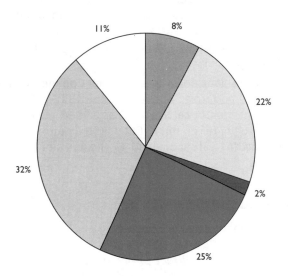

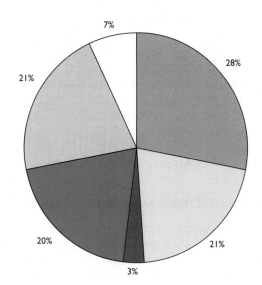

Source: Table II.17.

half). Expenditure on consumer subsidies has generally accounted for a large share of total expenditure, with more than 20 per cent since 1983-88, mainly as result of CONASUPO general consumer subsidies. Although it has declined compared with 1979-82, the importance of the share of expenditures on general services (around 15 per cent in 1995) and, although to a lesser extent, formal education (around 6 per cent in 1995) indicates efforts to modernise the agricultural sector. Within the general services, structures and infrastructures have generally accounted for the largest share (about three-quarters) over the review period, followed by research, training and extension (around 15 per cent). Over the review period, government transfers to state-owned enterprises for **price support** have generally accounted for less than 10 per cent of total expenditure. Expenditure on **sub-national and rural development measures** has remained limited, at around 2 per cent of total expenditure on agricultural policies.

The budget (*gasto programable*) of the Secretariat of Agriculture and Rural development (SAGAR) increased from M$ 3.6 (US$1.4) billion in 1989 to M$ 8.3 (US$1.3) billion in 1995, excluding, in 1995, government budgetary transfers to cover PROCAMPO and ASERCA payments [M$ 7.6 (US$1.2) billion]. SAGAR budget is mainly transferred to dependent institutions and agencies. Before its transfer to Secretariat of Environment, Natural Resources and Fisheries (SEMARNAP) in 1995, the National Water Commission (CNA) was the main institution depending on SAGAR, with a budget of M$ 2.4 (US$0.7) billion in 1994. Since its transfer from SECOFI to SAGAR in 1995, CONASUPO has accounted for the major share of SAGAR budget, with M$ 4.4 (US$0.7) billion. A 30 per cent cut in SAGAR staff occurred in 1995, which resulted in a decrease in salaries expenditures down to the 1991 level. In 1996, the resources allocated to SAGAR state delegations were substantially increased to implement the decentralisation process provided for in the 1995-2000 Alliance for Agriculture programme (see Box II.1).

The share of agriculture in federal government expenditure decreased from 18 per cent in 1980 to 8 per cent in 1995 (see Annex I, Table II.17). In 1995, total budgetary expenditures associated with agricultural policies amounted to around M$ 22 (US$3.4) billion, compared with federal government expenditure of M$ 291 (US$45) billion.

NOTES AND REFERENCES

1. Mexico was self-sufficient in food from the 1940s to the mid-1960s.

2. In the mid-1980s, the 77 Irrigation Districts and the 150 Rainfed Districts were placed under the supervision of 193 Rural Development Districts.

3. Information covers the review period and agencies are ranked according to their budgetary size.

4. FERRONALES is in the process of privatisation.

5. Nixtamal is the name of a manufacturing process to convert maize grains into dough (masa), which is then formed and cooked into tortillas. There are around 9 000 Nixtamal factories in Mexico, which supply around 32 000 tortilla factories across the country.

6. Until August 1996, the duty-free quota increase (relative to 1995) was 152 per cent (from 2.7 to 6.8 million tonnes).

7. The kgs of sugar recovered by factories from each tonne of cane is calculated using the KARBE formula which incorporates the average cane sucrose content of cane entering the mill, a national average fibre percentage in crushed cane, a national average mixed juice purity, and an implicit value for factory recovery rate (until the 1994/95 crop season, mills were subdivided into 8 groups and each group was allocated a recovery rate).

8. COFEMEX is composed of SAGAR, SHCP, SEDESOL, SECOFI, State governors, producers' associations, traders' organisations, the National Chamber of Processing Industries (CANACINTRA) and the National Association of Coffee Processors (ANACAFE).

9. *Source:* OECD (1996), *Trade liberalisation policies in Mexico,* Paris.

10. MERCOSUR is a trade agreement signed by Argentina, Brazil, Paraguay and Uruguay in 1991. Its main goal is to eliminate all tariffs for intra-regional trade, and to establish a common external tariff that would guide international trade between the member countries and the rest of the world.

11. The Asian Pacific Economic Cooperation is a forum of discussion which aims include promoting trade liberalisation between its 18 Member countries.

12. The corresponding values of export subsidy reduction for developed nations are: 36 per cent in value and 21 per cent in volume, over a six-year period.

13. In 1982, the government nationalised the commercial banks, and the Constitution was amended to reserve banking activities to the state. Many nationalised commercial banks that subsequently became insolvent were either merged or closed.

14. For more information on measures to assist the banking sector, see OECD (1995), *OECD Economic Surveys: Mexico 1995,* Paris.

15. For more information on debt restructuring mechanisms, see OECD (1996), *OECD Economic Surveys: Mexico,* Paris.

16. *Source:* The WEFA Group (1993), *Analysis of the Mexican Cattle and Beef Industries,* Final report presented to the Canadian International Trade Tribunal.

17. *Source:* VOCKE, G. (1994), *Global Review of Resource and Environmental Policies: Water resource Development and Management,* ERS-FAER No. 251, pp.52-54, Washington, DC.

18. The Mexican authorities estimate that people living in extreme poverty account for 24 per cent of the total population (*i.e.* 22 million people who lack the income necessary to purchase a minimum basket of foodstuffs), and that 63 per cent of the extremely poor live in rural areas.

BIBLIOGRAPHY

Anonymous (1995), "Effect of removal of sugar price controls in Mexico", *F.O. Licht's International Sugar and Sweetener Report*, Vol. 127, No. 28, pp. 627-631.

Anonymous (1996), "The Mexican sugar industry", *Sweetener Analysis*, Feb. 1996, 12 p.

American Farm Bureau Research Foundation (1991), *NAFTA effects on agriculture*, 4 volumes.

ASERCA (1994), "Programa de coberturas de algodón", *Claridades Agropecuarias*, No. 16, pp. 24-25.

ASERCA (1995), "El ganado vacuno en Mexico", *Claridades Agropecuarias*, No. 23, pp. 4-19.

ASERCA (1996), "Los apoyos directos al campo en México", *Claridades Agropecuarias*, No. 38, pp. 3-10.

ASERCA (1996), "Apoyos a la comercialización del arroz en Mexico", *Claridades Agropecuarias*, No. 38, pp. 14-17.

BANNISTER, G.J. (1993), "Rent-sharing in the Multi-Fibre Arrangement: the case of Mexico", *Policy Research Working Papers*, WPS 1191, The World Bank, September 1993.

BEAUMONT, M. (1993), "Mexico after NAFTA", *Meat and Livestock Review,* produced by the Australian Meat and Livestock Corporation – Market Intelligence Unit, November 1993, pp. 17-22.

BLANCO MENDOZA, H.(1994), *Las negociaciones comerciales de México con el Mundo,* ed. Una visión de la modernizacion de México, México DF.

BONILLA, J. and VIATTE, G. (1995), "A radical reform of Mexican agriculture" *The OECD Observer,* No. 191, December 94/January 95.

BORRELL, B. (1991), "The Mexican sugar industry: problems and prospects", *Policy Research Working Papers*, WPS 596, The World Bank, February 1991.

BUZZANELL, P. and LORD, R. (1995), "Mexico: sugar and corn sweeteners, an update", *Sugar and Sweetener*, S&O/SSSV20N2/June 1995, pp. 23-32.

CFCE (1981), *Le marché des produits agro-alimentaires au Mexique*, Centre Français du Commerce Extérieur, DEMA, Paris.

CIGA (1995), *Alianza para el campo*, Comisión Intersecretarial del Gabinete Agropecuario, Nov. de 1995.

CNA (1994), *Informe 1989-94*, Comisión Nacional del Agua.

CNG (1994), *Informe de actividades*, Consejo directivo de la Confederación Nacional Ganadera, Guadalajara, Jalisco, Mayo de 1994.

CONASUPO (1994), Memoria de gestion 1988-1994.

FAO (1994), "Mexican Cereal Policies and the North American Free Trade Agreement", *Cereal Policies Review*, 1993-94.

FIRA (1994), *Resultados 1989-1994*, Banco de México.

FOCIR (1994), *Informe de labores*, enero-septiembre 1994.

HJORT, K. and VALDES, C. (1993), "Potential effects of the NAFTA on Mexico's grain sector", USDA-ERS, *Western Hemisphere*, RS-93-2, pp. 82-87.

KLINDWORTH, K.A. and MARTINSEN, A.J. (1995), "Shipping US grain to Mexico", USDA-AMS, *Marketing Research Report*, No. 630.

LARSON, D.F. (1993), "Policies for coping with price uncertainty for Mexican maize", *Policy Research Working Papers*, WPS 1120, The World Bank, March 1993.

JANVRY, A. (de), SADOULET, E. and DAVIS, B. (1995), "NAFTA's impact on Mexico: Rural household-level effects", *the American Journal of Agricultural Economists*, No. 77, December 1995, pp. 1283-1291.

LEVY, S. and VAN WIJNBERGEN, S. (1995), "Transition problems in economic reform: agriculture in the North American Free Trade Agreement", *the American Economic Review*, September 1995.

McNALLY, M. (1995), "The Mexican beef industry", *Meat and Livestock Review,* produced by the Australian Meat and Livestock Corporation – Market Intelligence Unit, July 1995, pp. 11-13.

NELSON, F.J. (1993), "Producer Subsidy Equivalents for Canada, Mexico, and the United States", USDA-ERS, *Western Hemisphere,* RS-93-2, pp. 65-73.

NICHOLSON, C.F. (1995), "Mexico's Dairy Sector in the 1990s: a descriptive analysis", Department of Agricultural, Resource, and Managerial Economics, Cornell University.

OECD (1994), Reviews of National Science and Technology Policy: Mexico, Paris.

OECD (1995), The Uruguay Round: preliminary evaluation of the impacts of the agreement on agriculture in OECD countries, Paris.

OECD (1995), Agricultural Policies, Markets and Trade in OECD Countries: Monitoring and Outlook 1995, Paris.

OECD (1996), Agricultural Policies, Markets and Trade in OECD Countries: Monitoring and Evaluation 1996, Main Report and Summary and Conclusions, Paris.

OECD (1996), Trade Liberalisation Policies in Mexico, Paris.

PND (1995), *Plan Nacional de Desarrollo 1995-2000,* Poder Ejecutivo Federal.

PRONASOL (1994), Información básica sobre la ejecución y desarrollo del Programa Nacional de Solidaridad de 1988-94, SEDESOL, Secretaría General de la Federación, ed. Porrua, Mexico DF.

ROGOZINSKI, J.(1994), *La privatización de empresas paraestatales,* ed. Una visión de la modernización de México, México DF.

SAGAR (1996), Alianza para el campo.

SALINAS de GORTARI, C. (1994), *Sexto informe de Gobierno 1994,* Poder Ejecutivo Federal.

SARH (1990), Programa Nacional de Modernización del Campo 1990-94.

SARH (1992), Informe de labores 1991-92.

SARH (1992), Ley de Aguas Nacionales y su Reglamento, CNA.

SARH (1992), *Es tiempo de campo, es tiempo de progreso,* Articulo 27 Constitucional, Ley Agraria.

SARH (1993), El sector agropecuario en las negociaciones del Tratado de Libre Comercio Estados Unidos-México-Canada.

SARH (1994), *Produción y comercialización de maiz 1987-1993,* Subsecretaría de Planeación, Octubre de 1994.

SARH (1994), *Boletín estadístico azucarero,* Subsecretaria de Planeacion, Noviembre de 1994.

SARH (1994), *Ley Federal de Sanidad Vegetal,* Direccion General Juridica.

SARH (1995), *Producion y comercializacion de trigo 1987-1993,* Subsecretaria de Planeacion, Marzo de 1995.

SARH (1995), *Producion y comercializacion de frijol 1987-1993,* Subsecretaría de Planeación, Junio de 1995.

SARH (1995), *Producion y comercializacion de sorgo 1987-1993,* Subsecretaría de Planeación, Agosto de 1995.

SECOFI (1994), Tratado de Libre Comercio Estados Unidos-Mexico-Canada: Fracciones arancelarias y plazos de desgravacion, 4 tomos.

SEDESOL (1994), *Solidaridad: seis años de trabajo,* Subsecretaría de Desarrollo Regional, Programa Nacional de Solidaridad.

TELLEZ KUENZLER, L.(1994), *La modernización del sector agropecuario y forestal,* ed. Una visión de la modernización de México, México DF.

USDA-ERS (1995), "NAFTA: year one", a report by the NAFTA Economic Monitoring Taskforce, April 1995.

USDA-ERS (1996), "NAFTA: year two and beyond", a report by the NAFTA Economic Monitoring Taskforce, April 1996.

USDA-ERS (1996), "NAFTA: year three", a report by the NAFTA Economic Monitoring Taskforce, October 1996.

VALDES, C. (1993), "Mexico", USDA-ERS, *Western Hemisphere,* RS-93-2, pp. 29-32.

VALDES, C. (1994), "Mexico's PROCAMPO agricultural reform programme", USDA-ERS, *Western Hemisphere,* WRS-94-2, pp. 29-39.

VALDES, C. (1994), "Mexico", in "Global Review of Agricultural Policies: Western Hemisphere", USDA-ERS, *Statistical Bulletin,* n° 892, pp. 58-62.

VALDES, C. (1994), "Mexico", in "Estimates of Producer and Consumer Subsidy Equivalents: Government intervention in Agriculture, 1982-92", USDA-ERS, *Statistical Bulletin,* No. 913, pp. 221-240.

VALDES, C. (1995), "Peso devaluation: impact on agricultural trade", USDA-ERS, *Agricultural Outlook*, April 1995, pp. 12-16.

VITON, A. (1996), "The Mexican sugar economy on recovery path", *F.O. Licht's International Sugar and Sweetener Report*, Vol. 128, No. 11, pp. 239-244.

The WORLD BANK (1994), "Mexico's cotton price support scheme", *Commodity Markets and the Developing Countries*, p. 7.

ZARAGOZA, J.L. and MACIAS, R. (1980), *El desarrollo agrario de México y su marco jurídico*, Centro Nacional de Investigaciones Agrarias, México DF.

ZEDILLO PONCE de LEON, E. (1994), Primer *Informe de Gobierno 1995*, Poder Ejecutivo Federal.

3

ANALYSIS OF SUPPORT TO AGRICULTURE

Chapter II reviewed the main agricultural policy objectives and support measures in Mexico. Chapter III discusses the support measures in more detail, as they affect producers and consumers. For this purpose the key indicators are the estimates of the **Producer Subsidy Equivalent (PSE)** and the **Consumer Subsidy Equivalent (CSE),** as well as their components and derivatives. The definitions of the PSE/CSE indicators and their methods of calculation have already been presented in detail in a number of OECD publications. However, before proceeding with the analysis, it is useful to recall briefly the PSE/CSE concepts and to discuss some aspects specific to their use in the case of Mexican agricultural policy. Details of the calculation of PSE/CSE for each commodity studied and of the quality of data on which calculations are based are presented in Annex II.

A. METHODOLOGICAL ASPECTS

1. PSE/CSE concepts

The PSE is an indicator of the value of the monetary transfers to agriculture resulting from agricultural policies in a given year. Both transfers from consumers of agricultural products (through domestic market prices) and transfers from taxpayers (through budgetary or tax expenditures) are included. Five categories of agricultural policy measures are included in the OECD's calculations of PSEs:

- measures that transfer money to producers through affecting producer and consumer prices simultaneously, such as support prices and trade measures *(market price support)*;

- measures that transfer money directly from taxpayers to producers without raising prices to consumers, such as per tonne payments, area payments, and disaster payments *(direct payments)*;

- measures that transfer money to producers through lowering input costs, such as interest concessions and farm input subsidies *(reduction of input costs)*;

- measures that reduce the costs to the agricultural sector as a whole through transfers that are not received directly by producers, such as research, advisory, training, inspection, pest and disease control, structure and infrastructure improvement, and marketing and promotion *(general services)*;

- other measures, the main elements of which are *sub-national* such as measures funded by state or provincial governments, and certain tax concessions *(other support).*

All these categories of support measures (which are discussed in Chapter II) have been included in the PSE calculations for Mexico, except tax concessions, due to the lack of data.

The market price support (*MPS*) is generally estimated for each commodity by taking the difference between the price paid to domestic producers (at the farmgate) and the corresponding world market price at the Mexican border (the *reference price*), and multiplying this price difference by the quantity produced.[1] Because this price gap is the result of various, often interacting domestic and border measures taken to support market prices, it is not, however, possible (nor necessary) to estimate their separate contributions.

For the other four categories of support measures the amount of subsidy for the calculation of the PSE is the budget cost of the measures applied. The calculation of the PSE consists of allocating among the various commodities the budgetary expenditures due to each of the measures. The distribution method used in each case depends on how the measure is applied (and to which commodities if relevant), but if it is not possible to ascribe a specific basis for allocating the expenditure, allocation is done according to the share of each commodity in final agricultural output.

The PSE calculations include not only all the transfers to domestic producers that specifically result from the categories of policy measures indicated above, but also, if appropriate, **producer levies** on output, as negative transfers. In addition, if there is a MPS on grains, livestock producers pay an implicit tax on any feed that uses these grains as ingredients. Thus, when calculating the aggregate PSEs for all commodities the support is counted twice: firstly, directly under the feedgrains PSEs and secondly, indirectly under the livestock PSEs. To avoid double-counting a **Feed Adjustment** corresponding to the value of market price support for crops used in animal feed is deducted from effective support received by each livestock product. Accordingly, the term **Gross PSE** is used when referring to transfers to producers before the deduction of the feed adjustment, whereas the **Net PSE** is used when referring to transfers to producers after deduction of the feed adjustment.

The PSE is expressed in four ways:

- **total PSE:** the total value of transfers to producers;

- **percentage PSE:** the total value of transfers as a percentage of the total value of production (valued at domestic producer prices), adjusted to include direct payments and to exclude levies on production;

- **unit PSE:** the total value of transfers per tonne produced;

- **producer nominal assistance coefficient:** the ratio of the border price plus the unit PSE to the border price.

In algebraic form, these PSE expressions are written as:

gross total PSE: $Q \cdot (P - PW_{nc}) + DP - LV + OS$

net total PSE: $Q \cdot (P - PW_{nc}) + DP - LV + OS - FA$

unit PSE: $PSE_u = PSE / Q$

percentage PSE: $\%PSE = 100 \cdot PSE / (Q \cdot P + DP - LV)$

producer nominal assistance coefficient: $NAC_p = \dfrac{PW_{nc} + PSE_u}{PW_{nc}} = 1 + \dfrac{PSE_u}{PW_{nc}}$

where,

Q refers to the volume of production,

P refers to the domestic producer price,

PW_{nc} is the world price (reference price) at the border in domestic currency,

DP refers to direct payments,

LV refers to levies on production,

OS refers to all other budget financed support, and

FA refers to the feed adjustment (only for livestock products).

The CSE is an indicator of the value of the monetary transfers to consumers resulting from agricultural policies in a given year. Two categories of agricultural policy measures are included in the OECD calculations of CSEs:

- transfers to (if positive), or more commonly from (if negative), consumers due to market price support policies, plus estimated budget revenues from tariffs on agricultural imports **(market transfers)**;

- budgetary transfers to consumers resulting from agricultural policies, such as consumer subsidies *(other transfers)*.

Normally, "market transfers" are negative and are larger in absolute terms than "other transfers"; in such cases the CSE can be thought of as the implicit tax imposed on consumers by agricultural policies.

Like the PSE, the CSE is also expressed in four ways:

- *total CSE:* the total value of transfers to consumers, including transfers such as consumer subsidies;
- *percentage CSE:* the total value of transfers as a percentage of the total value of consumption (valued at producer prices);
- *unit CSE:* the total value of transfers per tonne consumed;
- *consumer nominal assistance coefficient:* the ratio of the border price plus the unit CSE to the border price.

In algebraic form, these CSE expressions, as measured by the OECD, are written as:

total CSE: $CSE = Q_c \cdot (PW_{nc} - P) + OT$

unit CSE: $CSE_u = CSE / Q_c$

percentage CSE: $\%CSE = 100 \cdot CSE / (Q_c \cdot P)$

consumer nominal assistance coefficient: $NAC_c = \dfrac{PW_{nc} + CSE_u}{PW_{nc}} = 1 + \dfrac{CSE_u}{PW_{nc}}$

where,

Q_c refers to the volume of consumption,

OT refers to budgetary subsidies to consumers resulting from agricultural policies,

and other parameters are the same as those used in the PSE expressions.

There is thus a very close relationship between the PSE and CSE indicators. All market price support policies that create a wedge between domestic and world prices raise consumer prices: a positive (negative) transfer from consumers to producers is equivalent to a subsidy (tax) to producers and a tax (subsidy) on consumption. Specific consumer subsidies paid from government budgets, such as food subsidies, may partly offset such taxes on consumption. Direct payments and other budgetary support paid to producers raise the effective price received by producers, but do not raise the price paid by consumers.

Both PSE and CSE are calculated at the farmgate level and the price received by farmers is the price paid by consumers at the first level of consumption. Thus, "consumption" means the first use (including on the farm) or purchase of the commodity concerned, and "consumers" means all those (including farmers) who use the commodity for the first time. The consumption price at the farmgate is thus the producer price, except when the level of consumption is larger than the level of production and the level of market price support on the quantities imported is different from the one on domestic production.

Nominal assistance coefficients (NACs) are indicators of the effective price wedges created by agricultural policies. The larger these effective price wedges, the greater are the distortions in production and consumption that stem from them.[2] A NAC equal to one indicates, *prima facie*, that domestic prices are not insulated from world prices. As the size of the wedge increases, the NAC increases in proportion: a NAC of 2.0 implies that the effective producer (or consumer) price is twice the world price, a NAC_p of 3.0 implies triple the world price, and so on (see Tables 15 and 16, Annex II). The advantage of using the NAC in this way as an indicator of the effective price wedge on the production side, rather than the percentage PSE, is that the percentage PSE measures transfers relative to the gross revenue of producers, but inadequately indicates the price relativities that are the key determinants of the production and trade effects associated with such transfers. Thus, the percentage PSE obscures the extent of the wedge between domestic and border prices and hence the degree of possible distortion in production.

Caution should be exercised in the interpretation of the producer NAC as an indicator of the insulation of domestic producer prices from border prices, insofar as the producer NAC also includes measures that are not received directly by producers, such as research and development. However, in most countries, market price support and direct payments received directly by farmers (based on output) are overwhelmingly the predominant form of assistance; thus the extent of bias is likely to be small. However, the consumer NAC is a better indicator of the degree of domestic price insulation, as it essentially includes market transfers in the calculations.

2. Commodities covered

The commodities for which PSE/CSE have been calculated for Mexico belong to the OECD standard list of PSE commodities. This list consists of: wheat, maize, other grains (barley, oats and sorghum), rice, oilseeds (soyabeans, rapeseed, sunflower), sugar (from sugarbeet or sugarcane), milk, beef and veal, pigmeat, poultrymeat (chicken, turkey, duck and goose), sheepmeat (mutton and lamb), wool (sheep) and eggs. All these commodities have been considered in the Mexican PSE, except oats, sheepmeat and wool which represent each less than 1 per cent of the total value of production. Over the review period, the PSE commodities have accounted on average for 65 per cent of the total value of agricultural production, almost all the value of total animal production in Mexico (97 per cent), but less than half (42 per cent) of that for total crop production. No PSE was calculated for avocados, bananas, beans, coffee, chillies, cotton, limes, mangoes, onions, oranges, potatoes, tobacco, and tomatoes, which are important agricultural commodities in Mexico, but are not included in the OECD standard list of PSE commodities.

3. Reference prices

In principle, the reference price represents the closest price of the alternative disposal or consumption possibilities open to a country for a commodity similar in quality and at the same stage in the production chain to that produced in Mexico. In other words, the reference price indicates the price that producers would receive and consumers would pay for a given commodity at the border (i.e. in the absence of trade measures, and assuming that world prices would not be affected by the removal of these trade measures). A c.i.f. import price (f.o.b. export price) should be in principle used as reference price when the country is a net importer (exporter).

The choice of actual prices depends on data availability, but the principle is to select prices that most closely express the value or cost of the alternatives to domestic production, and are most compatible with the approach used for other countries. In the case of milk, the reference price used is common to all OECD countries for which PSE calculations are made, being the producer price of milk in New Zealand, adjusted for the cost of transport to Mexico and for the relative fat content of milk. New Zealand is a low-cost milk producer and no price support is provided for its output.

For wheat, maize, sorghum, rice, and soyabeans, the reference prices used are the US c.i.f. import prices. The United States is the main supplier of these commodities to Mexico and the characteristics of the US products are broadly similar, except maize (yellow maize in the US, mainly white maize in Mexico). A quality premium of 20 per cent was applied on US reference prices to only white maize. For barley, the reference price used is the Minneapolis Board of Trade quotation for a quality similar to the malt barley produced in Mexico. In the case of sugar, the Caribbean f.o.b. price is used as reference price as its quality is close to Mexican raw sugar (sugarcane). In the case of beef and veal, the reference price used is the producer price in Australia. Australia does not provide any market price support for the production of the type of beef and veal that is similar to that in Mexico (grass fed). For pigmeat, poultrymeat and eggs, the reference prices used are the respective producer prices in the United States, where no market price support is provided. For all these commodities, reference prices were adjusted for the cost of transport to Mexico. Further details of prices used, sources and definitions can be found in Annex II.

4. MPS calculation method

Graph 1 illustrates, in simplified form, the basic concept behind the various price support measures applied in Mexico, with a view to explain the general PSE/CSE calculation associated with these measures. The diagram represents three possible trading positions: where domestic production equals domestic consumption at given prices and no trade is assumed to take place; where domestic production exceeds domestic consumption and there are net exports; and where domestic consumption exceeds domestic production and there are net imports. In Mexico, all these three situations have existed for some commodities and in some years.

For each commodity the graph depicts the world market price or reference price (PW) and the producer price (Pp). The relative position of supply (S) and demand (D) curves show whether at certain producer price (Pp) levels domestic supply (Q) is greater, equal or below domestic demand (Qc). The difference between the two (Qc – Q) is imported or exported (if negative). The calculation of market price support received by producers (MPS) and market transfers paid by consumers resulting from price support and trade measures (MT) is expressed in the graph as well. Market price support is simply the gap between producer price (Pp) and reference price (PW) multiplied by the quantity produced (Q), irrespective of the country's trading position. In the absence of appropriate data on producer prices for wheat, sorghum, and soyabeans over the period 1991-94, an implicit producer price was calculated by subtracting the unit budget payments of ASERCA from the concerted price for the respective commodities. Market price support was estimated as the gap between this implicit producer price (Pp*) and the reference price (PW) multiplied by the quantity produced (Q). It should be stressed that a number of interpretations – and thus methods of calculation – could be possible in the case of ASERCA payments, but it was felt that, within the context of the available data, the method outlined here reflects the objectives of ASERCA.

For exported commodities and commodities for which there is no trade, market transfers from consumers are assumed to be the price gap (Pp – PW) multiplied by the quantity consumed (Qc). For those imported commodities that are subject to an import tariff lower than (Pp – PW), the consumer price (Pc) is assumed to be the weighted average of the producer price (Pp) and the import price (Pi), the latter being defined as the reference price (PW) plus the import tariff (Ti). In that case, market transfers from consumers are assumed to be the price gap (Pc – PW) times the quantity consumed (Qc), which is equivalent to the price gap (Pp – PW) times the quantity produced (Q), plus the import tariff (Ti) times the quantity imported (Qc – Q). For commodities imported duty free, but subject to permits or tariff quotas, market transfers from consumers are assumed to be the price gap (Pp – PW) times the quantity domestically produced (Q), and zero for the quantity imported.

5. Total transfers

The PSE and CSE are estimates of **transfers to producers** from agricultural policies, but do not provide a complete picture of all transfers associated with agricultural policies. They do not cover all agricultural commodities, and exclude certain budgetary transfers that are not directly received by producers, such as outlays for public stockholding. In 1995, the percentage share of total value of agricultural production covered by the PSE and CSE calculations for Mexico was 63 per cent. That year, among other the OECD countries for which PSEs and CSEs were calculated, this share ranged from 40 per cent in Turkey to 84 per cent in Norway.

Total transfers resulting from agricultural policies are broadly defined as the sum of all transfers from taxpayers and all transfers from consumers (as measured by the *Total* CSE extrapolated to apply to all commodities), less budget revenues from tariffs on agricultural imports. Like the PSE, however, total transfers exclude outlays on general government administration (salaries of SAGAR staff), social security, taxation measures, formal education, and rural development.

◆ Graph 1. *Market price support and market transfers*

☐ MPS = (Pp – PW) * Q   ☐ MT = (Pc – PW) * Qc

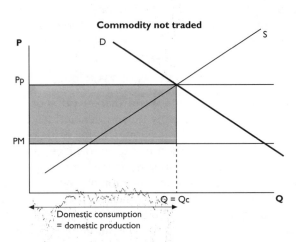

Commodity not traded

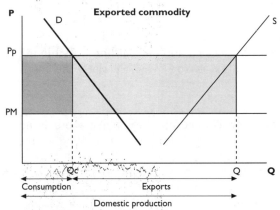

Exported commodity

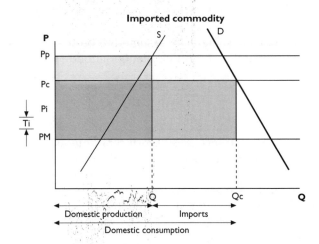

Imported commodity

Pp = Producer price	PW = World price	Pc = Consumer price
Pi = Import price	Q = Quantity produced	Qc = Quantity consumed
Ti = Import tariff	SPM = Market price support	MT = Market transfers

Source: OECD Secretariat, 1997.

B. AGGREGATE RESULTS

1. Evolution of total support

Over the review period, the **net total PSE** and total CSE, when expressed in Mexican pesos, have to be interpreted with great caution, as they include the effects of strong variations in inflation and exchange rates (see Chapter I, Section B.1). In 1982, the sharp peso depreciation heralded a period of rapid domestic inflation and large swings in exchange rates. From 1983 to 1988, inflation rates were very high and the exchange rate regime was modified repeatedly, including two devaluations in 1985 and 1987. From 1989 to 1994, as the exchange rate depreciated by less than the inflation differential between Mexico and its major trading partners, the currency appreciated in real terms. By the end of 1994, the exchange rate was allowed to float freely and the peso depreciated sharply. In 1995, inflation rose again, to around 50 per cent.

From 1983 to 1988, increases in the **net total PSE** expressed in pesos essentially reflected the government decision to keep agricultural prices rising in line with inflation, while decreases (in 1983 and 1986) can be attributed to devaluations of the peso (see Figure 1). Over the period 1989-94, total support in pesos increased substantially, mainly due to market price support and inflation. In 1995, the marked decrease in net total PSE coincided with the sharp devaluation of the peso. When measured in US dollars, total support since the mid-1980s increased much less, and then decreased sharply in 1995, as its measurement in US dollars reduces the effects of inflation and the associated currency volatility (see Figure 1).

It should be stressed that, as the net percentage PSE takes account of the effect of inflation on both support and the value of production, it is a more representative and appropriate measurement of support, and allows for comparison over time and across commodities. The evolution of the net percentage PSE throughout the period 1979-1995 may be divided into four periods: the 1979-82 period,

◆ Figure 1. **Net total PSE in Mexico, 1979-95**

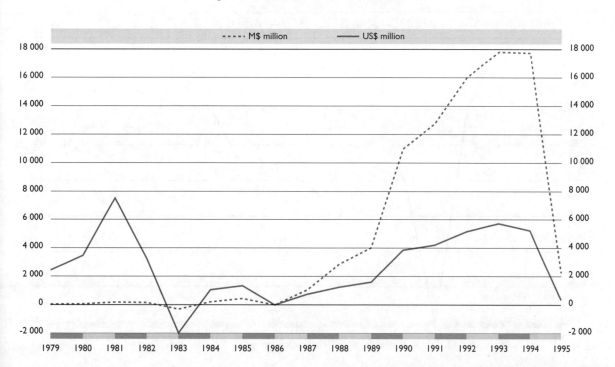

Source: Table 13, Annex II.

with four years where domestic prices exceeded reference prices, with an average percentage PSE of 34 per cent; the 1983-1988 period, with reference prices generally exceeding domestic prices and an average percentage PSE of 3 per cent; the 1989-1994 period, with six years where domestic prices exceeded again reference prices and an average percentage PSE of 30 per cent; and 1995, with reference prices exceeding domestic prices, resulting in a percentage PSE of 3 per cent (see Figure 2 and Annex I, Table III.1). The OECD averages in these periods were respectively 29 per cent, 39 per cent, 41 per cent, and, in 1995, 40 per cent (see Figure 3).

To analyse the agricultural policy reform initiated in 1990 as well as the entry into force of NAFTA and the launching of PROCAMPO direct payments in 1994, in order to understand the evolution of support, it is important to identify the main changes in the PSE components (see Section b below). In 1995, the ongoing reform process contributed to the reduction in the market price support. However, the sharp decrease of the percentage PSE to 3 per cent was mainly due to the sharp devaluation of the peso. Domestic prices were also depressed by lower domestic demand, in particular for animal products, due to the reduction in disposable consumer incomes following the drop in real wages in 1995.[3]

In general, changes in producer NACs have followed the evolution of the percentage PSE. The producer NAC decreased from 1.4 on average in 1979-82 to an average level of just over 1 in 1983-88. It increased from 1.2 in 1989 to 1.5 in 1993, and then decreased to just over 1 in 1995. The producer NAC for crops has generally been higher than the one for livestock products, except between 1983 and 1989. In 1994, the highest NAC was for maize, at 1.8.

The trend in support to agriculture, essentially the result of variations in the gap between world prices and domestic prices, as measured by the market price support (see Annex I, Table III.1), has been reflected in the evolution of the transfers from consumers to producers, as measured by the CSE. However, the evolution of the CSE has also been influenced by the Government's policy to keep food

◆ Figure 2. **Percentage PSE in Mexico and in the OECD, 1979-95**

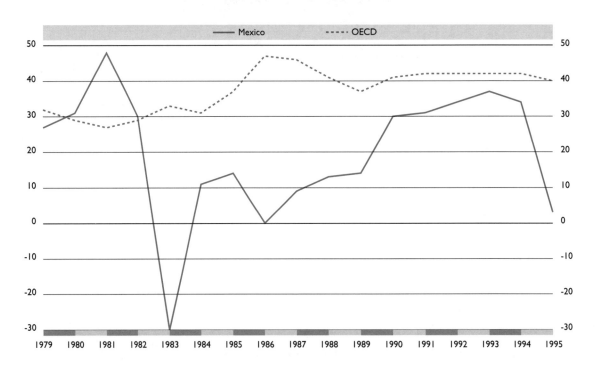

Note: The OECD average excludes the Czech Republic, Hungary, Mexico and Poland.
Source: Table 13, Annex II.

◆ Figure 3. **Support to agriculture: percentage PSE/CSE by country**

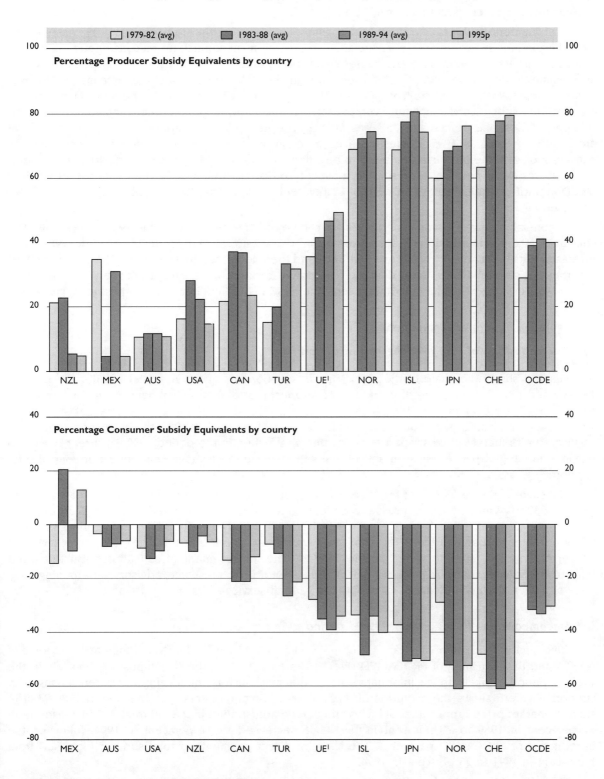

Notes: Countries are ranked according to 1995 PSE/CSE levels.
  The OECD average excludes the Czech Republic, Hungary, Mexico and Poland.
  Avg: average; p: provisional.
1. EU = EU-10 for 1979-85, EU-12 for 1986-94, EU-15 for 1995; includes ex-GDR from 1990.
Source: OECD Secretariat, 1997.

prices low, mainly through general subsidies to the processing sector and direct targeted subsidies to low-income consumers (see Chapter II, Section L).

Over the period 1979-82, transfers from consumers to producers were partly offset by consumption subsidies and the ***percentage CSE*** was negative, representing an implicit tax on consumption of around 8 per cent. In the following six years, reference (border) prices tended to exceed domestic prices and, as consumption continued to be subsidised through direct budgetary aids, the percentage CSE was positive, representing a subsidy on consumption of around 20 per cent. In the 1989-94 period, as consumption subsidies did not fully compensate for the growing gap between domestic prices and reference prices, the percentage CSE was negative, representing an implicit tax on consumption of around 10 per cent. In 1995, domestic prices were on average lower than reference prices and, as consumption of some products continued to be subsidised through direct budgetary aids, the percentage CSE was again positive, representing a subsidy on consumption of 12 per cent. The equivalent OECD implicit tax on consumption were of 22 per cent, 31 per cent, 33 per cent, and, in 1995, 29 per cent (see Figure 3).

In general, changes in consumer NACs have followed the evolution of the percentage CSE. The consumer NAC decreased from 1.1 on average in 1979-82 to an average level of 0.8 in 1983-88. It increased from just under 1 in 1989 to 1.3 in 1993, and then decreased to 0.9 in 1995. The consumer NAC for crops has generally been lower than the one for livestock products, except between 1991 and 1993, and in 1995. In 1994, wheat had the lowest consumer NAC (0.8), while it was the highest for sugar, at 1.2.

2. Evolution of support components

a) *Decomposition of PSE over the review period*[4]

Figure 4 shows the share of the main support components in the net total PSE for the periods 1979-82 and 1989-94. The share of ***market price support*** (net of feed adjustment) in the net total PSE rose from 40 per cent in 1979-1982 to 64 per cent in 1989-1994. Although the level of support in 1989-1994, as measured by the percentage PSE, was lower than in 1979-1982, the burden on consumers associated with market price support to agriculture was higher. In the period 1989-94, ***direct payments*** became an integral part of Mexican agricultural support, with an average share of 7 per cent of total support.

The share of the ***reduction of input costs*** in net total PSE fell from 42 per cent in 1979-82 to 21 per cent in 1989-94. While interest concessions on loans have generally accounted for a significant share of this support component, it has also included direct subsidies to reduce farm input prices, such as irrigation water and animal feed. The share of ***general services*** in net total support decreased from 18 per cent in 1979-1982 to 7 per cent in 1989-94. The improvement of agricultural structures and infrastructures (essentially irrigation schemes) and expenditure on research, advisory, and training have generally been the main elements of support to general services.

b) *Decomposition of PSE in the 1989-94 period*

Given that the reform of Mexican agricultural policy initiated in 1990 included the entry into force of NAFTA and the launching of PROCAMPO direct payments in 1994, the decomposition analysis in the 1989-94 period is likely to be informative as to the main factors influencing the recent changes in support. Figure 5 shows the evolution of the various PSE components over the period 1989-94. The share of **market price support** (net of levies and of feed adjustment) in the net total PSE increased from 37 per cent in 1989 to 77 per cent in 1991, but decreased to 47 per cent in 1994, following the introduction of PROCAMPO payments. The share of **direct payments** in total support increased from 1 per cent in 1991 to 26 per cent in 1994.

The share of the **reduction of input costs** in the net total PSE fell from 52 per cent in 1989 to 19 per cent in 1994. This decrease can be attributed to the removal of fertiliser subsidies after the privatisation of FERTIMEX in 1992, the decline of insurance subsidies resulting from the closure of ANAGSA in 1990, and the decrease in the share of interest concessions in total support. The share of **general services** in

◆ Figure 4. **Breakdown of total PSE, by type of support measure**

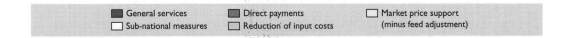

■ General services   ■ Direct payments   □ Market price support
□ Sub-national measures   □ Reduction of input costs   (minus feed adjustment)

A. Average 1979-82

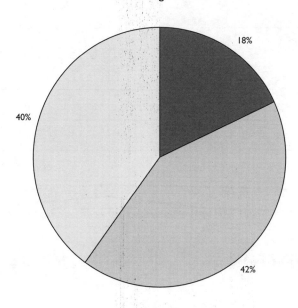

40%
18%
42%

B. Average 1989-94

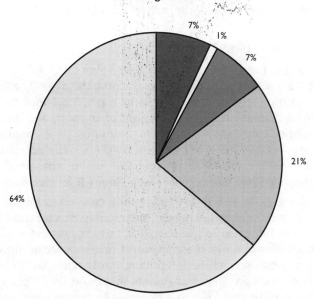

7% 1%
7%
21%
64%

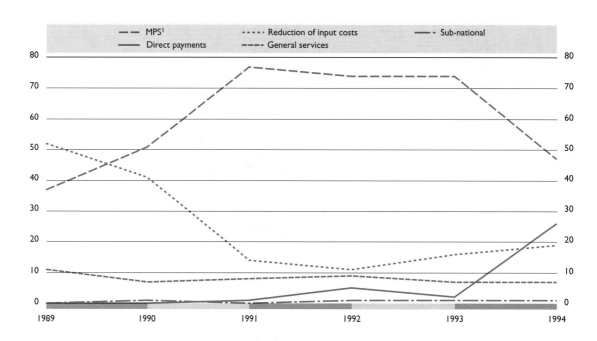

◆ Figure 5. **Evolution of support components over the period 1989-94**
%

1. MPS = Market price support net of levies and of feed adjustment.
Source: Table 13c, Annex II.

the net total PSE decreased from 11 per cent in 1989 to 7 per cent in 1994, mainly due to a decrease in the share of government transfers for irrigation infrastructure improvement in total support, which coincided with the transfer of operation and maintenance of irrigation works to producers initiated in 1992. The share of **subnational measures** in the net total PSE remained low, at 1 per cent in 1994.

c) Decomposition of PSE and CSE changes in 1995

The decomposition of the **Total PSE** and **Total CSE** helps to identify the relative importance of changes in the various PSE and CSE components in explaining the overall year-to-year changes in PSEs and CSEs. The decomposition analysis is presented in a graphical form using a "tree diagram" to illustrate the contribution of changes in each component of support, and the overall yearly change in support (Figure 6). The upper value shown for each component is its annual percentage change as measured by the Fisher ideal index. The lower value in brackets is the approximate contribution to the total change (*i.e.* the effect on the total PSE or total CSE of the change in the component, on the assumption that no other change had taken place) (see Annex II for details).

It is estimated that the net total PSE in 1995 sharply decreased to M$ 2.3 billion (US$354 million). As the volume of production only slightly decreased, the main reason for the PSE decline was the sharp decrease in the unit PSE. The decrease in the unit PSE, in turn, was essentially due to a decrease in market price support, as a result of an increase in world prices in Mexican pesos (mainly due to the depreciation of the Mexican peso against the US dollar), partly offset by an increase of 49 per cent in producer prices, in line with inflation. Direct payments increased by 11 per cent while other support decreased by about 17 per cent (mainly due to a decrease in interest concessions). The overall result was that the percentage PSE decreased from 34 per cent in 1994 to 3 per cent in 1995.

In 1995, the total CSE became positive, representing a subsidy on consumption of M$ 10.7 (US$1.7) billion. Since the quantity consumed and consumption subsidies only slightly increased, the shift from

◆ Figure 6. **Decomposition of PSE and CSE changes from 1994 to 1995**

Decomposition of PSE changes:

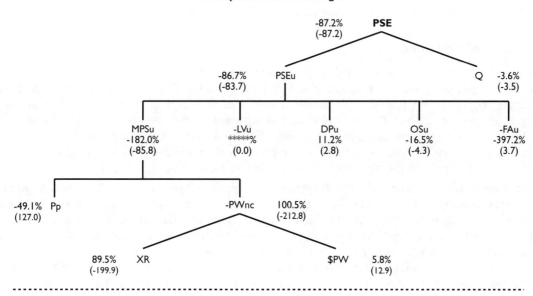

Decomposition of CSE changes:

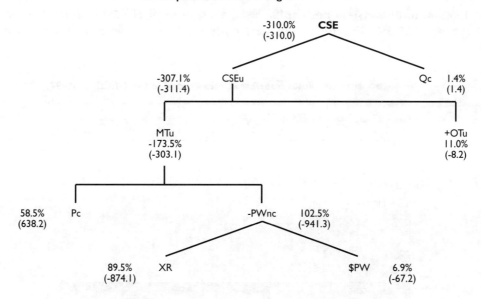

PSE	: net total PSE	MPS	: market price support	u	: per unit
CSE	: total CSE	MT	: market transfers	nc	: in national currency
Q	: quantity produced	LV	: levies on output	$	: in US$
Qc	: quantity consumed	DP	: direct payments	...%	: percentage change
Pp	: production price	FA	: feed adjustment	(...)	: contribution to total change
Pc	: consumption price	OS	: other support		in PSE or CSE
PW	: world price	OT	: other transfers		in percentage points
XR	: exchange rate/US$			***	: not applicable

1. For an explanation of decomposition see Annex II.
Source: OECD Secretariat 1997.

an implicit tax on consumption in 1994 to a subsidy on consumption in 1995 was essentially attributable to a sharp decline in market transfers. Higher border prices in Mexican pesos, partly offset by a rise in consumption prices, accounted for the fall in market transfers. The percentage CSE was negative in 1994, at −9 per cent, and became positive in 1995, at 12 per cent.

3. Evolution of total transfers

As for PSEs, the evolution of **total transfers expressed in US dollars** throughout the 1979-1995 period may be divided into four periods: the 1979-1982 period, with annual transfers of US$7.6 billion on average; the 1984-1988 period, with annual transfers of US$1.8 billion on average (excluding 1983 when transfers were negative); the 1989-1994 period, with annual transfers of US$7.7 billion on average; and 1995, when transfers were close to zero (US$0.3 billion) as a result of a negative MPS, which in turn was due to the sharp rise of border prices compared with domestic producer prices following the devaluation of the peso, implicitly subsidising consumers (see Annex I, Table III.2).

The share of **total transfers in GDP** decreased from about 3.7 per cent in 1979-82 to 2.6 per cent in 1989-94. This trend reflects not only the effects of the agricultural policy reform process but also the decreasing importance of agriculture in the economy. Over the period 1979-82, the share of total transfers in GDP was equivalent to about half the share of agriculture in GDP. In the 1989-94 period, the ratio decreased to around one third, while it was close to one for most OECD countries. The average share of total transfers in total GDP for the OECD as a whole was about 1.8 per cent in 1989-94 (Figure 7). Over the latter period and among the OECD countries for which PSEs and CSEs were calculated, the level of transfers in GDP in Mexico was quite similar to the level in the European Union[5] and Japan, and lower than the level in Turkey, Finland, Norway, Iceland, Switzerland, and Austria.

In 1989-94, **total transfers per capita**, at an average level of US$91, were about a quarter of the OECD average of US$369 (Figure 7). They were quite similar to the level in Australia and Hungary, and

◆ Figure 7. **Total transfers in Mexico and in the OECD, 1989-94**

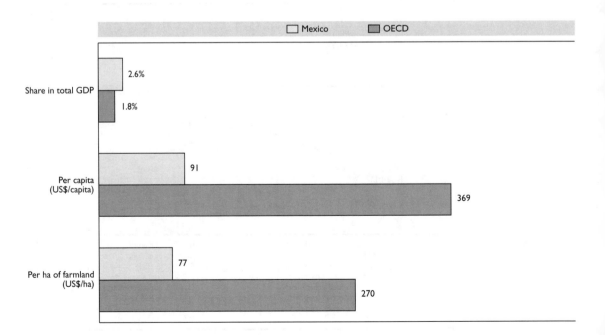

Note: The OECD average excludes the Czech Republic, Mexico and Poland.
Source: Table III.2.

lower than in all other OECD countries, except Poland and New Zealand. Over the same period, at an average level of US$77, **total transfers per hectare of agricultural land** were also much lower than the OECD average of US$270 (Figure 7). This comparison reflects the differences not only in the absolute level of transfers but also the amount of land used in agricultural production relative to other countries. The only OECD countries with a level of transfers per hectare lower than Mexico were Australia and New Zealand, and the level in Mexico is quite similar to the one in Poland.

C. ANALYSIS OF SUPPORT BY COMMODITY

This section analyses in more detail the evolution of support by commodity, as measured by the PSE and CSE. For comparison, Figures 8 and 9 present the percentage PSE and percentage CSE by commodity for Mexico and the OECD as a whole, for the periods 1979-82 and 1989-94. Figures 10 and 11 present the producer NAC and consumer NAC by commodity for Mexico and the OECD for the same periods. Figures 12a and 12b show the share of each support component in the net total PSE for the main commodities in 1989-94. Over that period, the share of market price support in total support was rather low for beef and veal, wheat, and sorghum (less than 20 per cent), while it was much higher for milk, pigmeat, maize, and sugar (more than 70 per cent).

1. Wheat (Table 1 – Annex II)

Wheat is mainly grown under irrigation in the north-western part of Mexico. **Total production** more than doubled between 1979 and 1985 to reach more than 5 million tonnes in 1985, mainly due to a doubling of the **cultivated area**, and an increase in **yields** by 12 per cent to 4.3 tonnes per hectare. Production subsequently decreased to stabilise at around 4 million tonnes in 1994. This evolution followed that of the area under cultivation, and can be attributed in some years to the limited availability of irrigation water and changes in relative prices following the replacement of guaranteed prices by concerted prices, that led to a shift to maize production from 1990. In 1995, production decreased by about 20 per cent due to drought. **Production/consumption ratios** increased from an average of 72 per cent between 1979 and 1981 to around 93 per cent over the period 1982-91, but decreased to an average of 73 per cent in the following four years, due to an increase in consumption.

The **total PSE** for wheat has generally been positive over the period under review, although it was negative in 1979, 1983, 1985, 1987, 1989, and 1995, often due to peso devaluations. Administered prices of wheat have generally been maintained at a low level compared with maize which is the main staple in Mexico. Until 1989, as part of the government policy to keep consumer prices low for bread and wheat flour, producer prices for wheat were artificially depressed by border measures (wheat flour exports were restricted as they required permits). The resulting negative MPS which implicitly taxed producers was, however, in some years, more than offset by budgetary support. In 1990, the export permit requirement for wheat flour was removed and producer prices for wheat were influenced by world prices, although imports continued to be regulated by permits. Over the 1990-1993 period, the positive MPS contributed to about one third of total support on average, with concerted prices exceeding border prices. In 1994, the MPS decreased due to the removal of import permits and the introduction of PROCAMPO payments. Budgetary support to wheat producers has mainly consisted of irrigation subsidies, interest concessions on loans, infrastructure development and, since 1992, direct payments. In 1995, despite an increase in the concerted price in pesos for the Autumn-Winter 1994/95 crop season and the removal of the concerted price for the Spring-Summer 1995 crop season, the MPS was negative as border prices exceeded domestic prices, due to the devaluation of the peso and an increase in border prices. That year, the net total PSE was negative as budgetary support (including PROCAMPO payments) only partly offset the negative MPS.

The **percentage PSE** for wheat was lower than the OECD average in the 1979-82 period (14 per cent compared with 23 per cent), and over the period 1989-94, at 23 per cent (compared with 45 per cent). In 1995, it decreased to –6 per cent, well below the OECD average of 33 per cent. Because of consumption subsidies (from CONASUPO until 1990, and ASERCA in 1992-94) and, to a lesser extent, due to domestic prices lower than border prices (except over the 1990-93 period), the percentage CSE has generally

◆   Figure 8. *Mexican percentage PSE and percentage CSE, by commodity*

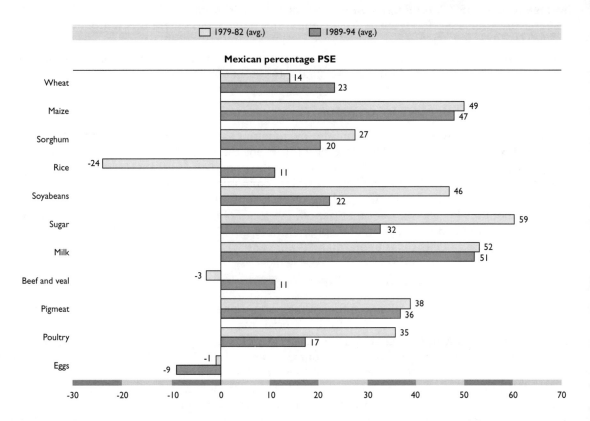

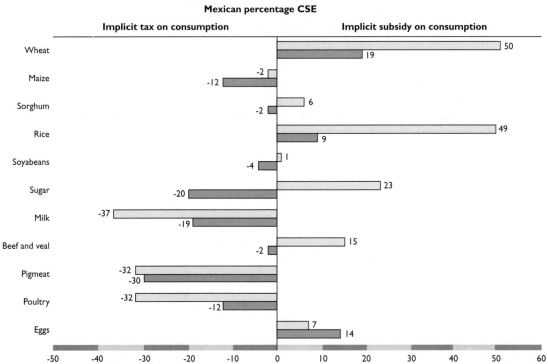

Note: avg.: average.
Source: Tables 15 and 16, Annex II.

◆ Figure 9. **OECD percentage PSE and percentage CSE, by commodity**

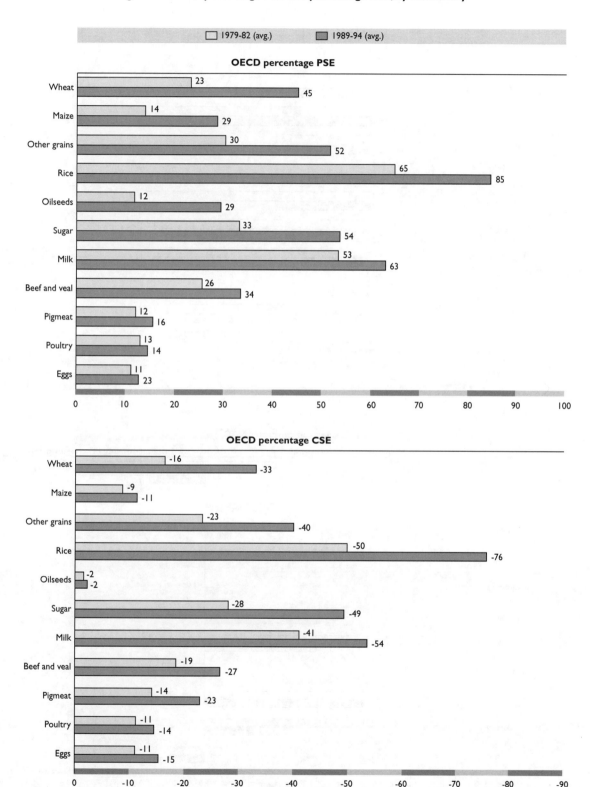

Note: avg.: average. The OECD average excludes the Czech Republic, Hungary, Mexico and Poland.
Source: OECD Secretariat, 1997.

125

◆ Figure 10. **Mexican producer NAC and consumer NAC, by commodity**

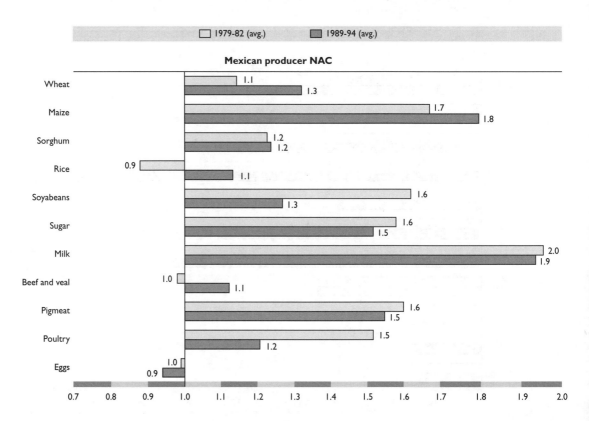

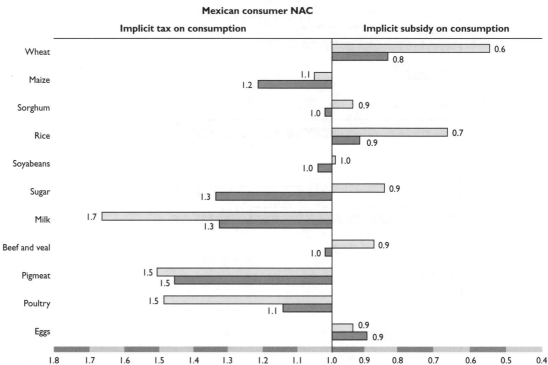

Note: avg.: average.
Source: Tables 15 and 16, Annex II.

◆ Figure 11. **OECD producer NAC and consumer NAC, by commodity**

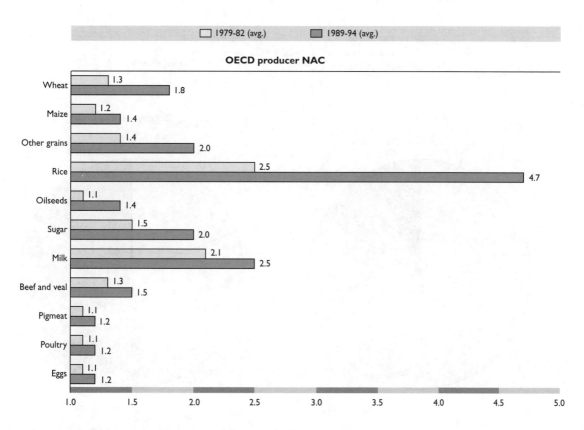

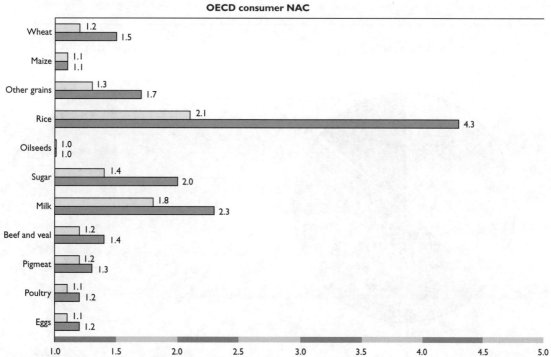

Note: avg.: average.
Source: OECD Secretariat, 1997.

◆ Figure 12a. **Breakdown of total PSE by type of support in 1989-94: main crops**

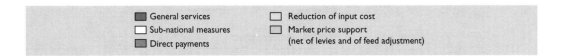

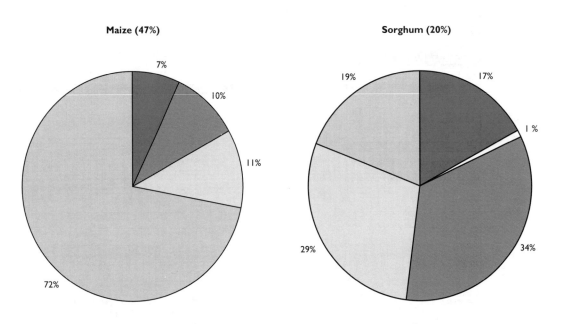

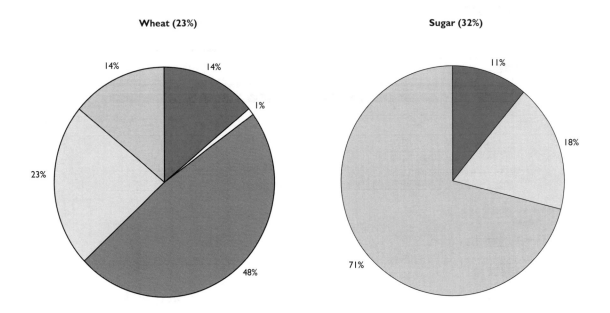

Note: The percentages in brackets after the name of each commodity refer to the average percentage PSE for that commodity in the period 1989-94.
Source: PSE Tables, Annex II.

◆ Figure 12b. **Breakdown of total PSE by type of support measure in 1989-94:**
main livestock products

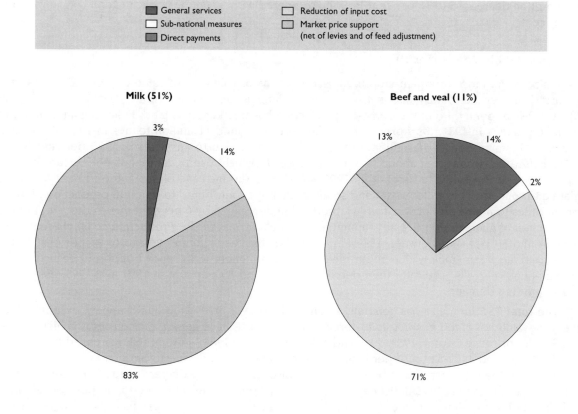

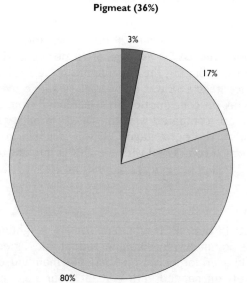

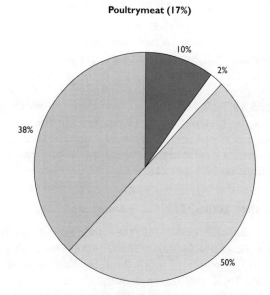

Note: The percentages in brackets after the name of each commodity refer to the average percentage PSE for that commodity in the period 1989-94.
Source: PSE Tables, Annex II.

been positive (except in 1991). The subsidy on consumption, as estimated by the percentage CSE, decreased from 50 per cent in the 1979-82 period to 19 per cent in the 1989-94 period, in contrast with the OECD implicit tax on consumption of 16 per cent and 33 per cent, respectively. The subsidy on consumption decreased to 18 per cent in 1995, compared with an OECD implicit tax on consumption of 11 per cent.

2. Maize (Table 2A – Annex II)

Maize is the most important crop in Mexico in terms of volume and value of production. Maize is produced all over the country, and is used mainly for human consumption (white maize), although, from 1991 to 1995, about a third of the domestic production has been used as feed. Following an increase to 15 million tonnes in 1981, *total production* decreased to around 11 million tonnes in 1989. Production then steadily increased to 18 million tonnes in 1994, partly due to an increase of 25 per cent in the maize *cultivated area* and of about 30 per cent in *yields*, which rose to 2.2 tonnes per hectare in 1994. The increase in the cultivated area from 1990 was due to the increase of guaranteed prices for maize relative to concerted prices for wheat and sorghum that has contributed to a shift in production of these commodities to maize production. In 1995, production decreased by 6 per cent due to drought, but the replacement of guaranteed prices by minimum prices also contributed. *Production/consumption ratios* were around 80 per cent between 1979 and 1990, but increased to an average of 94 per cent in the following three years, mainly due to an increase in production and reduced imports because of the large amount in stocks. The ratio then decreased to around 80 per cent in 1994 and 1995, essentially due to growing demand.

The *total PSE* for maize has generally been positive over the period under review, except in 1983 due to devaluation of the peso. Administered prices of maize have generally been set at a higher level than border prices, except in 1983, 1984 and 1995. The share of MPS in total PSE increased from 43 per cent in the period 1979-82 to 72 per cent over the 1989-94 period, due to an increase in guaranteed prices greater than the increase in border prices. However, the share decreased to 40 per cent in 1994, with the introduction of PROCAMPO payments, and to 20 per cent in 1995, due to the peso devaluation and the setting of minimum prices. Budgetary support to maize producers has mainly consisted of interest concessions on loans, infrastructure development, irrigation subsidies, research, advisory and training and, since 1994, PROCAMPO payments.

The *percentage PSE* for maize was higher than the OECD average over the periods 1979-82 (49 per cent compared with 14 per cent) and 1989-94 (47 per cent compared with 29 per cent). However, the percentage PSE decreased to 26 per cent in 1995, above the OECD average of 18 per cent, due to devaluation of the peso. Despite consumption subsidies, including the programme to subsidise the consumption of maize tortillas initiated in 1984, the percentage CSE was on average negative over the periods 1979-82 and 1989-94, representing an implicit tax on consumption that increased from 2 per cent in the first period to 12 per cent in the latter period (compared with the OECD implicit tax on consumption of 9 per cent and 11 per cent, respectively). The percentage CSE was positive in 1995, representing a subsidy on consumption of 6 per cent, which contrasted with the OECD implicit tax on consumption of 6 per cent).

3. Other grains (Table 2 – Annex II)

In the case of Mexico, the other grains considered in the OECD standard list are sorghum and barley. *Total production* of these two grains in Mexico is dominated by sorghum, with about 90 per cent of the total volume of production. Sorghum is essentially used for feed, while barley is mainly used for brewing. Total production of sorghum remained relatively unchanged until 1990, at around 5.5 million tonnes, but decreased since then to 3 million tonnes in 1995. This was mainly the result of the removal of guaranteed prices and import permits in 1989. Moreover, the maintenance of guaranteed prices for maize also encouraged a shift of production to maize. The decrease in sorghum production was due to decreases of more than 40 per cent in the *cultivated area* and 15 per cent in *yields*. Between 1979 and 1990, yields of sorghum were on average 3.3 tonnes per hectare, but decreased to 2.8 tonnes per hectare in 1995. **Production/consumption ratios** for sorghum increased from 70 per cent in 1979-85 to 85 per cent in 1986-88, but then decreased to 40 per cent in 1995, mainly due to a decrease in production. Production/consumption ratios for barley were around 92 per cent between 1979 and 1988, but decreased to an average of 76 per cent in the following seven years, mainly due to an increase in consumption.

Over the review period, the **total PSE** for other grains has generally been positive, except in 1983. Until 1994, administered prices of these grains were generally set at a higher level than border prices (except in the period 1982-86 for sorghum, and in 1983 and 1988 for barley). Over the period 1979-82, the budgetary support more than offset the generally negative MPS and the PSE was positive. In the 1989-94 period, the share of MPS in total support was 19 per cent for sorghum, mainly due to the setting of concerted prices for sorghum in Tamaulipas State above border prices. Over that period, the share was 81 per cent for barley, resulting from the commitment of brewers, through IASA, to buy all domestic production of barley at prices higher than border prices. Budgetary support to sorghum and barley producers was mainly in the form of interest concessions on loans, infrastructure development, and subsidies on irrigation. Since 1993, direct payments have become the main component of support for sorghum.

Although the average **percentage PSE** for other grains in the OECD increased from 30 per cent in the 1979-82 period to 52 per cent over the period 1989-94, it remained unchanged in Mexico, at around 22 per cent over these periods. In 1995, the percentage PSE decreased to 16 per cent, well below the OECD average of 49 per cent. Because of negative MPS, the subsidy on consumption, as measured by a positive percentage CSE, was on average 6 per cent in the 1979-82 period, in contrast with the OECD implicit tax on consumption of 23 per cent. However, because of positive MPS, the percentage CSE became negative in 1989-94. Over this period, the implicit tax on consumption was on average 5 per cent (compared with the OECD implicit tax on consumption of 40 per cent). In 1995, the percentage CSE was again positive, representing a subsidy on consumption of 1 per cent, which contrasted with the OECD implicit tax on consumption of 21 per cent.

4. Rice (Table 3 – Annex II)

The value of rice in total agricultural production is low compared with wheat, maize, and other grains. **Total production** decreased from an average of more than 500 000 tonnes until 1989 to about 350 000 tonnes in 1995, mainly due to a reduction by half of the **cultivated area**, partly offset by an increase in **yields** by 30 per cent to 4.5 tonnes per hectare. This decrease in cultivated area can be attributed to the replacement of guaranteed prices by concerted prices in 1989. On average, **production/consumption ratios** decreased from 86 per cent in 1979-89 to 53 per cent over the period 1990-95, mainly due to a decrease in production.

Until 1989, the **total PSE** for rice has generally been negative, except in 1981. Since 1990, it has become positive due to the introduction of ASERCA direct payments which more than offset the generally negative MPS. Until 1994, the generally negative MPS (except in 1992) was due to adminis-tered prices set below border prices. Budgetary support to rice growers has mainly been in the form of irrigation subsidies, infrastructure improvement, interest concessions on loans and, since 1991, direct payments. The **percentage PSE** increased from an average of –24 per cent in the 1979-82 period to an average of 11 per cent over the period 1989-94, and rose to 15 per cent in 1995. It has always been well below the OECD averages for these periods (65 per cent, 85 per cent, and 91 per cent respectively). Over the same periods, the subsidy on consumption, as measured by a positive percentage CSE, resulted from positive market transfers (except in 1992) and consumption aids through CONASUPO (until 1991). The percentage CSE decreased from 49 per cent in 1979-82 to 9 per cent in 1989-94, while in the OECD, over the same periods, the implicit tax on consumption, as measured by a negative percentage CSE, increased from 50 per cent to 76 per cent on average. The percentage CSE became negative in 1995, representing an implicit tax on consumption of 1 per cent, well below the OECD implicit tax on consumption of 78 per cent.

5.   Oilseeds (Table 4 – Annex II)

Oilseed production in Mexico consists mainly of soyabeans. **Total production** of soyabeans widely fluctuated around an average of about 700 000 tonnes until 1990, and subsequently decreased to 200 000 tonnes in 1995, mainly due to a decrease in the **cultivated area**. Over the same periods, the **production/consumption ratios** decreased dramatically from an average of 45 per cent to 5 per cent, mainly due to a sharp increase in imports to meet growing domestic demand.

The **total PSE** for soyabeans has generally been positive over the review period, except in 1983 and 1988. Until 1993, administered prices of soyabeans were set at a higher level than border prices, except in the period 1983-88. In the 1979-82 period, the positive PSE was mainly due to budgetary support, although the MPS contribution to total support was 39 per cent. From 1984 to 1987 and since 1989, the positive PSE continued to result mainly from budgetary support, mainly in the form of infrastructure improvement, irrigation subsidies, interest concessions on loans and, since 1991, direct payments.

The **percentage PSE** for soyabeans was higher than the OECD average in the 1979-82 period (46 per cent compared with 12 per cent), but was lower over the period 1989-94 (22 per cent compared with 29 per cent). In 1995, it decreased to 15 per cent, compared with an OECD average of 21 per cent. Over the period 1979-82, CONASUPO consumption subsidies more than offset the negative market transfers. The resulting subsidy on consumption was on average of 1 per cent in 1979-82. The percentage CSE became negative in the 1989-94 period, representing an implicit tax on consumption of 4 per cent. The OECD implicit tax on consumption for oilseeds was of 2 per cent for both periods. In 1995, the implicit tax on consumption increased to 6 per cent (compared with an OECD implicit tax on consumption of 1 per cent).

6.   Sugar (Table 5 – Annex II)

Although subject to variations, **total production** of sugarcane increased by 60 per cent over the review period, to about 4 million tonnes. The increase in production was the result of increases in the **cultivated area** until 1987, and **yields**, since 1990. The **production/consumption ratio** has traditionally been high with an average of 95 per cent over the review period and more than 100 per cent between 1983 and 1988, due to increases in domestic production in a situation of growing demand.

The **total PSE** for sugarcane has generally been positive over the review period, except in 1985, 1987, 1988, 1989, and 1995. The MPS was negative in the 1979-82 period and the positive PSE was due to the greater effect of budgetary support. From 1990 to 1994, concerted prices for sugarcane were set at levels higher than border prices, resulting in a positive MPS which contributed around 70 per cent of total support over that period. This substantial increase in MPS coincided with the privatisation of all sugar factories between 1988 and 1992, and the transfer of responsibility on producer price setting from the Secretariat of Energy, Mines, and State-owned Agencies (SEMIP) to the Secretariat of Agriculture. In 1995, the MPS became negative as the concerted price was set below border prices, mainly due to the sharp devaluation of the peso and an increase in border prices. Budgetary support to sugarcane growers has mainly been for infrastructure improvement, interest concessions on loans, irrigation subsidies, and research, advisory and training.

The **percentage PSE** for sugarcane decreased from 59 per cent in the 1979-82 period to 32 per cent over the period 1989-94. The OECD averages for these periods were 33 per cent and 54 per cent respectively. In 1995, the percentage PSE became negative (at –13 per cent), reflecting the decrease in MPS, which contrasted with the OECD positive average of 45 per cent. As consumption subsidies have never been granted to the sugar industry, the evolution of percentage CSE has followed the trend in MPS. In the 1979-82 period, the subsidy on consumption as measured by a positive percentage CSE of 23 per cent, contrasted with the OECD implicit tax on consumption of 28 per cent. Over the period 1989-94, the implicit tax on consumption, as measured by a negative percentage CSE, was below the OECD implicit tax on consumption (49 per cent), at around 20 per cent. In 1995, the percentage CSE was again positive and represented a subsidy on consumption of 17 per cent, which contrasted with the OECD implicit tax on consumption of 42 per cent.

7. Milk (Table 6 – Annex II)

Most of the milk produced in Mexico (98 per cent) comes from cows. Goat's milk comprises the remaining 2 per cent. Dairy cattle represent 14 per cent of the total bovine herd. Specialised dairy cattle accounts for only 16 per cent of the total dairy herd but produces more than half of the volume of milk. **Total production** of milk decreased from an average of 7 million tonnes between 1979 and 1985 to 6 million tonnes in 1989, and then increased to 8 million tonnes in 1995. The size of the **dairy herd** has remained relatively constant since 1985, and the trend in production can be largely attributed to changes in **yields.** Average yields vary between 4 000 to 6 000 litres per cow (intensive production); 1 600 to 2 800 litres per cow (semi-intensive farms); and 600 to 1 400 litres per cow (dual purpose). The **production/consumption ratio** decreased from 90 per cent in 1979 to 70 per cent in 1990, and then increased to 75 per cent in 1995. These trends mainly reflect the evolution of domestic production, except two peak years due to a marked decline in milk consumption (1981 and 1991),

The **net total PSE** for milk has generally been positive over the review period. Until 1994, domestic prices for milk exceeded border prices (except in 1983), resulting in a high share of MPS (net of feed adjustment) in total PSE (share from 81 per cent in 1979-82 to 83 per cent in 1989-94). Producer prices in Mexico have been kept above world prices through import controls by SECOFI. Budgetary support to milk producers have mainly been in the form of feed subsidies, interest concessions on loans, and research, advisory, and training. Adjusted for the implicit tax on feed, the annual **net percentage PSE** for milk slightly decreased from 52 per cent in the 1979-82 period to 51 per cent over the period 1989-94. The OECD averages for these periods were 53 per cent and 63 per cent respectively. In 1995, the percentage PSE sharply decreased (to 5 per cent), well below the OECD average of 57 per cent. Until 1994, despite consumption subsidies through the social programme of milk, the percentage CSE was generally negative due to higher levels of MPS. The implicit tax on consumption, as measured by the percentage CSE, decreased from 37 per cent in the 1979-82 period to 19 per cent over the period 1989-94, well below the OECD implicit tax on consumption for these periods (41 per cent and 54 per cent, respectively). In 1995, the percentage CSE became positive and represented a subsidy on consumption of 15 per cent, which contrasted with the OECD implicit tax on consumption of 46 per cent.

8. Beef and veal (Table 7 – Annex II)

Despite decreases in 1984 and 1989-90, **total production** has increased on average by about 40 per cent since 1979 to 1.4 million tonnes in 1995. Except in 1989-90, the trend in production has resulted from the increase in the total **number of cattle** by about 5 per cent from 1979 to more than 23 million in 1995. Generally, production exceeds consumption, Mexico being a net exporter. The **production/ consumption ratio** was 104 per cent on average over the period 1979-1990, decreased to 96 per cent in 1991-94 due to growing demand, and grew to 111 per cent in 1995 due to an increase in production.

Until 1988, the **net total PSE** for beef and veal was generally negative (except in 1979, and 1981), due to the existence of controls on live cattle exports and beef and veal imports, reflected in a negative MPS. Following the removal of these controls in 1989 and until 1994, domestic prices for beef and veal exceeded border prices, and total support became positive. From 1989 to 1992, the positive PSE resulted from budgetary support, mainly interest concessions on loans, feed subsidies, and research, advisory and training. With the introduction of an import tariff on beef and veal in 1993, the MPS accounted for 40 per cent of total support. MPS decreased to 13 per cent of total support in 1994, when the import tariff was removed for NAFTA partners. The MPS became negative in 1995 because the rise in domestic prices was much lower than the significant increase in border prices due to the sharp peso devaluation.

Adjusted for the implicit tax on feed, the **net percentage PSE** for beef and veal increased from –3 per cent in the 1979-82 period to 11 per cent over the period 1989-94, after a period of highly negative rates (–51 per cent over the period 1983-88). Mexico's net percentage PSE for beef and veal was well below the OECD averages in these periods (26 per cent and 34 per cent, respectively). In 1995, the percentage PSE became highly negative (at –23 per cent), due to the devaluation of the peso, which contrasted with the OECD average of 40 per cent. As consumption subsidies have never been granted to beef and veal, the evolution of percentage CSE has followed the trend in MPS. In the 1979-82 period, a subsidy on consumption of 15 per cent contrasted with an OECD implicit tax on consumption of 19 per cent. Over the period 1989-94, the implicit tax on consumption, as measured by a negative percentage CSE, was below the OECD implicit tax on consumption (2 per cent compared with 27 per cent). In 1995, the percentage CSE was again positive and represented a subsidy on consumption of 30 per cent, which contrasted with the OECD implicit tax on consumption of 31 per cent.

9. Pigmeat (Table 8 – Annex II)

Total production increased by 25 per cent between 1979 and 1983 to about 1.5 million tonnes, but it decreased by half from 1983 to 1989, and increased again by 30 per cent to 900 000 tonnes in 1995. Until 1989, the trend in production followed the evolution in the *number of pigs* that increased by about 12 per cent between 1979 and 1983, and then decreased by about 35 per cent to 10 million in 1995. The *production/consumption ratio* has declined to 90-95 per cent since 1988, due to an increase in consumption.

The *net total PSE* for pigmeat has generally been positive, except in 1983 and 1986 due to peso devaluations reflected in a negative MPS. Domestic prices for pigmeat have generally exceeded border prices, except in 1983-87, resulting in a high share of MPS (net of feed adjustment) in total PSE. The share slightly increased from 78 per cent in 1979-82 to 80 per cent in 1989-94. MPS decreased to 69 per cent of total support in 1995 because of the steady increase in border prices due to the sharp devaluation of the peso.

Adjusted for the implicit tax on feed, the *net percentage PSE* for pigmeat slightly decreased from 38 per cent in the period 1979-82 to 36 per cent over the period 1989-94. It was above the OECD averages for these periods (12 per cent and 16 per cent respectively). In 1995, the percentage PSE decreased to 16 per cent, close to the OECD average of 18 per cent. As consumption subsidies have never been granted to pigmeat, the evolution of percentage CSE has followed the trend in MPS. The implicit tax on consumption, as measured by a negative percentage CSE, slightly decreased from 32 per cent in 1979-82 to 30 per cent over the period 1989-94, above the OECD implicit tax on consumption of 14 per cent and 23 per cent, respectively. In 1995, the percentage CSE was still negative and represented an implicit tax on consumption of 10 per cent (compared with an OECD implicit tax on consumption of 22 per cent).

10. Poultrymeat (Table 9 – Annex II)

Most poultrymeat produced in Mexico (95 per cent) comes from chicken, turkey meat accounting for the remaining 5 per cent. Despite a decrease in 1986-89, *total production* increased on average almost threefold between 1979 and 1995, to about 1.2 million tonnes, mainly due to a shift in meat consumption. The trend in production followed the evolution in the *number of poultry* that increased by about 22 per cent between 1979 and 1985, decreased by about 23 per cent from 1985 to 1987, and then increased again to around 100 million in 1995. Consumption steadily increased to 1.3 million tonnes in 1995. The *production/consumption ratio* has declined since 1987 to 87 per cent in 1995, due to an increase in consumption.

The *net total PSE* for poultrymeat has generally been positive, except in 1986 and 1995. Domestic prices for poultrymeat have generally exceeded border prices, except in 1983-86 and 1995, resulting in a high share of MPS (net of feed adjustment) in total PSE. although the share sharply decreased from 70 per cent in 1979-82 to 38 per cent in 1989-94, period in which the reduction of input costs accounted for half of total support. Feed subsidies have been the most important component of budgetary support to poultry producers, accounting for 18 per cent of total support over the period 1989-94. MPS became negative in 1995 because the rise in domestic prices was much lower than the marked increase in border prices due to the sharp peso devaluation.

Adjusted for the implicit tax on feed, the *net percentage PSE* for poultrymeat sharply decreased from 35 per cent in the 1979-82 period to 17 per cent over the period 1989-94. It was above the OECD average over these periods (13 per cent and 14 per cent respectively). In 1995, the percentage PSE became negative, at –31 per cent, which contrasted with the OECD positive average of 15 per cent. As consumption subsidies have never been granted to poultrymeat, the evolution of percentage CSE has followed the trend in MPS. The implicit tax on consumption, as measured by a negative percentage CSE, decreased from 32 per cent in the 1979-82 period to 12 per cent over the period 1989-94 (compared with the OECD implicit tax on consumption of 11 per cent and 14 per cent, respectively). In 1995, the percentage CSE became positive and represented a subsidy on consumption of 33 per cent, which contrasted with the OECD implicit tax on consumption of 13 per cent.

11. Eggs (Table 12 – Annex II)

Since 1979, **total production** of eggs has almost doubled, to 1.2 million tonnes. This resulted from an increase by 50 per cent in the **number of laying hens**, to 90 million in 1995. Consumption was generally at the same level as production and the **production/consumption ratio** remained unchanged at 1.

The **net total PSE** for eggs has generally been negative, except in 1980, 1992, 1993 and 1994. Domestic prices for eggs have generally been exceeded by border prices, except in 1981, 1992 and 1993, resulting in a negative MPS. The main component of the PSE has thus been budgetary support, in particular feed subsidies. Adjusted for the implicit tax on feed, the **net percentage PSE** for eggs decreased from –1 per cent in the 1979-82 period to –9 per cent over the period 1989-94. It was well below the OECD average of 11 per cent and 13 per cent for the respective periods. In 1995, the percentage PSE decreased further to –18 per cent, which contrasted with the OECD positive average of 17 per cent. As consumption subsidies have never been granted to eggs, the evolution of percentage CSE has followed the trend in market transfers. The subsidy on consumption, as measured by a positive percentage CSE, increased from 7 per cent in the 1979-82 period to 14 per cent over the period 1989-94, in contrast with the OECD average implicit tax on consumption of 11 per cent and 15 per cent respectively. In 1995, the percentage CSE increased to 24 per cent, in contrast with an OECD implicit tax on consumption of 16 per cent.

NOTES AND REFERENCES

1. The volume of production considered in the calculation of PSEs includes the part of the production that is self-consumed by producers.

2. Producer nominal assistance coefficients (NAC$_p$), as defined in this report, are broader concepts than producer nominal protection coefficients (NPC). Conceptually, they lie between the nominal and the effective rate of assistance used in the literature. See, for example, G. Miller (1986), *The Political Economy of International Agricultural Policy Reform*, Department of Primary Industry, Canberra; H. Haszler and D. Parsons (1987), "The Price Adjustment Gap and World Agricultural Policy Reform", *Quarterly Review of the Rural Economy*, Vol. 9, No. 2, Australian Bureau of Agricultural Resource Economics.

3. *Source:* OECD (1997), *OECD Economic Surveys, Mexico*, Figure 22.

4. The periods 1983-87 and 1995 were excluded from this analysis as trends in support are masked by devaluations (see Table III.1).

5. EU-12.

Annex I

BACKGROUND TABLES

Table I.1. **Basic economic and agricultural indicators**[1]

	Units	1980	1981	1982	1983	1984	1985	1986	1987	1988
GDP (1)	M$ mn	4 470	4 862	4 831	4 628	4 796	4 920	4 735	4 823	4 883
Annual increase in GDP	%	9.2	8.8	(0.6)	(4.2)	3.6	2.6	(3.8)	1.9	1.2
Agricultural GDP (2)	M$ mn	368	391	383	391	401	416	405	410	395
Annual increase in agricultural GDP	%	7.2	6.1	(2.0)	2.0	2.7	3.8	(2.7)	1.4	(3.8)
Food processing GDP (3)	M$ mn	243	254	265	262	265	275	274	277	277
Annual increase in food processing GDP	%	4.8	4.3	4.5	(1.3)	1.5	3.8	(0.5)	0.9	0.2
(2)/(1) = (4)	%	8.2	8.0	7.9	8.4	8.4	8.5	8.5	8.5	8.1
(3)/(1) = (5)	%	5.4	5.2	5.5	5.7	5.5	5.6	5.8	5.7	5.7
(4) + (5)	%	13.7	13.2	13.4	14.1	13.9	14.1	14.3	14.2	13.8
Total employment (6)	mn	20.3	21.5	21.5	21.0	21.5	22.0	21.6	21.9	22.1
Agricultural employment (7)	mn	5.7	5.8	5.6	5.9	5.9	6.1	5.9	6.0	6.2
(7)/ (6)	%	28.0	27.0	26.2	28.0	27.7	27.8	27.5	27.6	28.1
Compensation of total employees (8)	M$ mn	1 611	1 793	1 697	1 278	1 243	1 268	1 133	1 121	1 019
Compensation of agric. employees (9)	M$ mn	94	104	90	79	76	78	76	72	62
Compensation per employee (8)/(6) = (10)	M$	79.4	83.2	79.0	60.9	57.9	57.8	52.3	51.3	46.2
Compensation per agric. employee (9)/(7) = (11)	M$	16.6	17.8	16.0	13.4	12.7	12.8	12.8	11.9	10.0
(11)/(10)	%	20.9	21.3	20.3	22.0	22.0	22.1	24.5	23.2	21.7
Agricultural labour productivity (2)/(7)	M$	64.9	67.0	67.9	66.5	67.5	68.3	68.1	68.0	63.8
Agricultural unit labour cost (9)/(2)	%	25.6	26.5	23.6	20.1	18.8	18.7	18.8	17.5	15.7
Private consumption (12)	M$ mn	2 918	3 110	3 082	2 951	3 030	3 131	3 054	3 062	3 101
Expenditure on food (13)	M$ mn	1 035	1 077	1 107	1 101	1 132	1 161	1 161	1 169	1 165
(13)/(12)	%	35.5	34.6	35.9	37.3	37.4	37.1	38.0	38.2	37.6

1. Based in 1980 pesos.
Source: INEGI; VI Informe de Gobierno, 1994; OECD Secretariat.

Table I.1. **Basic economic and agricultural indicators**[1] *(cont.)*

	Units	1989	1990	1991	1992	1993	1994	1995p
GDP (1)	M$ mn	5 049	5 277	5 469	5 620	5 659	5 858	5 452
Annual increase in GDP	%	3.4	4.5	3.6	2.8	0.7	3.5	(6.9)
Agricultural GDP (2)	M$ mn	388	414	419	413	423	432	416
Annual increase in agricultural GDP	%	(1.8)	6.8	1.1	(1.5)	2.6	2.0	(3.8)
Food processing GDP (3)	M$ mn	298	308	323	334	337	338	331
Annual increase in food processing GDP	%	7.7	3.1	5.1	3.4	0.8	0.4	(2.2)
(2)/(1) = (4)	%	7.7	7.8	7.7	7.3	7.5	7.4	7.6
(3)/(1) = (5)	%	5.9	5.8	5.9	5.9	5.9	5.8	6.1
(4) + (5)	%	13.6	13.7	13.6	13.3	13.4	13.1	13.7
Total employment (6)	mn	22.3	22.5	23.1	23.2	n.a.	n.a.	n.a.
Agricultural employment (7)	mn	6.0	5.7	6.0	5.9	n.a.	n.a.	n.a.
(7)/(6)	%	27.1	25.4	25.8	25.3	n.a.	n.a.	n.a.
Compensation of total employees (8)	M$ mn	1 098	1 138	1 207	1 306	1 370	n.a.	n.a.
Compensation of agric. employees (9)	M$ mn	59	53	51	49	49	n.a.	n.a.
Compensation per employee (8)/(6) = (10)	M$	49.1	50.5	52.2	56.2	n.a.	n.a.	n.a.
Compensation per agric. employee (9)/(7) = (11)	M$	9.7	9.3	8.6	8.4	n.a.	n.a.	n.a.
(11)/(10)	%	19.8	18.4	16.5	14.9	n.a.	n.a.	n.a.
Agricultural labour productivity (2)/(7)	M$	64.1	72.2	70.2	70.3	n.a.	n.a.	n.a.
Agricultural unit labour cost (9)/(2)	%	15.1	12.9	12.3	11.9	11.5	n.a.	n.a.
Private consumption (12)	M$ mn	3 303	3 489	3 652	3 790	3 789	n.a.	n.a.
Expenditure on food (13)	M$ mn	1 231	1 284	1 341	1 386	n.a.	n.a.	n.a.
(13)/(12)	%	37.3	36.8	36.7	36.6	n.a.	n.a.	n.a.

Note:
p: provisional.
n.a.:   not available.
1.   Based in 1980 pesos.
Source: INEGI; VI Informe de Gobierno, 1994; OECD Secretariat.

Table I.2. **Yields of major crops in Mexico (tonnes/hectare)**

Crop	1980	1985	1990	1991	1992	1993	1994	1995p
Maize	1.8	1.9	2.0	2.1	2.3	2.4	2.2	2.0
Beans	0.6	0.5	0.6	0.7	0.6	0.7	0.7	0.6
Wheat	3.8	4.3	4.2	4.1	4.0	4.1	4.3	3.9
Sorghum	3.0	3.5	3.3	3.1	3.9	2.9	3.0	2.8

p: provisional
Source: SAGAR.

Table I.3. **Distribution of private and ejido land in Mexican farm holdings in 1991**
(% share in total)

	Private	Ejido	Mixed[a]	Total
Farmland	62.6	34.0	3.4	100
Arable land	44.8	50.6	4.6	100
Irrigated land	44.8	50.2	5.0	100
Farmers	26.9	69.6	3.5	100

Note:
 a) Land in farm holdings with both private and ejido ownership.
Source: VII Agricultural-Livestock Census, 1991.

Table I.4. **Affiliates of CONASUPO (Mexican Basic Foods Company)**
in the marketing of agricultural commodities

Company	Activity	1996 status
MICONSA	manufacture of maize flour	privatised
TRICONSA	manufacture of wheat bread	liquidated
ICONSA	manufacture of staple foods	privatised
LICONSA	processing of milk	coordinated by SEDESOL
BORUCONSA	grain storage facilities	coordinated by SAGAR
IMPECSA[a]	wholesale distribution of staple food	coordinated by SAGAR
DICONSA	retailing of staple foods	coordinated by SEDESOL

Note:
 a) in process of liquidation.
Source: OECD Secretariat, 1997.

Table I.5. **Share in agro-food trade of Mexico with different regions, 1993-1994**
(in %)

	NAFTA			Other
	USA	Canada	Total	
Exports	88	1	89	11
Imports	70	6	76	24

Source: OECD Secretariat, 1997.

Table II.1. **Guaranteed prices for grains, beans, and oilseeds**

MS/Ton

Commodities	Crop season[a]	1979	1980	1981	1982	1983	1984	1985	1986	1987	1988	1989	1990	1991	1992	1993	1994	1995p
White maize	A.W.	3	4	7	9	16	26	44	75	160	320	370	600	680	715	750	650	715
	S.S.				10	19	33	53	96	245	370	435	636 [b]	715	750	750	600	815
Yellow maize	A.W.	[b]	[b]	[b]	[b]	[b]	[b]	[b]	[b]	[b]	[b]	[b]	[b]	565	595	595	540	595
	S.S.				[b]	[b]	[b]	[b]	[b]	[b]	[b]	[b]	530 [b]	565	625	625	500	680
Beans (preferred varieties)	A.W.	8	12	16	21	30	40	85	187	350	680	1 050	1 850	2 100	2 100	2 100	1 800	1 600
	S.S.				21	33	53	155	317	525	786	924	1 850		2 100	2 100	1 600	1 800
Beans (other varieties)	A.W.	[b]	[b]	[b]	[b]	[b]	[b]	[b]	[b]	[b]	[b]	[b]	1 650	1 860	1 860	1 860	1 595	1 415
	S.S.				[b]	[b]	[b]	[b]	[b]	[b]	[b]	[b]	1 650		1 860	1 860	1 415	1 700
Beans (highly preferred varieties)	A.W.																	1 800
	S.S.																	2 160
Wheat	A.W.	3	4	5	7	14	25	37	58	120	310	355	484	560	576	640	600	850
	S.S.				8	18	27	40	85			395					600	
Barley	A.W.	3	4	6	9	16	26	37	75	152	320	506	630	630	685	700		
	S.S.				9	19	37	53	112	225	440					700		
Sorghum	A.W.	2	3	4	5	11	19	29	50	117	225	320	360		460	400		
	S.S.				5	14	23	32	70	155	292	320	414			400		
Rice paddy	A.W.	4	5	7	9	18	34	54	98	98	379	445	550		685	550		
	S.S.				9	21										550		
Soyabeans	A.W.	6	8	11	15	27	56	88	165	238	860	986	850			940	856	
	S.S.				15	31										940		
Safflower	A.W.	5	6	8	11	23	35	63	113	408	500	680	700			850		
	S.S.				15	26	39											
Cottonseed	A.W.	4	5	7	9	17	20	48	81	225	430				460	475		
	S.S.				10	20	32			220						475		
Sesame	A.W.	9	12	16	21	38	75	150	277	700	1 250							
	S.S.				21	50	110											

Notes:
Data have been rounded. Prior to 1982, guaranteed prices were set only once a year. In 1989, guaranteed prices were replaced by concerted prices for wheat, barley, sorghum, rice and oilseeds; The concerted prices were abolished in 1995 (in the Spring/Summer 1995 crop season for wheat).
p: provisional.
a) A.W. = Autumn/Winter (sowing Oct.-Feb.: harvest Jan.-Feb.); S.S. = Spring/Summer (sowing Mar.-Sept.: harvest July-Mar.). Crop year 1995 = A.W. 1994/95 + S.S. 1995.
b) Administered prices were the same for white and yellow maize, or, in the case of beans, for all varieties of beans.
Source: SAGAR.

Table II.2. **Share of CONASUPO in the purchasing of domestic production (%)**

	Maize	Beans	Wheat	Sorghum	Milled rice	Soyabeans	Safflower	Cottonseed	Copra	Sesame
1970	13	4	43	7	0	0	0	0	7	0
1971	16	11	37	0	3	0	10	0	2	0
1972	16	16	35	0	3	0	37	0	0	0
1973	9	0	44	1	0	0	0	0	0	0
1974	10	2	26		2	17	0	0	0	0
1975	4	36	38	8	9	27	81	0	15	28
1976	12	33	44	12	34	0	2	0	18	22
1977	14	32	20	15	2	0	0	0	0	2
1978	17	18	43	14	20	0	0	0	0	0
1979	23	28	34	18	8	0	11	3	0	0
1980	7	14	42	7	8	0	1	1	0	14
1981	20	36	40	38	11	46	4	54	25	37
1982	32	50	55	24	20	28	0	45	12	7
1983	12	42	53	20	15	24	1	a	n.a.	0
1984	19	42	42	22	13	1	1	a	n.a.	0
1985	15	23	35	36	10	12	1	a	n.a.	5
1986	21	23	38	3	34	14	2	a	n.a.	1
1987	14	44	25	44	21	24	3	a	a	a
1988	16	31	30	16	38	2	a	a	a	a
1989	16	17	32	7	24	a	a	a	a	a
1990	16	10	9	32	17	a	a	a	a	a
1991	23	27	a	a	a	a	a	a	a	a
1992	30	40	a	a	a	a	a	a	a	a
1993	45	38	a	a	a	a	a	a	a	a
1994	45	25	a	a	a	a	a	a	a	a
1995p	26	11	a	a	a	a	a	a	a	a
Average[b]	*20*	*26*	*36*	*15*	*14*	*10*	*9*	*7*	*6*	*7*

Notes:
n.a.: not available.
p: provisional.
a) Years in which CONASUPO ceased purchasing domestic production.
b) Only the years in which CONASUPO purchased commodities have been included in the average.
Source: CONASUPO.

Table II.3. Marketing support provided by ASERCA

	Wheat [a]								Sorghum [a, b]				Rice [c]				Soyabeans [a, d]			
	Domestic production				Domestic consumption				Domestic production				Domestic production				Domestic production			
	Total	ASERCA payments [e]			Total	ASERCA payments [f]			Total	ASERCA payments			Total	ASERCA payments			Total	ASERCA payments [e]		
	mn tons	mn tons	MS mn	MS/ tons	mn tons	mn tons	MS mn	MS/ tons	mn tons	mn tons	MS mn	MS/ tons [e]	mn tons	mn tons	MS mn	MS/ tons	mn tons	mn tons	MS mn	MS/ tons
1991	3.6	3.1	546	175	4.7	4.3	392	91	4.3	0.4	19	47	0.4	0.3	18	60	0.7	0.7	71	107
1992	3.6	2.8	226	81	5.3	4.1	786	193	5.4	1.7	118	69	0.4	0.4	38	80	0.6	0.6	99	170
1993	4.2	2.1	453	217	5.3	3.1	497	161	2.6	1.0	101	104	0.3	0.4	46	120	0.5	0.5	66	138
1994	3.4	1.4	125	91	4.8	0	0	0	3.7	0.9	26	28	0.4	0.4	26	74	0.5	0.5	53	118
1995p									2.9	0	0	0	0.4	0.3	23	74	0.2	0	0	0

Notes:

p: provisional.

a) Payments provided to millers. In 1995, payments were provided for the Autumn/Winter crop season only.

b) ASERCA payments were provided only for the production of sorghum in Tamaulipas State.

c) Payments provided directly to producers.

d) In 1993-95, payments were also granted for other oilseeds, mainly safflower (not included in this Table).

e) Payments based on the volume of purchases of domestic production by millers.

f) Payments based on the volume of sales by millers.

In the 1991-95 period, ASERCA also provided marketing support to feed wheat producers and input subsidies to cotton producers (for seeds in 1992, for pesticides in 1993-95) (not included in this Table).

Source: ASERCA (SHCP in 1995).

Table II.4. **The Programme to Support Marketing in Ejidos (PACE)**

	Number of beneficiaries ('000)			Volume benefiting ('000 tonnes)			CONASUPO purchases[a] ('000 tonnes)			(1)/(2) (%)	PACE payments				
											(M$ mn)			(M$/tonne)	
	Maize	Beans	Total	Maize	Beans	(1) Total	Maize	Beans	(2) Total		Maize	Beans	Total	Maize	Beans
1980			12	198		198	863	132	995	20	0.0	0.0	0		0.1
1981			41	807	139	946	2 914	526	3 440	28	0.1	0.0	0	0.1	0.2
1982			96	1 725	324	2 049	3 272	547	3 819	54	0.3	0.0	0	0.2	0.3
1983	21	11	32	425	116	541	1 607	530	2 137	25	0.1	0.0	0	0.2	0.3
1984	43	9	52	1 191	123	1 314	2 493	392	2 885	46	0.4	0.1	0	0.4	0.5
1985	46	5	51	6 110	371	6 481	2 121	144	2 265	n.a.	0.6	0.1	1	0.1	0.1
1986	53	5	58	1 071	32	1 103	2 437	259	2 696	41	1.1	0.0	1	1.0	1.5
1987	42	8	49	753	59	812	1 679	465	2 144	38	1.7	0.1	2	2.3	2.4
1988	35	3	38	676	23	699	1 742	261	2 003	35	2.3	0.1	2	3.3	3.5
1989	39	4	44	757	31	788	1 753	103	1 856	42	5.4	0.3	6	7.2	9.5
1990	72	5	77	1 225	44	1 269	2 321	124	2 445	52	44.0	4.0	48	35.9	90.7
1991	78	22	101	1 756	137	1 893	3 255	367	3 622	52	87.5	13.6	101	49.8	99.2
1992	98	28	126	1 681	177	1 858	4 628	295	4 923	38	88.9	16.8	106	52.9	94.7
1993	145	24	170	2 910	172	3 082	8 115	393	8 508	36	153.7	16.1	170	52.8	93.4
1994	142	30	172	2 845	206	3 051	8 130	336	8 466	36	152.8	19.2	172	53.7	93.3
1995p	126	23	149	2 695	173	2 868	4 013	136	4 149	69	146.0	15.9	162	54.2	91.9
Average[b]										42					

Notes:
p: provisional.
n.a.:   not available.
a)   Total domestic production purchased by CONASUPO.
b)   Simple average 1980-95 excluding the year 1985.
Source: CONASUPO.

Table II.5. **Share of CONASUPO in total imports of grains, beans, and oilseeds**

% of total imports

	Maize	Beans	Wheat	Barley	Sorghum	Rice	Soyabeans
1979	100	88	100	n.a.	n.a.	56	n.a.
1980	76	66	85	[a]	63	100	13
1981	84	81	100	0	82	63	46
1982	90	91	100	[a]	78	46	100
1983	89	[a]	0	98	100	[a]	100
1984	99	0	0	94	98	99	100
1985	73	81	0	100	67	99	21
1986	71	93	0	[a]	50	[a]	3
1987	83	100	58	[a]	76	0	2
1988	80	100	100	n.a.	n.a.	[a]	n.a.
1989	57	100	100	n.a.	n.a.	90	n.a.
1990	47	100	58	n.a.	n.a.	33	[a]
1991	[a]	100	[a]	[a]	[a]	[a]	[a]
1992	[a]	[a]	[a]	[a]	[a]	[a]	[a]
1993	[a]	[a]	[a]	[a]	[a]	[a]	[a]
1994	[a]	[a]	[a]	[a]	[a]	[a]	[a]
1995p	[a]	[a]	[a]	[a]	[a]	[a]	[a]
Average[b]	79	83	58	73	77	65	48

Notes:
p: provisional.
n.a.: not available.
a) No imports.
b) Average calculated for the years in which CONASUPO imported.
Source: CONASUPO.

Table II.6. **Annual sales of maize by CONASUPO**

%

	Nixtamal factories	Flour companies[d]	DICONSA shops	Feed sector	Starch factories	Others[a]	Exports	Total
1989	55	14	14	[b]	[b]	17	0	100
1990	56	17	11	[b]	[b]	16	0	100
1991	34	20	17	18	8	2	1	100
1992	37	21	15	15	11	1	0	100
1993	22	11	6	48	12	0	1	100
1994	23	10	8	55	3	0	1	100
1995p	38	18	14	30[c]	0	0	0	100

Notes:
n.a.: not available.
p: provisional.
a) Selling to public organisations, State governments or directly to consumers.
b) Years in which CONASUPO did not sell maize to the feed sector and the starch factories.
c) CONASUPO sales to the feed sector ceased at the end of 1995.
d) Since 1985, flour companies buy maize directly from producers and receive payments from CONASUPO to lower selling prices to tortilla factories.
Source: CONASUPO.

Table II.7. **Purchasing and selling prices of maize by CONASUPO**

M$/Tonne

	Average purchasing prices[a]		Average selling prices							Consumer prices[d]			
			Nixtamal factories		Flour factories[b]	DICONSA shops[c]		Feed factories	Starch factories	Flour		Tortillas	
	White	Yellow	Mexico City	Other		White	Yellow			Mexico City	Other	Mexico City	Other
1985	43			16	n.a.	n.a.	n.a.	e	e	34	69	32	
1986	71		31	78	n.a.	n.a.	n.a.	e	e	69	117	77	127
1987	163		90	143	168	131		e	e	165	256	171	231
1988	308		140	241	293	236		e	e	252	413	275	375
1989	386		120	241	393	335		e	e	252	413	275	375
1990	527	475	258	380	636	520	450	e	e	642	731	563	787
1991	670	558	460	380	745	576	487	384	403	850	1 175	750	1 050
1992	724	603	442	632	760	622	530	378	392	735	963	750	1 050
1993	750	625	359	567	783	640	560	393	406	677	867	750	1 006
1994	671	558	289	520	n.a.	n.a.	n.a.	221	462	634	800	750	1 006
1995 A.W.p	771	582	265	440	n.a.	n.a.	n.a.	593	0	611	835	958	1 234
1995 S.S.p	1 234		350	550	n.a.	n.a.	n.a.	[f]	0	705	934	1 100	1 400

Notes:

n.a.: not available.

p: provisional.

a) Since the Spring/Summer 1990 crop season, purchasing prices differ between white and yellow maize (see Table II.1).

b) Since 1985, flour companies buy maize directly from producers and receive payments from CONASUPO to lower selling prices to tortilla factories.

c) Average purchasing price of the domestic production for the year: Spring/Summer 1994 + Autumn/Winter 1994/95 (*año oferta*).

d) Retail price ceilings set by the Government.

e) Years in which CONASUPO did not sell maize to the feed sector and the starch factories.

f) CONASUPO sales to the feed sector ceased at the end of 1995.

Source: CONASUPO.

Table II.8. **Targeted consumer subsidy programmes**

	Social supply of milk programme					Subsidised tortilla consumption programme[a]			
	Milk produced by LICONSA (bn litre)	Milk distributed per day (mn litre)	Number of children beneficiaries (mn)	Value of the subsidy (M$ mn)	Unit value of the subsidy (M$/child)	Tortillas distributed per day ('000 tonnes)	Number of families beneficiaries (mn)	Value of the subsidy (M$ mn)	Unit value of the subsidy (M$/family)
1980	0.6	1	0.4	2	5				
1981	0.8	1	0.5	3	5				
1982	0.8	1.6	0.6	6	10				
1983	1	1.7	0.7	11	15				
1984	1.1	1.9	0.8	22	27	n.a.	n.a.	n.a.	
1985	1.3	2.2	1	39	39	n.a.	n.a.	n.a.	
1986	1.4	2.5	1.2	76	63	0.3	0.1	8	81
1987	1.5	3.1	1.5	205	137	1.6	0.8	96	120
1988	1	3.3	3.8	478	126	2	1	214	214
1989	1.1	3.4	4.1	917	224	2.1	1	257	257
1990	1.1	3.5	4.8	861	179	1.6	0.8	261	326
1991	1.2	4	6.3	1 290	205	1.5	2	468	234
1992	1.2	4.1	6.7	1 452	217	1.7	2.1	517	246
1993	1.2	3.8	6.8	1 364	201	1.2	2.1	368	175
1994	1	3.4	4.9	1 254	256	1.4	2.1	403	192
1995p	1	3.4	5.6	1 725	308	1.6	2.8	468	167

Notes:
p: provisional.
n.a.: not available.
a) The Subsidised Tortilla Consumption Programme started to operate in 1984.
Source: Statistical Annex of President Zedillo's 1st report.

Table II.9. **Annual sales of beans by CONASUPO**

%

	DICONSA retail shops	LICONSA social programme	IMPECSA wholesale distribution	Traders	Private sector packers	Others	Social sector (DIF and other programmes)	Exports	Total
1989	40	3	9	13	22	5	8	0	100
1990	47	8	15	10	8	2	10	0	100
1991	21	3	7	30	21	0	18	0	100
1992	18	1	1	30	25	0	17	8	100
1993	12	1	0	44	21	9	8	5	100
1994	12	0	0	30	18	13	5	22	100

Source: CONASUPO.

Table II.10. **Feed consumption in Mexican agriculture**

%

	Sorghum		Maize				Wheat domestic production	Barley imports	Soya oil cake	Total
	Domestic production	Imports	Self/on-farm consumption	Sold by CONASUPO	Imports					
					Grade 3	Crushed				
1987	51	16	13						20	100
1988	55	15	10						20	100
1989	45	25	10						20	100
1990	44	22	12			a	2		20	100
1991	40	23	7	4	4	a	2	a	20	100
1992	33	31	4	4	4	2	2	a	20	100
1993	24	22	5	21		2	6		20	100

a) Only a small amount was consumed for feed.
Source: CONASUPO.

Table II.11. **Mexican import regime for major fruits and vegetables**

Commodity	1992[a] Import permit	1992[a] Tariff (AVE)	NAFTA Quota USA	NAFTA Quota Canada	NAFTA Tariff (%)	NAFTA Base US$/ton	NAFTA Base (AVE)	Rule of origin	UR Quota USA	UR Quota Canada	UR Quota Others	UR Tariff (%)	UR Base US$/ton	UR Base (AVE)	Applied rates in 1995 (AVE)	SS
Potatoes	x	0	15	4	0	354	272(C)	–	7		1	50	354	272(i)	251	x
Tomatoes	–	10				33	10(AB*//A)	–						50(ii)	10	–
Onions	–	10				39	10(C/B)	–						50(ii)	10	–
Cucumbers	–	10					10(ABC*//A)	–						50(ii)	10	–
Eggplants	–	10					10(A)	–						50(ii)	10	–
Chillies	–	10					10(B/A)	–						50(ii)	10	–
Bananas	–	20					20(A)	–						50(ii)	20	–
Avocados	–	20				132	20(C//A)	–						50(ii)	20	–
Mangos	–	20					20(A)	–						50(ii)	20	–
Oranges	–	20				22	20(AB*//A)	–						50(ii)	20	–
Limes	–	20					20(A)	–						50(ii)	20	–
Grapes	x	0					20(AC*)	–						50(i)	45	x
Watermelons	–	20					20(AC*)	–						50(ii)	20	–
Apples	–	20	55	1	20(C)		20(C)**	–						50(i)	20	x
Pears	–	20					15(B)	–						50(i)	20	–
Peaches	–	20					20(C)	–						50(i)	20	x
Strawberries	–	20					20(A)	–						50(i)	20	–

Notes:

(AVE) = *Ad Valorem* Equivalent. (SS) = Special Safeguard.

a) Trade regime applied by Mexico to imports from the United States in 1992.

b) All tariffs and tariff quotas will be gradually removed according to the following schedules:
(A) immediate;   (B) by 1998;   (C) by 2003.
The quotas will be increased each year by 3 per cent compared to previous year level.

c) From 1995 to 2004, the base tariffs will decrease by (i) 10 per cent; (ii) 28 per cent.

A different tariff reduction schedule applies to different seasons.

(*) Under a special safeguard provision, the 20 per cent tariff may be re-imposed on imports above the quota until 2003.

(//) Different tariff reduction schedules apply to the United States (left to //) and Canada (right to //).

Source: NAFTA and GATT schedules.

Table II.12.   **Food assistance to farmers affected by climatic hazard**

	Number of families assisted ('000) (1)	Value of food assistance (M$ mn) (2)	Value of food aid per family (M$ '000) (2)/(1)
1988	90	1.8	20
1989	148	4.6	31
1990	195	6.7	34
1991	166	9.4	57
1992	203	13.2	65
1993	170	8.7	51
1994	256	12.7	50
1995p	359	23.6	66

Note:
p: provisional.
Source: CONASUPO.

Table II.13. **Mexican import regime for major agricultural and agro-food commodities**

Commodity	1992[a] Import permit	1992[a] Tariff (AVE)	NAFTA schedule (1994-2008)[b] Quota ('000 tons) USA	NAFTA Quota ('000 tons) Canada	NAFTA Tariff (%)	NAFTA Base tariff[c] US$/ton	NAFTA Base tariff[c] (AVE)	UR Quota[d] ('000 tons) USA	UR Quota Canada	UR Quota Others	UR Tariff (%)	UR Base tariff[c] $US/ton	UR Base tariff[c] (AVE)	Applied rates in 1995 (AVE)	SS
Maize	x	0	2 500	1	0	206	215 (C+)	2 500	1	10[e]	50	206	215[g]	198	x
Beans	x	0	50	1.5	0	480	139 (C+)	50	1.5	5	50	401	139[g]	128	x
Common wheat	x	0					15 (C)	334	172.6	98	50	100	74[g]	67	x
Durum wheat	x	10					15 (C)						50[g]	15	x
Wheat flour	–	15			0	155	128 (C)					160	128[g]	118	x
Barley	x	5	120	30		212	175 (C)	1.2	2.3	1.2	50	212	175[g]	161	x
Malt	x	10					15/0 (A/D)						50[g]	15/0	x
Sorghum	–	15/0[f]					10 (C)						10[g]	10	x
Oats	–	10					10 (C)						50[g]	10	x
Rice-paddy	–	10					20 (C)						50[g]	20	x
Rice milled	–	20					10/0 (C/D)						50[g]	10/0	–
Soyabeans	–	10/0[f]					10 (C)						50[g]	10	
Soya oil	–	10	35	1	0	930	282 (C)	37.5	–	2.1	50	930	282[g]	260	x
Animal fats	x	20					10 (C)						50[g]	10	–
Cotton fibre	–	20					50 (C)						80[g]	50	x
Tobacco							20 (C)						72[g]	72	x
Coffee beans	x	20											156[g]	141	x
Coffee extract	x	20	0.2	0.03	20 (C)		20 (C)[j]		12 > 20.8		50	360	50[h]	1	x
Sugarcane[j]	–	1	variable	–	0		20 (C)[j]							1	
Refined sugar[j]	–	1				VIL	VIL (C+)						173[g]	128	x
Milk powder[j]	x	0	40	–	0	1 160	139 (C+)	40	110 > 183.8	80	50	400	139[g]	20	x
Butter[j]	–	20					20 (C)				0	1 160	50[h]	125	x
Cheese	x	20					20 (C)	7	–	2.4	50	1 160	139[g]	15	–
Live cattle	–	0					15 (A)						50[h]	25	
Beef and veal	–	0					25 (A)						50[g]	20	
Pigmeat	–	20	63.4	6	0	1 680	260 (C)	20 (C)[j]	–	1	50	1 680	260[g]	240	x
Poultrymeat[j]	x	10	95		0		50 (C)	39.5					50[h]	50	x
Eggs[j]	–	10	6.5		0		10 (C)						25[g]	10	x
Sheepmeat[j]	–	10					10 (C)						50[h]		x
Sheep wool	–	10													–

Notes:
(AVE) = *Ad Valorem* Equivalent. (SS) = Special Safeguard. (VIL) = Variable Import Levy.
a) Trade regime applied by Mexico on imports from the United States.
b) All tariffs and tariff quotas will be gradually removed according to the following schedules:
(A) immediate; (B) by 1998; (C) by 2003; (C+) by 2008; (D) duty-free imports already prevailed before 1994.
The quotas will be increased each year by 3 per cent (5 per cent for barley and, in the case of Canada, for pigmeat) compared to previous year level.
c) Base level for tariff reduction schedules (e.g. for a base tariff of 15 per cent under schedule C, the tariffs applied were 13.5 per cent in 1994 and 12 per cent in 1995).
d) The quotas will remain unchanged over the period 1995-2004, except for coffee and sugar.
e) To apply from year 2000.
f) Seasonal tariff: duty-free from mid-December to mid-May for sorghum; duty-free from beginning-February to end-July for soyabeans.
g) From 1995 to 2004, the base tariffs will decrease by 10 per cent.
h) From 1995 to 2004, the base tariffs will decrease by 25 per cent.
i) Under a special safeguard provision, the 20 per cent tariff may be re-imposed on imports above the quota up to 2003.
j) These products were not included in NAFTA for the trade between Mexico and Canada.
Source: NAFTA and GATT (Mexican Uruguay Round schedule).

Table II.14. **Export subsidy commitments under the Uruguay Round Agreement**

	Volume ('000 tonnes)			Value (US$ mn)		
	Average base level	Commitments		Average base level	Commitments	
	1990-91	1995	2004	1990-91	1995	2004
Maize	3 055.3	3 000	2 520	139.3	135.5	102.9
Beans	172.3	169.2	142.1	8.2	8	6.1
Wheat	402.6	395.3	332.1	12.2	11.8	9
Sorghum	522.5	513.1	431	18	17.5	13.3
Sugar	1 527.7	1 500	1 260	570.6	555	421.8

Source: Mexican Uruguay Round Schedule, GATT.

Table II.15a. **Interest rates applied to agricultural producers by BANRURAL and FIRA (%)**

	1993	1994	1995
CETES	14.93	14.02	32.57[a]
FIRA			
Working capital loans	CETES + 3 to 8	CETES + 3 to 8	CETES[b] or CETES + 2[c]
Investment loans	CETES + 2 to 6	CETES + 2 to 6	CETES[b] or CETES + 4[c]
BANRURAL			
Working capital loans	14.95[d]	13.06[d]	CETES[b] or more than CETES +30%[c]
Investment loans	14.6[d]	12.8[d]	CETES[b] or CETES +30%[c]

Notes:
CETES: treasury bills (*Certificado de Tesorería*), interest rate for 28 days.
a)   Rate as of February 1995.
b)   Until M$150 000 (US$23 360) and less than 1 000 times the minimum wage for the area.
c)   More than M$150 000 (US$23 360) and more than 1 000 times the minimum wage for the area.
d)   For primary industry and low-income producers.
Source: BANXICO, FIRA, and BANRURAL.

Table II.15b. **Agricultural lending and interest concessions**

US$ million

| | BANRURAL | | FIRA[b] | | | | FICART | FINA | FIDAZUCAR | FIMAIA | Total | Xrate |
| | Total lending[a] | Interest concessions | Total lending[a] | Interest concessions | | | Interest concessions | Interest concessions | Interest concessions | Interest concessions | Interest concessions | M$/$US |
				Total	% FONDO	% FEFA						
1980	2 502	n.a.	1 590	n.a.	n.a.	n.a.	n.a.	n.a.	n.a.	n.a.	n.a.	0.0229
1981	3 347	n.a.	1 869	n.a.	n.a.	n.a.	n.a.	n.a.	n.a.	n.a.	n.a.	0.0245
1982	1 986	1 667	1 366	284	27	73	116	190	31	1	2 289	0.0517
1983	1 056	474	786	201	32	68	45	138	18	6	882	0.1547
1984	1 583	890	1 164	141	1	99	82	138	9	14	1 275	0.1918
1985	1 317	279	1 219	330	41	59	0	98	10	11	728	0.3270
1986	1 235	310	835	257	31	69	0	22	0	7	597	0.6392
1987	1 733	258	848	200	34	66	0	9	0	5	472	1.4175
1988	1 576	309	1 179	27	38	62	0	14	0	2	352	2.2808
1989	1 135	164	1 473	192	35	65	0	8	0	1	365	2.4949
1990	971	136	1 950	110	29	71	0	1	0	1	248	2.8407
1991	1 290	134	2 678	58	25	75	0	0	0	1	193	3.0224
1992	1 700	147	3 286	121	27	73	0	0	0	2	271	3.0950
1993	1 521	173	4 007[c]	63	29	71	0	5	0	0	241	3.1151
1994	788	220	3 637[c]	140	14	86	0	10	5	0	375	3.3886
1995	n.a.	n.a.	2 229	n.a.	n.a.	n.a.	n.a.	n.a.	n.a.	n.a.	n.a.	6.4213

Notes:

From 1980 to 1987, data for BANRURAL and FIRA total lending were obtained from the Statistical Annex of President Salinas' Sixth Report.

n.a.: not available.

See list of acronyms for full title of Secretariats/agencies.

a) Including working capital (*crédito de avío*) and investment loans (*crédito refaccionario*).

b) Including FONDO (Trust Fund for Agriculture, Livestock and Poultry Development), and FEFA (Special Agricultural Trust Fund), but excluding FEGA (Technical Assistance and Loan Guarantee Trust Fund) and FOPESCA (Trust Fund for Fishery Development).

c) Excluding funds allocated to the System for the Restructuring of Agricultural Overdue Portfolio (SIRECA).

Source: SHCP.

Table II.16. **States and regions declared free of pest and disease by the Mexican authorities**

Situation in April 1996

State[a]	Salmonella (eggs)	Newcastle disease (poultry, eggs)	Aviar grippe	Aujesky disease	Classic fever (pig)	Fly (fruits)	Smut pest (wheat)
Aguascalientes							
Baja california	x	x		x	x		Mexicali
Baja California Sur	x	x		x	x	3M	
Campeche			x				
Chiapas							
Chihuahua	x	x	x	x	x	x	21M
Coahuila	CL	CL	CL		x		
Colima							
Durango	x	x	x				
Guanajuato							39M
Guerrero							
Hidalgo							
Jalisco							6M
Mexico							8M
Michoacan							35M
Morelos							
Nayarit							
Nuevo Leon	x	x			x		Anahuac
Oaxaca							
Puebla							5M
Queretaro							
Quintana Roo			x		x		
San Luis Potosi							
Sinaloa	x	x	x		x		
Sonora	x	x	x		x	67M	SLRC
Tabasco							
Tamaulipas					x		
Tlaxcala							
Veracruz							
Yucatan	x	x	x		x		
Zacatecas							

Note:
CL = Comarca Lagunera; M = Municipalities; SLRC = San Luis Rio Colorado.
a) Excluding Mexico City.
Source: SAGAR.

Table II.17a. **Total budgetary expenditures associated with agricultural policies**

M$ million

	1979	1980	1981	1982	1983	1984	1985	1986	1987	1988	Source
Price and income support	**5**	**9**	**14**	**29**	**47**	**113**	**152**	**368**	**336**	**574**	
a) Market price support	5	9	14	29	47	113	152	368	336	573	
CONASUPO (stockholding)	4	9	14	24	38	105	141	356	312	532	SHCP × 0.3
AZUCAR S.A.	0	0	0	0	0	0	0	0	0	0	SHCP
INMECAFE	1	0	0	5	9	8	10	11	22	38	SHCP
TABAMEX	0	0	0	0	0	0	0	0	0	0	SHCP
CONADECA	0	0	0	0	0	0	0	0	0	0	SHCP
PACE	0	0	0	0	0	1	1	1	2	2	CONASUPO
b) Direct payments	0	0	0	0	0	0	0	0	0	2	
PROCAMPO	0	0	0	0	0	0	0	0	0	0	SHCP
ASERCA	0	0	0	0	0	0	0	0	0	0	ASERCA (SHCP 95)
Disaster payments	0	0	0	0	0	0	0	0	0	2	CONASUPO (SHCP 95)
Reduction of input costs	**33**	**57**	**98**	**143**	**282**	**373**	**603**	**909**	**2 560**	**4 093**	
a) Interest concessions	24	36	58	80	150	139	248	364	1 190	2 025	
FONDO	0	0	0	0	4	0	0	0	0	0	SHCP
FEFA	1	4	1	1	10	0	0	0	0	0	SHCP
BANRURAL	16	22	40	51	105	125	181	339	1 144	1971	SHCP
FICART	2	0	2	5	6	7	8	7	10	19	SHCP
FINA	0	0	0	10	15	0	0	0	0	0	SHCP
FIDAZUCAR	5	9	13	8	4	1	52	11	10	13	SHCP
FIMAIA	0	0	1	2	1	1	1	1	3	5	SHCP
FIRCO	0	0	0	4	5	4	6	7	23	16	SHCP × 0.5
PRONASOL	0	0	0	0	0	0	0	0	0	0	SHCP (SEDESOL 90-91)
b) Fertilisers (FERTIMEX/ASERCA in 95)	2	3	9	23	73	79	121	236	505	872	SHCP
c) Insurance (ANAGSA/AGROASEMEX)	1	4	6	11	25	36	52	98	114	256	SHCP
d) Water	3	8	11	13	12	63	78	162	400	628	
Electric pumping (CFE)	0	0	0	0	0	33	48	123	302	537	SHCP
Irrigation operation and maintenance	3	8	11	13	12	29	29	38	98	91	SHCP partim
e) Feed	3	4	13	12	20	55	90	32	334	282	
CONASUPO	2	3	11	10	19	54	89	30	306	281	SHCP × 0.7 partim
ALBAMEX	1	1	2	2	1	1	1	2	28	1	SHCP
f) Seed (PRONASE/ASERCA)	0	2	2	3	2	2	2	4	4	12	SHCP (ASERCA 92)
g) Pesticides (cotton)	0	0	0	0	0	0	0	0	0	0	ASERCA (SHCP 95)
h) Machinery (SESA)	0	0	0	0	0	0	12	13	12	18	SHCP
i) Livestock breeding (FOGAN)	0	0	0	1	0	0	1	1	1	2	SHCP
General services	**19**	**48**	**67**	**90**	**92**	**178**	**266**	**352**	**583**	**882**	
a) Research/training/extension	1	2	4	8	11	19	28	44	111	176	
INIFAP	0	2	3	3	4	9	16	31	66	107	SHCP
IMTA	0	0	0	0	0	0	0	0	10	18	SHCP
FIRCO	0	0	0	4	5	4	6	7	23	16	SHCP × 0.5
FEGA	0	0	1	1	2	4	5	6	9	29	SHCP
INCA RURAL	0	0	0	0	0	1	1	1	3	7	SHCP
b) Pest and disease control	2	3	3	4	6	10	10	11	15	20	
Plant health	1	2	2	3	3	7	7	8	8	9	SHCP (SAGAR 89-95)
Animal health	1	1	1	2	2	3	3	4	7	11	SHCP (SAGAR 89-95)
c) Structures/Infrastructures	16	41	56	74	74	146	221	287	431	648	
Irrigated areas	6	16	22	29	26	57	96	145	218	352	SHCP partim
Rainfed areas	3	8	12	14	13	28	40	52	72	35	SHCP
Protection of river beds	1	3	2	4	5	5	12	25	58	128	SHCP
Crop production (excl. irrigation)	4	9	13	15	15	25	30	40	45	50	SHCP
Livestock production	0	2	1	2	3	7	8	12	26	30	SHCP
Roads	1	3	6	11	12	24	36	14	12	52	SHCP
d) Marketing and promotion	0	2	3	4	2	4	7	10	26	39	
ASERCA	0	0	0	0	0	0	0	0	0	0	SAGAR (SHCP 94-95)
CONAFRUT	0	1	2	2	2	3	4	7	16	30	SHCP
FOCIR	0	0	0	0	0	0	0	0	0	0	SHCP
Other	0	1	1	2	0	1	3	3	10	9	SHCP
Consumer subsidies	**7**	**20**	**25**	**53**	**81**	**214**	**280**	**884**	**722**	**1 654**	
LICONSA (milk)	0	2	3	6	11	22	39	76	205	478	I.P.95 p.123
CONASUPO/FIDELIST (maize tortilla)	0	0	0	0	0	0	0	8	96	214	I.P.95 p.123
ASERCA (wheat)	0	0	0	0	0	0	0	0	0	0	ASERCA (SHCP 95)
CONASUPO (grains, beans, oilseeds)	7	18	22	47	70	192	241	800	421	961	SHCP × 0.7 partim

Table II.17a. **Total budgetary expenditures associated with agricultural policies** *(cont.)*

M$ million

	1979	1980	1981	1982	1983	1984	1985	1986	1987	1988	Source
Formal education	**1**	**3**	**7**	**10**	**15**	**22**	**43**	**90**	**182**	**386**	
Agricultural Univ. A. Narro	0	0	0	1	1	2	3	5	16	36	SHCP
Chapingo Autonomous University	0	1	2	3	3	6	9	15	42	96	SHCP
Post-graduate College	0	1	1	2	2	3	4	7	17	37	SHCP
Agricultural technical institutes	0	0	1	1	1	2	3	5	13	26	I.P.94 p.372
Vocational agricultural schools	1	1	2	4	6	9	22	56	92	182	I.P.94 p.371
Other	0	0	0	0	1	1	2	2	3	9	SHCP
Rural development	**2**	**9**	**10**	**6**	**7**	**9**	**20**	**10**	**15**	**24**	
CONAZA	0	1	1	1	1	1	2	2	5	12	SHCP
PRONASOL (FONAES)											SEDESOL
	0	0	0	0	0	0	0	0	0	0	(unpubl.in 94-95)
PRONASOL (Indigenous communities)	0	0	0	0	0	0	0	0	0	0	SHCP
Other	2	8	9	5	6	8	18	8	10	12	SHCP
Sub-national measures (PRONASOL)	**0**	**0**	**0**	**0**	**0**	**0**	**0**	**0**	**0**	**0**	SEDESOL
Agricultural expenditures (1)	**67**	**146**	**220**	**332**	**523**	**909**	**1 364**	**2 613**	**4 398**	**7 612**	
Federal government expenditure (2)	**n.a.**	**818**	**1 335**	**2 703**	**4 639**	**7 105**	**11 573**	**23 012**	**60 440**	**105 857**	OECD[a]
% (1)/(2)	**n.a.**	**18**	**17**	**12**	**11**	**13**	**12**	**11**	**7**	**7**	

Table II.17a. **Total budgetary expenditures associated with agricultural policies** *(cont.)*

M$ million

	1989	1990	1991	1992	1993	1994	1995p	Source
Price and income support	**1 686**	**2 616**	**1 182**	**2 318**	**2 603**	**7 387**	**7 736**	
a) Market price support	1 681	2 610	1 065	1 259	1 920	1 727	1 623	
CONASUPO (stockholding)	833	2 351	904	1 070	1 656	1 553	1 461	SHCP × 0.3
AZUCAR S.A.	557	140	0	0	0	0	0	SHCP
INMECAFE	280	70	53	83	95	2	0	SHCP
TABAMEX	0	0	6	0	0	0	0	SHCP
CONADECA	5	0	0	0	0	0	0	SHCP
PACE	6	48	101	106	170	172	162	CONASUPO
b) Direct payments	5	7	118	1 059	682	5 660	6 113	
PROCAMPO	0	0	0	0	0	4 850	5 864	SHCP
ASERCA	0	0	109	1 046	674	798	172	ASERCA (SHCP 95)
Disaster payments	5	7	9	13	9	13	77	CONASUPO (SHCP 95)
Reduction of input costs	**5 017**	**7 252**	**4 333**	**3 972**	**5 182**	**5 235**	**4 595**	
a) Interest concessions	2 048	1 482	1 817	2 167	2 616	1 817	1 590	
FONDO	0	5	30	31	19	35	14	SHCP
FEFA	2	19	126	119	74	91	281	SHCP
BANRURAL	1 856	797	888	1 310	724	904	715	SHCP
FICART	22	23	39	41	39	0	0	SHCP
FINA	68	33	0	0	962	0	0	SHCP
FIDAZUCAR	55	60	168	20	77	0	0	SHCP
FIMAIA	9	19	18	0	0	0	0	SHCP
FIRCO	37	132	170	200	160	138	88	SHCP × 0.5
PRONASOL	0	395	379	446	561	650	491	SHCP (SEDESOL 90-91)
b) Fertilisers (FERTIMEX/ASERCA in 95)	592	745	889	475	0	0	68	SHCP
c) Insurance (ANAGSA/AGROASEMEX)	1 243	1 644	2	74	88	219	196	SHCP
d) Water	911	1 179	1 145	926	752	1 274	1 370	
Electric pumping (CFE)	759	925	807	610	570	1 055	1 140	SHCP
Irrigation operation and maintenance	152	254	338	316	182	219	230	SHCP partim
e) Feed	191	2 174	355	317	1 686	1 803	1 246	
CONASUPO	191	2 163	350	317	1 686	1 803	1 246	SHCP × 0.7 partim
ALBAMEX	0	11	5	0	0	0	0	SHCP
f) Seed (PRONASE/ASERCA)	14	8	109	6	0	0	0	SHCP (ASERCA 92)
g) Pesticides (cotton)	0	0	0	0	40	121	125	ASERCA (SHCP 95)
h) Machinery (SESA)	17	16	6	0	0	0	0	SHCP
i) Livestock breeding (FOGAN)	2	4	11	9	0	0	0	SHCP
General services	**1 351**	**2 220**	**2 197**	**3 104**	**2 938**	**4 176**	**3 198**	
a) Research/training/extension	255	477	579	747	800	935	943	
INIFAP	141	166	212	246	297	302	310	SHCP
IMTA	36	38	61	102	97	123	85	SHCP
FIRCO	37	132	170	200	160	138	88	SHCP × 0.5
FEGA	33	124	109	166	237	364	449	SHCP
INCA RURAL	9	18	27	32	9	9	11	SHCP
b) Pest and disease control	28	35	49	120	109	101	79	
Plant health	11	13	16	78	62	25	33	SHCP (SAGAR 89-95)
Animal health	17	22	33	42	48	76	46	SHCP (SAGAR 89-95)
c) Structures/Infrastructures	1 036	1 689	1 383	1 934	1 550	2 967	1992	
Irrigated areas	426	717	931	1 268	1 033	1 208	1 301	SHCP partim
Rainfed areas	46	94	117	137	97	119	88	SHCP
Protection of river beds	95	82	35	78	84	164	107	SHCP
Crop production (excl. irrigation)	76	47	211	205	152	183	89	SHCP
Livestock production	41	68	48	59	23	65	0	SHCP
Roads	352	680	40	188	162	1 227	407	SHCP
d) Marketing and promotion	33	19	187	302	478	173	185	
ASERCA	0	0	186	301	278	173	145	SAGAR (SHCP 94-95)
CONAFRUT	32	14	0	1	0	0	0	SHCP
FOCIR	0	0	0	0	200	0	40	SHCP
Other	1	5	1	0	0	0	0	SHCP
Consumer subsidies	**2 926**	**4 444**	**3 910**	**4 932**	**4 407**	**3 974**	**4 356**	
LICONSA (milk)	917	861	1 290	1 452	1 364	1 254	1 725	I.P.95 p.123
CONASUPO/FIDELIST (maize tortilla)	257	261	468	517	368	403	468	I.P.95 p.123
ASERCA (wheat)	0	0	0	392	786	497	0	ASERCA (SHCP 95)
CONASUPO (grains, beans, oilseeds)	1 752	3 322	1 760	2 178	2 178	1 820	2 163	SHCP × 0.7 partim

Table II.17a. **Total budgetary expenditures associated with agricultural policies** *(cont.)*

M$ million

	1989	1990	1991	1992	1993	1994	1995p	Source
Formal education	**558**	**645**	**792**	**903**	**1 143**	**1 363**	**1 439**	
Agricultural Univ. A. Narro	49	62	84	93	112	125	140	SHCP
Chapingo Autonomous University	122	147	180	215	234	265	304	SHCP
Post-graduate College	47	56	71	82	97	115	135	SHCP
Agricultural technical institutes	72	102	143	172	217	247	247	I.P.94 p.372
Vocational agricultural schools	257	265	308	334	476	602	602	I.P.94 p.371
Other	11	13	6	7	8	10	10	SHCP
Rural development	**32**	**26**	**33**	**472**	**493**	**385**	**462**	
CONAZA	18	21	31	31	56	66	45	SHCP
PRONASOL (FONAES)								SEDESOL
	0	0	0	407	362	213	335	(unpubl.in 94-95)
PRONASOL (Indigenous communities)	0	0	0	34	74	106	83	SHCP
Other	14	5	2	0	0	0	0	SHCP
Sub-national measures (PRONASOL)	**0**	**108**	**100**	**157**	**185**	**198**	**198**	SEDESOL
Agricultural expenditures (1)	**11 570**	**17 312**	**12 547**	**15 858**	**16 949**	**22 717**	**21 983**	
Federal government expenditure (2)	**115 795**	**137 147**	**147 419**	**163 920**	**185 189**	**221 178**	**291 337**	OECD[a]
% (1)/(2)	**10**	**13**	**9**	**10**	**9**	**10**	**8**	

p: provisional.

Table II.17b. **Total budgetary expenditures associated with agricultural policies**

US$ million

	1979	1980	1981	1982	1983	1984	1985	1986	1987	1988	Source
Price and income support	207	393	588	567	301	589	464	576	237	252	
a) Market price support	207	393	588	567	301	589	464	576	237	251	
CONASUPO (stockholding)	176	393	571	464	246	547	431	557	220	233	SHCP × 0.3
AZUCAR S.A.	0	0	0	0	0	0	0	0	0	0	SHCP
INMECAFE	31	0	0	95	55	39	30	17	15	17	SHCP
TABAMEX	0	0	0	0	0	0	0	0	0	0	SHCP
CONADECA	0	0	12	0	0	0	0	0	0	0	SHCP
PACE	0	0	4	8	0	3	2	2	1	1	CONASUPO
b) Direct payments	0	0	0	0	0	0	0	0	0	1	
PROCAMPO	0	0	0	0	0	0	0	0	0	0	SHCP
ASERCA	0	0	0	0	0	0	0	0	0	0	ASERCA (SHCP 95)
Disaster payments	0	0	0	0	0	0	0	0	0	1	CONASUPO (SHCP 95)
Reduction of input costs	1 460	2 488	4 015	2 772	1 825	1 947	1 844	1 423	1 806	1 795	
a) Interest concessions	1 053	1 576	2 351	1 556	972	722	758	570	839	888	
FONDO	4	4	8	2	23	0	0	0	0	0	SHCP
FEFA	26	192	37	10	66	0	0	0	0	0	SHCP
BANRURAL	718	978	1 637	994	678	651	554	530	807	864	SHCP
FICART	97	0	82	97	40	35	24	10	7	8	SHCP
FINA	0	0	0	201	98	0	0	0	0	0	SHCP
FIDAZUCAR	207	402	518	149	28	6	157	17	7	6	SHCP
FIMAIA	0	0	57	29	8	7	4	2	2	2	SHCP
FIRCO	0	0	12	74	30	23	18	11	16	7	SHCP × 0.5
PRONASOL	0	0	0	0	0	0	0	0	0	0	SHCP (SEDESOL 90-91)
b) Fertilisers (FERTIMEX/ASERCA in 95)	101	144	367	441	470	409	370	369	356	382	SHCP
c) Insurance (ANAGSA/AGROASEMEX)	48	166	245	221	162	188	158	153	80	112	SHCP
d) Water	127	335	431	260	79	327	237	253	282	275	
Electric pumping (CFE)	0	0	0	0	0	174	147	193	213	235	SHCP
Irrigation operation and maintenance	127	335	431	260	79	153	90	60	69	40	SHCP partim
e) Feed	115	170	522	222	130	287	276	50	236	123	
CONASUPO	88	131	449	193	123	282	272	47	216	123	SHCP × 0.7 partim
ALBAMEX	26	39	73	29	7	5	4	3	20	0	SHCP
f) Seed (PRONASE/ASERCA)	13	92	86	56	10	10	7	6	3	5	SHCP (ASERCA 92)
g) Pesticides (cotton)	0	0	0	0	0	0	0	0	0	0	ASERCA (SHCP 95)
h) Machinery (SESA)	0	0	0	0	0	2	35	21	8	8	SHCP
i) Livestock breeding (FOGAN)	3	4	12	15	3	2	2	1	1	1	SHCP
General services	815	2 109	2 727	1 750	595	930	815	551	411	387	
a) Research/training/extension	31	96	176	160	70	98	86	69	78	77	
INIFAP	18	79	106	62	28	49	50	48	46	47	SHCP
IMTA	0	0	0	0	0	0	0	0	7	8	SHCP
FIRCO	0	0	12	74	30	23	18	11	16	7	SHCP × 0.5
FEGA	13	17	49	19	10	21	16	9	6	12	SHCP
INCA RURAL	0	0	8	4	2	5	2	1	2	3	SHCP
b) Pest and disease control	79	114	139	81	36	51	29	18	10	9	
Plant health	53	79	94	52	22	35	21	12	6	4	SHCP (SAGAR 89-95)
Animal health	26	35	45	29	14	15	8	6	5	5	SHCP (SAGAR 89-95)
c) Structures/Infrastructures	696	1 808	2 302	1 431	475	760	676	448	304	284	
Irrigated areas	269	712	914	553	166	296	292	226	154	154	SHCP partim
Rainfed areas	132	349	473	275	86	145	122	81	51	16	SHCP
Protection of river beds	57	114	82	72	29	27	35	38	41	56	SHCP
Crop production (excl. irrigation)	176	393	531	290	97	130	92	63	32	22	SHCP
Livestock production	13	92	53	39	18	35	26	18	18	13	SHCP
Roads	48	148	249	203	79	127	109	22	9	23	SHCP
d) Marketing and promotion	9	92	110	77	14	21	22	15	19	17	
ASERCA	0	0	0	0	0	0	0	0	0	0	SAGAR (SHCP 94-95)
CONAFRUT	9	48	69	39	14	16	13	10	11	13	SHCP
FOCIR	0	0	0	0	0	0	0	0	0	0	SHCP
Other	0	44	41	39	0	5	9	5	7	4	SHCP
Consumer subsidies	308	865	1 000	1 021	522	1 114	856	1 383	509	725	
LICONSA (milk)	0	79	102	112	69	113	119	118	145	210	I.P.95 p.123
CONASUPO/FIDELIST (maize tortilla)	0	0	0	0	0	0	0	13	67	94	I.P.95 p.123
ASERCA (wheat)	0	0	0	0	0	0	0	0	0	0	ASERCA (SHCP 95)
CONASUPO (grains, beans, oilseeds)	308	786	898	909	452	1 001	737	1 252	297	421	SHCP × 0.7 partim

Table II.17*b*. **Total budgetary expenditures associated with agricultural policies** *(cont.)*

US$ million

	1979	1980	1981	1982	1983	1984	1985	1986	1987	1988	Source
Formal education	**40**	**144**	**273**	**193**	**95**	**113**	**131**	**140**	**129**	**169**	
Agricultural Univ. A. Narro	4	9	16	14	7	9	10	8	11	16	SHCP
Chapingo Autonomous											SHCP
University	4	48	65	48	21	29	28	23	29	42	
Post-graduate College	0	26	53	35	12	14	11	10	12	16	SHCP
Agricultural technical institutes	4	13	53	12	6	9	9	8	9	11	I.P.94 p.372
Vocational agricultural schools	26	48	86	85	41	46	66	88	65	80	I.P.94 p.371
Other	0	0	0	0	6	5	6	3	2	4	SHCP
Rural development	**101**	**371**	**396**	**116**	**43**	**47**	**61**	**15**	**11**	**10**	
CONAZA	13	22	29	19	4	6	6	3	4	5	SHCP
PRONASOL (FONAES)											SEDESOL
	0	0	0	0	0	0	0	0	0	0	(unpubl.in 94-95)
PRONASOL (Indigenous											SHCP
communities)	0	0	0	0	0	0	0	0	0	0	
Other	88	349	367	97	39	42	55	13	7	5	SHCP
Sub-national measures											SEDESOL
(PRONASOL)	**0**	**0**	**0**	**0**	**0**	**0**	**0**	**0**	**0**	**0**	
Agricultural expenditures (1)	**2 931**	**6 370**	**8 998**	**6 419**	**3 379**	**4 740**	**4 170**	**4 087**	**3 103**	**3 338**	
Federal government expenditure											OECD[a]
(2)	n.a.	35 721	54 490	52 282	29 987	37 044	35 391	36 001	42 638	46 412	
% (1)/(2)	**n.a.**	**18**	**17**	**12**	**11**	**13**	**12**	**11**	**7**	**7**	

Table II.17b. **Total budgetary expenditures associated with agricultural policies** *(cont.)*

US$ million

	1989	1990	1991	1992	1993	1994	1995p	Source
Price and income support	**676**	**921**	**391**	**749**	**835**	**2 180**	**1 205**	
a) Market price support	674	919	352	407	616	510	253	
CONASUPO (stockholding)	334	828	299	346	532	458	228	SHCP × 0.3
AZUCAR S.A.	223	49	0	0	0	0	0	SHCP
INMECAFE	112	25	18	27	30	1	0	SHCP
TABAMEX	0	0	2	0	0	0	0	SHCP
CONADECA	2	0	0	0	0	0	0	SHCP
PACE	2	17	33	34	55	51	25	CONASUPO
b) Direct payments	2	2	39	342	219	1 670	952	
PROCAMPO	0	0	0	0	0	1 431	913	SHCP
ASERCA	0	0	36	338	216	235	27	ASERCA (SHCP 95)
Disaster payments	2	2	3	4	3	4	12	CONASUPO (SHCP 95)
Reduction of input costs	**2 011**	**2 553**	**1 434**	**1 283**	**1 663**	**1 545**	**716**	
a) Interest concessions	821	522	601	700	840	536	248	
FONDO	0	2	10	10	6	10	2	SHCP
FEFA	1	7	42	38	24	27	44	SHCP
BANRURAL	744	281	294	423	232	267	111	SHCP
FICART	9	8	13	13	12	0	0	SHCP
FINA	27	12	0	0	309	0	0	SHCP
FIDAZUCAR	22	21	56	6	25	0	0	SHCP
FIMAIA	3	7	6	0	0	0	0	SHCP
FIRCO	15	46	56	65	51	41	14	SHCP × 0.5
PRONASOL	0	139	125	144	180	192	76	SHCP (SEDESOL 90-91)
b) Fertilisers (FERTIMEX/ASERCA in 95)	237	262	294	153	0	0	11	SHCP
c) Insurance (ANAGSA/AGROASEMEX)	498	579	0	24	28	65	31	SHCP
d) Water	365	415	379	299	241	376	213	
Electric pumping (CFE)	304	326	267	197	183	311	178	SHCP
Irrigation operation and maintenance	61	89	112	102	58	65	36	SHCP partim
e) Feed	77	765	117	102	541	532	194	
CONASUPO	77	761	116	102	541	532	194	SHCP × 0.7 partim
ALBAMEX	0	4	2	0	0	0	0	SHCP
f) Seed (PRONASE/ASERCA)	5	3	36	2	0	0	0	SHCP (ASERCA 92)
g) Pesticides (cotton)	0	0	0	0	13	36	19	ASERCA (SHCP 95)
h) Machinery (SESA)	7	6	2	0	0	0	0	SHCP
i) Livestock breeding (FOGAN)	1	1	4	3	0	0	0	SHCP
General services	**541**	**782**	**727**	**1 003**	**943**	**1 232**	**498**	
a) Research/training/extension	102	168	191	241	257	276	147	
INIFAP	56	58	70	80	95	89	48	SHCP
IMTA	14	13	20	33	31	36	13	SHCP
FIRCO	15	46	56	65	51	41	14	SHCP × 0.5
FEGA	13	44	36	54	76	107	70	SHCP
INCA RURAL	4	6	9	10	3	3	2	SHCP
b) Pest and disease control	11	12	16	39	35	30	12	
Plant health	4	5	5	25	20	7	5	SHCP (SAGAR 89-95)
Animal health	7	8	11	14	15	23	7	SHCP (SAGAR 89-95)
c) Structures/Infrastructures	415	594	457	625	498	876	310	
Irrigated areas	171	252	308	410	331	357	203	SHCP partim
Rainfed areas	18	33	39	44	31	35	14	SHCP
Protection of river beds	38	29	12	25	27	49	17	SHCP
Crop production (excl. irrigation)	30	17	70	66	49	54	14	SHCP
Livestock production	16	24	16	19	7	19	0	SHCP
Roads	141	239	13	61	52	362	63	SHCP
d) Marketing and promotion	13	7	62	98	153	51	29	
ASERCA	0	0	62	97	89	51	23	SAGAR (SHCP 94-95)
CONAFRUT	13	5	0	0	0	0	0	SHCP
FOCIR	0	0	0	0	64	0	6	SHCP
Other	0	2	0	0	0	0	0	SHCP
Consumer subsidies	**1 173**	**1 564**	**1 294**	**1 594**	**1 415**	**1 173**	**678**	
LICONSA (milk)	368	303	427	469	438	370	269	I.P.95 p.123
CONASUPO/FIDELIST (maize tortilla)	103	92	155	167	118	119	73	I.P.95 p.123
ASERCA (wheat)	0	0	0	127	252	147	0	ASERCA (SHCP 95)
CONASUPO (grains, beans, oilseeds)	702	1 169	582	704	699	537	337	SHCP × 0.7 partim

Table II.17b. **Total budgetary expenditures associated with agricultural policies** *(cont.)*

US$ million

	1989	1990	1991	1992	1993	1994	1995p	Source
Formal education	**224**	**227**	**262**	**292**	**367**	**402**	**224**	
Agricultural Univ. A. Narro	20	22	28	30	36	37	22	SHCP
Chapingo Autonomous University	49	52	60	69	75	78	47	SHCP
Post-graduate College	19	20	23	27	31	34	21	SHCP
Agricultural technical institutes	29	36	47	56	70	73	38	I.P.94 p.372
Vocational agricultural schools	103	93	102	108	153	178	94	I.P.94 p.371
Other	4	5	2	2	3	3	2	SHCP
Rural development	**13**	**9**	**11**	**152**	**158**	**114**	**72**	
CONAZA	7	7	10	10	18	20	7	SHCP
PRONASOL (FONAES)								SEDESOL
	0	0	0	131	116	63	52	(unpubl.in 94-95)
PRONASOL (Indigenous communities)	0	0	0	11	24	31	13	SHCP
Other	6	2	1	0	0	0	0	SHCP
Sub-national measures (PRONASOL)	**0**	**38**	**33**	**51**	**59**	**58**	**31**	SEDESOL
Agricultural expenditures (1)	**4 637**	**6 094**	**4 151**	**5 124**	**5 441**	**6 704**	**3 423**	
Federal government expenditure (2)	**46 413**	**48 279**	**48 775**	**52 963**	**59 449**	**65 271**	**45 370**	OECD[a]
% (1)/(2)	**10**	**13**	**9**	**10**	**9**	**10**	**8**	

p: provisional.

Table III.1. **Decomposition of net total PSE, 1979-1995**

	1979-82		1983-1988		1989-1994		1995p	
	mn $US[a]	%[b]	mn $US[a]	%[b]	mn $US[a]	%[b]	mn $US	%
General policy measures								
A. *Market price support*	1 960	43	−1 096	−37	2 934	68	−1 141	−322
B. *Levies*	0	0	0	0	0	0	0	0
C. *Direct payments*	0	0	0	0	298	7	771	218
Payment per tonne (ASERCA)	0	0	0	0	7	0	4	1
Area and headage payments	0	0	0	0	196	5	740	209
Disaster	0	0	0	0	2	0	7	2
Price premium (ASERCA)	0	0	0	0	93	2	19	5
D. *Reduction of input costs*	1 629	42	994	97	914	21	418	118
Interest concessions	1 008	26	413	34	240	6	117	33
Fertilizer	109	3	178	20	63	1	4	1
Insurance	113	3	98	9	128	3	19	5
Irrigation	121	3	111	14	136	3	84	24
Seeds	26	1	3	0	3	0	0	0
Machinery	0	0	6	1	1	0	0	0
Feed	242	6	183	19	342	8	194	55
Animal breeding improvement	9	0	1	0	1	0	0	0
E. *General services*	719	18	264	24	337	8	204	58
Research, advisory, training	77	2	55	6	127	3	91	26
Inspection	0	0	0	0	0	0	0	0
Pest and disease control	61	1	16	1	17	0	9	3
Structures/infrastructures	581	14	192	16	167	4	91	26
Marketing and promotion	0	0	0	0	26	1	13	4
F. *Sub-national*	0	0	0	0	24	1	19	5
G. *Other*	0	0	0	0	0	0	0	0
Total other support (D + E + F + G)	2 348	60	1 257	120	1 276	29	641	181
Gross total PSE	4 308		161		4 508		271	
Feed adjustment	−139	−3	245	17	−203	−5	83	24
Net total PSE	4 169	100	406	100	4 305	100	354	100
Percentage PSE	34		3		30		3	

Notes:
p: provisional.
a)   Simple average for the period.
b)   The share of PSE components in net total PSE was calculated based on simple averages in M$.
Source: Table 13, Annex II.

Table III.2. **Total transfers, 1979-1995**

	Note	1979	1980	1981	1982	1983	1984	1985	1986	1987	1988	1989	1990	1991	1992	1993	1994	1995p
Share of PSE commodities (%)	(1)	67	67	67	66	64	70	73	69	66	68	67	63	61	62	61	60	62
Total CSE (M$ bn)	(2)	0.0	0.0	0.1	0.0	-0.7	-0.4	-0.4	-1.5	-0.8	-1.2	-1.0	2.1	7.3	8.4	10.5	5.1	-10.7
Budget revenues in Total CSE (M$ bn)	(3)	0.0	0.0	0.0	0.0	0.0	0.0	0.0	0.0	0.0	0.1	0.1	0.1	0.3	0.3	0.3	0.3	0.6
Transfers from taxpayers (M$ bn)	(4)	0.1	0.1	0.2	0.3	0.5	0.9	1.3	2.5	4.2	7.2	11.0	16.6	11.7	14.5	15.3	21.0	20.1
Transfers from consumers (M$ bn) (2)/(1)	5	0.0	0.0	0.1	0.0	-1.1	-0.6	-0.5	-2.2	-1.2	-1.7	-1.6	3.3	11.9	13.4	17.2	8.5	-17.2
Total budget revenues (M$ bn) (3)/(1)	6	0.0	0.0	0.0	0.0	0.0	0.0	0.0	0.0	0.0	0.1	0.1	0.1	0.4	0.5	0.5	0.6	0.9
Total transfers:																		
– in billion M$ (4) + (5) – (6)		0.1	0.1	0.3	0.3	-0.6	0.3	0.8	0.3	3.0	5.4	9.3	19.8	23.3	27.4	32.0	28.9	2.0
– in billion US$		4.2	6.5	13.8	5.9	-3.6	1.5	2.3	0.5	2.1	2.4	3.7	7.0	7.7	8.8	10.3	8.5	0.3
– share of total GDP	(7)	3.0	3.3	5.5	3.1	-3.1	1.0	1.6	0.4	1.5	1.4	1.8	2.9	2.7	2.7	2.9	2.4	0.1
– in US$ per capita	(8)	n.a.	97	201	84	-50	21	31	7	27	30	47	86	92	104	119	97	3
– in US$ per ha of farmland	(9)	43	66	139	60	-36	15	23	5	21	24	37	70	78	89	104	86	3

Notes:

p: provisional.

n.a.: not available.

(1) Share of PSE commodities in total value of agricultural production in Mexico (OECD PSE/CSE database).

(2), (3) Table 13B, Annex II.

(4) Table II.17, excluding formal education and rural development.

(5) Total CSE extrapolated to apply to the total value of agricultural production.

(6) Budget revenues from import tariffs extrapolated to apply to the total value of agricultural production.

(7) GDP: OECD *Economic Outlook* database.

(8) Mexican population: OECD *Labour force statistics* database for the years 1980 to 1994, and INEGI, *Conteo de población y vivienda 1995* for 1995.

(10) Source: FAO AGROSTAT database for the years 1986-93 and OECD estimates for the most recent years.

Source: OECD Secretariat, 1997.

ASSISTANCE TO MEXICAN AGRICULTURE

INTRODUCTION

Chapter III presented the basic concepts of the PSE and CSE, the general methodology used to calculate them, and the results (aggregate and by commodities) in the case of Mexican agriculture. This Annex presents the main assumptions made in estimating the Mexican PSEs and CSEs (Section A). Section B presents the PSE and CSE calculation tables,[1] including detailed notes on definitions and sources used for the calculations. The calculations should be integrated with care, in particular given a number of problems with the availability and quality of some data.[2]

A. ASSUMPTIONS RELATED TO THE PSE/CSE CALCULATIONS[3]

I. Market price support

The general methodology presented in Chapter III to calculate market price support to producers (MPS) requires appropriate **reference prices**, which are given in Table 14 of section B. The **exchange rates** used in the PSE/CSE calculations are those published by the OECD.[4] The calculation of market price support for each commodity is detailed in Tables 1c to 12c *of section B.*

For grains and oilseeds, in the absence of reliable information on average **producer prices** at the farmgate until 1994, the *administered prices* were used to calculate the MPS. For 1995, estimates of producer prices were provided by SAGAR. In the case of sugar, the price gap between the producer price and the reference price is calculated at the wholesale level (ex-factory). A ratio between the wholesale (raw sugar) and producer (sugarcane) prices is applied to the price gap to express it at the farmgate level. Until 1993, the average producer price (*precio medio rural*) of sugarcane was used to calculate the ratio. In 1994 and 1995, the ratio was estimated as being the coefficient fixed by the government between wholesale and producer prices (54 per cent and 55 per cent respectively), in accordance with the 1991 Sugar Ordinance (see Chapter II, Section B1.*b*). Producer prices for milk were provided by the National Livestock Confederation (CNG). For beef and veal, the only available producer price published by SAGAR (*precio medio ponderado*) represents the price middlemen receive from the slaughterhouse upon delivery of the live animal. Therefore producers receive a lower price because of the commission charged by middlemen, and a "marketing margin" was deducted from the published average producer prices. Producer prices for pigmeat were provided by the Mexican Council of Pig producers (CMP). For poultrymeat and eggs, producer prices at the farmgate were provided by the National Union of Poultry Producers (UNA). In the case of wheat, sorghum and soyabeans, an implicit producer price was calculated for the period 1991-95, during which ASERCA price premiums were in place.

For all the PSE commodities, the **MPS** was estimated as being the difference between the producer price and the corresponding reference price (price gap), multiplied by the quantity produced (including for self-consumption). However, there were exceptions for some years in the case of sorghum and beef and veal. For sorghum, between 1991 and 1994, the price gap system was considered for Tamaulipas State, the only State for which a concerted price is fixed. The price gap consisted of the difference between the concerted price and the reference price. For the other parts of the country, where the government did not set administered prices and where the seasonal tariff did not apply on imports originated in the United States during the harvest period, the MPS was not calculated. In the case of beef and veal (1989-92), sorghum (1990), and soyabeans (1990), the MPS was not calculated since neither administered prices nor trade measures were in place.

2. Total CSE

The total CSE consists of **Market Transfers** (MT) and **Other Transfers** (OT). Market transfers in turn consist of the MPS on domestic production (see above) and **budget revenues**, or the MPS on domestic consumption, for commodities and years in which Mexico was a net exporter (sugar, beef and veal). Budget revenues arising from border policy measures were estimated by applying the tariff on imports originated in the United States on all the quantities imported, as measured by the difference between the level of consumption in the CSE and the level of production in the PSE. No budget revenues were included in the MT when imports from the United States were duty-free or subject to duty-free permits or tariff quotas, assuming in the latter case that the tariff was never applied on any imports above the quota. Other transfers included in the CSE calculation consist of **consumption subsidies** (see Chapter II, Section L). Over the review period, the consumption subsidies granted by the Mexican government have been allocated to the CSE according to the commodity concerned or, in the case of CONASUPO, in proportion of domestic purchases.

3. Budgetary support[5]

Budgetary support consists of direct or indirect transfers from taxpayers (through budgetary or tax expenditures) to producers of PSE commodities (see Table 13, Section B). Data on the value of budgetary expenditures associated with agricultural policies were essentially provided by the Secretariat of Finance and Public Credit (SHCP) (see Table II.17). The way to allocate these budgetary expenditures among commodities and within the four categories of budgetary support measures (see Chapter III, Section A1) is presented below.

a) Direct payments

PROCAMPO *area payments* have been allocated to the crops that farmers must have cultivated in the past to be eligible to receive payments (except barley for which payments were not authorised until 1996), assuming that producers continued to grow the same crops. The allocation was done among the PSE crops according to their share in the total area cultivated with "eligible crops". ASERCA *per tonne payments* (rice) and *price premiums* (wheat, sorghum, soyabeans) have been allocated to the corresponding commodities. For *disaster payments*, allocation was done among all commodities according to their share in the value of total agricultural production.

b) Reduction of input costs

For BANRURAL and FIRA, **interest concessions** have been allocated between crops and livestock products according to their share in the total value of loans granted to farmers, and the sub-totals allocated among the PSE commodities according to their respective share in the value of total crop production and the value of total animal production. FICART, FIRCO, and PRONASOL interest concessions have been allocated among all commodities according to their share in the value of total agricultural production. FINA, FIDAZUCAR and FIMAIA credit subsidies have been entirely allocated to sugar production.

ANAGSA and AGROASEMEX **insurance subsidies** have been allocated to all commodities according to their share in the value of total agricultural production. Subsidies on the purchase of **fertilisers and seeds,** on the electricity rate for groundwater pumping, on the operation and maintenance cost of on-farm **irrigation** schemes, and on the rent of **machinery** have been allocated among crops according to their share in the total value of crop production. **Pesticide and seed** subsidies granted by ASERCA have been entirely allocated to cotton production. **Feed** subsidies provided by CONASUPO and ALBAMEX have been allocated among livestock products according to their share in the total value of animal production. Subsidies on **livestock breeding services** provided by FOGAN have been entirely allocated to beef and veal production.

c) General services

Concerning **research, advisory and training**, government transfers to INIFAP, IMTA, FIRCO, FEGA, and INCARURAL have been allocated to all commodities according to their share in the value of total agricultural production. Concerning **pest and disease control**, the budgetary expenditures on plant health have been allocated among crops according to their share in total value of crop production, while the budgetary expenditures on animal health have been allocated among livestock products according to their share in total value of animal production.

With regard to **structures and infrastructures**, the major part of the government transfers (for irrigated and rainfed areas, and crop production) has been allocated among crops according to their share in the total value of crop production, the remainder being allocated among livestock products according to their share in total value of livestock production. **Marketing and promotion** activities of CONAFRUT have been entirely allocated to fruit and vegetable production, while those undertaken by ASERCA and FOCIR have been allocated to all commodities according to their share in the value of total agricultural production.

d) Other

This category includes programmes which are not accounted for in any of the above categories of budgetary support measures. **Tax concessions** that are applied to agriculture were not included by lack of information (see Chapter II, Section E). **Sub-national measures** include programmes that are funded at the local or regional level. They should not be confused with regional policies that are funded centrally and administered locally. The operating cost of the PRONASOL Solidarity Fund for Production is shared between central and sub-national governments, and the part funded by State governments has been allocated to all commodities according to their share in the value of total agricultural production.

4. Feed adjustment

This adjustment takes into account the implicit taxes or subsidies associated with market price support on the PSE feed commodities: sorghum, maize, soyabeans, and wheat (see Table II.10). The feed adjustment is the unit market price support of each of these commodities multiplied by the corresponding quantity of the domestic production used as feed. This represents the intra-sectoral transfer that have to be deducted from the Gross PSE of livestock products to obtain a Net PSE and avoid double-counting. The quantities of PSE commodities used as feed have been distributed every year among the various animal products according to a "feed matrix" estimated on the basis of the production of compound feed by the private sector. The coefficients of the feed matrix are relatively stable within the 1979-86 and 1987-95 periods (see Figure 1).

Figure 1. **Allocation of feed adjustment among livestock products (%)**

Livestock products	Period	
	1979-86	1987-95
Milk	12	21
Beef and veal	4	5
Pigmeat	29	26
Poultrymeat	41	35
Eggs	12	11
Others	2	2
Total	100	100

Source: OECD Secretariat.

5. PSE and CSE decomposition

The PSE and CSE decomposition has a number of advantages. First, it identifies the relative importance of changes in the various PSE and CSE components in explaining the overall year-to-year change in total PSEs and CSEs for Mexico. Second, it allows for the condensation of a large volume of data into a concise form.

The methodology is based on expressing the net total PSE for a given commodity in terms of its components, a *production volume* component and a *unit PSE*. The unit PSE is in turn broken down into a series of *unit value* components: *market price support, output levies, direct payments, other support* (i.e. the categories described as "Reduction in Input Costs", "General Services" and "Other" in Part III. Section 1a) and *feed adjustment*. Market price support is itself further decomposed into a *domestic producer price* component and a *border price in domestic currency*. The latter in turn is made up of an *exchange rate* component and a *border price in US dollars* component.

Likewise, the total CSE is broken down into a *consumption volume* component and a *unit CSE*. The unit CSE has two unit value components: *market transfers* and *other transfers*. As it is the mirror image of market price support, "market transfers" consist of a *domestic consumer price* (as consumption is usually valued at the farm gate, this is also the producer price) and a *border price in domestic currency*. The latter is broken down into an *exchange rate* and a *border price in US dollars* component.

For each component, two indicators are calculated: the *percentage change* in that component and the *contribution*, in terms of percentage points, of that change to the overall change in the total PSE. The contribution of a change in a component to the total PSE can also be interpreted as the change that would have occurred in the total PSE if nothing else other than that component had changed. The sum of the contributions from all components equals the change in total PSE. Similarly, the changes in CSEs can be expressed in terms of shares in the total CSE and changes in its components. CSE indices are constructed and contributions estimated as for PSEs.

For the total PSE and for each of its components, year-to-year percentage changes in Fisher ideal indices are calculated for the aggregate of each commodity.[6] Aggregation across commodities is done by weighting these commodity indices for each individual PSE and CSE component. Weighted Fisher ideal indices are calculated from weighted Laspeyres and Paasche indices.[7] The weights used are component specific and are evaluated at base period prices for the Laspeyres indices and at current period prices for the Paasche indices.

Algebraically the **decomposition analysis** for PSE, in terms of percentage changes, is presented as follows:

$$\overset{\circ}{PSE} = \overset{\circ}{PSE}_u + \overset{\circ}{Q} + \overset{\circ}{PSE}_u \cdot \overset{\circ}{Q} \tag{1}$$

$$\overset{\circ}{PSE}_u = S_{mps} \cdot \overset{\circ}{MPS} - S_{lv} \cdot \overset{\circ}{LV}_u + S_{dp} \cdot \overset{\circ}{DP}_u + S_{os} \cdot \overset{\circ}{OS}_u - S_{fa} \cdot \overset{\circ}{FA}_u \tag{2}$$

$$\overset{\circ}{MPS}_u = (S_p \cdot \overset{\circ}{P} - S_{pwnc} \cdot \overset{\circ}{PW}_{nc}) / S_{mps} \tag{3}$$

$$\overset{\circ}{PW}_{nc} = \overset{\circ}{XR} + \overset{\circ}{\$PW} + \overset{\circ}{XR} \cdot \overset{\circ}{\$PW} \tag{4}$$

where,

$\circ$ indicates the percentage change in the nominated variable;

MPS_u is unit market price support (per tonne);

LV_u is unit levies on output (per tonne);

DP_u is unit direct payments (per tonne);

OS_u is unit other support (per tonne);

FA_u is feed adjustment per unit (per tonne);

XR is the exchange rate in units of domestic currency per US$;

S_{mps}, S_{lv}, S_{dp}, S_{os} and S_{fa} are, respectively, the shares of market price support, levies, direct payments, other support and feed adjustment in the total PSE;

S_p and S_{pwnc} each measure the value of production as a share of the total PSE, in the former case using the producer price to calculate the value of production, in the latter case using the border price (measured in national currency units) to calculate it;

$PW is the *implicit* border price in US dollars; it is calculated as the difference between domestic prices and unit market price support.[8]

Equation [2] shows that the change in the unit PSE is equal to the sum of the percentage changes in its components weighted by the shares of those components in the base year. However, as the changes are expressed by Fisher Ideal indices the above expressions are not exact. Thus, approximation techniques are used to preserve the additivity of the decomposition formulae.

The decomposition analysis is based on the assumption that components of assistance are independent of one another, which is a useful simplification but needs to be interpreted carefully. In many cases the components are related; for instance, market price support and direct payments may both be influenced by border price changes. In the case where market price support is provided solely by a tariff, changes in the internal price would be a direct consequence of changes in the border price.

The choice of the numéraire currency to be used for international comparison is arbitrary from a technical point of view. By convention the United States dollar has been used predominantly in OECD PSE work and is therefore used in this study. However, it can be shown that the use of an alternative numéraire currency affects only the values and contributions of the exchange rate and border price in the numéraire currency indices. No other PSE components are affected, and the differences in the exchange rate and border price indices are fully determined by the change in the exchange rate between the "old" and "new" numéraire currencies. Likewise, the contributions are determined using the share weights, which remain unaltered by any change in the choice of numéraire currency.

6. Limitations of PSEs and CSEs

In any use of **PSE** and **CSE** indicators, such as for comparison between countries, it is important to bear in mind the recognised limits of these indicators with respect to policy coverage, commodity coverage, data availability and methodology applied, as well as to the specific characteristics of agriculture. When the PSE and CSE concepts are used to infer the degree of economic distortion in domestic prices, it is assumed that all policy measures induce the same degree of distortion per unit of support, which is not really the case. However, because the measures for which the distortion effect is expected to be minimal (e.g. expenditure on services of a general nature) account for only a small share in total assistance in most countries, the error implied is likely to be minor. Moreover, the methodology used in the calculations continues to evolve through a process of constant review within the OECD.

The PSE and CSE calculations for Mexico are, in general, based on actual data, albeit often of a preliminary nature, especially for recent years. Obviously, as actual data may well depart from what has been assumed, the calculations may be revised in due course as more reliable data become available. It should be stressed, however, that there is often a lack of good, detailed and consistent statistical information available on Mexican agricultural policies, including average farmgate producer prices. Each agency involved in agricultural policy tends to manage its own data sources and publications.

In the case of **total transfers**, the grossing up procedure applied to the Total CSE and budget revenues assumes that the average rate of market transfers calculated for PSE commodities can also be applied to non-PSE commodities. However, because PSE commodities accounted for around two-thirds of the total value of agricultural production over the review period, the error implied is likely to be limited.

B. TABLES OF PRODUCER SUBSIDY EQUIVALENTS (PSE) AND CONSUMER SUBSIDY EQUIVALENTS (CSE) FOR MEXICAN AGRICULTURE

General Notes:

Tables 2C (oats), 10 (sheepmeat) and 11 (wool) were not included as their respective production accounts for less than one per cent of the gross value of total agricultural production in Mexico, and their level of consumption is not significant in Mexico.
Table 4 (oilseeds) only includes soyabeans as the production of the other PSE oilseed commodities (rapeseed and sunflower) accounts each for less than one per cent of the gross value of total agricultural production in Mexico.

Table 1. Producer subsidy equivalent – wheat

	Units	1979	1980	1981	1982	1983	1984	1985	1986	1987	1988	1989	1990	1991	1992	1993	1994	1995p
I. Level of production	'000 t	2 287	2 785	3 193	4 391	3 463	4 505	5 214	4 770	4 415	3 665	4 375	3 931	4 061	3 621	3 582	4 151	3 468
II. Production price (farm gate)	M$/t	3	4	5	7	16	26	39	72	120	310	358	484	560	425	577	491	910
III. Value of production	M$ mn	7	10	15	32	56	118	201	341	530	1 136	1 566	1 903	2 274	1 540	2 066	2 038	3 157
IV. Levies	M$ mn	0	0	0	0	0	0	0	0	0	0	0	0	0	0	0	0	0
V. Direct payments	M$ mn	0	0	0	0	0	0	0	0	0	0	0	0	0	546	226	811	513
VI. Adjusted value of production	M$ mn	7	10	15	32	56	118	201	341	530	1 136	1 566	1 903	2 274	2 086	2 293	2 848	3 671
VII. Policy transfers	M$ mn	-1	1	5	7	-19	11	-9	7	-163	5	-166	537	794	503	773	853	-235
A. Market price support	M$ mn	-2	-2	0	-4	-30	-19	-46	-52	-254	-160	-374	298	568	-251	389	-175	-936
1. Trade measures	M$ mn	-2	-2	0	-4	-30	-19	-46	-52	-254	-160	-374	298	568	-251	389	-175	-936
2. PACE	M$ mn																	
B. Levies	M$ mn	0	0	0	0	0	0	0	0	0	0	0	0	0	0	0	0	0
C. Direct payments	M$ mn	0	0	0	0	0	0	0	0	0	0	0	0	0	546	226	811	513
1. Per tonne payment (Aserca)	M$ mn	0	0	0	0	0	0	0	0	0	0	0	0	0	0	0	357	387
2. Area and headage payments	M$ mn	0	0	0	0	0	0	0	0	0	0	0	0	0	0	0	0	0
3. Disaster	M$ mn	0	0	0	0	0	0	0	0	0	0	0	0	0	0	0		2
4. Price premium (Aserca)	M$ mn	0	0	0	0	0	0	0	0	0	0	0	0	0	546	226	453	125
D. Reduction of input costs	M$ mn	1	1	2	7	8	21	25	43	71	135	166	180	137	99	66	113	97
E. General services	M$ mn	1	1	2	4	3	8	12	16	20	29	41	56	87	104	87	99	86
F. Sub national	M$ mn	0	0	0	0	0	0	0	0	0	0	0	3	3	4	4	5	5
G. Other	M$ mn																	
VIII. Gross total PSE	M$ mn	-1	1	5	7	-19	11	-9	7	-163	5	-166	537	794	503	773	853	-235
IX. Gross unit PSE	M$/t	0	0	2	2	-6	2	-2	2	-37	1	-38	137	196	139	216	205	-68
X. Gross percentage PSE	%	-8	10	34	21	-35	9	-5	2	-31	0	-11	28	35	24	34	30	-6

Notes to Table 1
PSE: Wheat

Definitions and Notes :

I **Level of production**: SAGAR statistics on grain wheat (*trigo grano*) [1].

II **Production price (farm gate)**: From 1979 to 1981, guaranteed prices [2]. From 1982 to 1986, the annual production price was estimated as the simple average of the guaranteed prices for the Autumn-Winter and Spring-Summer crop seasons [2]. From 1987 to 1994, a weighted average of the administered prices for the Autumn-Winter and Spring-Summer crop seasons [2]. For the period 1992-94, an implicit production price was calculated by subtracting the unit budget payments of ASERCA [3] from the concerted price. For 1995, implicit production price for the Autumn-Winter 1994-95 crop season and average producer price [4] for the Spring-Summer 1995 crop season.

III **Value of production**: Level of production (I) multiplied by the production price (II).

A.1 **Trade measures**: Production price (II) minus reference price (see Table 14) multiplied by the level of production (I).

C.2 **Area and headage payments:** See notes to Table 13.

C.3 **Disaster payments**: See notes to Table 13.

C.4 **Price premiums**: ASERCA payments [3] to the buyers of domestic production at concerted prices.

D. **Reduction of input costs:** See notes to Table 13.

E. **General services**: See notes to Table 13.

Source:

[1] SAGAR, as reported in *Sexto Informe de Gobierno* 1994, *Anexo*, page 167 and *Primer Informe de Gobierno* 1995, *Anexo*, page 79. Estimates provided directly by SAGAR for 1995.

[2] SAGAR, as reported in Sexto Informe de Gobierno 1994, Anexo, pages 165 and 166 and *Primer Informe de Gobierno* 1995, *Anexo*, page 84.

[3] Data provided directly by ASERCA. Data provided by SHCP for 1995.

[4] Estimate provided directly by SAGAR.

Table 1. **Consumer subsidy equivalent – wheat** (cont.)

	Units	1979	1980	1981	1982	1983	1984	1985	1986	1987	1988	1989	1990	1991	1992	1993	1994	1995p
I. Level of consumption	'000 t	3 434	3 684	4 316	4 702	3 864	4 839	5 534	4 994	4 830	4 687	4 574	4 267	4 602	4 697	5 324	5 476	4 400
II. Consumption price (farm gate)	M$/t	3	4	5	7	17	26	39	72	125	320	362	478	544	441	541	518	997
III. Value of consumption	M$ mn	11	14	20	35	66	128	216	360	603	1 497	1 654	2 040	2 502	2 072	2 882	2 839	4 389
IV. Policy transfers	M$ mn	4	11	5	21	60	94	147	352	381	481	1 098	86	–568	643	397	577	804
A. Market transfers	M$ mn	2	2	0	4	30	19	46	52	254	160	374	–298	–568	251	–389	80	804
1. MPS on domestic production	M$ mn	2	2	0	4	30	19	46	52	254	160	374	–298	–568	251	–389	175	936
2. Tariffs	M$ mn	0	0	0	0	0	0	0	0	0	0	0	0	0	0	0	–95	–132
B. Other transfers	M$ mn	2	9	5	17	31	75	101	300	127	321	723	384	0	392	786	497	0
1. Conasupo subsidy	M$ mn	2	9	5	17	31	75	101	300	127	321	723	384	0	0	0	0	0
2. Aserca payment	M$ mn	0	0	0	0	0	0	0	0	0	0	0	0	0	392	786	497	0
V. Total CSE	M$ mn	4	11	5	21	60	94	147	352	381	481	1 098	86	–568	643	397	577	804
VI. Unit CSE	M$/t	1	3	1	4	16	19	27	71	79	103	240	20	–123	137	75	105	183
VII. Percentage CSE	%	33	82	24	61	92	73	68	98	63	32	66	4	–23	31	14	20	18

p. provisional.

Notes to Table 1
CSE: Wheat

Definitions and Notes:

I   **Level of consumption**: Apparent consumption of grain wheat defined as production plus imports minus exports [1].

II   **Consumption price (farm gate)**: Implicit price measured at the farm gate; equal to the production price (Pp) minus the sum of unit market price support (MPS_u) and unit market transfers (M_{tu}) [Pp − (MPS_u + MT_u)].

III   **Value of consumption**: Level of consumption (I) multiplied by the consumption price (II).

A.1   **MPS on domestic production**: The inverse of the market price support component of the PSE.

A.2   **Tariffs**: Not applicable for the 1979-93 period in which imports required permit, but were duty-free. For the other periods: import tariff multiplied by reference price multiplied by the difference between the consumption (I) and production (see PSE I) levels. The following tariffs were considered: 15 per cent in 1994 and 13.5 per cent in 1995.

B.1   **CONASUPO subsidy**: Government transfers to CONASUPO [2] net of stockholding expenditure (estimated as 30 per cent of transfers) and feed subsidies (see PSEs for livestock products). Consumption subsidies were allocated among wheat, maize, rice and soyabeans according to their share in domestic purchases by CONASUPO [3].

B.2   **ASERCA payment**: Payments to the wheat millers [4].

Source:

[1]   For the years 1979-93, SAGAR, as reported in *Sexto Informe de Gobierno* 1994, *Anexo*, page 168. 1994: BIOSA, número 126, Junio 1996, page 7; 1995: data provided by SAGAR.

[2]   Data provided by SHCP.

[3]   CONASUPO, as reported in *Sexto Informe de Gobierno* 1994, *Anexo*, page 264 and *Primer Informe de Gobierno* 1995, *Anexo*, page 86. Estimates provided directly by SAGAR for 1995.

[4]   Data provided directly by ASERCA. Data provided by SHCP for 1995.

Table 1. **Calculation of market price support and of market transfers – wheat** (cont.)

WHEAT (TRIGO)

PSE-MARKET PRICE SUPPORT (MPS)

	Units	1979	1980	1981	1982	1983	1984	1985	1986	1987	1988	1989	1990	1991	1992	1993	1994	1995p
(1) Production	'000T	2 287	2 785	3 193	4 391	3 463	4 505	5 214	4 770	4 415	3 665	4 375	3 931	4 061	3 621	3 582	4 151	3 468
(1)a Production Otoño Invierno	'000 T									4 190	3 443	4 063	3 540	3 671	3 306	3 318	3 781	3 082
(1)b Production Primavera Verano	'000 T									225	222	312	391	390	314	264	370	386
(2)a Administered price O-I	MS/T				7	14	25	37	58	120	310	355	484	560	576	640	600	850
(2)b Administered price P-V	MS/T				8	18	27	40	85	120	310	395	484	560	576	640	600	1 393
(2) Average price	MS/T	3	4	5	7	16	26	39	72	120	310	358	484	560	576	640	600	
(3) Aserca payment	MS Mio														546	226	453	125
(4) Unit Aserca payment (3/(1) * 1 000	MS/T														151	63	109	109
(5) Producer price net of the payment	MS/T	3	4	5	7	16	26	39	72	120	310	358	484	560	425	577	491	910
(6) Value of production (5) * (1)/1 000	MS Mio	7	10	15	32	56	118	201	341	530	1 136	1 566	1 903	2 274	1 540	2 066	2 038	3 157
(7) Hard red winter No. 2	US$/bu	4	5	5	4	4	4	4	3	3	4	5	4	4	4	4	4	5
(8) HRW per tonne (7) * 36.7437	US$/T	164	171	176	161	158	153	137	117	114	146	171	137	129	152	141	150	177
(9) Exchange rate	MS/US$	0	0	0	0	0	0	0	1	1	2	2	3	3	3	3	3	6
(10) Hard red winter in MS (8) * (9)	MS/T	4	4	4	8	24	29	45	75	162	333	426	388	391	470	438	509	1 137
(11) Soft red winter No. 2	US$/T	154	171	165	135	139	141	131	119	114	142	163	129	127	146	138	142	168
(12) Soft red winter in MS (11) * (9)	MS/T	3	4	4	7	21	27	43	76	162	324	406	366	383	451	430	482	1 082
(13) Average of HRW and SRW	MS/T	4	4	4	8	23	28	44	75	162	328	416	377	387	461	434	496	1 110
(14) Transport cost to Veracruz	US$/T	11	11	11	11	11	11	11	11	11	11	11	11	11	11	11	11	11
(15) Transport cost in MS (14) * (9)	MS/T	0	0	0	0	2	2	4	7	16	25	27	31	33	34	34	37	71
(16) Adjusted reference price (13) + (15)	MS/T	4	4	4	8	25	30	47	82	177	354	443	408	420	495	468	533	1 180
(17) Unit market price support (5) − (16)	MS/T	-1	-1	0	-1	-9	-4	-9	-11	-57	-44	-86	76	140	-69	109	-42	-270
(18) Market price support (1) * (17)/1 000	MS Mio	-2	-2	0	-4	-30	-19	-46	-52	-254	-160	-374	298	568	-251	389	-175	-936
(19) Market price support in %	%	-28	-19	3	-13	-53	-16	-23	-15	-48	-14	-24	16	25	-16	19	-9	-30

CSE-MARKET TRANSFERS (MT)

	Units	1979	1980	1981	1982	1983	1984	1985	1986	1987	1988	1989	1990	1991	1992	1993	1994	1995p
(20) MPS on domestic prod. − (18)	MS Mio	2	2	0	4	30	19	46	52	254	160	374	-298	-568	251	-389	175	936
(21) Consumption	'000T	3 434	3 684	4 316	4 702	3 864	4 839	5 534	4 994	4 830	4 687	4 574	4 267	4 602	4 697	5 324	5 476	4 400
(22) Consumption − Prod. (21) − (1)	'000T	1 147	899	1 123	311	401	334	320	224	415	1 022	199	336	541	1 076	1 742	1 325	932
(23) Rate of the tariff on imports	%																14	12
(24) Tariffs on imports	MS Mio																-95	-132
(25) Total market transfers (20) + (24)	MS Mio	2	2	0	4	30	19	46	52	254	160	374	-298	-568	251	-389	80	804

Notes:

p. provisional
(1) Sources: SAGAR. 1979-93. *Informe para cuenta pública, 1994*. 1994. *Anuario estadístico de la producción agrícola de los Estados Unidos Mexicanos, 1994*; 1995. *BIOSA, number 126, June 1996, page 5. Data refer to crop year (año agrícola)*.
(1)a, (1)b Sources: 1987-92. SAGAR. *Producción y comercialización de trigo, 1987-1993*; 1993 and 1994. *Anuario estadístico de la producción agrícola de los Estados Unidos Mexicanos*, several issues; 1995. SAGAR.
(2)a, (2)b Guaranted prices *(precios de garantía)* up to spring-summer 1990, then concerted prices *(precios de concertación)*. Source: *Sexto Informe de Gobierno, 1994*; 1995. SAGAR.
(2) Weighted average of the prices of the two crop seasons. (2) = [(1)a * (2)a + (1)b * (2)b]/[(1)a + (1)b]
(3) Source: Aserca.
(5) = (2) − (4) for all years except 1995 where (5) = [[(2)a − (3)/(1)a] * (1)a + ((2)b − (1)b] * (1)a + (1)b] because in 1995 the concerted price applies only to Otoño Invierno.
(7) US exports: wheat No.2, hard red winter, ordinary protein, fob, vessel, Gulf portts, source: USDA, *Agricultural Outlook*, various issues.
(8) One metric tonne is equivalent to 36.7437 bushel for wheat.
(9) Source: OECD, *Main Economic Indicators*.
(11) US export price, Gulf, wheat No.2, soft red winter; source: IWC, *World wheat statistics*, London.
(14) Source: USDA, Agricultural Marketing Service, *Marketing Research Report number 630, Shipping US grain to Mexico*, September 1995.
(19) = (18)/(6) * 100.
(21) Sources: 1979-93. *Informe para cuenta pública 1994*; 1994. *BIOSA, Number 126, June 1996, page 7*; 1995. data provided by SAGAR.
(24) Tariffs on imports − (22) * (16) * (23)/100 000.

Table 2A.   **Producer subsidy equivalent – maize**

	Units	1979	1980	1981	1982	1983	1984	1985	1986	1987	1988	1989	1990	1991	1992	1993	1994	1995p
I. Level of production	'000 t	8 458	12 374	14 550	10 120	13 188	12 788	14 103	11 721	11 607	10 600	10 953	14 635	14 252	16 929	18 125	18 236	18 353
II. Production price (farm gate)	M$/t	3	4	7	10	18	29	48	86	239	363	428	627	704	739	744	609	1 070
III. Value of production	M$ mn	29	55	95	96	232	377	683	1 002	2 774	3 846	4 690	9 182	10 026	12 518	13 480	11 097	19 640
IV. Levies	M$ mn	0	0	0	0	0	0	0	0	0	0	0	0	0	0	0	0	0
V. Direct payments	M$ mn	0	0	0	0	0	0	0	0	0	0	1	1	1	2	1	3 001	3 643
VI. Adjusted value of production	M$ mn	29	55	95	96	232	377	683	1 002	2 774	3 846	4 691	9 183	10 028	12 520	13 482	14 097	23 283
VII. Policy transfers	M$ mn	6	26	63	57	-68	61	150	345	1 492	1 085	1 373	4 403	5 052	6 703	7 079	6 663	6 054
A. Market price support	M$ mn	0	8	35	22	-124	-52	8	124	1 092	490	747	3 335	4 091	5 501	6 083	2 638	1 209
1. Trade measures	M$ mn	0	8	35	22	-124	-52	7	123	1 090	488	741	3 291	4 003	5 412	5 929	2 485	1 063
2. PACE	M$ mn	0	0	0	0	0	0	1	1	2	2	5	44	88	89	154	153	146
B. Levies	M$ mn	0	0	0	0	0	0	0	0	0	0	0	0	0	0	0	0	0
C. Direct payments	M$ mn	0	0	0	0	0	0	0	0	0	0	0	1	1	2	1	3 001	3 643
1. Per tonne payment (Aserca)	M$ mn																	
2. Area and headage payments	M$ mn																	
3. Disaster	M$ mn	0	0	0	0	0	0	0	0	0	0	0	0	0	0	0	2 999	3 631
4. Price premium (Aserca)	M$ mn	0	0	0	0	0	0	0	0	0	0	0	1	1	2	1	2	12
D. Reduction of input costs	M$ mn	4	9	15	23	42	81	94	161	312	489	501	803	581	576	417	535	623
E. General services	M$ mn	2	9	13	12	14	32	47	60	88	106	125	250	367	600	550	465	549
F. Sub national	M$ mn	0	0	0	0	0	0	0	0	0	0	0	14	12	24	28	25	30
G. Other	M$ mn																	
VIII. Gross total PSE	M$ mn	6	26	63	57	-68	61	150	345	1 492	1 085	1 373	4 403	5 052	6 703	7 079	6 663	6 054
IX. Gross unit PSE	M$/t	1	2	4	6	-5	5	11	29	129	102	125	301	354	396	391	365	330
X. Gross percentage PSE	%	21	47	66	60	-29	16	22	34	54	28	29	48	50	54	53	47	26

Notes to Table 2A
PSE: Maize

Definitions and Notes:

I **Level of production**: SAGAR statistics on grain maize (*maíz grano*) [1].

II **Production price (farm gate)**: From 1979 to 1981, guaranteed prices [2]. From 1982 to 1986, the annual production price was estimated as the simple average of the guaranteed prices for the Autumn-Winter and Spring-Summer crop seasons [2]. From 1987 to 1994, a weighted average of the guaranteed prices for the Autumn-Winter and Spring-Summer crop seasons [2]. From 1979 to 1994, a weighted average of the guaranteed prices for white maize and yellow maize was used, assuming that white maize accounts for 95 per cent of total maize production and yellow maize for the remaining 5 per cent. For 1995, average producer price [3].

III **Value of production**: Level of production (I) multiplied by the production price (II).

A.1 **Trade measures**: Production price (II) minus reference price (see Table 14) multiplied by the level of production (I).

A.2 **PACE (Programme to Support the Marketing in Ejidos)**: Marketing subsidy provided to ejido farmers for each tonne of maize sold to CONASUPO rural stores (BORUCONSA) [4].

C.2 **Area and headage payments**: See notes to Table 13.

C.3 **Disaster payments**: See notes to Table 13.

D. **Reduction of input costs:** See notes to Table 13.

E. **General services**: See notes to Table 13.

Sources:

[1] SAGAR, as reported in Sexto Informe de Gobierno 1994, Anexo, page 167 and Primer Informe de Gobierno 1995, Anexo, page 79. Estimates provided directly by SAGAR for 1995.

[2] SAGAR, as reported in Sexto Informe de Gobierno 1994, Anexo, pages 165 and 166 and *Primer Informe de Gobierno* 1995, *Anexo*, page 84. Data provided by SHCP for 1994 and 1995.

[3] Estimate provided directly by SAGAR.

[4] CONASUPO, as reported in Sexto Informe de Gobierno 1994, Anexo, pages 262 and *Primer Informe de Gobierno* 1995, *Anexo*, page 86.

Table 2A. **Consumer subsidy equivalent – maize** *(cont.)*

	Units	1979	1980	1981	1982	1983	1984	1985	1986	1987	1988	1989	1990	1991	1992	1993	1994	1995p
I. Level of consumption	'000 t	9 203	16 561	17 504	10 370	17 833	15 216	16 323	13 420	15 201	13 896	14 600	18 737	15 659	18 224	18 126	20 913	20 390
II. Consumption price (farm gate)	M$/t	3	4	6	9	20	30	48	84	217	352	411	578	678	716	744	590	1 064
III. Value of consumption	M$ mn	32	71	108	98	357	458	789	1 129	3 295	4 889	6 004	10 821	10 612	13 055	13 481	12 338	21 686
IV. Policy transfers	M$ mn	4	-1	-23	0	151	151	113	287	-798	238	405	-350	-2 086	-2 956	-3 716	-559	1 202
A. Market transfers																		
1. MPS on domestic production	M$ mn	0	-8	-35	-22	124	52	-8	-124	-1 092	-490	-747	-3 335	-4 091	-5 501	-6 083	-2 638	-1 209
1. Tariffs	M$ mn	0	-8	-35	-22	124	52	-8	-124	-1 092	-490	-747	-3 335	-4 091	-5 501	-6 083	-2 638	-1 209
B. Other transfers	M$ mn	5	7	12	23	27	99	121	411	294	728	1 152	2 985	2 005	2 545	2 367	2 079	2 411
1. Conasupo subsidy	M$ mn	5	7	12	23	27	99	121	403	199	514	895	2 724	1 537	2 029	2 000	1 676	1 943
2. Tortilla consumption subsidy	M$ mn	0	0	0	0	0	0	0	8	96	214	257	261	468	517	368	403	468
V. Total CSE	M$ mn	4	-1	-23	0	151	151	113	287	-798	238	405	-350	-2 086	-2 956	-3 716	-559	1 202
VI. Unit CSE	M$/t	0	0	-1	0	8	10	7	21	-52	17	28	-19	-133	-162	-205	-27	59
VII. Percentage CSE	%	13	-2	-21	0	42	33	14	25	-24	5	7	-3	-20	-23	-28	-5	6

p: provisional.

Notes to Table 2A
CSE: Maize

Definitions and Notes:

I   **Level of consumption**: Apparent consumption of grain maize defined as production plus imports minus exports [1].

II **Consumption price (farm gate)**: Implicit price measured at the farm gate; equal to the production price (Pp) minus the sum of unit market price support (MPS_u) and unit market transfers (M_{tu}) [$Pp - (MPS_u + MT_u)$].

III **Value of consumption**: Level of consumption (I) multiplied by the consumption price (II).

A.1 **MPS on domestic production**: The inverse of the market price support component of the PSE.

A.2 **Tariffs**: Not applicable for the entire review period in which imports were duty-free (even if import permit or tariff quotas were in place).

B.1 **CONASUPO subsidy**: Government transfers to CONASUPO [2] net of stockholding expenditure (estimated as 30 per cent of transfers) and feed subsidies (see PSEs for livestock products). Consumption subsidies were allocated among wheat, maize, rice and soyabeans according to their share in domestic purchases by CONASUPO [3].

B.2 **Tortilla consumption subsidy**: CONASUPO programme to subsidise maize tortilla consumption for a targeted low-income population [4].

Sources:

[1]   For the years 1979-93, SAGAR, as reported in *Sexto Informe de Gobierno* 1994, *Anexo*, page 168. Estimates from the OECD Secretariat for 1994 and 1995.

[2]   Data provided by SHCP.

[3]   CONASUPO, as reported in *Sexto Informe de Gobierno* 1994, *Anexo*, page 264 and *Primer Informe de Gobierno* 1995, *Anexo*, page 86. Estimates provided directly by SAGAR for 1995.

[4]   CONASUPO, as reported in Sexto Informe de Gobierno 1994, Anexo, page 261 and Primer Informe de Gobierno 1995, Anexo, page 123.

Table 2A. Calculation of market price support and of market transfers – maize (cont.)

	Units	1979	1980	1981	1982	1983	1984	1985	1986	1987	1988	1989	1990	1991	1992	1993	1994	1995p
MAIZE (MAIZ)																		
PSE-MARKET PRICE SUPPORT (MPS)																		
(1) Production	'000 T	8 458	12 374	14 550	10 120	13 188	12 788	14 103	11 721	11 607	10 600	10 953	14 635	14 252	16 929	18 125	18 236	18 353
(1)a Production Otoño Invierno	'000 T									815	1 520	1 214	1 402	1 708	2 104	3 823	4 974	3 733
(1)b Production Primavera Verano	'000 T									10 792	9 080	9 739	13 233	12 544	14 825	14 302	13 262	14 620
(2)a Administered price white O-I	M$/T				9	16	26	44	75	160	320	370	600	680	715	750	650	747
(2)b Administered price white P-V	M$/T				10	19	33	53	96	245	370	435	636	715	750	750	600	1 179
(2)c Price white	M$/T	3	4	7	10	18	29	48	86	239	363	428	633	711	746	750	614	1 092
(2)d Administered price yellow O-I	M$/T													565	595	625	540	595
(2)e Administered price yellow P-V	M$/T												530	565	625	625	500	680
(2)f Price yellow	M$/T												530	565	621	625	511	663
(2) Weighted admin. price	M$/T	3	4	7	10	18	29	48	86	239	363	428	627	704	739	744	609	1 070
(3) Value of production (2) * (1)/1 000	M$ Mio	29	55	95	96	232	377	683	1 002	2 774	3 846	4 690	9 182	10 026	12 518	13 480	11 097	19 640
YELLOW MAIZE (MAIZ AMARILLO)																		
(4) Production	'000 T	423	619	728	506	659	639	705	586	580	530	548	732	713	846	906	912	918
(5) Producer price (administered)	M$/T	3	4	7	10	18	29	48	86	239	363	428	530	565	621	625	511	663
(6) Reference price fob	US$/bu	3	3	3	3	3	4	3	2	2	3	3	3	3	3	3	3	3
(7) Reference price (6) * 39.3679	US$/T	118	129	134	110	137	138	114	89	77	107	112	110	108	105	103	108	123
(8) Exchange rate	M$/US$	0	0	0	0	0	0	0	1	1	2	2	3	3	3	3	3	6
(9) Reference price (7) * (8)	M$/T	3	3	3	6	21	26	37	57	109	245	280	312	327	324	321	366	791
(10) Transport cost to Veracruz	US$/T	11	11	11	11	11	11	11	11	11	11	11	11	11	11	11	11	11
(11) Transport cost in M$ (10) * (8)	M$/T	0	0	1	1	2	7	4	7	16	25	27	31	33	34	34	37	71
(12) Adjusted reference price (9) + (11)	M$/T	3	3	4	6	23	29	41	64	124	270	307	343	360	358	356	403	862
(13) Unit market price support (5) – (12)	M$/T	1	1	3	3	-5	1	8	21	115	93	121	187	205	263	269	108	-199
(14) Market price support (13) * (4)/1 000	M$ Mio	0	3	2	2	-4	1	5	13	67	49	66	137	146	223	244	99	-183
WHITE MAIZE (MAIZ BLANCO)																		
(15) Production	'000 T	8 035	11 755	13 823	9 614	12 529	12 149	13 398	11 135	11 027	10 070	10 405	13 903	13 539	16 083	17 219	17 324	17 435
(16) Producer price (administered)	M$/T	3	4	4	10	18	29	48	86	239	363	428	633	711	746	750	614	1 092
(17) Ref. price yellow adjusted to white	M$/T	3	4	4	7	26	32	45	69	131	294	336	374	393	389	386	439	949
(18) Adjusted reference price (17) + (11)	M$/T	3	4	4	7	27	34	48	76	146	319	363	406	426	423	420	476	1 020
(19) Unit market price support (18) – (16)	M$/T	0	1	2	2	-10	-4	0	10	93	44	65	227	285	323	330	138	71
(20) Market price support (19) * (15)/1 000	M$ Mio	0	8	32	20	-120	-53	2	110	1 024	439	675	3 154	3 857	5 190	5 685	2 386	1 246
Market price support for total maize																		
(21) Total trade measures (14) + (20)	M$ Mio	0	8	35	22	-124	-52	7	123	1 090	488	741	3 291	4 003	5 412	5 929	2 485	1 063
(22) PACE	M$ Mio	0	0	0	0	0	0	1	1	2	2	5	44	88	89	154	153	146
(23) Total MPS (21) + (22)	M$ Mio	0	8	35	22	-124	-52	8	124	1 092	490	747	3 335	4 091	5 501	6 083	2 638	1 209
(24) Unit market price support	M$/T	0	1	2	2	-9	-4	1	11	94	46	68	228	287	325	336	145	66
(25) Market price support in %	%	1	15	36	23	-53	-14	1	12	39	13	16	36	41	44	45	24	6

Table 2A. Calculation of market price support and of market transfers – maize *(cont.)*

	Units	1979	1980	1981	1982	1983	1984	1985	1986	1987	1988	1989	1990	1991	1992	1993	1994	1995p
CSE-MARKET TRANSFERS (MT)																		
(26) MPS on domestic prod. – (23)	MS Mio	0	–8	–35	–22	124	52	–8	–124	–1 092	–490	–747	–3 335	–4 091	–5 501	–6 083	–2 638	–1 209
(27) Consumption	'000 T	9 203	16 561	17 504	10 370	17 833	15 216	16 323	13 420	15 201	13 896	14 600	18 737	15 659	18 224	18 126	20 913	20 390
(28) Consumption – Production (27) – (1)	'000 T	745	4 187	2 954	250	4 645	2 428	2 220	1 699	3 594	3 296	3 647	4 102	1 407	1 295	1	2 677	2 037
(29) Rate of the tariff on imports	%																	
(30) Tariffs on imports	MS Mio																	
(31) Total market transfers (26) + (30)	MS Mio	0	–8	–35	–22	124	52	–8	–124	–1 092	–490	–747	–3 335	–4 091	–5 501	–6 083	–2 638	–1 209

Notes:
p: provisional
(1) Sources: SAGAR, 1979-93: *Informe para cuenta pública, 1994*; 1994: *Anuario estadístico de la producción agrícola de los Estados Unidos Mexicanos, 1994*; 1995: *BIOSA*, number 126, June 1996, page 5. Data refer to crop year *año agrícola*.
(1)a. (1)b Sources: 1987-92: SAGAR, *Producción y comercialización de maíz*, 1987-1993; 1993 and 1994: *Anuario estadístico de la producción agrícola de los Estados Unidos Mexicanos*, several issues; 1995: SAGAR.
(2)a, (2)b Guaranted prices (*Precios de garantía*). Source: *Sexto Informe de Gobierno 1994*, and for 1995: SAGAR.
(2)c Weighted average of the prices of the two crop seasons. (2)c = [(1)a * (2)a + (1)b * (2)b]/[(1)a + (1)b].
(2)d From mid-1990, the government set separate prices for white maize and yellow maize.
(2)f 1991-95: weighted average of the prices of the two crop seasons. (2)f = [(1)a * (2)d + (1)b * (2)e]/[(1)a + (1)b].
(2) f=(2)c * 0.95+(2)f * 0.05 however (2) =(2)c when only (2)c is available.
(4) Yellow maize accounts for 5 per cent of total production.
(6) US exports: corn n° 2, fob, vessel, Gulf ports, source: USDA, *Agricultural Outlook*, various issues.
(7) One metric tonne is equivalent to 39.3679 bu for maize.
(8) Source: OECD, *Main Economic Indicators*.
(10) Source: USDA, Agricultural Marketing Service, *Marketing Research Report number 630*, Shipping US grain to Mexico, September 1995.
(15) White maize accounts for 95 per cent of total production.
(17) US exports: corn n° 2, fob, vessel, Gulf ports, source: USDA, *Agricultural Outlook*, various issues.This price is increased by 20 per cent to take account of the difference between white and yellow maize. This is based on the fact that the administrative price for white maize was set 20% above the administrative price for yellow maize for the years 1992 to 1995.
(20) Market price support. (20) = (19) * (15)/1 000.
(22) PACE: *Programa de apoyo a la comercialización ejidal*. Source: *Sexto Informe de Gobierno, 1994, Anexo*, page 262, table "*Programa de apoyo a la comercialización rural*", 1994 and 1995: *Primer Informe de Gobierno*, 1995, page 86.
(24) Unit market price support. (24) = (23)/(1) * 1 000.
(25) Market price support in %. (25) = (23)/(3) * 100.
(27) Source: 1979-92: *Informe para cuenta pública 1994*, 1993-94: *BIOSA*, Number 126, June 1996, page 7; 1995 estimated from coarse grains consumption growth rate shown in OECD, *The Agricultural Outlook, Trends and Issues to 2000*, Paris 1996.
(29) The rate of the tariff was zero for all the period under review.
(30) Tariffs on imports. (30) = – (28) * (12) * (29)/100 000.

Table 2B. **Producer subsidy equivalent – barley**

	Units	1979	1980	1981	1982	1983	1984	1985	1986	1987	1988	1989	1990	1991	1992	1993	1994	1995p
I. Level of production	'000 t	368	530	551	424	558	619	536	515	617	350	435	492	580	550	541	307	487
II. Production price (farm gate)	M$/t	3	4	3	9	18	31	45	94	189	380	506	630	630	685	700	700	1 003
III. Value of production	M$ mn	1	2	3	4	10	19	24	48	116	133	220	310	365	377	379	215	488
IV. Levies	M$ mn	0	0	0	0	0	0	0	0	0	0	0	0	0	0	0	0	0
V. Direct payments	M$ mn	0	0	0	0	0	0	0	0	0	0	0	0	0	0	0	0	0
VI. Adjusted value of production	M$ mn	1	2	3	4	10	19	24	48	116	133	220	310	365	377	379	215	488
VII. Policy transfers	M$ mn	0	0	2	1	-2	5	5	15	24	7	30	126	162	173	177	74	-51
A. Market price support	M$ mn	0	0	1	0	-3	2	1	10	15	-6	10	98	133	144	156	60	-75
1. Trade measures	M$ mn	0	0	1	0	-3	2	1	10	15	-6	10	98	133	144	156	60	-75
2. PACE	M$ mn																	
B. Levies	M$ mn	0	0	0	0	0	0	0	0	0	0	0	0	0	0	0	0	0
C. Direct payments	M$ mn	0	0	0	0	0	0	0	0	0	0	0	0	0	0	0	0	0
1. Per tonne payment (Aserca)	M$ mn																	
2. Area and headage payments	M$ mn																	
3. Disaster	M$ mn	0	0	0	0	0	0	0	0	0	0	0	0	0	0	0	0	0
4. Price premium (Aserca)	M$ mn																	
D. Reduction of input costs	M$ mn	0	0	0	0	1	2	2	3	7	10	15	20	16	11	5	5	9
E. General services	M$ mn	0	0	0	0	1	1	2	2	3	3	5	8	13	18	15	8	13
F. Sub national	M$ mn	0	0	0	0	0	0	0	0	0	0	0	0	0	1	1	0	1
G. Other	M$ mn																	
VIII. Gross total PSE	M$ mn	0	0	2	1	-2	5	5	15	24	7	30	126	162	173	177	74	-51
IX. Gross unit PSE	M$/t	0	1	3	3	-3	8	9	29	40	19	69	256	280	315	328	240	-105
X. Gross percentage PSE	%	-10	16	47	31	-16	25	19	31	21	5	14	41	44	46	47	34	-10

Notes to Table 2B
PSE: Barley

Definitions and Notes:

I   **Level of production**: SAGAR statistics on grain barley (*cebada grano*) [1].

II   **Production price (farm gate)**: From 1979 to 1981, guaranteed prices [2]. From 1982 to 1986, the annual production price was estimated as the simple average of the guaranteed prices for the Autumn-Winter and Spring-Summer crop seasons [2]. From 1987 to 1994, a weighted average of the administered prices for the Autumn-Winter and Spring-Summer crop seasons [2]. For 1995, average producer price [3].

III   **Value of production**: Level of production (I) multiplied by the production price (II).

A.1   **Trade measures**: Production price (II) minus reference price (see Table 14) multiplied by the level of production (I).

C.3   **Disaster payments**: See notes to Table 13.

D.   **Reduction of input costs:** See notes to Table 13.

E.   **General services**: See notes to Table 13.

Sources:

[1]   SAGAR, as reported in *Sexto Informe de Gobierno* 1994, *Anexo*, page 167 and *Primer Informe de Gobierno* 1995, *Anexo*, page 79. Estimates provided directly by SAGAR for 1995.

[2]   SAGAR, as reported in Sexto Informe de Gobierno 1994, Anexo, pages 165 and 166 and *Primer Informe de Gobierno* 1995, *Anexo*, page 84.

[3]   Estimate provided directly by SAGAR.

Table 2B. **Consumer subsidy equivalent – barley** (cont.)

	Units	1979	1980	1981	1982	1983	1984	1985	1986	1987	1988	1989	1990	1991	1992	1993	1994	1995p
I. Level of consumption	'000 t	413	704	642	426	645	645	574	519	618	358	560	603	671	682	641	649	633
II. Consumption price (farm gate)	M$/t	3	4	6	9	18	31	45	93	188	381	506	597	602	638	658	597	1 038
III. Value of consumption	M$ mn	1	3	4	4	12	20	26	48	116	136	283	360	404	435	422	387	657
IV. Policy transfers	M$ mn	0	0	-1	0	3	-2	-1	-10	-15	6	-14	-100	-134	-147	-158	-60	75
A. Market transfers																		
1. MPS on domestic production	M$ mn	0	0	-1	0	3	-2	-1	-10	-15	6	-14	-98	-133	-144	-156	-60	75
2. Tariffs	M$ mn	0	0	0	0	0	0	0	0	0	0	0	-2	-2	-3	-2	0	0
B. Other transfers																		
1. Consumption subsidies	M$ mn	0	0	0	0	0	0	0	0	0	0	0	0	0	0	0	0	0
2. Aserca payment	M$ mn																	
V. Total CSE	M$ mn	0	0	-1	0	3	-2	-1	-10	-15	6	-14	-100	-134	-147	-158	-60	75
VI. Unit CSE	M$/t	1	0	-2	-1	4	-3	-2	-19	-24	17	-24	-167	-200	-216	-247	-93	118
VII. Percentage CSE	%	19	2	-26	-12	24	-9	-4	-20	-13	4	-5	-28	-33	-34	-38	-16	11

p. provisional.

Notes to Table 2B
CSE: Barley

Definitions and Notes:

I   **Level of consumption**: Apparent consumption of grain barley defined as production plus imports minus exports [1].

II   **Consumption price (farm gate)**: Implicit price measured at the farm gate; equal to the production price (Pp) minus the sum of unit market price support (MPS_u) and unit market transfers (M_{tu}) [Pp – (MPS_u + MT_u)].

III   **Value of consumption**: Level of consumption (I) multiplied by the consumption price (II).

A.1   **MPS on domestic production**: The inverse of the market price support component of the PSE.

A.2   **Tariffs**: Not applicable for the 1994-95 period in which imports were duty-free (even if tariff quotas were in place). For the 1979-93 period: import tariff of 10 per cent multiplied by reference price multiplied by the difference between the consumption (I) and production (see PSE I) levels.

Sources:

[1]   For the years 1979-93, SAGAR, as reported in *Sexto Informe de Gobierno* 1994, *Anexo*, page 168. Estimates from the OECD Secretariat for 1994 and 1995.

Table 2B. **Calculation of market price support and of market transfers – barley** (cont.)

BARLEY (CEBADA EN GRANO)

PSE-MARKET PRICE SUPPORT (MPS)

	Units	1979	1980	1981	1982	1983	1984	1985	1986	1987	1988	1989	1990	1991	1992	1993	1994	1995p
(1) Production	'000T	368	530	551	424	558	619	536	515	617	350	435	492	580	550	541	307	487
(1)a Production Otoño Invierno	'000 T																	202
(1)b Production Primavera Verano	'000 T																	285
(2)a Administered price O-I	M$/T				9	16	26	37	75	152	320							752
(2)b Administered price P-V	M$/T				9	19	37	53	112	225	440							1 180
(3) Average price	M$/T	3	4	6	9	18	31	45	94	189	380	506	630	630	685	700	700	1 003
Value of production (2) * (1)/1 000	M$ Mio	1	2	3	4	10	19	24	48	116	133	220	310	365	377	379	215	488
(4) Malting barley price, Minneapolis	US$/bu	3	3	3	3	3	3	2	2	2	3	4	3	2	2	2	3	3
(5) Malt. reference price (4) * 45.9296	US$/T	126	148	155	126	123	125	107	92	91	150	168	127	108	112	107	124	155
(6) Exchange rate	M$/US$	0	0	0	0	0	0	0	1	1	2	2	3	3	3	3	3	6
(7) Malt. reference price in M$ (5) * (6)	M$/T	3	3	4	6	19	24	35	59	129	341	420	360	327	346	334	420	997
(8) Transport cost to Gulf	US$/bu	0	0	0	0	0	0	0	0	0	0	0	0	0	0	0	0	0
(9) Transport cost to Gulf (8) * 45.9296	US$/T	14	14	14	14	14	14	14	14	14	14	14	14	14	14	14	14	14
(10) Transport cost to Veracruz	US$/T	11	11	11	11	11	11	11	11	11	11	11	11	11	11	11	11	11
(11) Total transport cost in M$	M$/T	1	1	1	1	4	5	8	16	35	57	62	70	75	77	77	84	159
(12) Adjusted reference price (7) + (11)	M$/T	4	4	4	8	23	29	43	75	164	398	482	431	401	423	411	504	1 156
(13) Unit market price support (2) – (12)	M$/T	-1	0	2	1	-5	3	2	19	24	-18	24	199	229	262	289	196	-154
(14) Market price support (1) * (13)/1 000	M$ Mio	0	0	1	0	-3	2	1	10	15	-6	10	98	133	144	156	60	-75
(15) Market price support in %	%	-23	-4	29	12	-30	9	4	20	13	-5	5	32	36	38	41	28	-15
CSE-MARKET TRANSFERS (MT)																		
(16) MPS on domestic prod. – (14)	M$ Mio	0	0	-1	0	3	-2	-1	-10	-15	6	-10	-98	-133	-144	-156	-60	75
(17) Consumption	'000T	413	704	642	426	645	645	574	519	618	358	560	603	671	682	641	649	633
(18) Consumption – Production (17) – (1)	'000T	45	174	91	2	87	26	38	4	1	8	125	111	91	132	100	342	146
(19) Rate of the tariff on imports	%	5	5	5	5	5	5	5	5	0	5	5	5	5	5	5	0	0
(20) Tariffs on imports	M$ Mio	0	0	-1	0	0	0	0	0	0	0	-3	-2	-2	-3	-2	0	0
(21) Total market transfers (16) + (20)	M$ Mio	0	0	-1	0	3	-2	-1	-10	-15	6	-14	-100	-134	-147	-158	-60	75

Notes:

p. provisional

(1) Sources: SAGAR: 1979-93: *Informe para cuenta pública 1994.* 1994: *Anuario estadístico de la producción agrícola de los Estados Unidos Mexicanos, 1994; 1995:* SAGAR. Data refer to crop year (*año agrícola*).

(2a), (2b) Guaranteed prices (*precios de garantía*) up to spring-summer 1990, then concerted prices (*precios de concertación*). Source: *Sexto Informe de Gobierno 1994,* page 166. For 1995, data provided by SAGAR.

(2) Weighted average of the prices of the two crop seasons. (2) = [(1)a * (2)a + (1)b * (2)b]/[(1)a + (1)b].

(4) Cash price of barley at Minneapolis for barley, no. 3 or better malting, 65% or better plump. Source: USDA ERS, *Feed situation and outlook.* October 1994, appendix table 14 page 53. For most recent years, USDA, *Agricultural Outlook,* various issues.

(5) One metric tonne is equivalent to 45.9296 bushel for barley.

(8) Transport cost from US production areas to Gulf port. Source USDA, Agricultural Marketing Service, *Marketing Research Report number 630.* Shipping US grain to Mexico, September 1995.

(10) Transport cost from US production areas to Gulf port. Source: USDA, Agricultural Marketing Service, *Marketing Research Report number 630,* Shipping US grain to Mexico. September 1995.

(11) = [(9) + (10)] * (6).

(15) = [(14)/(3)] * 100.

(17) Sources 1973-93: *Informe para cuenta pública 1994.* 1994: Data provided by SAGAR. 1995 estimated from coarse grains consumption growth rate shown in OECD, *The Agricultural Outlook. Trends and Issues to 2000,* Paris 1996.

(20) = – [(18)] * (12) * (19)/100 000.

Table 2D. **Producer subsidy equivalent – sorghum**

	Units	1979	1980	1981	1982	1983	1984	1985	1986	1987	1988	1989	1990	1991	1992	1993	1994	1995p
I. Level of production	'000 t	3 988	4 689	6 086	4 719	4 687	5 039	6 597	4 833	6 298	5 895	5 002	5 978	4 308	5 353	2 581	3 701	4 170
II. Production price (farm gate)	MS/t	2	3	4	5	12	21	30	60	142	269	320	397	410	438	361	393	942
III. Value of production	MS mn	9	14	24	25	56	106	200	290	897	1 586	1 601	2 375	1 764	2 344	931	1 454	3 926
IV. Levies	MS mn	0	0	0	0	0	0	0	0	0	0	0	0	0	0	0	0	0
V. Direct payments	MS mn	0	0	0	0	0	0	0	0	0	0	0	0	19	118	101	518	641
VI. Adjusted value of production	MS mn	9	14	24	25	56	106	200	290	897	1 586	1 601	2 375	1 784	2 463	1 033	1 972	4 567
VII. Policy transfers	MS mn	0	3	10	6	-34	13	-5	73	280	384	318	244	276	532	194	642	876
A. Market price support	MS mn	-2	-2	3	-5	-47	-19	-48	-7	138	104	137	0	81	195	14	-5	0
1. Trade measures	MS mn	-2	-2	3	-5	-47	-19	-48	-7	138	104	137	0	81	195	14	-5	0
2. PACE	MS mn																	
B. Levies	MS mn	0	0	0	0	0	0	0	0	0	0	0	0	0	0	0	0	0
C. Direct payments	MS mn	0	0	0	0	0	0	0	0	0	0	0	0	19	118	101	518	641
1. Per tonne payment (Aserca)	MS mn																	
2. Area and headage payments	MS mn	0	0	0	0	0	0	0	0	0	0	0	0	0	0	0	491	638
3. Disaster	MS mn	0	0	0	0	0	0	0	0	0	0	0	0	0	0	0	0	2
4. Price premium (Aserca)	MS mn	0	0	0	0	0	0	0	0	0	0	0	0	19	118	101	26	0
D. Reduction of input costs	MS mn	1	2	4	7	9	23	29	58	111	230	145	184	107	105	33	67	122
E. General services	MS mn	1	2	3	4	3	9	14	22	31	50	36	57	67	110	44	59	108
F. Sub national	MS mn	0	0	0	0	0	0	0	0	0	0	0	3	2	4	2	3	6
G. Other	MS mn																	
VIII. Gross total PSE	MS mn	0	3	10	6	-34	13	-5	73	280	384	318	244	276	532	194	642	876
IX. Gross unit PSE	MS/t	0	1	2	1	-7	3	-1	15	44	65	64	41	64	99	75	173	210
X. Gross percentage PSE	%	2	21	43	24	-61	12	-2	25	31	24	20	10	16	22	19	33	19

Notes to Table 2D
PSE: Sorghum

Definitions and Notes:

I   **Level of production**: SAGAR statistics on grain sorghum (*sorgo grano*) [1].

II **Production price (farm gate)**: From 1979 to 1981, guaranteed prices [2]. From 1982 to 1986, the annual production price was estimated as the simple average of the guaranteed prices for the Autumn-Winter and Spring-Summer crop seasons [2]. From 1987 to 1994, a weighted average of the administered prices for the Autumn-Winter and Spring-Summer crop seasons [2]. For the period 1991-94, an implicit production price was calculated by subtracting the unit budget payments of ASERCA [3] from the concerted price. For 1995, average producer price [4].

III **Value of production**: Level of production (I) multiplied by the production price (II).

A.1 **Trade measures**: Production price (II) minus reference price (see Table 14) multiplied by the level of production (I). In the 1991-94 period, the price gap was multiplied by the level of production of the Autumn-Winter crop season in the Tamaulipas State (as the concerted price only applied to that State and the seasonal import tariff only applied during the harvest season in that State [5]). In 1990, the MPS was not calculated as there were no trade measures in place and concerted prices were not yet implemented.

C.2 **Area and headage payments:** See notes to Table 13.

C.3 **Disaster payments**: See notes to Table 13.

C.4 **Price premiums:** ASERCA payments [3] to the buyers of domestic production at concerted prices.

D. **Reduction of input costs:** See notes to Table 13.

E. **General services**: See notes to Table 13.

Sources:

[1] SAGAR, as reported in *Sexto Informe de Gobierno* 1994, Anexo, page 167 and *Primer Informe de Gobierno* 1995, Anexo, page 79. Estimates provided directly by SAGAR for 1995.

[2] SAGAR, as reported in Sexto Informe de Gobierno 1994, Anexo, pages 165 and 166 and *Primer Informe de Gobierno* 1995, Anexo, page 84.

[3] Data provided directly by ASERCA. Data provided by SHCP for 1995.

[4] Estimate provided directly by SAGAR.

[5] SAGAR (1994), *Producción y comercialización de sorgo*, 1987-1993, pages 4-9.

Table 2D. **Consumer subsidy equivalent – sorghum** (cont.)

	Units	1979	1980	1981	1982	1983	1984	1985	1986	1987	1988	1989	1990	1991	1992	1993	1994	1995p
I. Level of consumption	'000 t	5 251	6 941	8 718	6 360	8 198	7 350	8 819	5 614	7 064	7 042	7 667	8 835	7 508	10 080	6 326	7 563	7 373
II. Consumption price (farm gate)	M$/t	2	3	4	5	16	22	32	60	140	266	310	397	402	421	358	394	942
III. Value of consumption	M$ mn	13	21	33	35	134	163	284	338	989	1 874	2 380	3 510	3 015	4 243	2 263	2 977	6 942
IV. Policy transfers	M$ mn	2	2	-3	5	47	19	48	7	-138	-104	-137	0	-81	-195	-14	5	0
A. Market transfers																		
1. MPS on domestic production	M$ mn	2	2	-3	5	47	19	48	7	-138	-104	-137	0	-81	-195	-14	5	0
2. Tariffs	M$ mn	0	2	-3	5	47	19	48	7	-138	-104	-137	0	-81	-195	-14	5	0
B. Other transfers	M$ mn	0	0	0	0	0	0	0	0	0	0	0	0	0	0	0	0	0
1. Consumption subsidies	M$ mn																	
2. Aserca payment	M$ mn																	
V. Total CSE	M$ mn	2	2	-3	5	47	19	48	7	-138	-104	-137	0	-81	-195	-14	5	0
VI. Unit CSE	M$/t	0	0	0	1	6	3	5	1	-19	-15	-18	0	-11	-19	-2	1	0
VII. Percentage CSE	%	14	9	-9	15	35	12	17	2	-14	-6	-6	0	-3	-5	-1	0	0

p: provisional.

Notes to Table 2D
CSE: Sorghum

Definitions and Notes:

I   **Level of consumption**: Apparent consumption of grain sorghum defined as production plus imports minus exports [1].

II   **Consumption price (farm gate)**: Implicit price measured at the farm gate; equal to the production price (Pp) minus the sum of unit market price support (MPS_u) and unit market transfers (M_{tu}) $[Pp - (MPS_u + MT_u)]$.

III **Value of consumption**: Level of consumption (I) multiplied by the consumption price (II).

A.1 **MPS on domestic production**: The inverse of the market price support component of the PSE.

A.2 **Tariffs**: Not applicable for the 1979-90 and 1994-95 periods in which imports were duty-free (even if import permits were in place). For the 1991-93 period: import tariff of 15 per cent multiplied by reference price multiplied by the difference between the consumption (I) and production (see PSE I) levels.

Sources:

[1]   For the years 1979-93, SAGAR, as reported in *Sexto Informe de Gobierno* 1994, *Anexo*, page 168. Estimates from the OECD Secretariat for 1994 and 1995.

Table 2D. **Calculation of market price support and of market transfers – sorghum** (cont.)

SORGHUM (SORGO (GRANO))

PSE-MARKET PRICE SUPPORT (MPS)

	Units	1979	1980	1981	1982	1983	1984	1985	1986	1987	1988	1989	1990	1991	1992	1993	1994	1995p
(1) Production	'000 T	3 988	4 689	6 086	4 719	4 687	5 039	6 597	4 832	6 298	5 895	5 002	5 978	4 308	5 353	2 581	3 701	4 170
(1)a Production Otoño Invierno	'000 T									2 100	2 021	1 143	1 852	1 550	2 458	1 190	1 626	908
(1)b Production Primavera Verano	'000 T									4 198	3 872	3 859	4 126	2 758	2 895	1 391	2 075	3 262
(1)c Tamaulipas Otoño Invierno	'000 T												1 693	1 438	2 331	1 069	1 447	
(1)d Tamaulipas Primavera Verano	'000 T												199	167	117	58	206	
(1)e Production Tamaulipas (1)c + (1)d	'000 T												1 893	1 605	2 448	1 127	1 653	1 835
(2)a Administered price O-I	MS/T					11	19	29	50	117	225	320	360	414	460	400	400	712
(2)b Administered price P-V	MS/T					14	23	32	70	155	292	320	414	414	460	400	400	1 006
(2) Average price	MS/T	2	3	4	5	12	21	30	60	142	269	320	397	414	460	400	400	942
(3) Aserca payment	MS Mio													19	118	101	26	0
(4) Unit Aserca payment (3)/(1) * 1 000	MS/T													4	22	39	7	0
(5) Producer price net of the payment	MS/T	2	3	4	5	12	21	30	60	142	269	320	397	410	438	361	393	942
(6) Value of production (5) * (1)/1 000	MS Mio	9	14	24	25	56	106	200	290	897	1 586	1 601	2 375	1 764	2 344	931	1 454	3 926
(7) Reference price fob	US$/bu	3	3	3	3	3	3	3	2	2	3	3	3	3	3	3	3	3
(8) Reference price (7) * 39.3679	US$/T	112	133	129	111	131	118	104	85	74	99	106	104	106	104	101	106	123
(9) Exchange rate	MS/US$	0	0	0	0	0	0	0	1	1	2	2	3	3	3	3	3	6
(10) Reference price in MS (8) * (9)	MS/T	3	3	3	6	20	23	34	54	105	226	265	296	320	320	314	359	791
(11) Transport cost to Veracruz	US$/T	11	11	11	11	11	11	11	11	11	11	11	11	11	11	11	11	11
(12) Transport cost in MS (11) * (9)	MS/T	0	0	0	0	2	2	4	7	16	25	27	31	33	34	34	37	71
(13) Adjusted reference price (10) + (12)	MS/T	3	3	3	6	22	25	38	61	121	251	293	328	353	354	348	396	862
(14) Price gap (5) – (13)	MS/T	-1	0	1	-1	-10	-4	-7	-1	22	18	27	70	56	83	13	-3	80
(15) Market price support	MS Mio	-2	-2	3	-5	-47	-19	-48	-7	138	104	137	0	81	195	14	-5	0
(16) Market price support in %	%	-20	-14	13	-21	-83	-18	-24	-2	15	7	9	0	5	8	1	0	0

CSE-MARKET TRANSFERS (MT)

	Units	1979	1980	1981	1982	1983	1984	1985	1986	1987	1988	1989	1990	1991	1992	1993	1994	1995p
(20) MPS on domestic prod. – (15)	MS Mio	2	2	-3	5	47	19	48	7	-138	-104	-137	0	-81	-195	-14	5	0
(21) Consumption	'000 T	5 251	6 941	8 718	6 360	8 198	7 350	8 819	5 614	7 064	7 042	7 667	8 835	7 508	10 080	6 326	7 563	7 373
(22) Consumption – Production (21) – (1)	'000 T	1 263	2 252	2 631	1 641	3 510	2 311	2 222	782	766	1 147	2 665	2 856	3 200	4 726	3 745	3 861	3 204
(23) Rate of the tariff on imports	%	0	0	0	0	0	0	0	0	0	0	0	0	0	0	0	0	0
(24) Tariffs on imports	MS Mio	0	0	0	0	0	0	0	0	0	0	0	0	0	0	0	0	0
(25) Total market transfers (20) + (24)	MS Mio	2	2	-3	5	47	19	48	7	-138	-104	-137	0	-81	-195	-14	5	0

Notes:

p: provisional

(1) Sources: SAGAR. 1979-93: *Informe para cuenta pública 1994*. 1994: *Anuario estadístico de la producción agrícola de los Estados Unidos Mexicanos*. 1994. 1995: SAGAR. Data refer to crop year *(año agrícola)*.

(1)e For 1995, the production in Tamaulipas was estimated as equal to 44% of total production as it was in 1993 and 1994.

(2)a, (2)b Guaranteed prices *(Precios de garantía)* up to spring-summer 1990, then concerted prices *(precios de concertación)*. Source: *Sexto Informe de Gobierno 1994*. The price for 1994 was estimated as equal to the one in 1993. the one for 1995 was provided directly by SAGAR.

(2) Weighted average of the prices of the two crop seasons. (2) = [(1)a * (2)a + (1)b * (2)b]/[(1)a + (1)b]

(3) Source: Aserca.

(5) Producer price net of the payment. (5) = (2) – (4)

(7) US exports: grain sorghum. fob. vessel. Gulf ports. source: USDA. *Agricultural Outlook*. various issues.

(8) One metric tonne is equivalent to 39.3679 bu for sorghum.

(9) Source: OECD. *Main Economic Indicators*.

(11) Source: USDA. Agricultural Marketing Service. *Marketing Research Report number 630. Shipping US grain to Mexico*. September 1995

(15) Market price support (1) * (14)/1 000 until 1989. (1)c * (14)/1 000 from 1991 to 1994; for 1990, it was agreed not to calculate market price support as imports were duty free and the concerted price was not yet applied.

(16) Market price support in %. (16) = (15)/(6) * 100.

(21) Consumption is 100% feed. Source: 1979-93: *Informe para cuenta pública 1994*. 1994: OECD estimation. 1995 estimated from coarse grains consumption growth rate shown in OECD. *The Agricultural Outlook. Trends and Issues to 2000*. Paris 1996.

(24) Tariffs on imports. (24) = – (22) * (13) * (23)/100 000.

Table 2. **Producer subsidy equivalent – other grains**

	Units	1979	1980	1981	1982	1983	1984	1985	1986	1987	1988	1989	1990	1991	1992	1993	1994	1995p
I. Level of production	'000 t	4 356	5 219	6 637	5 143	5 245	5 658	7 133	5 348	6 915	6 245	5 437	6 470	4 888	5 903	3 122	4 008	4 657
II. Production price (farm gate)	M$/t	2	3	4	6	13	22	31	63	146	275	335	415	436	461	420	417	948
III. Value of production	M$ mn	10	16	27	28	66	125	224	338	1 013	1 719	1 821	2 685	2 130	2 721	1 310	1 670	4 414
IV. Levies	M$ mn	0	0	0	0	0	0	0	0	0	0	0	0	0	0	0	0	0
V. Direct payments	M$ mn	0	0	0	0	0	0	0	0	0	0	0	0	19	118	101	518	641
VI. Adjusted value of production	M$ mn	10	16	27	28	66	125	224	338	1 013	1 719	1 821	2 685	2 149	2 840	1 411	2 187	5 055
VII. Policy transfers	M$ mn	0	3	12	7	-36	18	0	88	304	391	348	370	439	705	371	716	825
A. Market price support	M$ mn	-2	-2	4	-5	-50	-17	-47	3	153	98	147	98	213	339	170	56	-75
1. Trade measures	M$ mn	-2	-2	4	-5	-50	-17	-47	3	153	98	147	98	213	339	170	56	-75
2. PACE	M$ mn	0	0	0	0	0	0	0	0	0	0	0	0	0	0	0	0	0
B. Levies	M$ mn	0	0	0	0	0	0	0	0	0	0	0	0	0	0	0	0	0
C. Direct payments	M$ mn	0	0	0	0	0	0	0	0	0	0	0	0	19	118	101	518	641
1. Per tonne payment (Aserca)	M$ mn	0	0	0	0	0	0	0	0	0	0	0	0	0	0	0	0	0
2. Area and headage payments	M$ mn	0	0	0	0	0	0	0	0	0	0	0	0	0	0	0	491	638
3. Disaster	M$ mn	0	0	0	0	0	0	0	0	0	0	0	0	0	0	0	0	3
4. Price premium (Aserca)	M$ mn	0	0	0	0	0	0	0	0	0	0	0	0	19	118	101	26	0
D. Reduction of input costs	M$ mn	1	2	4	7	10	25	31	61	118	240	160	203	123	116	38	72	131
E. General services	M$ mn	1	3	4	4	4	10	16	24	34	53	41	65	81	127	59	67	121
F. Sub national	M$ mn	0	0	0	0	0	0	0	0	0	0	0	4	3	5	3	4	7
G. Other	M$ mn	0	0	0	0	0	0	0	0	0	0	0	0	0	0	0	0	0
VIII. Gross total PSE	M$ mn	0	3	12	7	-36	18	0	88	304	391	348	370	439	705	371	716	825
IX. Gross unit PSE	M$/t	0	1	2	1	-7	3	0	16	44	63	64	57	90	119	119	179	177
X. Gross percentage PSE	%	1	20	43	25	-54	14	0	26	30	23	19	14	20	25	26	33	16

Table 2. **Consumer subsidy equivalent – other grains** (cont.)

	Units	1979	1980	1981	1982	1983	1984	1985	1986	1987	1988	1989	1990	1991	1992	1993	1994	1995p
I. Level of consumption	'000 t	5 664	7 645	9 360	6 786	8 843	7 995	9 393	6 133	7 682	7 400	8 227	9 438	8 179	10 762	6 967	8 212	8 006
II. Consumption price (farm gate)	M$/t	2	3	4	6	17	23	33	63	144	273	326	410	418	435	390	409	955
III. Value of consumption	M$ mn	14	24	37	39	146	184	310	387	1 108	2 019	2 682	3 874	3 422	4 685	2 717	3 362	7 643
IV. Policy transfers	M$ mn	2	2	–4	5	50	17	47	–3	–153	–98	–150	–100	–215	–342	–172	–56	75
A. Market transfers																		
1. MPS on domestic production	M$ mn	2	2	–4	5	50	17	47	–3	–153	–98	–150	–100	–215	–342	–172	–56	75
2. Tariffs	M$ mn	2	2	–4	5	50	17	47	–3	–153	–98	–147	–98	–213	–339	–170	–56	75
	M$ mn	0	0	0	0	0	0	0	0	0	0	–3	–2	–2	–3	–2	0	0
B. Other transfers																		
1. Consumption subsidies	M$ mn	0	0	0	0	0	0	0	0	0	0	0	0	0	0	0	0	0
2. Aserca payment	M$ mn	0	0	0	0	0	0	0	0	0	0	0	0	0	0	0	0	0
V. Total CSE	M$ mn	2	2	–4	5	50	17	47	–3	–153	–98	–150	–100	–215	–342	–172	–56	75
VI. Unit CSE	M$/t	0	0	0	1	6	2	5	0	–20	–13	–18	–11	–26	–32	–25	–7	9
VII. Percentage CSE	%	15	8	–11	12	34	9	15	–1	–14	–5	–6	–3	–6	–7	–6	–2	1

p: provisional.

Notes to Table 2
PSE: Other Grains

Definitions and Notes:

This table is the aggregation of PSE Tables 2B (barley) and 2D (sorghum).

Notes to Table 2
CSE: Other Grains

Definitions and Notes:

This table is the aggregation of CSE Tables 2B (barley) and 2D (sorghum).

REVIEW OF AGRICULTURAL POLICIES IN MEXICO

Table 3. **Producer subsidy equivalent – rice (paddy)**

	Units	1979	1980	1981	1982	1983	1984	1985	1986	1987	1988	1989	1990	1991	1992	1993	1994	1995p
I. Level of production	'000 t	494	445	652	519	416	484	808	545	591	456	527	394	347	394	287	374	367
II. Production price (farm gate)	M$/t	4	5	7	9	19	34	54	98	168	379	445	550	630	685	550	550	1 066
III. Value of production	M$ mn	2	2	4	5	8	17	43	53	99	173	235	217	219	270	158	205	391
IV. Levies	M$ mn	0	0	0	0	0	0	0	0	0	0	0	0	0	0	0	0	0
V. Direct payments	M$ mn	0	0	0	0	0	0	0	0	0	0	0	0	18	38	46	58	59
VI. Adjusted value of production	M$ mn	2	2	4	5	8	17	43	53	99	173	235	217	237	308	204	263	451
VII. Policy transfers	M$ mn	-1	-1	1	-1	-6	0	-9	-15	-57	-15	-18	16	28	69	38	36	67
A. **Market price support**	M$ mn	-1	-2	0	-3	-7	-5	-18	-26	-76	-44	-50	-10	-10	10	-19	-43	-16
1. Trade measures	M$ mn	-1	-2	0	-3	-7	-5	-18	-26	-76	-44	-50	-10	-10	10	-19	-43	-16
2. PACE	M$ mn																	
B. **Levies**	M$ mn	0	0	0	0	0	0	0	0	0	0	0	0	0	0	0	0	0
C. **Direct payments**	M$ mn	0	0	0	0	0	0	0	0	0	0	0	0	18	38	46	58	59
1. Per tonne payment (Aserca)	M$ mn	0	0	0	0	0	0	0	0	0	0	0	0	18	38	46	26	23
2. Area and headage payments	M$ mn	0	0	0	0	0	0	0	0	0	0	0	0	0	0	0	32	36
3. Disaster	M$ mn	0	0	0	0	0	0	0	0	0	0	0	0	0	0	0	0	0
4. Price premium (Aserca)	M$ mn																	
D. **Reduction of input costs**	M$ mn	0	0	1	1	1	3	6	8	15	24	26	19	12	10	5	11	12
E. **General services**	M$ mn	0	0	1	1	0	1	3	3	4	5	6	6	8	10	6	10	11
F. **Sub national**	M$ mn	0	0	0	0	0	0	0	0	0	0	0	0	0	0	0	1	1
G. **Other**	M$ mn																	
VIII. Gross total PSE	M$ mn	-1	-1	1	-1	-6	0	-9	-15	-57	-15	-18	16	28	69	38	36	67
IX. Gross unit PSE	M$/t	-2	-2	1	-2	-14	-1	-12	-27	-96	-34	-34	40	80	175	133	98	182
X. Gross percentage PSE	%	-56	-42	20	-18	-70	-3	-21	-28	-57	-9	-8	7	12	22	19	14	15

Notes to Table 3
PSE: Rice (Paddy)

Definitions and Notes:

I   **Level of production**: SAGAR statistics on paddy rice (*arroz palay*) [1].

II **Production price (farm gate)**: From 1979 to 1981, guaranteed prices [2]. From 1982 to 1986, the annual production price was estimated as the simple average of the guaranteed prices for the Autumn-Winter and Spring-Summer crop seasons [2]. From 1987 to 1994, a weighted average of the administered prices for the Autumn-Winter and Spring-Summer crop seasons [2]. For 1995, average producer price [3].

III **Value of production**: Level of production (I) multiplied by the production price (II).

A.1 **Trade measures**: Production price (II) minus reference price (see Table 14) multiplied by the level of production (I).

C.1 **Per tonne payments**: Direct payments by ASERCA to rice producers [4].

C.2 **Area and headage payments:** See notes to Table 13.

C.3 **Disaster payments**: See notes to Table 13.

D. **Reduction of input costs:** See notes to Table 13.

E. **General services**: See notes to Table 13.

Sources:

[1]   SAGAR, as reported in *Sexto Informe de Gobierno* 1994, Anexo, page 167 and *Primer Informe de Gobierno* 1995, Anexo, page 79. Estimates provided directly by SAGAR for 1995.

[2]   SAGAR, as reported in Sexto Informe de Gobierno 1994, Anexo, pages 165 and 166 and *Primer Informe de Gobierno* 1995, Anexo, page 84.

[3]   Estimate provided directly by SAGAR.

[4]   Data provided directly by ASERCA.

Table 3. **Consumer subsidy equivalent – rice (paddy)** (cont.)

	Units	1979	1980	1981	1982	1983	1984	1985	1986	1987	1988	1989	1990	1991	1992	1993	1994	1995p
I. Level of consumption	'000 t	548	589	792	552	417	741	1 058	547	617	458	805	623	470	868	497	621	621
II. Consumption price (farm gate)	M$/t	4	6	7	9	19	39	61	98	175	379	497	580	655	707	604	620	1 120
III. Value of consumption	M$ mn	2	3	5	5	8	29	64	54	108	173	400	361	308	614	300	385	696
IV. Policy transfers	M$ mn	1	2	1	3	8	7	20	56	90	91	113	65	14	–41	6	29	–7
A. Market transfers	M$ mn	1	1	0	3	7	4	16	26	75	44	35	–3	2	–41	6	29	–7
1. MPS on domestic production	M$ mn	1	2	0	3	7	5	18	26	76	44	50	10	10	–10	19	43	16
2. Tariffs	M$ mn	0	0	0	0	0	–1	–2	0	–1	0	–15	–13	–8	–31	–13	–15	–23
B. Other transfers	M$ mn	0	0	0	1	1	2	4	31	15	47	77	68	12	0	0	0	0
1. Conasupo subsidy	M$ mn	0	0	0	1	1	2	4	31	15	47	77	68	12	0	0	0	0
2. Aserca payment	M$ mn																	
V. Total CSE	M$ mn	1	2	1	3	8	7	20	56	90	91	113	65	14	–41	6	29	–7
VI. Unit CSE	M$/t	3	3	1	6	20	9	19	103	146	198	140	104	29	–48	12	46	–11
VII. Percentage CSE	%	66	54	12	66	105	23	31	105	83	52	28	18	4	–7	2	7	–1

p: provisional.

Notes to Table 3
CSE: Rice (Paddy)

Definitions and Notes:

I   **Level of consumption**: Apparent consumption of paddy rice defined as production plus imports minus exports [1].

II   **Consumption price (farm gate)**: Implicit price measured at the farm gate; equal to the production price (Pp) minus the sum of unit market price support (MPS_u) and unit market transfers (M_{tu}) [Pp – (MPS_u + MT_u)].

III   **Value of consumption**: Level of consumption (I) multiplied by the consumption price (II).

A.1   **MPS on domestic production**: The inverse of the market price support component of the PSE.

A.2   **Tariffs**: Import tariff multiplied by reference price multiplied by the difference between the consumption (I) and production (see PSE I) levels. The following tariffs were considered: 10 per cent in 1979-94 and 9 per cent in 1995.

B.1   **CONASUPO subsidy**: Government transfers to CONASUPO [2] net of stockholding expenditure (estimated as 30 per cent of transfers) and feed subsidies (see PSEs for livestock products). Consumption subsidies were allocated among wheat, maize, rice and soyabeans according to their share in domestic purchases by CONASUPO [3].

Sources:

[1]   For the years 1979-93, SAGAR, as reported in *Sexto Informe de Gobierno* 1994, Anexo, page 168. Estimates from the OECD Secretariat for 1994 and 1995.

[2]   Data provided by SHCP.

[3]   CONASUPO, as reported in *Sexto Informe de Gobierno* 1994, Anexo, page 264 and *Primer Informe de Gobierno* 1995, Anexo, page 86. Estimates provided directly by SAGAR for 1995.

Table 3. **Calculation of market price support and of market transfers – rice** (cont.)

RICE (ARROZ PALAY)

	Units	1979	1980	1981	1982	1983	1984	1985	1986	1987	1988	1989	1990	1991	1992	1993	1994	1995p
PSE-MARKET PRICE SUPPORT (MPS)																		
(1) Production of paddy rice	'000T	494	445	652	519	416	484	808	545	591	456	527	394	347	394	287	374	367
(1)a Production Otoño Invierno	'000 T																	54
(1)b Production Primavera Verano	'000 T																	313
(2)a Administered price O-I	MS/T					18	34	54	98	98	379	445	550	630	685	550	550	854
(2)b Administered price P-V	MS/T					21				238								
(2) Average price	MS/T	4	5	7	9	19	34	54	98	168	379	445	550	630	685	550	550	1 066
(3) Value of production (2) * (1)/1 000	MS Mio	2	2	4	5	8	17	43	53	99	173	235	217	219	270	158	205	391
(4) Fob Gulf medium grain	US$/T	425	517	429	395	349	338	338	327	300	299	312	290	314	306	283	371	324
(5) Exchange rate	MS/US$	0	0	0	0	0	0	0	1	1	2	2	3	3	3	3	3	6
(6) Reference price in MS/T (4) * (5)	MS/T	10	12	11	20	54	65	111	209	425	682	778	824	949	947	882	1 258	2 078
(7) Ref price in paddy equivalent	MS/T	6	8	7	13	36	43	73	138	281	450	514	544	626	625	582	629	1 039
(8) Transport cost to Veracruz	US$/T	11	11	11	11	11	11	11	11	11	11	11	11	11	11	11	11	71
(9) Transport cost in MS (8) * (5)	MS/T	0	0	0	1	2	2	4	7	16	25	27	31	33	34	34	37	71
(10) Adjusted reference price (7) + (9)	MS/T	7	8	7	14	37	45	77	145	296	475	541	575	660	659	616	666	1 110
(11) Unit market price support (2) – (10)	MS/T	-3	-4	-1	-5	-18	-11	-23	-47	-128	-97	-96	-25	-30	26	-66	-116	-44
(12) Market price support (1) * (11)/1 000	MS Mio	-1	-2	0	-3	-7	-5	-18	-26	-76	-44	-50	-10	-10	10	-19	-43	-16
(13) Market price support in %	%	-78	-79	-11	-56	-93	-32	-42	-48	-76	-26	-21	-5	-5	4	-12	-21	-4
CSE-MARKET TRANSFERS (MT)																		
(14) MPS on domestic prod. – (12)	MS Mio	1	2	0	3	7	5	18	26	76	44	50	10	10	-10	19	43	16
(15) Consumption of milled rice	'000T	362	389	523	364	275	489	698	361	407	302	531	411	310	573	328	410	410
(16) Consumption of paddy rice	'000T	548	589	792	552	417	741	1 058	547	617	458	805	623	470	868	497	621	621
(17) Consumption – Production (16) – (1)	'000T	55	144	140	32	1	257	250	2	26	2	278	228	123	474	210	248	254
(18) Rate of the tariff on imports	%	10	10	10	10	10	10	10	10	10	10	10	10	10	10	10	9	8
(19) Tariffs on imports	MS Mio	0	0	0	0	0	-1	-2	0	-1	0	-15	-13	-8	-31	-13	-15	-23
(20) Total market transfers (14) + (19)	MS Mio	1	1	0	3	7	4	16	26	75	44	35	-3	2	-41	6	29	-7

Notes:

p: provisional

(1) Sources: 1989-93: *Boletín mensual de información básica del sector agropecuario y forestal, avance a marzo de 1995*, page 3, *arroz palay*; 1994. *Anuario estadístico de la producción agrícola de los Estados Unidos Mexicanos, 1994*; 1995: BIOSA, number 126, June 1996, page 5.

(2)|a Guaranted prices *(precios de garantía)* up to spring-summer 1990, then concerted prices *(precios de concertación)*. Source: *Sexto Informe de Gobierno 1994*, page 166, the price for 1995 was provided directly by SAGAR.

(2) Weighted average of the prices of the two crop seasons. (2) = [(1)a * (2)a + (1)b * (2)b]/[(1)a + (1)b].

(4) USA n° 5, 20% medium grain FOB, Gulf. Source: *FAO Quarterly Bulletin of Statistics* (series discontinued). 1994 and 1995 were estimated from the Houston long grain series by applying to it the average ratio fob Gulf medium grain / Houston long grain.

(7) For the years 1979-93, (7) = (6) * 0.66, the source for this coefficient is: *Sexto Informe de Gobierno 1994, Anexo*, page 167. For the years 1994-95, (7) = (6) * 0.5 as provided by USDA-ERS.

(8) Source: USDA, Agricultural Marketing Service, *Marketing Research Report number 630, Shipping US grain to Mexico*, September 1995.

(13) = (12)/(3) * 100.

(15) 1993 and 1994 source: BIOSA, Number 126, June 1996, page 7, 1995 estimated as equal to 1994.

(16) = (15)/0.66.

ASSISTANCE TO MEXICAN AGRICULTURE

Table 4. Producer subsidy equivalent – oilseeds

	Units	1979	1980	1981	1982	1983	1984	1985	1986	1987	1988	1989	1990	1991	1992	1993	1994	1995p
I. Level of production	'000 t	707	322	707	649	688	685	929	709	828	226	992	575	725	594	498	523	190
II. Production price (farm gate)	M$/t	6	8	11	15	29	44	72	122	282	408	697	888	702	643	807	755	1 474
III. Value of production	M$ mn	5	3	8	10	20	30	67	86	233	92	691	511	509	382	402	394	280
IV. Levies	M$ mn	0	0	0	0	0	0	0	0	0	0	0	0	0	0	0	0	0
V. Direct payments	M$ mn	0	0	0	0	0	0	0	0	0	0	0	0	71	99	66	167	61
VI. Adjusted value of production	M$ mn	5	3	8	10	20	30	67	86	233	92	692	511	580	481	468	562	340
VII. Policy transfers	M$ mn	1	1	5	5	-5	3	14	14	38	-36	139	56	156	112	114	156	53
A. Market price support	M$ mn	0	0	3	2	-10	-7	-2	-9	-19	-61	22	0	-2	-44	13	-49	-25
1. Trade measures	M$ mn	0	0	3	2	-10	-7	-2	-9	-19	-61	22	0	-2	-44	13	-49	-25
2. PACE	M$ mn	0	0	0	0	0	0	0	0	0	0	0	0	0	0	0	0	0
B. Levies	M$ mn	0	0	0	0	0	0	0	0	0	0	0	0	0	0	0	0	0
C. Direct payments	M$ mn	0	0	0	0	0	0	0	0	0	0	0	0	71	99	66	167	61
1. Per tonne payment (Aserca)	M$ mn	0	0	0	0	0	0	0	0	0	0	0	0	0	0	0	0	61
2. Area and headage payments	M$ mn	0	0	0	0	0	0	0	0	0	0	0	0	0	0	0	114	0
3. Disaster	M$ mn	0	0	0	0	0	0	0	0	0	0	0	0	0	0	0	0	0
4. Price premium (Aserca)	M$ mn	0	0	0	0	0	0	0	0	0	0	0	0	71	99	66	53	0
D. Reduction of input costs	M$ mn	1	0	1	2	4	8	10	17	44	21	93	42	53	27	15	20	9
E. General services	M$ mn	0	0	1	1	1	3	5	6	12	4	23	13	33	28	20	17	8
F. Sub national	M$ mn	0	0	0	0	0	0	0	0	0	0	0	0	1	1	1	1	0
G. Other	M$ mn	0	0	0	0	0	0	0	0	0	0	0	0	0	0	0	0	0
VIII. Gross total PSE	M$ mn	1	1	5	5	-5	3	14	14	38	-36	139	56	156	112	114	156	53
IX. Gross unit PSE	M$/t	1	4	7	8	-7	5	15	20	46	-160	140	98	216	188	229	299	278
X. Gross percentage PSE	%	18	47	65	53	-25	11	21	16	16	-39	20	11	27	23	24	28	15

Notes to Table 4
PSE: Oilseeds

Definitions and Notes:

I   **Level of production**: SAGAR statistics on soyabeans (*soya*) [1].

II   **Production price (farm gate)**: From 1979 to 1981, guaranteed prices [2]. From 1982 to 1986, the annual production price was estimated as the simple average of the guaranteed prices for the Autumn-Winter and Spring-Summer crop seasons [2]. From 1987 to 1994, a weighted average of the administered prices for the Autumn-Winter and Spring-Summer crop seasons [2]. For the period 1991-94, an implicit production price was calculated by subtracting the unit budget payments of ASERCA [3] from the concerted price. For 1995, average producer price [4].

III   **Value of production**: Level of production (I) multiplied by the production price (II).

A.1   **Trade measures**: Production price (II) minus reference price (see Table 14) multiplied by the level of production (I). In 1990, the MPS was not calculated as there were no trade measures in place and concerted prices were not yet implemented.

C.2   **Area and headage payments:** See notes to Table 13.

C.3   **Disaster payments**: See notes to Table 13.

C.4   **Price premiums:** ASERCA payments [3] to the buyers of domestic production at concerted prices.

D.   **Reduction of input costs:** See notes to Table 13.

E.   **General services**: See notes to Table 13.

Sources:

[1]   SAGAR, as reported in *Sexto Informe de Gobierno* 1994, Anexo, page 167 and *Primer Informe de Gobierno* 1995, Anexo, page 79. Estimates provided directly by SAGAR for 1995.

[2]   SAGAR, as reported in Sexto Informe de Gobierno 1994, Anexo, pages 165 and 166 and *Primer Informe de Gobierno* 1995, Anexo, page 84.

[3]   Data provided directly by ASERCA. Data provided by SHCP for 1995.

[4]   Estimate provided directly by SAGAR.

Table 4. **Consumer subsidy equivalent – oilseeds** (cont.)

	Units	1979	1980	1981	1982	1983	1984	1985	1986	1987	1988	1989	1990	1991	1992	1993	1994	1995p
I. Level of consumption	'000 t	1 296	844	1 817	1 130	1 571	1 993	2 148	1 536	1 890	1 324	2 102	1 472	2 213	2 669	2 672	2 115	1 997
II. Consumption price (farm gate)	M$/t	6	7	8	14	37	50	73	129	295	633	685	888	752	757	850	883	1 708
III. Value of consumption	M$ mn	8	6	15	16	58	101	157	198	557	838	1 440	1 307	1 663	2 020	2 271	1 868	3 410
IV. Policy transfers	M$ mn	0	0	0	1	13	8	9	32	44	64	-18	0	-103	-105	-183	-72	-207
A. Market transfers		0	0	-3	-2	10	7	2	9	19	61	-22	0	-103	-105	-183	-72	-207
1. MPS on domestic production	M$ mn	0	0	-3	-2	10	7	2	9	19	61	-22	0	2	44	-13	49	25
2. Tariffs	M$ mn	0	0	0	0	0	0	0	0	0	0	0	0	-105	-149	-170	-122	-232
B. Other transfers		0	0	3	2	3	0	7	23	26	3	4	0	0	0	0	0	0
1. Conasupo subsidy	M$ mn	0	0	3	2	3	0	7	23	26	3	4	0	0	0	0	0	0
2. Aserca payment	M$ mn	0	0	0	0	0	0	0	0	0	0	0	0	0	0	0	0	0
V. Total CSE	M$ mn	0	0	0	1	13	8	9	32	44	64	-18	0	-103	-105	-183	-72	-207
VI. Unit CSE	M$/t	0	0	0	1	8	4	4	21	24	48	-9	0	-46	-39	-68	-34	-104
VII. Percentage CSE	%	4	-5	1	4	22	8	6	16	8	8	-1	0	-6	-5	-8	-4	-6

p: provisional.

Notes to Table 4
CSE: Oilseeds

Definitions and Notes:

I   **Level of consumption**: Apparent consumption of soyabeans defined as production plus imports minus exports [1].

II   **Consumption price (farm gate)**: Implicit price measured at the farm gate; equal to the production price (Pp) minus the sum of unit market price support (MPS_u) and unit market transfers (M_{tu}) [Pp − (MPS_u + MT_u)].

III   **Value of consumption**: Level of consumption (I) multiplied by the consumption price (II).

A.1   **MPS on domestic production**: The inverse of the market price support component of the PSE.

A.2   **Tariffs**: Not applicable for the 1979-90 period in which imports were duty-free (even if import permits were in place) For the other periods: import tariff multiplied by reference price multiplied by the difference between the consumption (I) and production (see PSE I) levels. The following tariffs were considered: 10 per cent in 1991-94 and 9 per cent in 1995.

B.1   **CONASUPO subsidy**: Government transfers to CONASUPO [2] net of stockholding expenditure (estimated as 30 per cent of transfers) and feed subsidies (see PSEs for livestock products). Consumption subsidies were allocated among wheat, maize, rice and soyabeans according to their share in domestic purchases by CONASUPO [3].

Sources:

[1]   For the years 1979-93, SAGAR, as reported in *Sexto Informe de Gobierno* 1994, Anexo, page 168. Estimates from the OECD Secretariat for 1994 and 1995.

[2]   Data provided by SHCP.

[3]   CONASUPO, as reported in *Sexto Informe de Gobierno* 1994, Anexo, page 264 and *Primer Informe de Gobierno* 1995, Anexo, page 86. Estimates provided directly by SAGAR for 1995.

Table 4. **Calculation of market price support and of market transfers – soyabeans** *(cont.)*

SOYABEANS (SOYA)

	Units	1979	1980	1981	1982	1983	1984	1985	1986	1987	1988	1989	1990	1991	1992	1993	1994	1995p
PSE-MARKET PRICE SUPPORT (MPS)																		
(1) Production	'000T	707	322	707	649	688	685	929	709	828	226	992	575	725	594	498	523	190
(1)a Production Otoño Invierno	'000 T																0	0
(1)b Production Primavera Verano	'000 T														593	497	522	190
(2)a Administered price O-I	MS/T				15	27	31	56	88	156	408	408	986	790	810	940	940	1 163
(2)b Administered price P-V	MS/T			11	15	31	56	88	156	408	408	986	790	810	810	940	856	1 474
(2) Average price	MS/T	6	8	11	15	29	44	72	122	282	408	697	888	800	810	940	856	1 474
(3) Aserca payment	MS Mio													71	99	66	53	0
(4) Unit Aserca payment (3)/(1) * 1 000	MS/T													98	167	133	101	0
(5) Producer price net of the payment	MS/T	6	8	11	15	29	44	72	122	282	408	697	888	702	643	807	755	1 474
(6) Value of production (5) * (1)/1 000	MS Mio	5	3	8	10	20	30	67	86	233	92	691	511	509	382	402	394	280
(7) Reference price	US$/bu	8	7	7	6	7	7	6	5	6	8	7	6	6	6	7	7	7
(8) Reference price per tonne	US$/T	279	272	272	234	269	271	214	200	204	287	259	229	222	221	240	240	239
(9) Exchange rate	MS$/US$	0	0	0	0	0	0	0	1	1	2	2	3	3	3	3	3	6
(10) Reference price in MS (8) * (9)	MS/T	6	6	7	12	42	52	70	128	289	655	647	651	672	683	747	812	1 534
(11) Transport cost to Veracruz	US$/T	11	11	11	11	11	11	11	11	11	11	11	11	11	11	11	11	11
(12) Transport cost in MS (11) * (9)	MS/T	0	0	0	1	2	2	4	7	16	25	27	31	33	34	34	37	71
(13) Adjusted reference price (10) + (12)	MS/T	7	6	7	13	43	54	74	135	305	680	675	683	705	718	782	849	1 604
(14) Unit market price support (5) – (13)	MS/T	0	2	4	3	-14	-11	-2	-13	-23	-272	22	205	-3	-74	26	-94	-131
(15) Market price support (1) * (14)/1 000	MS Mio	0	0	3	2	-10	-7	-2	-9	-19	-61	22	0	-2	-44	13	-49	-25
(16) Market price support in %	%	-3	19	36	17	-49	-24	-2	-11	-8	-67	3	0	0	-12	3	-13	-9
CSE-MARKET TRANSFERS (MT)																		
(17) MPS on domestic prod. – (15)	MS Mio	0	0	-3	-2	10	7	2	9	19	61	-22	0	2	44	-13	49	25
(18) Consumption	'000T	1 296	844	1 817	1 130	1 571	1 993	2 148	1 536	1 890	1 324	2 102	1 472	2 213	2 669	2 672	2 115	1 997
(19) Consumption – Production (18) – (1)	'000T	589	522	1 110	481	883	1 308	1 219	827	1 062	1 098	1 110	897	1 488	2 075	2 174	1 592	1 807
(20) Rate of the tariff on imports	%												0	10	10	10	9	8
(21) Tariffs on imports	MS Mio	0	0	0	0	0	0	0	0	0	0	0	0	-105	-149	-170	-122	-232
(22) Total market transfers (17) + (21)	MS Mio	-3	0	-3	-2	10	7	2	9	19	61	-22	0	-103	-105	-183	-72	-207

Notes:

p: provisional

(1) Sources: SAGAR, 1979-93: *Informe para cuenta pública 1994*; 1994: *Anuario estadístico de la producción agrícola de los Estados Unidos Mexicanos, 1994*; 1995: *BIOSA*, number 126, June 1996, page 5. Data refer to crop year *(año agrícola)*.

(2)a Guaranteed prices *(precios de garantía)* up to spring-summer 1990, then concerted prices *(precios de concertación)*. Source: *Sexto Informe de Gobierno, 1995*. SAGAR.

(2)b Weighted average of the prices of the two crop seasons. (2) = [(1)a * (2)a + (1)b * (2)b]/[(1)a + (1)b].

(2) Source: Aserca.

(5) Producer price net of the payment (5) = (2) – (4).

(7) US export price, soybeans, fob vessel, Gulf ports; source: USDA, *Agricultural Outlook*.

(8) One metric tonne is equivalent to 36.7437 bu for soybeans. Reference price per tonne (8) = (7) * 36.7437.

(9) Source: OECD, *Main Economic Indicators*.

(11) Source: USDA, Agricultural Marketing Service, *Marketing Research Report number 630, Shipping US grain to Mexico*, September 1995.

(15) For 1990, it was agreed not to calculate market price support as imports were duty free and the concerted price was not yet applied.

(16) Market price support in %. (16) = (15)/(6) * 100.

(18) Consumption: 100% is feed use. Source: 1979-92: *Informe para cuenta pública 1994*; 1993-94: *BIOSA, Numero 126, Junio 1996*, page 7. 1995 was estimated from oilseed consumption growth rate shown in OECD, *The Agricultural Outlook, Trends and Issues to 2000*, Paris 1996.

(21) Tariffs on imports. (21) = – (19) * (13) * (20)/100 000.

Table 5. **Producer subsidy equivalent – sugar (refined equivalent)**

	Units	1979	1980	1981	1982	1983	1984	1985	1986	1987	1988	1989	1990	1991	1992	1993	1994	1995p
I. Level of production	'000 t	2 742	2 542	2 512	2 533	3 064	3 058	3 203	3 677	3 825	3 546	3 351	3 248	3 591	3 480	3 988	3 529	3 860
II. Production price (farm gate)	M$/t	4	5	7	11	21	26	46	84	186	375	639	663	770	910	989	1 172	1 338
III. Value of production	M$ mn	10	13	17	29	65	80	147	310	712	1 329	2 141	2 155	2 764	3 166	3 945	4 135	5 166
IV. Levies	M$ mn	0	0	0	0	0	0	0	0	0	0	0	0	0	0	0	0	0
V. Direct payments	M$ mn	0	0	0	0	0	0	0	0	0	0	0	0	0	1	0	1	3
VI. Adjusted value of production	M$ mn	10	13	17	29	65	80	147	310	712	1 329	2 141	2 155	2 764	3 166	3 945	4 136	5 168
VII. Policy transfers	M$ mn	6	0	18	20	12	35	-3	59	-94	-262	-221	483	1 341	1 599	1 881	1 321	-686
A. **Market price support**	M$ mn	-1	-13	-1	-1	-27	-17	-70	-22	-219	-490	-506	187	1 078	1 269	1 599	896	-949
1. Trade measures	M$ mn	-1	-13	-1	-1	-27	-17	-70	-22	-219	-490	-506	187	1 078	1 269	1 599	896	-949
2. PACE	M$ mn																	
B. **Levies**	M$ mn	0	0	0	0	0	0	0	0	0	0	0	0	0	0	0	0	0
C. **Direct payments**	M$ mn	0	0	0	0	0	0	0	0	0	0	0	0	0	1	0	1	3
1. Per tonne payment (Aserca)	M$ mn																	
2. Area and headage payments	M$ mn																	
3. Disaster	M$ mn																	
4. Price premium (Aserca)	M$ mn	0	0	0	0	0	0	0	0	0	0	0	0	0	1	0	1	3
D. **Reduction of input costs**	M$ mn	6	11	17	18	35	46	58	64	102	194	233	224	160	162	127	246	135
E. **General services**	M$ mn	1	2	2	4	4	6	9	17	23	34	52	68	99	161	147	169	119
F. **Sub national**	M$ mn	0	0	0	0	0	0	0	0	0	0	0	4	3	6	7	9	7
G. **Other**	M$ mn																	
VIII. Gross total PSE	M$ mn	6	0	18	20	12	35	-3	59	-94	-262	-221	483	1 341	1 599	1 881	1 321	-686
IX. Gross unit PSE	M$/t	2	0	7	8	4	11	-1	16	-25	-74	-66	149	373	459	472	374	-178
X. Gross percentage PSE	%	56	-1	110	71	19	44	-2	19	-13	-20	-10	22	49	50	48	32	-13

Notes to Table 5
PSE: Sugar (refined equivalent)

Definitions and Notes:

I   **Level of production**: SAGAR statistics on refined (*azúcar refinado*) and partly-refined (*azúcar estandar*) sugar [1].

II   **Production price (farm gate)**: Implicit production price for sugar cane expressed in refined sugar equivalent obtained by dividing the value of production of sugar cane (production price of sugar cane [2] multiplied by the level of sugar cane production [3]) by the level of production of refined sugar (I).

III   **Value of production**: Level of production (I) multiplied by the production price (II).

A.1   **Trade measures**: Wholesale price of raw sugar (*azúcar mascabado al mayoreo*) [4] minus reference price of raw sugar (see Table 14). For the years 1979 to 1993, this price gap is converted in sugar cane equivalent by dividing it by the ratio of the wholesale price of raw sugar to the production price of sugar cane [2], and then multiplied by the level of sugar cane production [3]. In 1994 and 1995, farmers received respectively 54 and 55 per cent of the raw sugar value realised by processors, hence the MPS was assumed to be this percentage of the value of the price gap multiplied by the level of refined sugar production (I).

C.3   **Disaster payments**: See notes to Table 13.

D.   **Reduction of input costs:** See notes to Table 13.

E.   **General services**: See notes to Table 13.

Sources:

[1]   SAGAR, as reported in *Sexto Informe de Gobierno* 1994, Anexo, page 177 for 1979, and SAGAR (1994) *Boletín Estadístico Azucarero* for the years 1980-95.

[2]   Data provided directly by SAGAR (1979-81) and COAAZUCAR (1990-95).

[3]   Data provided directly by SAGAR.

[4]   Cámara Nacional de las industrias azucarera y alcoholera.

Table 5. **Consumer subsidy equivalent – sugar (refined equivalent)** (cont.)

	Units	1979	1980	1981	1982	1983	1984	1985	1986	1987	1988	1989	1990	1991	1992	1993	1994	1995p
I. Level of consumption	'000 t	2 855	2 922	3 020	3 226	3 023	3 088	3 095	3 190	3 428	3 511	3 734	3 872	4 056	3 923	4 026	4 124	4 145
II. Consumption price (farm gate)	M$/t	4	6	7	12	21	26	46	84	186	375	654	654	735	868	985	1 135	1 355
III. Value of consumption	M$ mn	11	17	20	37	64	81	142	269	638	1 316	2 443	2 533	2 982	3 407	3 967	4 681	5 617
IV. Pol.cy transfers	M$ mn	1	13	1	1	26	17	68	19	197	485	506	–187	–1 078	–1 269	–1 599	–896	949
A. Market transfers	M$ mn	1	13	1	1	26	17	68	19	197	485	506	–187	–1 078	–1 269	–1 599	–896	949
1. Trade measures	M$ mn	1	13	1	1	26	17	68	19	197	485	506	–187	–1 078	–1 269	–1 599	–896	949
i. Other	M$ mn																	
B. Other transfers	M$ mn	0	0	0	0	0	0	0	0	0	0	0	0	0	0	0	0	0
1. Consumption subsidies	M$ mn																	
2. Aserca payment	M$ mn																	
V. Total CSE	M$ mn	1	13	1	1	26	17	68	19	197	485	506	–187	–1 078	–1 269	–1 599	–896	949
VI. Unit CSE	M$/t	0	4	0	0	9	5	22	6	57	138	136	–48	–266	–324	–397	–217	229
VII. Percentage CSE	%	10	77	3	4	41	21	47	7	31	37	21	–7	–36	–37	–40	–19	17

p: provisional.

Notes to Table 5
CSE: Sugar (refined equivalent)

Definitions and Notes:

I   **Level of consumption**: Sum of industrial and household consumption of sugar [1].

II **Consumption price (farm gate)**: Implicit price measured at the farm gate; equal to the production price (Pp) minus the sum of unit market price support (MPS_u) and unit market transfers (M_{tu}) [$Pp - (MPS_u + MT_u)$].

III **Value of consumption**: Level of consumption (I) multiplied by the consumption price (II).

A.1 **MPS on domestic production**: The inverse of the market price support component of the PSE. In the 1983 and 1985-88 periods, as the level of production exceeded the level of consumption, the MPS was applied on domestic consumption: production price (see PSE II) minus reference price (see Table 14) multiplied by the level of consumption (I).

A.2 **Tariffs**: Not applicable as imports of sugar were subject to permits, but duty-free until 1990 and are imported duty-free within an import quota since 1994. The rate of the variable import levy applied from 1991 to 1993 was not available.

Source:

[1] SAGAR, as reported in *Sexto Informe de Gobierno* 1994, *Anexo*, page 178 for the years 1979-94, and SAGAR (1994) *Boletín Estadístico Azucarero* for 1995.

Table 5. **Calculation of market price support and of market transfers – sugar** (cont.)

SUGAR (AZUCAR (CANA DE))

PSE-MARKET PRICE SUPPORT (MPS)

	Units	1979	1980	1981	1982	1983	1984	1985	1986	1987	1988	1989	1990	1991	1992	1993	1994	1995p
(1) Sugarcane production	'000 T	35 768	35 081	33 165	35 511	34 232	34 970	34 400	44 219	45 813	42 673	43 894	39 908	38 387	41 652	42 880	40 539	42 562
(2) Sugar production (calen. year)	'000 T	2 742	2 542	2 512	2 533	3 064	3 058	3 203	3 677	3 825	3 546	3 351	3 248	3 591	3 480	3 988	3 529	3 860
(3) Producer price (cane)	MS/T	0	0	1	1	2	2	4	7	16	31	49	60	71	83	87	107	121
(4) Producer price for cane	MS/T												54	72	76	92	102	121
(5) Producer price for cane (3); (4)	MS/T	0	0	1	1	2	2	4	7	16	31	49	54	72	76	92	102	121
(6) Value of production (1) * (5)/1 000	MS Mio	10	13	17	29	65	80	147	310	712	1 329	2 141	2 155	2 764	3 166	3 945	4 135	5 166
(7) Implicit sugar producer price	MS/T	4	5	7	11	21	26	46	84	186	375	639	663	770	910	989	1 172	1 338
(8) Wholesale price of raw sugar	MS/T	5	8	10	12	26	26	31	110	215	457	670	1 016	1 235	1 294	1 420	1 546	1 777
(9) Wholesale price of raw sugar	MS/T												1 033	1 310	1 428	1 567	1 692	1 945
(10) Ratio raw sugar/cane (8)/(5)		19	21	20	14	14	11	7	16	14	15	14	19	17	17	15	15	15
(11) World price for raw sugar	c/lb	10	29	17	8	8	5	4	6	7	10	13	13	9	9	10	12	13
(12) World price per tonne (11) * 22.046	US$/T	213	640	373	186	187	114	89	133	148	224	282	277	199	200	221	267	296
(13) Transport costs Mexican ports	US$/T	50	50	50	50	50	50	50	50	50	50	50	50	50	50	50	50	50
(14) World price (12) + (13)	US$/T	263	690	423	236	237	164	139	183	198	274	332	327	249	250	271	317	346
(15) Exchange rate	MS/US$	0	0	0	0	0	0	0	1	1	2	3	3	3	3	3	3	6
(16) World price in MS/T (14) * (15)	MS/T	6	16	10	13	37	31	45	117	281	625	828	928	753	775	845	1 076	2 224
(17) Price gap for raw sugar (8) – (16)	MS/T	-1	-8	0	-1	-11	-5	-15	-8	-66	-168	-158	88	482	519	576	470	-447
(18) Price gap in sugarcane equivalent	MS/T	0	0	0	0	-1	0	-2	0	-5	-11	-12	5	28	30	37		
(19) Market price support	MS Mio	-1	-13	-4	-1	-27	-17	-70	-22	-219	-490	-506	187	1 078	1 269	1 599	896	-949
(20) Market price support in %	%	-11	-100	-4	-5	-41	-21	-47	-7	-31	-37	-24	9	39	40	41	22	-18

CSE-MARKET TRANSFERS (MT)

	Units	1979	1980	1981	1982	1983	1984	1985	1986	1987	1988	1989	1990	1991	1992	1993	1994	1995p
(21) Industrial consumption sugar	'000 T	1 463	1 592	1 693	1 767	1 666	1 666	1 654	1 719	1 673	1 755	2 135	2 246	2 404	2 244	2 320	2 393	
(22) Household consumption sugar	'000 T	1 392	1 330	1 327	1 459	1 357	1 422	1 441	1 471	1 755	1 756	1 599	1 626	1 652	1 679	1 706	1 731	
(23) Total consumption of sugar	'000 T	2 855	2 922	3 020	3 226	3 023	3 088	3 095	3 190	3 428	3 511	3 734	3 872	4 056	3 923	4 026	4 124	4 145
(24) Market transfer – (19)/(2) * (23)	MS Mio	1	15	1	2	26	17	68	19	197	485	564	-223	-1 218	-1 431	-1 614	-1 046	1 019
(25) MPS on domestic prod. – (19)	MS Mio	1	13	1	1	27	17	70	22	219	490	506	-187	-1 078	-1 269	-1 599	-896	949
(26) Market transfer (24), (25)	MS Mio	1	13	1	1	26	17	68	19	197	485	506	-187	-1 078	-1 269	-1 599	-896	949

Notes:

p: provisional

(1) The data on production on a calendar year basis was provided directly by SAGAR, except for 1993 and 1994 data whose source is: Anuario estadístico de la producción agrícola de los Estados Unidos Mexicanos 1993 and 1994. 1995: OECD Secretariat estimate.

(2) Source: SAGAR, Boletín Estadístico Azucarero, 1994, pages 21- 24 and 31; estimation for 1995 is from page 32; 1979 was estimated as the average of 1978/79 and 1979/80 data presented in Sexto Informe de Gobierno, p.177.

(3) Precio medio rural; this data was provided directly by SAGAR.

(4) Source: Comité de la Agroindustria Azucarera

(7) = 6/(2) * 1 000.

(8) Mascabado. Source: Cámara Nacional de las industrias azucarera y alcoholera. 1995 was estimated by applying the growth rate of the wholesale price of raw sugar provided by Coaazucar.

(9) Precio Azúcar Base Estándar. Source: Comité de la Agroindustria Azucarera.

(11) Source: USDA, Sugar and sweetener Outlook and Situation, world raw sugar price, contract no 11, FOB stowed Caribbean port, bulk spot price. (source: New York, Coffee, Sugar and Cocoa Exchange).

(13) Source: FORMA.

(15) Source: OECD, Main Economic Indicators.

(18) = :17/(10).

(19) = :18] * (1)/1 000 for the years 1979-1993, (19) = (17) * 0.54 * (2) for 1994 and (19) = (17) * 0.55 * (2) for 1995.

(20) = :19/(6) * 100.

(23) = :21] + (22); 1995 is from Boletín Estadístico Azucarero, 1994, page 34.

(26) = :24] for the years 1983 and 1985-88, (26) = (25) for the years 1979-82 , 1984 and 1989-95.

Table 6. Producer subsidy equivalent – milk

	Units	1979 1980	1981	1982	1983	1984	1985	1986	1987	1988	1989	1990	1991	1992	1993	1994	1995p
I. Level of production	'000 t	6 848	6 951	7 069	7 138	6 978	7 073	7 395	6 571	6 393	6 350	5 750	6 332	6 925	7 182	7 634	7 547 7 628
II. Production price (farm gate)	M$/t	5	6	8	12	20	42	63	105	227	407	601	629	802	863	901	912 1 174
III. Value of production	M$ mn	35	44	60	88	143	295	463	690	1 451	2 587	3 458	3 980	5 555	6 200	6 875	6 881 8 952
IV. Levies	M$ mn	0	0	0	0	0	0	0	0	0	0	0	0	0	0	0	0 0
V. Direct payments	M$ mn	0	0	0	0	0	0	0	0	0	0	0	0	0	1	1	1 6
VI. Adjusted value of production	M$ mn	35	44	60	88	143	295	463	690	1 451	2 587	3 458	3 980	5 556	6 201	6 875	6 882 8 959
VII. Policy transfers	M$ mn	17	24	38	35	-5	160	298	407	560	486	1 350	2 477	3 013	3 204	4 047	3 673 361
A. Market price support	M$ mn	16	21	31	27	-19	124	248	364	426	360	1 110	1 631	2 778	2 930	3 457	3 027 -120
1. Trade measures	M$ mn	16	21	31	27	-19	124	248	364	426	360	1 110	1 631	2 778	2 930	3 457	3 027 -120
2. PACE	M$ mn																
B. Levies	M$ mn	0	0	0	0	0	0	0	0	0	0	0	0	0	0	0	0 0
C. Direct payments	M$ mn	0	0	0	0	0	0	0	0	0	0	0	0	0	1	1	1 6
1. Per tonne payment (Aserca)	M$ mn																
2. Area and headage payments	M$ mn																
3. Disaster	M$ mn	0	0	0	0	0	0	0	0	0	0	0	0	0	1	1	1 6
4. Price premium (Aserca)	M$ mn																
D. Reduction of input costs	M$ mn	1	2	6	7	12	30	43	34	117	103	202	767	157	178	475	522 368
E. General services	M$ mn	0	1	1	2	2	5	7	9	18	23	38	68	69	83	99	107 91
F. Sub national	M$ mn	0	0	0	0	0	0	0	0	0	0	0	11	9	13	15	16 16
G. Other	M$ mn																
VIII. Gross total PSE	M$ mn	17	24	38	35	-5	160	298	407	560	486	1 350	2 477	3 013	3 204	4 047	3 673 361
IX. Gross unit PSE	M$/t	3	4	5	5	-1	23	40	62	88	77	235	391	435	446	530	487 47
X. Gross percentage PSE	%	50	56	63	40	-3	54	64	59	39	19	39	62	54	52	59	53 4
XI. Feed adjusment	M$ mn	0	0	-2	0	14	7	7	3	-19	107	-58	-161	-105	-118	-341	-38 119
1. Excess feed cost	M$ mn	0	0	-1	0	7	3	3	2	-23	27	-34	-60	-61	-56	-299	-88 67
i. Other feed cost	M$ mn	0	0	-1	0	7	3	2	2	4	80	-24	-101	-44	-62	-42	50 53
XII. Net total PSE	M$ mn	18	24	24	36	9	166	305	410	541	593	1 292	2 316	2 908	3 086	3 707	3 636 480
XIII. Net unit PSE	M$/t	3	3	5	5	1	24	41	62	85	93	225	366	420	430	486	482 63
XIV. Net percentage PSE	%	51	55	60	40	7	56	66	59	37	23	37	58	52	50	54	53 5

Notes to Table 6
PSE: Milk

Definitions and Notes:

I   **Level of production**: SAGAR statistics on cow milk (*leche de bovino*) production [1]. To express the level of production in tonnes, data in thousand litres has been multiplied by a coefficient 1.031 which corresponds to the density of milk.

II   **Production price (farm gate)**: Cow milk production price per litre [2], divided by a coefficient 1.031 to obtain the production price per tonne.

III   **Value of production**: Level of production (I) multiplied by the production price (II).

A.1   **Trade measures**: Production price (II) minus reference price (see Table 14) multiplied by the level of production (I).

C.3   **Disaster payments**: See notes to Table 13.

D.   **Reduction of input costs:** See notes to Table 13.

E.   **General services**: See notes to Table 13.

XI   **Feed adjustment:** See notes to Table 13.

Sources:

[1]   SAGAR, as reported in *Sexto Informe de Gobierno* 1994, Anexo, page 182 for the years 1979-93, and SAGAR *Boletín mensual de información básica del sector agropecuario y forestal*, for 1994 and 1995.

[2]   *Diario Oficial de la Federación* for the years 1979-85, SECOFI for the years 1986-89, CONAFOPALE for the years 1986-91, and CNG for the years 1992-95.

Table 6. **Consumer subsidy equivalent – milk** (cont.)

	Units	1979	1980	1981	1982	1983	1984	1985	1986	1987	1988	1989	1990	1991	1992	1993	1994	1995p
I. Level of consumption	'000 t	7 608	8 981	7 069	8 243	8 367	8 207	9 045	8 196	8 143	8 509	8 451	9 596	7 581	9 600	10 265	10 388	10 388
II. Consumption price (farm gate)	M$/t	5	6	8	12	21	39	57	94	213	393	540	541	767	761	784	802	1 178
III. Value of consumption	M$ mn	37	51	60	97	175	322	511	770	1 732	3 344	4 561	5 191	5 818	7 301	8 053	8 332	12 235
IV. Policy transfers	M$ mn	-16	-19	-28	-21	29	-103	-209	-288	-221	118	-193	-770	-1 488	-1 478	-2 093	-1 773	1 845
A. Market transfers	M$ mn																	
1. MPS on domestic production	M$ mn	-16	-21	-31	-27	19	-124	-248	-364	-426	-360	-1 110	-1 631	-2 778	-2 930	-3 457	-3 027	120
2. Tariffs	M$ mn	-16	-21	-31	-27	19	-124	-248	-364	-426	-360	-1 110	-1 631	-2 778	-2 930	-3 457	-3 027	120
B. Other transfers	M$ mn																	
1. Consumption subsidies	M$ mn	0	2	3	6	11	22	39	76	205	478	917	861	1 290	1 452	1 364	1 254	1 725
2. Aserca payment	M$ mn	0	2	3	6	11	22	39	76	205	478	917	861	1 290	1 452	1 364	1 254	1 725
V. Total CSE	M$ mn	-16	-19	-28	-21	29	-103	-209	-288	-221	118	-193	-770	-1 488	-1 478	-2 093	-1 773	1 845
VI. Unit CSE	M$/t	-2	-2	-4	-3	4	-13	-23	-35	-27	14	-23	-80	-196	-154	-204	-171	178
VII. Percentage CSE	%	-43	-38	-47	-21	17	-32	-41	-37	-13	4	-4	-15	-26	-20	-26	-21	15

p: provisional

Notes to Table 6
CSE: Milk

Definitions and Notes:

I **Level of consumption**: Domestic apparent consumption of cow milk [1].

II **Consumption price (farm gate)**: Implicit price measured at the farm gate; equal to the production price (Pp) minus the sum of unit market price support (MPS_u) and unit market transfers (M_{tu}) [$Pp - (MPS_u + MT_u)$].

III **Value of consumption**: Level of consumption (I) multiplied by the consumption price (II).

A.1 **MPS on domestic production**: The inverse of the market price support component of the PSE.

A.2 **Tariffs**: Not applicable over the review period, as milk powder has always been imported duty-free by CONASUPO.

B.1 **Consumption subsidy**: LICONSA social programme for milk targeted to low-income families [2].

Sources:

[1] For the years 1979-93 data directly provided by SAGAR; 1994 was estimated by applying a coefficient derived from CNG (1995), *Información Económica Pecuaria*, May 1995, page 50; and 1995 was estimated to be equivalent to 1994.

[2] CONASUPO, as reported in Sexto Informe de Gobierno 1994, Anexo, page 261 and Primer Informe de Gobierno 1995, Anexo, page 123.

Table 6. **Calculation of market price support and of market transfers – milk** *(cont.)*

	Units	1979	1980	1981	1982	1983	1984	1985	1986	1987	1988	1989	1990	1991	1992	1993	1994	1995p
MILK (LECHE DE BOVINO)																		
PSE-MARKET PRICE SUPPORT (MPS)																		
(1) Production	Litres Mio	6 642	6 742	6 856	6 924	6 768	6 860	7 173	6 373	6 201	6 159	5 577	6 142	6 717	6 966	7 404	7 320	7 399
(2) Production converted into tonnes	'000 T	6 848	6 951	7 069	7 138	6 978	7 073	7 395	6 571	6 393	6 350	5 750	6 332	6 925	7 182	7 634	7 547	7 628
(3) Producer price	M$/L	0	0	0	0	0	0	0	0	0	1	1	1	1	1	1	1	1
(4) Producer price per tonne	M$/T	5	6	8	12	20	42	63	105	227	407	601	629	802	863	901	912	1 174
(5) Value of production (4) * (2)/1 000	M$ Mio	35	44	60	88	143	295	463	690	1 451	2 587	3 458	3 980	5 555	6 200	6 875	6 881	8 952
(6) Price of milk (New Zealand)	US$/T	109	132	153	153	138	114	73	68	105	151	162	122	129	144	138	147	184
(7) Transport cost, butter	US$/T	324	365	421	387	335	298	273	237	269	276	277	298	264	268	264	251	273
(8) Transport cost, SMP	US$/T	150	157	177	177	164	150	164	88	106	109	115	126	110	123	155	154	166
(9) Transport cost, milk equivalent	US$/T	30	33	38	36	32	29	29	21	24	24	25	27	24	25	27	27	29
(10) NZ price + transport cost (6) + (9)	US$/T	140	165	191	189	171	143	101	88	129	175	187	149	152	169	165	174	213
(11) Fat content (New Zealand)	%	4.7	4.7	4.6	4.6	4.7	4.6	4.6	4.6	4.6	4.7	4.6	4.7	4.7	4.7	4.7	4.8	4.7
(12) Fat content (Mexico)	%	3.5	3.5	3.5	3.5	3.5	3.5	3.5	3.5	3.5	3.5	3.5	3.5	3.5	3.5	3.5	3.5	3.5
(13) NZ price+transport, adjusted to Mexico fat content	US$/T	122	144	168	166	149	126	89	78	113	154	164	131	133	147	144	151	185
(14) Exchange rate	M$/US$	0	0	0	0	0	0	0	1	1	2	2	3	3	3	3	3	6
(15) Reference price (13) * (14)	M$/T	3	3	4	9	23	24	29	50	160	351	408	371	401	455	448	511	1 189
(16) Unit market price support (4) – (15)	M$/T	2	3	4	4	-3	18	34	55	67	57	193	258	401	408	453	401	-16
(17) Market price support (16) * (2)/1 000	M$ Mio	16	21	31	27	-19	124	248	364	426	360	1 110	1 631	2 778	2 930	3 457	3 027	-120
(18) Market price support in %	%	45	48	51	30	-13	42	54	53	29	14	32	41	50	47	50	44	-1
CSE-MARKET TRANSFERS (MT)																		
(19) MPS on domestic prod. – (17)	M$ Mio	-16	-21	-31	-27	19	-124	-248	-364	-426	-360	-1 110	-1 631	-2 778	-2 930	-3 457	-3 027	120
(20) Consumption	Litres Mio	7 379	8 711	6 856	7 995	8 115	7 960	8 773	7 950	7 898	8 253	8 197	9 307	7 353	9 311	9 956	10 075	10 075
(21) Consumption converted into tonnes	'000 T	7 608	8 981	7 069	8 243	8 367	8 207	9 045	8 196	8 143	8 509	8 451	9 596	7 581	9 600	10 265	10 388	10 388
(22) Consumption – Production (21) – (2)	'000 T	760	2 031	0	1 105	1 388	1 134	1 650	1 625	1 750	2 159	2 701	3 264	656	2 417	2 631	2 841	2 760

Notes:

p. provisional
(1) Cow milk production. Sources: 1979-93: *Sexto Informe de Gobierno 1994*. 1994-95: SAGAR, *Boletín mensual de información básica del sector agropecuario y forestal, avance a septiembre de 1996*.
(2) Milk production in litres has been transformed into weight on the basis of a coefficient 1.031 corresponding to the density of milk.(2) = (1) * 1.031
(3) Sources: 1979-85: *Diario Oficial de la Federación*; 1986-89: *Oficios de la Secofi*; 1990-91: CONAFOPALE; 1992-95: *Confederación Nacional Ganadera*.
(4) Producer price per tonne (3)/1.031 * 1 000.
(6) Information provided by New Zealand Authorities, Ministry of Agriculture and Fisheries to OECD Secretariat.
(7). Transport costs from New Zealand to Mexico. Information provided by New Zealand Authorities to OECD Secretariat for the years 1992-95. 1979-91 was estimated by extrapolating back the average of the freight differential with the
(8) US costs over the period 1992 to 1995.
(9) = (7) * 0.056 + (8) * 0.082.
(12) Source: Mexican Authorities.
(13) = (10) * ((11) + (12))/(2 * (11)).
(14) Source: OECD, *Main Economic Indicators*.
(16) Unit market price support (4) = (17)/(5) * 100.
(18) Market price support in % = (18) = (17)/(5) * 100.
(20) Cow milk apparent consumption. Source SAGAR. 1994 was estimated by applying the growth rate as in *Confederación Nacional Ganadera, Información económica pecuaria*, p. 50, and 1995 was estimated as equal to 1994.
(21) = (20) * 1.031.

Table 7. **Producer subsidy equivalent – beef and veal**

	Units	1979	1980	1981	1982	1983	1984	1985	1986	1987	1988	1989	1990	1991	1992	1993	1994	1995p
I. Level of production	'000 t	989	1 062	1 148	1 186	1 029	931	955	1 237	1 265	1 174	1 143	1 049	1 145	1 198	1 232	1 334	1 404
II. Production price (farm gate)	M$/t	30	32	37	60	108	168	379	628	1 178	3 074	5 026	5 376	5 943	5 726	5 845	5 691	7 406
III. Value of production	M$ mn	29	34	43	71	111	157	362	777	1 490	3 610	5 746	5 641	6 802	6 861	7 199	7 593	10 398
IV. Levies	M$ mn	0	0	0	0	0	0	0	0	0	0	0	0	0	0	0	0	0
V. Direct payments	M$ mn	0	0	0	0	0	0	0	0	0	0	1	1	1	2	1	2	9
VI. Adjusted value of production	M$ mn	29	34	43	71	111	157	362	777	1 490	3 610	5 747	5 642	6 803	6 863	7 200	7 595	10 407
VII. Policy transfers	M$ mn	2	-5	5	-11	-126	-111	-11	-256	-1 009	-821	382	1 056	334	415	1 426	1 061	-2 457
A. Market price support	M$ mn	0	-9	-2	-22	-140	-135	-53	-307	-1 171	-1 036	0	0	0	0	622	151	-3 117
1. Trade measures	M$ mn	0	-9	-2	-22	-140	-135	-53	-307	-1 171	-1 036	0	0	0	0	622	151	-3 117
2. PACE	M$ mn																	
B. Levies	M$ mn	0	0	0	0	0	0	0	0	0	0	0	0	0	0	0	0	0
C. Direct payments	M$ mn																	
1. Per tonne payment (Aserca)	M$ mn																	
2. Area and headage payments	M$ mn																	
3. Disaster	M$ mn																	
4. Price premium (Aserca)	M$ mn											1	1	1	2	1	2	9
D. Reduction of input costs	M$ mn	2	3	6	9	12	20	37	41	140	176	321	957	226	272	646	735	504
E. General services	M$ mn	0	1	1	2	2	3	6	10	21	39	59	85	95	123	135	151	125
F. Sub national	M$ mn	0	0	0	0	0	0	0	0	0	0	0	13	12	19	21	23	22
G. Other	M$ mn																	
VIII. Gross total PSE	M$ mn	2	-5	5	-11	-126	-111	-11	-256	-1 009	-821	382	1 056	334	415	1 426	1 061	-2 457
IX. Gross unit PSE	M$/t	2	-5	4	-9	-122	-119	-12	-207	-798	-699	334	1 006	292	347	1 158	795	-1 750
X. Gross percentage PSE	%	7	-16	12	-15	-113	-71	-3	-33	-68	-23	7	19	5	6	20	14	-24
XI. Feed adjustment	M$ mn	0	0	-1	0	4	2	3	2	-4	28	-14	-34	-27	-25	-84	-9	30
1. Excess feed cost	M$ mn	0	0	0	0	2	1	2	1	-5	7	-8	-13	-16	-12	-74	-22	17
2. Other feed cost	M$ mn	0	0	0	0	2	1	1	1	1	21	-6	-21	-11	-13	-10	12	13
XII. Net total PSE	M$ mn	2	-5	4	-11	-121	-109	-8	-254	-1 014	-793	367	1 022	307	390	1 342	1 052	-2 428
XIII. Net unit PSE	M$/t	2	-5	4	-9	-118	-117	-9	-206	-801	-675	321	974	268	326	1 089	788	-1 729
XIV. Net percentage PSE	%	7	-16	10	-15	-109	-70	-2	-33	-68	-22	6	18	5	6	19	14	-23

Notes to Table 7
PSE: Beef and veal

Definitions and Notes:

I   **Level of production**: Gross indigenous production defined as live weight beef production expressed in carcass weight (*carne de bovino en canal*) (including exports of live animals in carcass weight equivalent) [1] minus imports of live animals in carcass weight equivalent [2]. For 1995, estimate provided directly by SAGAR.

II   **Production price (farm gate)**: Weighted average live weight price to middlemen at slaughter-house (*precio promedio ponderado*), of beef in carcass weight equivalent [3] multiplied by a margin (of 30 to 40 per cent) to bring this price to the farm gate level [4]. For 1995, average producer price [5].

III **Value of production**: Level of production (I) multiplied by the production price (II).

A.1 **Trade measures**: Production price (II) minus reference price (see Table 14) multiplied by the level of production (I). For the period 1989-92, the MPS was not calculated as there were neither administered prices or trade measures in place.

C.3 **Disaster payments**: See notes to Table 13.

D.   **Reduction of input costs**: See notes to Table 13.

E.   **General services**: See notes to Table 13.

XI   **Feed adjustment**: See notes to Table 13.

Sources:

[1] SAGAR, as reported in *Sexto Informe de Gobierno* 1994, *Anexo*, page 182 for the years 1979-93, and SAGAR *Boletín mensual de información básica del sector agropecuario y forestal*, for 1994 and 1995.

[2] OECD (AGLINK database).

[3] SAGAR (1986), *Subsector pecuario, Precios y valorización de la producción 1972-1985*; SAGAR (1994); *Compendio estadístico de la producción pecuaria 1989-1993*. Data provided directly by SAGAR for the periods 1986-88 and 1994.

[4] For the years 1982 to 1991, the margin is given in The WEFA Group (1993), *Analysis of the Mexican Cattle and Beef Industries, Final report presented to the Canadian International Trade Tribunal*, April 1993. The margin was estimated at 30 per cent for the 1979-81 period and 40 per cent over the period 1992-95.

[5] Estimate provided directly by SAGAR.

Table 7. **Consumer subsidy equivalent – beef and veal** (cont.)

	Units	1979	1980	1981	1982	1983	1984	1985	1986	1987	1988	1989	1990	1991	1992	1993	1994	1995p
I. Level of consumption	'000 t	933	1 032	1 135	1 174	969	917	969	1 160	1 169	1 143	1 095	1 008	1 215	1 298	1 212	1 380	1 301
II. Consumption price (farm gate)	M$/t	30	32	37	60	108	168	379	628	1 178	3 074	5 026	5 376	5 943	5 726	5 845	5 687	7 406
III. Value of consumption	M$ mn	28	33	42	71	105	154	368	728	1 377	3 515	5 502	5 419	7 223	7 432	7 086	7 848	9 635
IV. Policy transfers	M$ mn	0	9	2	22	132	133	53	288	1 082	1 009	0	0	0	0	-612	-151	2 888
A. **Market transfers**	M$ mn	0	9	2	22	132	133	53	288	1 082	1 009	0	0	0	0	-612	-151	2 888
1. Trade measures	M$ mn	0	9	2	22	132	133	53	288	1 082	1 009	0	0	0	0	-612	-151	2 888
2. Tariffs	M$ mn																	
B. **Other transfers**	M$ mn	0	0	0	0	0	0	0	0	0	0	0	0	0	0	0	0	0
1. Consumption subsidies	M$ mn																	
2. Aserca payment	M$ mn																	
V. Total CSE	M$ mn	0	9	2	22	132	133	53	288	1 009	1 009	0	0	0	0	-612	-151	2 888
VI. Unit CSE	M$/t	0	8	2	19	136	145	55	248	925	882	0	0	0	0	-505	-109	2 220
VII. Percentage CSE	%	0	26	4	31	126	86	15	40	79	29	0	0	0	0	-9	-2	30

p: provisional

Notes to Table 7
CSE: Beef and veal

Definitions and Notes:

I   **Level of consumption**: Domestic apparent consumption of beef in carcass weight, defined as gross indigenous production plus total imports minus total exports. Total imports (exports) include meat and live animals in carcass weight equivalent [1].

II **Consumption price (farm gate)**: Implicit price measured at the farm gate; equal to the production price (Pp) minus the sum of unit market price support (MPS_u) and unit market transfers (M_{tu}) $[Pp - (MPS_u + MT_u)]$.

III **Value of consumption**: Level of consumption (I) multiplied by the consumption price (II).

A.1 **MPS on domestic production**: In 1985, 1991 and 1992, the inverse of the market price support component of the PSE. For all the other years of the review period, as the level of production exceeded the level of consumption, the MPS was applied on domestic consumption: production price (see PSE II) minus reference price (see Table 14) multiplied by the level of consumption (I).

A.2 **Tariffs**: Not applicable over the review period, as beef has generally been imported duty-free, although subject to permits until 1988.

Sources:

[1]   OECD (AGLINK database).

Table 7. **Calculation of market price support and of market transfers – beef and veal** (cont.)

BEEF AND VEAL (BOVINO)
PSE-MARKET PRICE SUPPORT (MPS)

	Units	1979	1980	1981	1982	1983	1984	1985	1986	1987	1988	1989	1990	1991	1992	1993	1994	1995p
(1) Produccion carne en canal	'000 T	994	1 065	1 164	1 201	1 030	963	980	1 248	1 273	1 217	1 163	1 114	1 189	1 247	1 256	1 365	
(2) Beef & veal imports, live animals	'000 T	5	3	16	15	2	32	25	11	8	43	19	65	44	49	25	30	
(3) Gross indigenous production (1) – (2)	'000 T	989	1 062	1 148	1 186	1 029	931	955	1 237	1 265	1 174	1 143	1 049	1 145	1 198	1 232	1 334	1 404
(4) Producer price (en canal)	MS/T	49	54	62	102	180	267	549	910	1 840	4 880	7 180	7 680	8 490	8 180	8 350	8 130	10 580
(5) Margin producer / wholesale	%	40	40	40	41	40	37	31	31	36	37	30	30	30	30	30	30	30
(6) Adjusted producer price	MS/T	30	32	37	60	108	168	379	628	1 178	3 074	5 026	5 376	5 943	5 726	5 845	5 691	7 406
(7) Value of prod (3) * (6)/1 000	MS Mio	29	34	43	71	111	157	362	777	1 490	3 610	5 746	5 641	6 802	6 861	7 199	7 593	10 398
(8) Australia production price	AS/t	1 420	1 299	1 089	1 225	1 446	1 584	1 566	1 732	1 779	1 877	2 252	2 003	1 924	1 899	2 204	2 000	1 751
(9) Australia/US exchange rate	AS/US$	.89	.88	.87	.99	1.11	1.14	1.43	1.5	1.43	1.28	1.26	1.28	1.28	1.36	1.47	1.37	1.35
(10) Australia production price in US$	US$/T	1 587	1 481	1 253	1 243	1 304	1 389	1 094	1 158	1 245	1 465	1 781	1 563	1 498	1 394	1 496	1 461	1 297
(11) Mexico/US exchange rate	MS/US$	0	0	0	0	0	0	0	1	1	2	2	3	3	3	3	3	6
(12) Australia production price MS	MS/T	36	34	31	64	202	266	358	740	1 765	3 341	4 442	4 439	4 529	4 315	4 661	4 950	8 331
(13) Transport cost Australia to the US	$A/t cwe		217	239	229	253	232	280	266	284	288	296	274	246	238	267	211	227
(14) Transport cost to Mexico	MS/T		7	8	14	42	47	77	136	338	615	701	729	696	650	679	628	1 295
(15) Australia prod. price + transport	MS/T		41	39	79	244	313	435	876	2 103	3 957	5 143	5 168	5 225	4 964	5 340	5 578	9 626
(16) Unit market price support (6) – (15)	MS/T		-8	-2	-19	-136	-145	-56	-248	-925	-882	-117	208	718	762	505	113	-2 220
(17) Market price support (16) * (3)/1 000	MS Mio		-9	-2	-22	-140	-135	-53	-307	-1 171	-1 036	-134	218	822	913	622	151	-3 117
(18) Agreed market price support(17)	MS/T		-9	-2	-22	-140	-135	-53	-307	-1 171	-1 036	0	0	0	0	622	151	-3 117
(19) Agreed market price support in %	MS Mio		-26	-4	-31	-126	-86	-15	-40	-79	-29	0	0	0	0	9	2	-30
CSE-MARKET TRANSFERS (MT)																		
(20) Beef & veal consumption	'000 T	933	1 032	1 135	1 174	969	917	969	1 160	1 169	1 143	1 095	1 008	1 215	1 298	1 212	1 380	1 301
(21) Consumption – Production (20) – (3)	'000 T	-55	-30	-13	-12	-60	-13	14	-77	-96	-31	-49	-41	71	100	-19	46	-103
(22) Market transfer – (18)/(3) * (20)	MS Mio	0	9	2	22	132	133	54	288	1 082	1 009	0	0	0	0	-612	-156	2 888
(23) MPS on domestic production – (18)	MS Mio							53									-151	
(24) Market transfer (22),(23)	MS Mio	0	9	2	22	132	133	53	288	1 082	1 009	0	0	0	0	-612	-151	2 888

Notes:
p: provisional
(1) Sources: 1979-93: Sexto Informe de Gobierno 1994; 1994: SAGAR, Boletín mensual de información básica del sector agropecuario y forestal, avance a septiembre de 1996. Carcass weight equivalent (Ganancia en peso vivo expresada en carne en canal). Production including live exports.
(2) Source: OECD (AGLINK database).
(3) 1995: OECD (AGLINK estimate).
(4) Precio promedio ponderado. Sources: 1979-85: SAGAR, Subsector pecuario, precios y valorización de la producción 1972-1985; 1986-88: printout provided by SAGAR; 1989-93: SAGAR, Compendio estadístico de la producción pecuaria, 1989-1993; 1994-1995: data provided directly by SAGAR.
(5) Estimates of the margin between the producer prices and wholesale prices for the years 1982 to 1991 are given in The WEFA Group, Analysis of the Mexican Cattle and Beef Industries, Final report, April 1993.
(6) = (4) * (1-(5)/100).
(8) PSE database for Australia.
(9), (11) Source: OECD, Main Economic Indicators.
(10) = (8)/(9).
(12) = (10) * (11).
(13) Frozen rates based on the difference between CIF and FAS prices for 90CL cow beef sold to the US
(14) = (13)/(9) * (11) * 1.2; 20% was added to the transport cost from Australia to the US, on the basis of what was done in the case of milk for the transport from New Zealand to Mexico.
(18) As no measure was in place at the border for the years 1989-92, it was agreed to assume the market price support was zero for those years.
(19) = (18)/(7) * 100.
(20) Source: OECD (AGLINK database); 1995: AGLINK estimate.
(24) = (22) except for the years 1985 and 1994 where (24) = (23).

Table 8. **Producer subsidy equivalent – pigmeat**

	Units	1979	1980	1981	1982	1983	1984	1985	1986	1987	1988	1989	1990	1991	1992	1993	1994	1995p
I. Level of production	'000 t	1 166	1 250	1 304	1 364	1 486	1 455	1 293	959	914	824	708	750	750	798	816	838	897
II. Production price (farm gate)	MS/t	47	46	61	102	144	285	452	623	2 320	4 510	4 940	6 100	7 130	6 780	6 230	6 680	9 050
III. Value of production	MS mn	55	58	80	139	214	415	584	598	2 121	3 718	3 499	4 574	5 350	5 411	5 082	5 595	8 120
IV. Levies	MS mn	0	0	0	0	0	0	0	0	0	0	0	0	0	0	0	0	0
V. Direct payments	MS mn	0	0	0	0	0	0	0	0	0	0	0	0	1	1	1	0	5
VI. Adjusted value of production	MS mn	55	58	80	139	214	415	584	598	2 121	3 718	3 500	4 574	5 351	5 412	5 083	5 596	8 125
VII. Policy transfers	MS mn	20	25	41	34	-117	33	40	-339	60	1 307	1 281	1 546	1 907	2 332	2 007	2 589	1 115
A. Market price support	MS mn	17	22	35	21	-136	-9	-15	-374	-59	1 148	1 078	934	1 710	2 099	1 547	2 110	722
1. Trade measures	MS mn	17	22	35	21	-136	-9	-15	-374	-59	1 148	1 078	934	1 710	2 099	1 547	2 110	722
2. PACE	MS mn																	
B. Levies	MS mn	0	0	0	0	0	0	0	0	0	0	0	0	0	0	0	0	0
C. Direct payments	MS mn	0	0	0	0	0	0	0	0	0	0	0	0	1	1	1	1	5
1. Per tonne payment (Aserca)	MS mn																	
2. Area and headage payments	MS mn																	
3. Disaster	MS mn	0	0	0	0	0	0	0	0	0	0	0	0	1	1	1	1	5
4. Price premium (Aserca)	MS mn																	
D. Reduction of input costs	MS mn	2	2	6	10	16	35	48	29	103	130	171	555	131	151	370	387	300
E. General services	MS mn	0	1	1	2	3	6	7	7	16	29	32	50	58	70	77	80	74
F. Sub national	MS mn	0	0	0	0	0	0	0	0	0	0	0	8	7	11	12	12	13
G. Other	MS mn																	
VIII. Gross total PSE	MS mn	20	25	41	34	-117	33	40	-339	60	1 307	1 281	1 546	1 907	2 332	2 007	2 589	1 115
IX. Gross unit PSE	MS/t	17	20	32	25	-78	22	31	-353	65	1 585	1 808	2 062	2 542	2 922	2 460	3 091	1 243
X. Gross percentage PSE	%	36	43	52	24	-54	8	7	-57	3	35	37	34	36	43	39	46	14
XI. Feed adjustment	MS mn	1	0	-5	0	35	16	20	9	-24	136	-71	-169	-120	-143	-433	-48	152
1. Excess feed cost	MS mn	1	0	-2	1	18	8	14	4	-28	34	-41	-63	-70	-68	-380	-112	85
i. Other feed cost	MS mn	0	0	-3	-1	17	8	6	5	5	102	-29	-106	-50	-75	-53	64	67
XII. Net total PSE	MS mn	20	25	37	34	-81	49	60	-330	36	1 443	1 210	1 377	1 787	2 189	1 574	2 541	1 267
XIII. Net unit PSE	MS/t	17	20	28	25	-55	33	47	-344	39	1 750	1 708	1 836	2 382	2 743	1 929	3 034	1 412
XIV. Net percentage PSE	%	37	43	46	24	-38	12	10	-55	2	39	35	30	33	40	31	45	16

Notes to Table 8
PSE: Pigmeat

Definitions and Notes:

I   **Level of production**: Gross indigenous production defined as live weight pigmeat production expressed in carcass weight (*carne de porcino en canal*) [1] minus imports of live animals in carcass weight equivalent [2].

II   **Production price (farm gate)**: Producer price (*precio del cerdo*) of pigmeat in carcass weight equivalent [3].

III **Value of production**: Level of production (I) multiplied by the production price (II).

A.1 **Trade measures**: Production price (II) minus reference price (see Table 14) multiplied by the level of production (I).

C.3 **Disaster payments**: See notes to Table 13.

D.   **Reduction of input costs:** See notes to Table 13.

E.   **General services**: See notes to Table 13.

XI   **Feed adjustment:** See notes to Table 13.

Sources:

[1]   SAGAR, as reported in *Sexto Informe de Gobierno* 1994, Anexo, page 182 for the years 1979-93, and SAGAR *Boletín mensual de información básica del sector agropecuario y forestal*, for 1994 and 1995.
[2]   OECD (AGLINK database).
[3]   Data provided directly by CMP (Mexican Council of Pig Producers).

Table 8. **Consumer subsidy equivalent – pigmeat** (cont.)

	Units	1979	1980	1981	1982	1983	1984	1985	1986	1987	1988	1989	1990	1991	1992	1993	1994	1995p
I. Level of consumption	'000 t	1 166	1 251	1 307	1 365	1 485	1 455	1 293	959	914	905	783	787	860	875	868	963	1 004
II. Consumption price (farm gate)	M$/t	47	46	61	102	144	285	452	623	2 320	4 442	4 860	6 087	6 963	6 622	6 168	6 460	9 140
III. Value of consumption	M$ mn	55	58	80	139	214	415	585	597	2 120	4 018	3 806	4 789	5 988	5 793	5 351	6 221	9 176
IV. Policy transfers	M$ mn	-17	-22	-35	-21	136	9	15	374	59	-1 198	-1 129	-969	-1 816	-2 162	-1 592	-2 214	-898
A. Market transfers	M$ mn	-17	-22	-35	-21	136	9	15	374	59	-1 198	-1 129	-969	-1 816	-2 162	-1 592	-2 214	-898
1. MPS on domestic production	M$ mn	-17	-22	-35	-21	136	9	15	374	59	-1 148	-1 078	-934	-1 710	-2 099	-1 547	-2 110	-722
2. Tariffs	M$ mn	0	0	0	0	0	0	0	0	0	-50	-51	-36	-106	-64	-45	-104	-176
B. Other transfers	M$ mn	0	0	0	0	0	0	0	0	0	0	0	0	0	0	0	0	0
1. Consumption subsidies	M$ mn																	
2. Aserca payment	M$ mn																	
V. Total CSE	M$ mn	-17	-22	-35	-21	136	9	15	374	59	-1 198	-1 129	-969	-1 816	-2 162	-1 592	-2 214	-898
VI. Unit CSE	M$/t	-15	-17	-27	-15	91	6	12	390	64	-1 324	-1 442	-1 232	-2 112	-2 472	-1 835	-2 299	-895
VII. Percentage CSE	%	-32	-38	-44	-15	64	2	3	63	3	-30	-30	-20	-30	-37	-30	-36	-10

p: provisional.

Notes to Table 8
CSE: Pigmeat

Definitions and Notes:

I   **Level of consumption**: Domestic apparent consumption of pigmeat in carcass weight, defined as gross indigenous production plus total imports minus total exports. Total imports (exports) include meat and live animals in carcass weight equivalent [1].

II   **Consumption price (farm gate)**: Implicit price measured at the farm gate; equal to the production price (Pp) minus the sum of unit market price support (MPS_u) and unit market transfers (M_{tu}) $[Pp - (MPS_u + MT_u)]$.

III   **Value of consumption**: Level of consumption (I) multiplied by the consumption price (II).

A.1   **MPS on domestic production**: The inverse of the market price support component of the PSE.

A.2   **Tariffs**: Not applicable over the period 1979-87 in which imports were subject to permits, but duty-free. For the 1988-95 period, import tariff of 20 per cent multiplied by reference price multiplied by the difference between the consumption (I) and production (I in PSE) levels.

Sources:

[1]   OECD (AGLINK database).

Table 8. **Calculation of market price support and of market transfers – pigmeat** (cont.)

PIGMEAT (PORCINO)

	Units	1979	1980	1981	1982	1983	1984	1985	1986	1987	1988	1989	1990	1991	1992	1993	1994	1995p
PSE-MARKET PRICE SUPPORT (MPS)																		
(1) Pigmeat production	'000 T	1 167	1 251	1 307	1 365	1 486	1 455	1 293	959	915	861	727	757	812	820	822	873	
(2) Pigmeat imports, live animals	'000 T	1	1	2	2	1	1	1	0	0	37	18	8	61	22	6	35	
(3) Gross indigenous production (1) – (2)	'000 T	1 166	1 250	1 304	1 364	1 486	1 455	1 293	959	914	824	708	750	750	798	816	838	897
(4) Producer price	M$/T	47	46	61	102	144	285	452	623	2 320	4 510	4 940	6 100	7 130	6 780	6 230	6 680	9 050
(5) Value of production (3) * (4)/1 000	M$ Mio	55	58	80	139	214	415	584	598	2 121	3 718	3 499	4 574	5 350	5 411	5 082	5 595	8 120
(6) US Reference price	US$/T	1 334	1 180	1 322	1 599	1 442	1 437	1 338	1 505	1 602	1 287	1 290	1 629	1 525	1 261	1 311	1 148	1 204
(7) Transport cost	US$/T	80	80	80	80	80	80	80	80	80	80	80	80	80	80	80	80	80
(8) US price landed (6) + (7)	US$/T	1 414	1 260	1 402	1 679	1 522	1 517	1 418	1 585	1 682	1 367	1 370	1 709	1 605	1 341	1 391	1 228	1 284
(9) Exchange rate	M$/US$	0	0	0	0	0	0	0	0	1	2	2	3	3	3	3	3	6
(10) US Reference price landed (8) * (9)	M$/T	32	29	34	87	235	291	464	1 013	2 384	3 118	3 418	4 855	4 851	4 150	4 333	4 161	8 245
(11) Unit market price support (4) – (10)	M$/T	15	17	27	15	-91	-6	-12	-390	-64	1 392	1 522	1 245	2 279	2 630	1 897	2 519	805
(12) Market price support (11) * (3)/1 000	M$ Mio	17	22	35	21	-136	-9	-15	-374	-59	1 148	1 078	934	1 710	2 099	1 547	2 110	722
(13) Market price support in %	%	32	38	44	15	-64	-2	-3	-63	-3	31	31	20	32	39	30	38	9
CSE-MARKET TRANSFERS (MT)																		
(14) MPS on domestic prod. – (12)	M$ Mio	-17	-22	-35	-21	136	9	15	374	59	-1 148	-1 078	-934	-1 710	-2 099	-1 547	-2 110	-722
(15) Pigmeat consumption	'000 T	1 166	1 251	1 307	1 365	1 485	1 455	1 293	959	914	905	783	787	860	875	868	963	1 004
(16) Consumption – Production (15) – (3)	'000 T	0	0	2	2	-1	0	1	0	-1	80	75	37	109	77	52	125	107
(17) Rate of the tariff on imports	%										20	20	20	20	20	20	20	20
(18) Tariffs on imports	M$ Mio	-17	-22	-35	-21	-64	-9	-3	-63	-3	-50	-51	-36	-106	-64	-45	-104	-176
(19) Total market transfers (14) + (18)	M$ Mio	-17	-22	-35	-21	136	9	15	374	59	-1 198	-1 129	-969	-1 816	-2 162	-1 592	-2 214	-898

Notes:

p: provisional

(1) Sources: 1979-93: *Sexto Informe de Gobierno 1994*, 1994 and 1995: SAGAR, *Boletín mensual de información básica del sector agropecuario y forestal*, avance a septiembre de 1996. Carcass weight equivalent (*Ganancia en peso vivo expresada en carne en canal*).

(3) 1995: OECD (AGLINK estimate).

(4) Sources: 1979-80: SAGAR, *Subsector pecuario, precios y valorización de la producción 1972-1985, Precio promedio ponderado*, 1981-86: IDA, 1987-95: SNIM.

(6) Pigmeat reference price in the US PSE database: 1979: implicit price derived by substracting the US tariff from the US producer price, 1980-95: US producer price.

(7) Transport costs US-Canada used in the canadian PSE database to calculate US poultry price landed.

(9) Source: OECD, *Main Economic Indicators*.

(13) Market price support in %. (13) = (12)/(5) * 100. It should be noted here that the difference in import regime between pigmeat (tariff) and poultrymeat (tariff quota) may not be sufficiently reflected in their respective MPS (see Table 9 continued for the MPS of poultrymeat). The MPS for poultrymeat will be subject to revision when more accurate data on producer prices will become available.

(15) Source: OECD (AGLINK database).

(18) Tariffs on imports: (18) = – (16) * (10) * (17)/100 000.

Table 9. Producer subsidy equivalent – poultrymeat

	Units	1979	1980	1981	1982	1983	1984	1985	1986	1987	1988	1989	1990	1991	1992	1993	1994	1995p
I. Level of production	'000 t	395	429	457	482	502	525	625	703	699	654	632	773	879	922	1 058	1 144	1 299
II. Production price (farm gate)	M$/t	28	32	39	69	115	201	311	521	1 255	2 682	3 355	3 595	4 001	3 634	4 110	3 960	5 160
III. Value of production	M$ mn	11	14	18	33	58	106	195	366	878	1 755	2 120	2 778	3 517	3 350	4 348	4 532	6 704
IV. Levies	M$ mn	0	0	0	0	0	0	0	0	0	0	0	0	0	0	0	0	0
V. Direct payments	M$ mn	0	0	0	0	0	0	0	0	0	0	0	0	1	1	1	1	5
VI. Adjusted value of production	M$ mn	11	14	18	33	58	106	195	366	878	1 755	2 120	2 779	3 517	3 351	4 349	4 533	6 710
VII. Policy transfers	M$ mn	3	6	9	14	-10	4	-1	-105	198	280	377	975	972	544	1 117	725	-2 267
A. Market price support	M$ mn	3	4	7	10	-17	-9	-22	-131	105	186	226	397	794	357	641	169	-2 673
1. Trade measures	M$ mn	3	4	7	10	-17	-9	-22	-131	105	186	226	397	794	357	641	169	-2 673
2. PACE	M$ mn																	
B. Levies	M$ mn	0	0	0	0	0	0	0	0	0	0	0	0	0	0	0	0	0
C. Direct payments	M$ mn	0	0	0	0	0	0	0	0	0	0	0	0	1	1	1	1	5
1. Per tonne payment (Aserca)	M$ mn																	
2. Area and headage payments	M$ mn																	
3. Disaster	M$ mn																	
4. Price premium (Aserca)	M$ mn	0	0	0	0	0	0	0	0	0	0	0	0	1	1	1	1	5
D. Reduction of input costs	M$ mn	1	1	2	3	6	11	19	21	80	77	127	524	119	121	383	448	310
E. General services	M$ mn	0	0	0	1	1	2	3	5	12	17	24	47	52	56	80	92	77
F. Sub national	M$ mn	0	0	0	0	0	0	0	0	0	0	0	7	7	9	12	14	14
G. Other	M$ mn																	
VIII. Gross total PSE	M$ mn	3	6	9	14	-10	4	-1	-105	198	280	377	975	972	544	1 117	725	-2 267
IX. Gross unit PSE	M$/t	9	13	20	30	-20	7	-1	-150	282	428	596	1 261	1 106	590	1 055	633	-1 745
X. Gross percentage PSE	%	31	41	52	43	-17	4	0	-29	23	16	18	35	28	16	26	16	-34
XI. Feed adjustment	M$ mn	1	0	-7	0	49	22	29	15	-37	206	-93	-249	-190	-201	-485	-54	170
1. Excess feed cost	M$ mn	1	0	-3	1	25	12	20	7	-45	52	-55	-93	-111	-95	-426	-125	95
i. Other feed cost	M$ mn	0	-1	-4	-1	24	11	8	8	7	154	-38	-156	-80	-105	-59	72	75
XII. Net total PSE	M$ mn	5	5	3	15	39	26	28	-91	160	487	284	725	782	343	632	671	-2 098
XIII. Net unit PSE	M$/t	12	12	6	31	78	50	44	-129	229	744	449	939	889	373	597	587	-1 614
XIV. Net percentage PSE	%	42	38	14	45	67	25	14	-25	18	28	13	26	22	10	15	15	-31

Notes to Table 9
PSE: Poultrymeat

Definitions and Notes:

I **Level of production**: Gross indigenous production defined as live weight poultry (chicken and turkey) production expressed in carcass weight (*carne de ovino y guajolotes en canal*) [1].

II **Production price (farm gate)**: Producer price (*precio al productor*) of poultrymeat in carcass weight equivalent [2].

III **Value of production**: Level of production (I) multiplied by the production price (II).

A.1 **Trade measures**: Production price (II) minus reference price (see Table 14) multiplied by the level of production (I).

C.3 **Disaster payments**: See notes to Table 13.

D. **Reduction of input costs:** See notes to Table 13.

E. **General services**: See notes to Table 13.

XI **Feed adjustment:** See notes to Table 13.

Sources:

[1] SAGAR, as reported in *Sexto Informe de Gobierno* 1994, Anexo, page 182 for the years 1979-93, and SAGAR *Boletín mensual de información básica del sector agropecuario y forestal*, for 1994 and 1995.

[2] Data provided directly by UNA (National Union of Poultry Producers).

Notes to Table 9
CSE: Poultrymeat

Definitions and Notes:

I **Level of consumption**: Domestic apparent consumption of poultrymeat in carcass weight, defined as gross indigenous production plus imports minus exports [1].

II **Consumption price (farm gate)**: Implicit price measured at the farm gate; equal to the production price (Pp) minus the sum of unit market price support (MPS_u) and unit market transfers (M_{tu}) $[Pp - (MPS_u + MT_u)]$.

III **Value of consumption**: Level of consumption (I) multiplied by the consumption price (II).

A.1 **MPS on domestic production**: The inverse of the market price support component of the PSE.

A.2 **Tariffs**: For the 1979-93 period, import tariff of 10 per cent multiplied by reference price multiplied by the difference between the consumption (I) and production (I in PSE) levels. Not applicable in 1994 and 1995 as poultrymeat could be imported duty-free within quotas.

Sources:

[1] OECD (AGLINK database).

Table 9. **Consumer subsidy equivalent – poultrymeat** (cont.)

	Units	1979	1980	1981	1982	1983	1984	1985	1986	1987	1988	1989	1990	1991	1992	1993	1994	1995p
I. Level of consumption	'000 t	396	431	471	489	506	537	644	722	717	706	680	828	979	1 065	1 214	1 321	1 494
II. Consumption price (farm gate)	MS/t	28	32	38	69	116	202	314	527	1 254	2 679	3 350	3 582	3 940	3 626	4 077	3 940	5 428
III. Value of consumption	MS mn	11	14	18	34	59	108	202	381	900	1 892	2 278	2 965	3 857	3 861	4 950	5 203	8 110
IV. Policy transfers	MS mn	-3	-4	-7	-10	17	9	22	130	-107	-199	-241	-414	-825	-403	-695	-169	2 673
A. **Market transfers**	MS mn	-3	-4	-7	-10	17	9	22	130	-107	-199	-241	-414	-825	-403	-695	-169	2 673
1. MPS on domestic production	MS mn	-3	-4	-7	-10	17	9	22	131	-105	-186	-226	-397	-794	-357	-641	-169	2 673
2. Tariffs	MS mn	0	0	0	0	0	0	-1	-1	-2	-12	-14	-17	-31	-46	-55	0	0
B. **Other transfers**	MS mn	0	0	0	0	0	0	0	0	0	0	0	0	0	0	0	0	0
1. Consumption subsidies	MS mn																	
2. Aserca payment	MS mn																	
V. Total CSE	MS mn	-3	-4	-7	-10	17	9	22	130	-107	-199	-241	-414	-825	-403	-695	-169	2 673
VI. Unit CSE	MS/t	-7	-10	-15	-21	33	16	34	180	-150	-281	-354	-500	-842	-379	-573	-128	1 789
VII. Percentage CSE	%	-25	-32	-39	-31	28	8	11	34	-12	-11	-11	-14	-21	-10	-14	-3	33

p: provisional.

Table 9. **Calculation of market price support and of market transfers – poultrymeat** *(cont.)*

	Units	1979	1980	1981	1982	1983	1984	1985	1986	1987	1988	1989	1990	1991	1992	1993	1994	1995p
POULTRY (AVES)																		
PSE-MARKET PRICE SUPPORT (MPS)																		
(1)a Poultry production	'000 T	367	399	426	450	469	490	589	673	673	627	611	750	858	898	1 040	1 126	1 284
(1)b Turkey production	'000 T	28	30	31	33	34	35	37	31	26	27	21	22	21	23	18	18	15
(1) Gross indigenous prod. (1)a + (1)b	'000 T	395	429	457	482	502	525	625	703	699	654	632	773	879	922	1 058	1 144	1 299
(2) Producer price	M$/T	28	32	39	69	115	201	311	521	1 255	2 682	3 355	3 595	4 001	3 634	4 110	3 960	5 160
(3) Value of production (1) * (2)/1 000	M$ Mio	11	14	18	33	58	106	195	366	878	1 755	2 120	2 778	3 517	3 350	4 348	4 532	6 704
(4) US Reference price	US$/T	831	864	874	841	880	1 056	982	1 026	699	971	1 121	1 005	945	969	1 045	1 045	1 044
(5) Transport cost US-Canada	US$/T	80	80	80	80	80	80	80	80	80	80	80	80	80	80	80	80	80
(6) US price landed (4) + (5)	US$/T	911	944	954	921	960	1 136	1 062	1 106	779	1 051	1 201	1 085	1 025	1 049	1 125	1 125	1 124
(7) Exchange rate	M$/US$	0	0	0	0	0	0	0	1	1	2	2	3	3	3	3	3	6
(8) US Reference price landed (6) * (7)	M$/T	21	22	23	48	149	218	347	707	1 104	2 397	2 996	3 082	3 098	3 247	3 504	3 812	7 218
(9) Unit market price support (2) – (8)	M$/T	7	10	16	21	-33	-17	-36	-186	151	285	358	513	903	387	606	148	-2 058
(10) Market price support (9) * (1)/1 000	M$ Mio	3	4	7	10	-17	-9	-22	-131	105	186	226	397	794	357	641	169	-2 673
(11) Market price support in %	%	25	32	40	31	-29	-8	-12	-36	12	11	11	14	23	11	15	4	-40
CSE-MARKET TRANSFERS (MT)																		
(12) MPS on domestic prod. – (10)	M$ Mio	-3	-4	-7	-10	17	9	22	131	-105	-186	-226	-397	-794	-357	-641	-169	2 673
(13) Volume of imports	'000 T	0	2	14	7	4	12	19	19	22	79	54	66	105	147	156	176	
(14) Volume of exports	'000 T	0	0	0	0	0	0	0	0	4	27	6	11	5	4	0	0	
(15) Apparent consumption	'000 T	396	431	471	489	506	537	644	722	717	706	680	828	979	1 065	1 214	1 321	1 494
(16) Consumption – Production (15) – (1)	'000 T	1	2	14	7	4	12	19	19	18	52	48	55	100	143	156	176	195
(17) Rate of the tariff on imports	%	10	10	10	10	10	10	10	10	10	10	10	10	10	10	10	0	0
(18) Tariffs on imports	M$ Mio	10	10	0	0	0	0	-1	-1	-2	-12	-14	-17	-31	-46	-55	0	0
(19) Total market transfers (12) + (18)	M$ Mio	-3	-4	-7	-10	17	9	22	130	-107	-199	-241	-414	-825	-403	-695	-169	2 673

Notes:
p: provisional
(1)a: aves, (1)b: guajolotes. Sources: 1979-93: *Sexto Informe de Gobierno 1994*, 1994-95: *Primer Informe de Gobierno 1995*, page 88 and SAGAR, *Boletín mensual de información básica del sector agropecuario y forestal, avance a septiembre de 1996*. Carcass weight equivalent (*Ganancia en peso vivo expresada en carne en canal*).
(2) Source: *Unión nacional de avicultores*.
(4) Poultry reference price in the US PSE database: 1979-85: US producer price, 1986-94: implicit price derived by substracting the US tariff from the US producer price.
(5) Transport costs used in the canadian database to calculate US poultry price landed.
(7) Source: OECD, *Main Economic Indicators*
(11) Market price support in %. (11) = (10)/(3) * 100.
(13), (14) Source: OECD database. (13) 1994 data updated from US exports to Mexico.
(15) = (1) + (13) – (14): Source: OECD database. 1995: Source: OECD (AGLINK database).
(18) Tariffs on imports. (18)=(16) * (8) * (17)/100 000.

227

Table 12. **Producer subsidy equivalent – eggs**

	Units	1979	1980	1981	1982	1983	1984	1985	1986	1987	1988	1989	1990	1991	1992	1993	1994	1995p
I. Level of production	'000 t	601	644	664	690	715	740	826	998	975	1 090	1 047	1 010	1 141	1 161	1 234	1 246	1 242
II. Production price (farm gate)	M$/t	18	19	24	39	72	109	174	369	845	1 561	1 951	2 385	2 182	2 761	2 780	2 620	4 550
III. Value of production	M$ mn	11	12	16	27	51	80	144	368	824	1 702	2 043	2 408	2 490	3 206	3 429	3 265	5 651
IV. Levies	M$ mn	0	0	0	0	0	0	0	0	0	0	0	0	0	0	0	0	0
V. Direct payments	M$ mn	0	0	0	0	0	0	0	0	0	0	0	0	0	0	0	1	3
VI. Adjusted value of production	M$ mn	11	12	16	27	51	80	144	368	824	1 702	2 043	2 409	2 491	3 207	3 430	3 266	5 654
VII. Policy transfers	M$ mn	-1	1	2	-3	-46	-63	-93	-239	-172	-98	-555	-252	-796	350	498	124	-1 092
A. **Market price support**	M$ mn	-1	0	0	-5	-51	-72	-107	-260	-241	-170	-659	-576	-892	230	216	-202	-1 348
1. Trade measures	M$ mn	-1	0	0	-5	-51	-72	-107	-260	-241	-170	-659	-576	-892	230	216	-202	-1 348
2. PACE	M$ mn																	
B. **Levies**	M$ mn	0	0	0	0	0	0	0	0	0	0	0	0	0	0	0	0	0
C. **Direct payments**	M$ mn	0	0	0	0	0	0	0	0	0	0	0	0	0	0	0	1	3
1. Per tonne payment (Aserca)	M$ mn																	
2. Area and headage payments	M$ mn																	
3. Disaster	M$ mn	0	0	0	0	0	0	0	0	0	0	0	0	0	0	0	1	3
4. Price premium (Aserca)	M$ mn																	
D. **Reduction of input costs**	M$ mn	0	1	2	2	4	8	12	17	60	59	87	293	64	78	227	263	196
E. **General services**	M$ mn	0	0	0	0	1	1	2	4	9	13	16	26	28	36	47	54	48
F. **Sub national**	M$ mn	0	0	0	0	0	0	0	0	0	0	0	4	4	6	7	8	9
G. **Other**	M$ mn																	
VIII. Gross total PSE	M$ mn	-1	1	2	-3	-46	-63	-93	-239	-172	-98	-555	-252	-796	350	498	124	-1 092
IX. Gross unit PSE	M$/t	-1	1	4	-4	-64	-85	-113	-239	-176	-90	-531	-249	-697	302	404	100	-879
X. Gross percentage PSE	%	-6	5	15	-10	-89	-79	-65	-65	-21	-6	-27	-10	-32	11	15	4	-19
XI. Feed adjustment	M$ mn	0	0	-2	0	15	7	8	4	-12	69	-31	-68	-37	-45	-186	-21	65
1. Excess feed cost	M$ mn	0	0	-1	0	8	4	6	2	-15	17	-18	-25	-22	-22	-164	-48	36
i. Other feed cost	M$ mn	0	0	-1	0	7	3	2	2	2	51	-13	-43	-16	-24	-23	28	29
XII. Net total PSE	M$ mn	0	1	0	-2	-31	-56	-85	-235	-184	-29	-587	-320	-833	305	312	104	-1 027
XIII. Net unit PSE	M$/t	0	1	2	-4	-43	-76	-103	-235	-189	-27	-560	-317	-730	263	253	83	-827
XIV. Net percentage PSE	%	-3	4	2	-9	-60	-70	-59	-64	-22	-2	-29	-13	-33	10	9	3	-18

Notes to Table 12
PSE: Eggs

Definitions and Notes:

I   **Level of production**: SAGAR statistics on egg (*huevo*) production [1].

II   **Production price (farm gate)**: Producer price (*precio al productor*) of eggs [2].

III   **Value of production**: Level of production (I) multiplied by the production price (II).

A.1   **Trade measures**: Production price (II) minus reference price (see Table 14) multiplied by the level of production (I).

C.3   **Disaster payments**: See notes to Table 13.

D.   **Reduction of input costs:** See notes to Table 13.

E.   **General services**: See notes to Table 13.

XI   **Feed adjustment:** See notes to Table 13.

Sources:

[1]   SAGAR, as reported in *Sexto Informe de Gobierno* 1994, *Anexo*, page 182 for the years 1979-93, and SAGAR *Boletín mensual de información básica del sector agropecuario y forestal*, for 1994 and 1995.

[2]   Data provided directly by UNA (National Union of Poultry Producers).

Notes to Table 12
CSE: Eggs

Definitions and Notes:

I   **Level of consumption**: Domestic apparent consumption of eggs, defined as production plus imports minus exports [1].

II   **Consumption price (farm gate)**: Implicit price measured at the farm gate; equal to the production price (Pp) minus the sum of unit market price support (MPS_u) and unit market transfers (M_{tu}) [$Pp - (MPS_u + MT_u)$].

III   **Value of consumption**: Level of consumption (I) multiplied by the consumption price (II).

A.1   **MPS on domestic production**: The inverse of the market price support component of the PSE.

A.2   **Tariffs**: For the 1979-93 period, import tariff of 10 per cent multiplied by reference price multiplied by the difference between the consumption (I) and production (I in PSE) levels. Not applicable in 1994 and 1995 as fresh eggs could be imported duty-free within quotas.

Sources:

[1]   OECD (AGLINK database).

Table 12. **Consumer subsidy equivalent – eggs** (cont.)

	Units	1979	1980	1981	1982	1983	1984	1985	1986	1987	1988	1989	1990	1991	1992	1993	1994	1995p
I. Level of consumption	'000 t	605	647	667	702	716	740	825	998	975	1 101	1 056	1 015	1 149	1 173	1 245	1 262	1 242
II. Consumption price (farm gate)	MS/t	18	19	24	39	72	109	174	369	845	1 564	1 959	2 389	2 190	2 762	2 781	2 622	4 550
III. Value of consumption	MS mn	11	12	16	27	52	80	143	368	824	1 723	2 068	2 425	2 517	3 240	3 461	3 308	5 651
IV. Policy transfers	MS mn	1	0	0	5	51	72	107	260	241	168	657	574	889	-233	-219	202	1 348
A. **Market transfers**	MS mn	1	0	0	5	51	72	107	260	241	168	657	574	889	-233	-219	202	1 348
1. MPS on domestic production	MS mn	1	0	0	5	51	72	107	260	241	170	659	576	892	-230	-216	202	1 348
2. Tariffs	MS mn	0	0	0	0	0	0	0	0	0	-2	-2	-1	-2	-3	-3	0	0
B. **Other transfers**	MS mn	0	0	0	0	0	0	0	0	0	0	0	0	0	0	0	0	0
1. Consumption subsidies	MS mn																	
2. Aserca payment	MS mn																	
V. Total CSE	MS mn	1	0	0	5	51	72	107	260	241	168	657	574	889	-233	-219	202	1 348
VI. Unit CSE	MS/t	2	1	-1	7	71	98	130	261	247	153	622	566	774	-199	-176	160	1 086
VII. Percentage CSE	%	11	3	-3	19	98	90	75	71	29	10	32	24	35	-7	-6	6	24

p. provisional.

Table 12. **Calculation of market price support and of market transfers – eggs** (cont.)

	Units	1979	1980	1981	1982	1983	1984	1985	1986	1987	1988	1989	1990	1991	1992	1993	1994	1995p
EGGS (HUEVO)																		
PSE-MARKET PRICE SUPPORT (MPS)																		
(1) Production	'000 T	601	644	664	690	715	740	826	998	975	1 090	1 047	1 010	1 141	1 161	1 234	1 246	1 242
(2) Producer price	M$/T	18	19	24	39	72	109	174	369	845	1 561	1 951	2 385	2 182	2 761	2 780	2 620	4 550
(3) Value of production (1) * (2)/1 000	M$ Mio	11	12	16	27	51	80	144	368	824	1 702	2 043	2 408	2 490	3 206	3 429	3 265	5 651
(4) US reference price	US$/T	819	793	889	838	860	1 018	873	931	714	692	971	976	915	766	778	766	823
(5) Transport cost	C$/T	75	75	75	75	75	75	75	75	75	75	75	75	75	75	75	75	75
(6) Exchange rate Canada/US$	C$/US$	1	1	1	1	1	1	1	1	1	1	1	1	1	1	1	1	1
(7) Transport cost (5)/(6)	US$/T	64	64	63	61	61	58	55	54	57	61	63	64	65	62	58	55	55
(8) US price landed (4) + (7)	US$/T	883	857	952	899	921	1 076	928	985	771	753	1 034	1 040	980	828	836	821	878
(9) Exchange rate	M$/US$	0	0	0	0	0	0	0	1	1	2	2	3	3	3	3	3	6
(10) US Reference price landed (8) * (9)	M$/T	20	20	23	46	142	206	303	630	1 092	1 717	2 581	2 955	2 963	2 563	2 605	2 782	5 636
(11) Unit market price support (2) – (10)	M$/T	–2	–1	1	–8	–71	–98	–129	–261	–247	–156	–630	–570	–781	198	175	–162	–1 086
(12) Market price support (1) * (11)/1 000	M$ Mio	–1	0	0	–5	–51	–72	–107	–260	–241	–170	–659	–576	–892	230	216	–202	–1 348
(13) Market price support in %	%	–11	–3	3	–19	–98	–90	–74	–71	–29	–10	–32	–24	–36	7	6	–6	–24
CSE-MARKET TRANSFERS (MT)																		
(14) MPS on domestic prod. – (12)	M$ Mio	1	0	0	5	51	72	107	260	241	170	659	576	892	–230	–216	202	1 348
(15) Volume of imports	'000 T	4	3	3	12	1	0	0	0	0	11	9	5	8	12	11	16	
(16) Volume of exports	'000 T	0	0	0	0	0	0	1	0	0	0	0	0	0	0	0	0	
(17) Apparent consumption	'000 T	605	647	667	702	716	740	825	998	975	1 101	1 056	1 015	1 149	1 173	1 245	1 262	1 242
(18) Consumption-Production (17) – (1)	'000 T	4	3	3	12	1	0	–1	0	0	11	9	5	8	12	11	16	0
(19) Rate of the tariff on imports	%	10	10	10	10	10	10	10	10	10	10	10	10	10	10	10	10	0
(20) Tariffs on imports	M$ Mio	0	0	0	0	0	0	0	0	0	–2	–2	–2	–3	–3	–3	0	0
(21) Total market transfers (14) + (20)	M$ Mio	1	0	0	5	51	72	107	260	241	168	657	574	889	–233	–219	202	1 348

Notes:

p: provisional
(1) Sources: 1979-93: Sexto Informe de Gobierno 1994; 1994-95: SAGAR, Boletín mensual de información básica del sector agropecuario y forestal, avance a septiembre de 1996.
(2) Source: Union nacional de avicultores.
(4) Eggs reference price in the US PSE database: 1979-86: US producer price, 1987-95: implicit price derived by substracting the tariff from the US producer price.
(5) Transport costs US-Canada used in the canadian PSE database to calculate US eggs price landed.
(6), (9) Source: OECD, Main Economic Indicators.
(13) = (12)/(3) * 100.
(15), (16) Source: OECD (AGLINK database).
(17) = (1) + (15) – (16).
(20) = – (18) * (10) * (19)/100 000.

Table 13A.   **Detail of general policy measures: production – aggregate of all commodities 1979 to 1995**

	Units	1979	1980	1981	1982	1983	1984	1985	1986	1987	1988	1989	1990	1991	1992	1993	1994	1995p
Adjusted value of production	M$ mn	203	260	382	559	1 024	1 798	3 113	4 929	12 126	21 667	28 013	36 038	41 750	46 434	48 740	51 964	77 822
A. Market price support	M$ mn	28	28	112	42	-609	-218	-124	-691	-262	321	1 741	6 294	10 327	12 440	14 718	8 576	-7 328
B. Levies	M$ mn	0	0	0	0	0	0	0	0	0	0	0	0	0	0	0	0	0
C. Direct payments	M$ mn	0	0	0	0	0	0	0	0	0	1	3	4	114	809	444	4 560	4 948
D. Reduction of input costs	M$ mn	18	33	61	92	149	290	382	497	1 160	1 646	2 087	4 567	1 762	1 790	2 768	3 352	2 686
Interest concessions	M$ mn	13	21	35	57	78	142	145	201	342	531	436	669	608	840	795	1 018	750
Fertilizer	M$ mn	1	1	4	9	30	37	60	111	224	374	245	297	332	199	0	0	27
Insurance	M$ mn	1	3	4	8	16	25	38	69	76	177	829	1 035	1	46	53	130	122
Irrigation	M$ mn	1	3	5	5	5	30	38	76	178	269	378	469	428	389	292	462	539
Seeds	M$ mn	0	1	1	1	1	1	1	2	2	5	6	6	41	3	0	0	0
Machinery	M$ mn	0	0	0	0	0	0	6	6	5	8	7	6	2	0	0	0	0
Feed	M$ mn	2	4	12	11	19	54	93	32	332	279	183	2 083	339	306	1 628	1 742	1 248
Animal breeding improvement	M$ mn	0	0	0	1	0	0	1	0	1	2	2	4	11	9	0	0	0
E. General services	M$ mn	7	19	27	32	35	78	117	161	258	354	457	734	976	1 399	1 308	1 312	1 309
Research, advisory, training	M$ mn	0	1	3	6	7	13	21	31	74	122	170	300	353	467	488	556	586
Inspection	M$ mn	0	0	0	0	0	0	0	0	0	0	0	0	0	0	0	0	0
Pest and disease control	M$ mn	1	2	2	2	3	6	6	7	10	15	20	27	38	73	70	83	59
Structures/infrastructures	M$ mn	5	16	22	24	25	59	90	122	174	217	267	407	516	733	520	610	582
Marketing and promotion	M$ mn	0	0	0	0	0	0	0	0	0	0	0	0	70	126	230	63	82
F. Sub national	M$ mn	0	0	0	0	0	0	0	0	0	0	0	68	61	98	113	118	123
G. Other	M$ mn	0	0	0	0	0	0	0	0	0	0	0	0	0	0	0	0	0
Total other support (D + E + F + G)	M$ mn	25	53	88	124	185	368	499	658	1 418	1 999	2 544	5 369	2 799	3 287	4 189	4 783	4 118
Gross total PSE	M$ mn	53	81	200	166	-424	150	375	-33	1 156	2 322	4 288	11 667	13 240	16 536	19 351	17 918	1 738
Feed adjustment	M$ mn	3	-1	-16	1	118	54	67	32	-97	546	-267	-682	-480	-533	-1 529	-169	535
Net total PSE	M$ mn	56	80	184	167	-306	204	441	-1	1 060	2 868	4 021	10 985	12 760	16 004	17 822	17 749	2 273
Net percentage PSE	%	27	31	48	30	-30	11	14	0	9	13	14	30	31	34	37	34	3
Net total PSE	US$ mn	2 450	3 488	7 507	3 230	-1 980	1 064	1 349	-1	747	1 257	1 612	3 867	4 222	5 171	5 721	5 238	354

p: provisional.

Tableau 13B. **Detail of general policy measures: consumption – aggregate of all commodities 1979 to 1995**

	Unités	1979	1980	1981	1982	1983	1984	1985	1986	1987	1988	1989	1990	1991	1992	1993	1994	1995p
Value of consumption	M$ mn	221	304	423	602	1 308	2 070	3 507	5 270	13 329	25 413	33 150	42 087	47 396	53 961	55 071	56 937	88 799
A. Market transfers	M$ mn	–28	–29	–112	–42	600	214	119	667	148	–418	–1 827	–6 364	–10 582	–12 736	–14 996	–8 912	6 537
MPS on domestic production		–28	–28	–112	–42	600	216	122	669	151	–353	–1 741	–6 294	–10 327	–12 440	–14 708	–8 576	7 099
Tariffs		0	0	0	0	0	–1	–3	–1	–3	–65	–86	–70	–254	–296	–287	–336	–563
B. Other transfers	M$ mn	7	19	23	49	72	198	272	841	667	1 577	2 873	4 298	3 306	4 389	4 517	3 830	4 136
C. Total CSE	M$ mn	–21	–10	–90	7	672	412	391	1 509	815	1 159	1 047	–2 065	–7 276	–8 347	–10 478	–5 082	10 673
D. Percentage CSE	%	–10	–3	–21	1	51	20	11	29	6	5	3	–5	–15	–15	–19	–9	12
Total CSE	US$ mn	–947	–435	–3 654	127	4 342	2 150	1 196	2 360	575	508	420	–727	–2 407	–2 697	–3 364	–1 500	1 662

p: provisional.

Tableau 13C. **Shares of general policy measures in net total PSE/CSE – aggregate of all commodities 1979 to 1995**

	Units	1979	1980	1981	1982	1983	1984	1985	1985	1987	1988	1989	1990	1991	1992	1993	1994	1995p
A. Market price support net of levies and of feed adjustment	%	55	34	52	25	-160	-80	-13	-82 965	-34	30	37	51	77	74	74	47	-299
C. Direct payments	%	0	0	0	0	0	0	0	0	0	0	0	0	1	5	2	26	218
D. Reduction of input costs	%	33	42	33	55	49	142	87	62 601	110	57	52	42	14	11	16	19	118
E. General services	%	12	24	15	19	11	38	27	20 265	24	12	11	7	8	9	7	7	58
F. Sub national	%	0	0	0	0	0	0	0	0	0	0	0	1	0	1	1	1	5
G. Other	%	0	0	0	0	0	0	0	0	0	0	0	0	0	0	0	0	0
Total of PSE elements	%	100	100	100	100	-100	100	100	-100	100	100	100	100	100	100	100	100	100
A. Market transfers	%	131	287	125	-639	89	52	31	44	18	-36	-174	308	145	153	143	175	61
B. Other transfers	%	-31	-187	-25	739	11	48	69	56	82	136	274	-208	-45	-53	-43	-75	39
Total of CSE elements	%	100	100	100	100	100	100	100	100	100	100	100	100	100	100	100	100	100

p: provisional.

Notes to Table 13
Details of General Policy Measures

Aggregate of all Commodities

Definitions and Notes:

I   **Market price support**: Sum of market price support for all PSE commodities.

B.   **Levies**: Not applicable.

C.   **Direct payments**

C.1   **Per tonne payments**: ASERCA payments [1] to rice producers.

C.2   **Area and headage payments**: PROCAMPO payments [2] allocated to maize, wheat, sorghum, rice, and soyabeans: for 1994, in proportion to their share in the average area cultivated in the 1991-93 (base) with the crops eligible for PROCAMPO payments; for 1995, in proportion to their share in the area cultivated in 1995 with the crops eligible for PROCAMPO payments.

C.3   **Disaster payments**: Payments by CONASUPO [3] and, in 1995, FIRCO [4] and ASERCA [2] to farmers affected by climatic hazard, allocated to all commodities in proportion to their share in the value of total agricultural production.

C.4   **Price premiums**: Sum of ASERCA payments [1] for wheat, sorghum and soyabeans.

D.   **Reduction of input costs**

D.1   **Capital grants**: Not applicable.

D.2   **Interest concessions**: For BANRURAL, FONDO, FEFA, FICART, FINA, FIDAZUCAR, and FIMAIA, difference between commercial loan rates (*tasa de interes activa de mercado*) and preferential rates applied to agricultural loans, multiplied by the total value of agricultural loans [2]. For PRONASOL, federal government transfers [5]. For FIRCO, half of federal government transfers to FIRCO [2] (the other half was allocated to E.1). For BANRURAL and FIRA, interest concessions first allocated in proportion of the share of total crops and total livestock products in total lending by BANRURAL [6] and FIRA [2], and then allocated to all crops according to their respective share in total value of crop production and to all livestock products according to their respective share in total value of animal production. For FICART, FIRCO and PRONASOL, interest concessions allocated to all commodities in proportion to their share in the value of total agricultural production. For FINA, FIDAZUCAR and FIMAIA, interest concessions entirely allocated to sugar production.

D.3   **Fuel**: Not reported in PSE calculations.

D.4   **Fertiliser**: Federal government transfers to FERTIMEX [2] and, in 1995, ASERCA [2] allocated to all crops according to their respective share in the total value of crop production.

D.5   **Transport**: Not applicable.

D.6   **Insurance**: Federal government transfers to ANAGSA [2] and AGROASEMEX [2] allocated to all products according to their respective share in the value of total agricultural production.

D.7   **Irrigation**: Subsidy on the tariff rate for electricity used for groundwater pumping [2]. Share of public investment on "small irrigation schemes" in total public investment on irrigation schemes (excluding activities on protection and residual water) [7] applied on government transfers for infrastructure development in irrigated areas [2] (the other part was allocated to E.4). Both transfers (water pumping and small irrigation schemes) allocated to all crops according to their respective share in the total value of crop production.

D.8   **Seed**: Federal government transfers to PRONASE [2] allocated to all crops according to their respective share in the total value of crop production.

D.9   **Machinery**: Federal government transfers to SESA [2] allocated to all crops according to their respective share in the total value of crop production.

D.10   **Feed**: Federal government transfers to CONASUPO [2] net of stockholding [8] allocated to sorghum, maize feedgrains, and soya oil cake according to their respective share in total domestic purchases by CONASUPO [9]. The amounts allocated to sorghum, maize (the share of maize sold by CONASUPO for feed [10].) and soya oil cake are then summed up and allocated to all livestock products according to their respective share in total value of animal production.

D.11   **Animal breeding improvement**: Federal government transfers to FOGAN [2] (livestock fund for cattle genetic improvement) entirely allocated to beef and veal.

E.   **General services**

E.1   **Research, advisory, training**: Federal government transfers to INIFAP [2], IMTA [2], FEGA [2], INCARURAL [2], and half of federal government transfers to FIRCO [2] (see also D.2), allocated to all products according to their respective share in the value of total agricultural production.

E.2   **Inspection**: Not available.

E.3   **Pest and disease control**: Government transfers for plant health [11] allocated to all crops according to their respective share in total value of crop production. Government transfers for animal health [11] allocated to all livestock products according to their respective share in total value of animal production.

E.4   **Structures/infrastructures**: Part of government transfers for infrastructure development in irrigated areas [2] (see D.7), plus government transfers for infrastructure development in rainfed areas [2] and for crop production [2] allocated to crops according to their share in the total value of crop production. Government transfers for infrastructure development for livestock production [2] allocated to livestock products according to their share in the total value of livestock production.

E.5   **Marketing and promotion**: Government transfers to ASERCA [12] and FOCIR [2] allocated to all products according to their respective share in the value of total agricultural production.

F.   **Sub national**: State governments contribution to the PRONASOL Solidarity Fund for Production [13] allocated to all products according to their respective share in the value of total agricultural production.

G.   **Other**: Tax concessions: Not available.

XI.   **Feed adjustment**

XI.1   **Excess feed cost**: Volumes of domestically produced sorghum, maize feed grains [10], and soya oil cake [9] allocated to the various livestock products according to their share in the production of compound feed sold by commercial enterprises to livestock producers (*producción de alimentos balanceados por los fabricantes comerciales*) [14] (see matrix in Figure 1, Section A) and multiplied by the respective unit market price support for sorghum, maize, and soyabeans (see relevant PSE Tables).

XI.2   **Other feed cost**: Volumes of imported sorghum [15], maize feed grains [10], and soya oil cake [9] allocated to the various livestock products according to their share in the production of compound feed [14] and multiplied by the respective unit market price support for sorghum, maize, and soyabeans (see relevant PSE Tables).

Sources:

[1]   Data provided directly by ASERCA in 1991-94, and by SHCP for 1995.

[2]   Data provided directly by SHCP.

[3]   Data provided directly by CONASUPO.

[4]   SAGAR (1995), *Analisis coyuntural*, May 1995.

[5]   In 1990-91: SEDESOL (1994), *Solidaridad: seis años de trabajo*, page 190. Data provided directly by SHCP for the period 1992-95.

[6]   Data provided directly by BANRURAL.

[7]   CNA, as reported in *Sexto Informe de Gobierno* 1994, *Anexo*, page 181.

[8]   Throughout the review period, 30 per cent of transfers to CONASUPO were allocated to stockholding on the basis of CONASUPO (1995), *Memoria de gestion* 1988-94, Anexo A, cuadro 1.

[9]   CONASUPO, as reported in *Sexto Informe de Gobierno* 1994, *Anexo*, page 264. Data provided directly by CONASUPO for 1995.

[10]   SAGAR (1994), *Producción y comercialización de sorgo*, 1987-1993, page 47. Data provided directly by CONASUPO for 1994 and 1995.

[11]   Data provided by SHCP for the 1979-88 period; SAGAR (1995) *Carpeta presupuestal* 1989-95 for the 1989-95 period.

[12]   Data provided directly by SAGAR in 1991-93, and by SHCP in 1994-95.

[13]   SEDESOL (1994), *Solidaridad: seis años de trabajo*, page 190.

[14]   Consejo Nacional Agropecuario, 10 *años de actividad agropecuario en México*, 1984-1993, page 75.

[15]   PSE table for sorghum.

Table 14. **Reference prices**

M$/T

Commodity	1979	1980	1981	1982	1983	1984	1985	1986	1987	1988	1989	1990	1991	1992	1993	1994	1995p
Wheat	4	4	4	8	25	30	47	82	177	354	443	408	420	495	468	533	1 180
White maize	3	4	4	7	27	34	48	76	146	319	363	406	426	423	420	476	1 020
Yellow maize	3	3	4	6	23	29	41	64	124	270	307	343	360	358	356	403	862
Barley	3	4	4	8	23	29	43	75	164	398	482	431	401	423	411	504	1 156
Sorghum	3	3	3	6	22	25	38	61	121	251	293	328	353	354	348	396	862
Rice	7	8	7	14	37	45	77	145	296	475	541	575	660	659	616	666	1 110
Soyabeans	7	6	7	13	43	54	74	135	305	680	675	683	705	718	782	849	1 604
White sugar	6	16	10	12	37	31	45	117	281	625	828	928	753	775	845	1 076	2 224
Milk	3	3	4	9	23	24	29	50	160	351	408	371	401	455	448	511	1 189
Beef and Veal	n.a.	41	39	79	244	313	435	876	2 103	3 957	5 143	5 168	5 225	4 964	5 340	5 578	9 626
Pigmeat	32	29	34	87	235	291	464	1 013	2 384	3 118	3 418	4 855	4 851	4 150	4 333	4 161	8 245
Poultrymeat	21	22	23	48	149	218	347	707	1 104	2 397	2 997	3 082	3 098	3 247	3 504	3 812	7 218
Eggs	20	20	23	46	142	206	303	630	1 092	1 717	2 581	2 955	2 963	2 563	2 605	2 782	5 636

p: provisional.

Notes to Table 14
Reference Prices

Definitions and Notes:

Wheat: Simple average of US export prices for Hard Red Winter No. 2, f.o.b. Gulf ports [1] and Soft Red Winter No. 2, f.o.b. Gulf ports [2], plus US$11 per tonne for transport cost from US Gulf to Veracruz [3].

White maize: US export price of yellow corn No. 2, f.o.b. Gulf ports [1], increased by 20 per cent (quality premium), plus US$11 per tonne for transport cost from US Gulf to Veracruz [3].

Yellow maize: US export price of yellow corn No. 2, f.o.b. Gulf ports [1], plus US$11 per tonne for transport cost from US Gulf to Veracruz [3].

Barley: Cash price at Minneapolis board of trade of barley No. 3 or better malting, 65 per cent or better plump [4], plus transport cost from US production areas to Gulf ports [3] plus US$11 per tonne for transport cost from US Gulf to Veracruz [3].

Sorghum: US export price of grain sorghum, f.o.b. Gulf ports [1], plus US$11 per tonne for transport cost from US Gulf to Veracruz [3].

Rice: In 1979-93, US export price of 20 per cent medium grain, f.o.b. Gulf ports [5], expressed in paddy rice equivalent by multiplying it by 0.66 [6], plus US$11 per tonne for transport cost from US Gulf to Veracruz [3]. For 1994 and 1995, US export price, long grain, f.o.b. mill, Houston [1]multiplied by an average ratio between medium and long grain prices (0.88), expressed in paddy rice equivalent by multiplying it by 0.5 [7], plus US$11 per tonne for transport cost from US Gulf to Veracruz [3].

Soyabeans: US export price, f.o.b. Gulf ports [1], plus US$11 for transport cost from US Gulf to Veracruz [3].

Sugar: World price of raw sugar, contract No. 11, f.o.b. stowed Caribbean port, bulk spot price [8] plus US$50 per tonne for transport costs to the Mexican border [9].

Milk: Farm gate price of milk at actual fat content in New Zealand [10], plus transport cost for butter and skim-milk powder in milk equivalent (56 kg and 82 kg per tonne of milk, respectively) from New Zealand to Mexico [10], adjusted to Mexico's fat content [11].

Beef and veal: Australian beef production price [12] plus transport costs from Australia to Mexico (estimated as the difference between c.i.f. and f.o.b. prices for 90 CL cow beef sold to the United States, increased by 20 per cent).

Pigmeat: Implicit pigmeat reference price for the United States PSE calculation [13].

Poultrymeat: Implicit poultrymeat reference price for the United States PSE calculation [13].

Eggs: Implicit egg reference price for the United States PSE calculation [13].

Sources:

[1] USDA, ERS, *Agricultural Outlook*, various issues.
[2] Data provided directly by the International Wheat Council, London.
[3] USDA, AMS, Marketing Research Report No. 630, *Shipping US grain to Mexico*, September 1995.
[4] USDA, ERS, *Feed Situation and Outlook*, October 1994, appendix table 14 page 53 and *Agricultural Outlook*, various issues.
[5] FAO, *Production yearbook*, various issues.
[6] SAGAR, as reported in *Sexto Informe de Gobierno* 1994, Anexo, page 167.

[7]   Coefficient provided directly by USDA, ERS.

[8]   USDA, ERS, Sugar and sweetener Outlook and Situation, various issues.

[9]   Data provided directly by SAGAR.

[10]   Information provided directly by the New Zealand Ministry of Agriculture and Fisheries.

[11]   Data provided directly by LICONSA.

[12]   OECD PSE database for Australia.

[13]   OECD PSE database for the United States.

Table 15. **Producer subsidy equivalents by commodity**

	Units	1979-82 (average)	1983-88 (average)	1989-94 (average)	1989	1990	1991	1992	1993	1994	1995p
Wheat											
Total PSE	M$ mn	3	−28	549	−166	537	794	503	773	853	−235
Percentage PSE	%	14	−10	23	−11	28	35	24	34	30	−6
Producer NAC		1.1	0.9	1.3	0.9	1.3	1.5	1.3	1.5	1.4	0.9
Maize											
Total PSE	M$ mn	38	511	5 212	1 373	4 403	5 052	6 703	7 079	6 663	6 054
Percentage PSE	%	49	21	47	29	48	50	54	53	47	26
Producer NAC		1.6	1.3	1.8	1.3	1.8	1.9	2.0	2.0	1.8	1.3
Other grains [1]	M$ mn										
Total PSE	%	5	127	491	348	370	439	705	371	716	825
Percentage PSE		22	6	23	19	14	20	25	26	33	16
Producer NAC		1.2	1.1	1.3	1.2	1.1	1.2	1.3	1.3	1.4	1.2
Rice											
Total PSE	M$ mn	0	−17	28	−18	16	28	69	38	36	67
Percentage PSE	%	−24	−31	11	−8	7	12	22	19	14	15
Producer NAC		0.9	0.8	1.1	0.9	1.1	1.1	1.3	1.2	1.2	1.2
Oilseeds											
Total PSE	M$ mn	3	5	122	139	56	156	112	114	156	53
Percentage PSE	%	46	0	22	20	11	27	23	24	28	15
Producer NAC		1.6	1.0	1.3	1.2	1.1	1.3	1.3	1.3	1.4	1.2
Sugar (refined equivalent)											
Total PSE	M$ mn	11	−42	1 067	−221	483	1 341	1 599	1 881	1 321	−686
Percentage PSE	%	59	8	32	−10	22	49	50	48	32	−13
Producer NAC		1.6	1.1	1.5	0.9	1.2	1.8	1.8	1.8	1.4	0.9
Crops											
Total PSE	M$ mn	61	556	7 470	1 454	5 865	7 810	9 690	10 257	9 745	6 078
Percentage PSE	%	40	11	37	13	35	43	45	47	40	16
Producer NAC		1.4	1.1	1.6	1.1	1.5	1.7	1.7	1.8	1.6	1.2
Milk											
Net total PSE	M$ mn	28	338	2 824	1 292	2 316	2 908	3 086	3 707	3 636	480
Net percentage PSE	%	52	41	51	37	58	52	50	54	53	5
Producer NAC		1.9	1.8	1.9	1.6	2.0	2.0	1.9	2.1	1.9	1.1
Beef and Veal											
Net total PSE	M$ mn	−2	−383	747	367	1 022	307	390	1 342	1 052	−2 428
Net percentage PSE	%	−3	−51	11	6	18	5	6	19	14	−23
Producer NAC		1.0	0.7	1.1	1.1	1.2	1.0	1.1	1.2	1.1	0.8
Pigmeat											
Net total PSE	M$ mn	29	196	1 780	1 210	1 377	1 787	2 189	1 574	2 541	1 267
Net percentage PSE	%	38	−5	36	35	30	33	40	31	45	16
Producer NAC		1.6	1.0	1.5	1.5	1.4	1.5	1.7	1.5	1.7	1.2
Poultry											
Net total PSE	M$ mn	7	108	573	284	725	782	343	632	671	−2 098
Net percentage PSE	%	35	21	17	13	26	22	10	15	15	−31
Producer NAC		1.5	1.2	1.2	1.2	1.3	1.3	1.1	1.2	1.2	0.8
Sheepmeat											
Net total PSE	M$ mn	0	0	0	0	0	0	0	0	0	0
Net percentage PSE	%	0	0	0	0	0	0	0	0	0	0
Producer NAC		0	0	0	0	0	0	0	0	0	0
Wool											
Net total PSE	M$ mn	0	0	0	0	0	0	0	0	0	0
Net percentage PSE	%	0	0	0	0	0	0	0	0	0	0
Producer NAC		0	0	0	0	0	0	0	0	0	0
Eggs											
Net total PSE	M$ mn	0	−103	−170	−587	−320	−833	305	312	104	−1 027
Net percentage PSE	%	−1	−46	−9	−29	−13	−33	10	9	3	−18
Producer NAC		1.0	0.7	0.9	0.8	0.9	0.8	1.1	1.1	1.0	0.9
Livestock products											
Net total PSE	M$ mn	61	155	5 753	2 567	5 120	4 950	6 313	7 566	8 004	−3 805
Net percentage PSE	%	30	−3	24	15	26	21	25	28	29	−10
Producer NAC		1.4	1.2	1.3	1.2	1.3	1.3	1.3	1.4	1.4	0.9
All products											
Net total PSE	M$ mn	122	711	13 224	4 021	10 985	12 760	16 004	17 822	17 749	2 273
Net percentage PSE	%	34	3	30	14	30	31	34	37	34	3
Producer NAC		1.4	1.0	1.4	1.2	1.4	1.4	1.5	1.5	1.5	1.0
Net total PSE	*US$ mn*	*4 169*	*406*	*4 305*	*1 612*	*3 867*	*4 222*	*5 171*	*5 721*	*5 238*	*354*

p: provisional.
n.c.:   not calculated.
1)   Barley and sorghum.

Table 16. **Consumer subsidy equivalents by commodity**

	Units	1979-82 (average)	1983-88 (average)	1989-94 (average)	1989	1990	1991	1992	1993	1994	1995p
Wheat											
Total CSE	M$ mn	10	253	372	1 098	86	−568	643	397	577	804
Percentage CSE	%	50	71	19	66	4	−23	31	14	20	18
Consumer NAC		0.6	0.4	0.8	0.5	1.0	1.3	0.7	0.8	0.8	0.9
Maize											
Total CSE	M$ mn	−5	23	−1 543	405	−350	−2 086	−2 956	−3 716	−559	1 202
Percentage CSE	%	−2	16	−12	7	−3	−20	−23	−28	−5	6
Consumer NAC		1.0	0.9	1.2	0.9	1.0	1.3	1.4	1.5	1.1	0.9
Other grains [1]	M$ mn										
Total CSE	%	1	−23	−173	−150	−100	−215	−342	−172	−56	75
Percentage CSE		6	7	−5	−6	−3	−6	−7	−6	−2	1
Consumer NAC		1.0	1.0	1.1	1.1	1.0	1.1	1.1	1.1	1.0	1.0
Rice											
Total CSE	M$ mn	2	45	31	113	65	14	−41	6	29	−7
Percentage CSE	%	49	67	9	28	18	4	−7	2	7	−1
Consumer NAC		0.7	0.6	0.9	0.7	0.8	1.0	1.1	1.0	0.9	1.0
Oilseeds											
Total CSE	M$ mn	0	28	−80	−18	0	−103	−105	−183	−72	−207
Percentage CSE	%	1	11	−4	−1	0	−6	−5	−8	−4	−6
Consumer NAC		1.0	0.9	1.0	1.0	1.0	1.1	1.1	1.1	1.0	1.1
Sugar (refined equivalent)											
Total CSE	M$ mn	4	135	−754	506	−187	−1 078	−1 269	−1 599	−896	949
Percentage CSE	%	23	31	−20	21	−7	−36	−37	−40	−19	17
Consumer NAC		0.9	0.8	1.3	0.8	1.1	1.6	1.6	1.7	1.2	0.9
Crops											
Total CSE	M$ mn	12	461	−2 147	1 953	−487	−4 036	−4 070	−5 266	−977	2 816
Percentage CSE	%	10	23	−8	13	−2	−19	−16	−21	−4	6
Consumer NAC		0.9	0.8	1.1	0.9	1.0	1.3	1.2	1.3	1.0	0.9
Milk											
Total CSE	M$ mn	−21	−112	−1 299	−193	−770	−1 488	−1 478	−2 093	−1 773	1 845
Percentage CSE	%	−37	−17	−19	−4	−15	−26	−20	−26	−21	15
Consumer NAC		1.7	1.3	1.3	1.1	1.2	1.5	1.3	1.5	1.3	0.9
Beef and Veal											
Total CSE	M$ mn	8	450	−127	0	0	0	0	−612	−151	2 888
Percentage CSE	%	15	62	−2	0	0	0	0	−9	−2	30
Consumer NAC		0.9	0.6	1.0	1.0	1.0	1.0	1.0	1.1	1.0	0.8
Pigmeat											
Total CSE	M$ mn	−24	−101	−1 647	−1 129	−969	−1 816	−2 162	−1 592	−2 214	−898
Percentage CSE	%	−32	17	−30	−30	−20	−30	−37	−30	−36	−10
Consumer NAC		1.5	0.9	1.5	1.4	1.3	1.4	1.6	1.4	1.6	1.1
Poultry											
Total CSE	M$ mn	−6	−22	−458	−241	−414	−825	−403	−695	−169	2 673
Percentage CSE	%	−32	10	−12	−11	−14	−21	−10	−14	−3	33
Consumer NAC		1.5	0.9	1.1	1.1	1.2	1.3	1.1	1.2	1.0	0.8
Sheepmeat											
Total CSE	M$ mn	0	0	0	0	0	0	0	0	0	0
Percentage CSE	%	0	0	0	0	0	0	0	0	0	0
Consumer NAC		0	0	0	0	0	0	0	0	0	0
Wool											
Total CSE	M$ mn	0	0	0	0	0	0	0	0	0	0
Percentage CSE	%	0	0	0	0	0	0	0	0	0	0
Consumer NAC		0	0	0	0	0	0	0	0	0	0
Eggs											
Total CSE	M$ mn	2	150	312	657	574	889	−233	−219	202	1 348
Percentage CSE	%	7	62	14	32	24	35	−7	−6	6	24
Consumer NAC		0.9	0.6	0.9	0.8	0.8	0.7	1.1	1.1	0.9	0.8
Livestock products											
Total CSE	M$ mn	−41	365	−3 220	−906	−1 578	−3 240	−4 277	−5 212	−4 105	7 857
Percentage CSE	%	−21	19	−12	−5	−7	−13	−15	−18	−13	17
Consumer NAC		1.3	0.9	1.1	1.0	1.1	1.1	1.2	1.2	1.1	0.8
All products											
Total CSE	M$ mn	−29	826	−5 367	1 047	−2 065	−7 276	−8 347	−10 478	−5 082	10 673
Percentage CSE	%	−8	20	−10	3	−5	−15	−15	−19	−9	12
Consumer NAC		1.1	0.8	1.1	1.0	1.1	1.2	1.2	1.3	1.1	0.9
Total CSE	*US$ mn*	*−1 227*	*1 855*	*−1 713*	*420*	*−727*	*−2 407*	*−2 697*	*−3 364*	*−1 500*	*1 662*

p: provisional.
n.c.: not calculated.
1) Barley and sorghum.

NOTES AND REFERENCES

1. The numbering of PSE/CSE tables is the same for all OECD countries for which the PSE/CSE calculations have been carried out and is retained whether or not a commodity is actually included in the calculations.

2. However, the PSE/CSE calculations presented below are considered to accurately reflect the developments of Mexican agricultural policies, in line with the standard OECD methodology.

3. See definitions of PSE and CSE terms in the glossary in Annex III.

4. OECD *Economic Outlook* database.

5. See list of acronyms for full title of agencies or programmes.

6. The Fisher ideal index has been developed expressly to deal with large changes in weights when measuring economic aggregates. The Fisher ideal index has been demonstrated to be a "superlative" index, meaning that in situations where quantities produced and consumed undergo large changes between year t and $t + 1$, the Fisher ideal index of changes in prices and unit support is the best approximation of the underlying "true" theoretical index. The changes in unit aggregates, in other words, do not suffer a bias.

7. The Laspeyres price index is a weighted average of price changes between year 1 and year 0 with the weights being the quantity for year 0:

$$L = \frac{\Sigma \, P_1 \cdot Q_0}{\Sigma \, P_0 \cdot Q_0}$$

The Paasche price index is a weighted average of price changes between year 1 and year 0 with the weights being the quantity for year 1:

$$P = \frac{\Sigma \, P_1 \cdot Q_1}{\Sigma \, P_0 \cdot Q_1}$$

The Fisher ideal index is the geometric average of the Laspeyres and Paasche indices:

$$F = \sqrt{L \cdot P} = \sqrt{\left(\frac{\Sigma \, P_1 \cdot Q_0}{\Sigma \, P_0 \cdot Q_0} \right) \cdot \left(\frac{\Sigma \, P_1 \cdot Q_1}{\Sigma \, P_0 \cdot Q_1} \right)}$$

Readers interested in the properties of the Fisher ideal index are referred to the following papers: W.E. Diewert, "Fisher ideal output, input and productivity indexes revisited", *Journal of Productivity Analysis*, No. 3, 1992, pp. 211-248; W.E. Diewert, "Exact and superlative index numbers", *Journal of Econometrics*, No. 4, 1976, pp. 115-145; and W. Eichhorn, R. Henn, O. Optiz and R.W. Shephard (editors), *Theory and Application of Economic Indexes*, Physica Verlag, Wurzburg, 1978.

8. It may not therefore equate exactly with the actual reference price used in estimating the PSE, as transport costs, quality adjustment factors etc., are all reflected in this implicit price.

Annex III

GLOSSARY OF PSE/CSE AND POLICY TERMS

This glossary is designed to provide a concise list the main PSE, CSE and policy terms used in this report.

Administered price: Prices that are fixed by policy makers in order to determine, directly or indirectly, domestic market or producer prices (guaranteed prices, concerted prices, minimum prices).

Area payments: Direct payments made under PROCAMPO to individual producers on the basis of eligible land (areas that were planted in the 1990-93 period with grains, beans or oilseeds). Payments are made to individual producers per hectare of eligible land devoted to any crop, livestock, or forestry activity, or placed in an approved environmental programme, as compensation for decreases in (or abolishment of) administered prices for grains, beans, and oilseeds. All eligible producers receive the same per-hectare payment. There is no upper limit to the number of hectares eligible for area payments, although farmers must be in conformity with the provisions of the Agrarian Law on maximum cultivated area per farm. The payments are not conditional on the implementation of a set-aside programme, but one year land set aside may be authorised as part of an approved environmental programme.

Border price: See Reference price.

Calendar year: The PSE and CSE estimates are given on a *calendar year* basis. However, for crops, in many cases, production and price data are available only on a marketing year basis. In such cases, in order to preserve comparability of the PSE and CSE estimates among countries and commodities, *crop year* data are assigned to the closest calendar year. When the crop runs from January through March of the following year for example, the data are assigned to the calendar year in which the first month falls. In Mexico, the crop year (*año agrícola*) 1995 consists of the sum of the Autumn/Winter 1994/95 crop season and the Spring/Summer 1995 crop season. Budget data are in all cases on a *fiscal year* basis and budget items are in general allocated to individual commodities when they actually appear in the budget.

Consumer Subsidy Equivalent, CSE: An indicator of the value of the monetary transfers to consumers resulting from agricultural policies. When negative, it measures the implicit tax imposed on consumers by agricultural policy. The major component is *market transfers* due to *market price support* to production. It also includes *other transfers* such as subsidies to consumption from government budget. The CSE can be expressed in money terms (*total* CSE), in percentage terms (*percentage* CSE) or in money terms per tonne of consumption (*unit* CSE).

Direct payments: Budgetary payments paid directly to producers. The category includes a wide range of different types of payments, such as per tonne payments, area payments, and disaster payments, each which may have different effects on the agricultural sector.

Disaster payments: Budgetary payments to compensate farmers for the adverse effects of natural events such as droughts, floods and diseases.

Farm gate price: see Producer price.

Feed adjustment: The sum of the additional costs of animal feed to livestock producers resulting from *market price support* on feeds for which PSEs are calculated and taxes on feeds and processed feedstuffs. Its purpose is to allow commodity *total* PSEs to be summed up to give a total for the agricultural sector without double counting the market price support paid by livestock producers to

245

producers of PSE feed grains and oilseeds, and also to deduct any other taxes on feeds or on processed feedstuffs.

Gross total PSE: Total value of transfers to agriculture by means of *market price support* (net of *levies on output*), *direct payments* and other support, but before deduction of the *feed adjustment*. In the case of crop products, where there is no animal feed input, gross and *net total* PSEs are identical.

Import licence: A government-issued permit or document required of importers. In their most innocuous form, import licences are used simply to identify legitimate importers, usually for tax purposes. Sometimes, however, they are used to impose special restrictions, or to load additional burdens, on importers so as to make importing of a particular good more difficult and costly, thereby benefiting domestic producers of the good.

Import quota: A quantitative restriction on the level of imports, imposed by a country.

Interest concession: A reduction, compared with commercial interest rates, in the interest rate charged on a loan taken out by a farmer, typically provided directly by a government agency or by a government grant to the lending bank (in the case of a commercial loan).

Levies on output: Taxes on farm output which reduce the price received by producers as a result of *market price support*. None applied in Mexico for PSE commodities over the review period.

Market price support, MPS: Transfers to producers resulting from measures that raise prices to consumers of farm commodities by way of tariffs, import quotas, *administered prices* or trade licensing arrangements. Market price support per unit of volume (tonne) of production is referred to as the *unit* MPS.

Market transfers: Transfers to (when positive), or from (when negative) consumers due to *market price support* policies.

Net total PSE: *Gross total* PSE minus the *feed adjustment*. In the case of crop products, where there is no animal feed input, the gross and net total PSEs are identical.

Nominal assistance coefficient, NAC: Nominal Assistance Coefficients are indicators of the effective price wedge between domestic and world markets created by agricultural policies. The producer NAC is the ratio of the *border price* in national currency plus the unit PSE, relative to the border price. It expresses the transfers to producers in relation to border prices. The higher the producer NAC, the greater the level of support. The consumer NAC is the ratio of the border price in national currency plus the unit CSE, relative to the border price. It is an indicator of the gap between domestic consumer prices (measured at the farm gate) and world prices. A consumer NAC higher (lower) than one is equivalent to an implicit tax (subsidy) to consumers.

Oilseeds: Generally, seeds grown primarily for the production of edible (*i.e.* cooking) oils. When used as a collective term in the context of PSE and CSE estimates, the composition generally refer to soya beans. In a few cases, statistical difficulties prevent the separating out of data on soya beans from those for other oilseeds, mainly safflower, cotton seed, copra and sesame.

Other grains: Generally refers to cereal grains other than wheat, maize and rice that are used primarily for animal feed or brewing (sorghum and barley).

Other support: The value of transfers other than market price support and direct payments that are included in the PSE calculation. These include explicit or implicit subsidies on purchased farm inputs, farm credit, and government transfers to agricultural research and development, extension services, training and agricultural infrastructure. This category also includes sub -national assistance measures and taxation concessions specific to agriculture.

Other transfers: The value of those budgetary transfers to consumers included in the CSE calculation.

Percentage PSE: The *gross total* PSE or, in the case of livestock products, *net total* PSE, expressed as a percentage of the value of production, valued at the farm gate. A *percentage* CSE is also calculated, which measures the implicit tax on consumers (if negative), or the implicit subsidy on consumption (if positive).

Producer price: The average price or unit value received by farmers for a specific agricultural commodity produced within a specified 12-month period. This price is measured at the *farm gate* – that is, at the point that the commodity leaves the farm – and therefore does not incorporate cost of transport and processing.

Producer Subsidy Equivalent, PSE: An indicator of the value of monetary transfers to agriculture resulting from agricultural policies in a given year. Both transfers from consumers of agricultural products (through domestic *market price support*) and transfers from taxpayers (through budgetary or tax expenditures) are included. The PSE can be expressed in money terms (*total* PSE), in percentage terms (*percentage* PSE), or in money terms per tonne of production (*unit* PSE).

PSE commodity: A commodity that belong to the OECD standard list of 17 commodities (wheat, maize, barley, oats, sorghum, rice, rapeseed, soyabeans, sunflower, sugarcane or sugarbeet, milk, beef and veal, pigmeat, poutrymeat, sheepmeat, wool, eggs) and which production value exceeds one per cent of the gross value of total agricultural production. In Mexico, oats, rapeseed, sunflower, sheepmeat, and wool were not included in the list of commodities for which PSEs have been calculated.

Reference price: The import (c.i.f.) or export (f.o.b.) price of a commodity. An implicit reference price may be calculated as the *producer price* in the foreign country less the *unit* MPS and may differ slightly from the explicit reference price. Board of trade quotations may also be used as reference price.

Supply control: A wide range of measures designed to affect the level of production or supply, including measures which restrict output directly (such as milk quotas) and those which restrict the use of an input (production licences, set-aside). None applied in Mexico for PSE commodities over the review period.

Support price: See Administered price.

Tariff: A tax imposed on commodity imports. A tariff may be either a specific tariff (fixed charge per unit of product imported) or an *ad valorem* tariff (a fixed percentage of value). See also *Variable Import Levy*.

Tarification: The conversion of non-tariff barriers to tariffs.

Tariff quota: A quantitative threshold (quota) on imports during a given period beyond which a higher tariff is applied. The lower tariff rate applies to imports within the quota.

Tariff-rate quota: A term used interchangeably with the term tariff quota.

Total consumption: The total volume of domestic consumption (in metric tonnes) of a PSE commodity in a given crop year.

Total production: The total volume of production (in metric tonnes) of a PSE commodity at the farm level. This includes the production used for human and animal consumption on the farm, and the production sold to state-owned agencies and the private sector. All production data are on a crop year basis.

Total PSE: The aggregate PSE in money terms. For livestock products, the term "net *total* PSE" refer to monetary transfers to producers after the deduction of the *feed adjustment*.

Total transfers: An indicator defined as the sum of all transfers from taxpayers and all transfers from consumers resulting from agricultural policies, less budget revenues from tariffs on imports.

Unit direct payments: The total value of *direct payments* to production, including per tonne, area, and disaster payments, divided by the volume of production, measured in tonnes.

Unit market price support: The total transfers to production resulting from measures that tax consumers of farm commodities, divided by the volume of commodity production.

Unit PSE: The *gross* or *net total* PSE for a commodity, divided by the volume of its production in tonnes. A *unit* CSE is similarly calculated.

World price: See Reference price.

MAIN SALES OUTLETS OF OECD PUBLICATIONS
PRINCIPAUX POINTS DE VENTE DES PUBLICATIONS DE L'OCDE

AUSTRALIA – AUSTRALIE
D.A. Information Services
648 Whitehorse Road, P.O.B 163
Mitcham, Victoria 3132   Tel. (03) 9210.7777
                             Fax: (03) 9210.7788

AUSTRIA – AUTRICHE
Gerold & Co.
Graben 31
Wien I   Tel. (0222) 533.50.14
                             Fax: (0222) 512.47.31.29

BELGIUM – BELGIQUE
Jean De Lannoy
Avenue du Roi, Koningslaan 202
B-1060 Bruxelles   Tel. (02) 538.51.69/538.08.41
                             Fax: (02) 538.08.41

CANADA
Renouf Publishing Company Ltd.
5369 Canotek Road
Unit 1
Ottawa, Ont. K1J 9J3   Tel. (613) 745.2665
                             Fax: (613) 745.7660

Stores:
71 1/2 Sparks Street
Ottawa, Ont. K1P 5R1   Tel. (613) 238.8985
                             Fax: (613) 238.6041

12 Adelaide Street West
Toronto, QN M5H 1L6   Tel. (416) 363.3171
                             Fax: (416) 363.5963

Les Éditions La Liberté Inc.
3020 Chemin Sainte-Foy
Sainte-Foy, PQ G1X 3V6   Tel. (418) 658.3763
                             Fax: (418) 658.3763

Federal Publications Inc.
165 University Avenue, Suite 701
Toronto, ON M5H 3B8   Tel. (416) 860.1611
                             Fax: (416) 860.1608

Les Publications Fédérales
1185 Université
Montréal, QC H3B 3A7   Tel. (514) 954.1633
                             Fax: (514) 954.1635

CHINA – CHINE
Book Dept., China National Publications
Import and Export Corporation (CNPIEC)
16 Gongti E. Road, Chaoyang District
Beijing 100020   Tel. (10) 6506-6688 Ext. 8402
                             (10) 6506-3101

CHINESE TAIPEI – TAIPEI CHINOIS
Good Faith Worldwide Int'l. Co. Ltd.
9th Floor, No. 118, Sec. 2
Chung Hsiao E. Road
Taipei   Tel. (02) 391.7396/391.7397
                             Fax: (02) 394.9176

**CZECH REPUBLIC –
RÉPUBLIQUE TCHÈQUE**
National Information Centre
NIS – prodejna
Konviktská 5
Praha 1 – 113 57   Tel. (02) 24.23.09.07
                             Fax: (02) 24.22.94.33
E-mail: nkposp@dec.niz.cz
Internet: http://www.nis.cz

DENMARK – DANEMARK
Munksgaard Book and Subscription Service
35, Nørre Søgade, P.O. Box 2148
DK-1016 København K   Tel. (33) 12.85.70
                             Fax: (33) 12.93.87

J. H. Schultz Information A/S,
Herstedvang 12,
DK – 2620 Albertslung   Tel. 43 63 23 00
                             Fax: 43 63 19 69
Internet: s-info@inet.uni-c.dk

EGYPT – ÉGYPTE
The Middle East Observer
41 Sherif Street
Cairo   Tel. (2) 392.6919
                             Fax: (2) 360.6804

FINLAND – FINLANDE
Akateeminen Kirjakauppa
Keskuskatu 1, P.O. Box 128
00100 Helsinki

Subscription Services/Agence d'abonnements :
P.O. Box 23
00100 Helsinki   Tel. (358) 9.121.4403
                             Fax: (358) 9.121.4450

*FRANCE
OECD/OCDE
Mail Orders/Commandes par correspondance :
2, rue André-Pascal
75775 Paris Cedex 16   Tel. 33 (0)1.45.24.82.00
                        Fax: 33 (0)1.49.10.42.76
                        Telex: 640048 OCDE
Internet: Compte.PUBSINQ@oecd.org

Orders via Minitel, France only/
Commandes par Minitel, France exclusivement :
36 15 OCDE

OECD Bookshop/Librairie de l'OCDE :
33, rue Octave-Feuillet
75016 Paris   Tel. 33 (0)1.45.24.81.81
                        33 (0)1.45.24.81.67

Dawson
B.P. 40
91121 Palaiseau Cedex   Tel. 01.89.10.47.00
                             Fax: 01.64.54.83.26

Documentation Française
29, quai Voltaire
75007 Paris   Tel. 01.40.15.70.00

Economica
49, rue Héricart
75015 Paris   Tel. 01.45.78.12.92
                             Fax: 01.45.75.05.67

Gibert Jeune (Droit-Économie)
6, place Saint-Michel
75006 Paris   Tel. 01.43.25.91.19

Librairie du Commerce International
10, avenue d'Iéna
75016 Paris   Tel. 01.40.73.34.60

Librairie Dunod
Université Paris-Dauphine
Place du Maréchal-de-Lattre-de-Tassigny
75016 Paris   Tel. 01.44.05.40.13

Librairie Lavoisier
11, rue Lavoisier
75008 Paris   Tel. 01.42.65.39.95

Librairie des Sciences Politiques
30, rue Saint-Guillaume
75007 Paris   Tel. 01.45.48.36.02

P.U.F.
49, boulevard Saint-Michel
75005 Paris   Tel. 01.43.25.83.40

Librairie de l'Université
12a, rue Nazareth
13100 Aix-en-Provence   Tel. 04.42.26.18.08

Documentation Française
165, rue Garibaldi
69003 Lyon   Tel. 04.78.63.32.23

Librairie Decitre
29, place Bellecour
69002 Lyon   Tel. 04.72.40.54.54

Librairie Sauramps
Le Triangle
34967 Montpellier Cedex 2   Tel. 04.67.58.85.15
                             Fax: 04.67.58.27.36

A la Sorbonne Actual
23, rue de l'Hôtel-des-Postes
06000 Nice   Tel. 04.93.13.77.75
                             Fax: 04.93.80.75.69

GERMANY – ALLEMAGNE
OECD Bonn Centre
August-Bebel-Allee 6
D-53175 Bonn   Tel. (0228) 959.120
                             Fax: (0228) 959.12.17

GREECE – GRÈCE
Librairie Kauffmann
Stadiou 28
10564 Athens   Tel. (01) 32.55.321
                             Fax: (01) 32.30.320

HONG-KONG
Swindon Book Co. Ltd.
Astoria Bldg. 3F
34 Ashley Road, Tsimshatsui
Kowloon, Hong Kong   Tel. 2376.2062
                             Fax: 2376.0685

HUNGARY – HONGRIE
Euro Info Service
Margitsziget, Európa Ház
1138 Budapest   Tel. (1) 111.60.61
                             Fax: (1) 302.50.35
E-mail: euroinfo@mail.matav.hu
Internet: http://www.euroinfo.hu//index.html

ICELAND – ISLANDE
Mál og Menning
Laugavegi 18, Pósthólf 392
121 Reykjavik   Tel. (1) 552.4240
                             Fax: (1) 562.3523

INDIA – INDE
Oxford Book and Stationery Co.
Scindia House
New Delhi 110001   Tel. (11) 331.5896/5308
                        Fax: (11) 332.2639
E-mail: oxford.publ@axcess.net.in

17 Park Street
Calcutta 700016   Tel. 240832

INDONESIA – INDONÉSIE
Pdii-Lipi
P.O. Box 4298
Jakarta 12042   Tel. (21) 573.34.67
                             Fax: (21) 573.34.67

IRELAND – IRLANDE
Government Supplies Agency
Publications Section
4/5 Harcourt Road
Dublin 2   Tel. 661.31.11
                             Fax: 475.27.60

ISRAEL – ISRAËL
Praedicta
5 Shatner Street
P.O. Box 34030
Jerusalem 91430   Tel. (2) 652.84.90/1/2
                             Fax: (2) 652.84.93

R.O.Y. International
P.O. Box 13056
Tel Aviv 61130   Tel. (3) 546 1423
                             Fax: (3) 546 1442
E-mail: royil@netvision.net.il

Palestinian Authority/Middle East:
INDEX Information Services
P.O.B. 19502
Jerusalem   Tel. (2) 627.16.34
                             Fax: (2) 627.12.19

ITALY – ITALIE
Libreria Commissionaria Sansoni
Via Duca di Calabria, 1/1
50125 Firenze   Tel. (055) 64.54.15
                             Fax: (055) 64.12.57
E-mail: licosa@ftbcc.it

Via Bartolini 29
20155 Milano   Tel. (02) 36.50.83

Editrice e Libreria Herder
Piazza Montecitorio 120
00186 Roma   Tel. 679.46.28
                             Fax: 678.47.51

Libreria Hoepli
Via Hoepli 5
20121 Milano   Tel. (02) 86.54.46
                             Fax: (02) 805.28.86

Libreria Scientifica
Dott. Lucio de Biasio 'Aeiou'
Via Coronelli, 6
20146 Milano   Tel. (02) 48.95.45.52
                        Fax: (02) 48.95.45.48

JAPAN – JAPON
OECD Tokyo Centre
Landic Akasaka Building
2-3-4 Akasaka, Minato-ku
Tokyo 107   Tel. (81.3) 3586.2016
                        Fax: (81.3) 3584.7929

KOREA – CORÉE
Kyobo Book Centre Co. Ltd.
P.O. Box 1658, Kwang Hwa Moon
Seoul   Tel. 730.78.91
                        Fax: 735.00.30

MALAYSIA – MALAISIE
University of Malaya Bookshop
University of Malaya
P.O. Box 1127, Jalan Pantai Baru
59700 Kuala Lumpur
Malaysia   Tel. 756.5000/756.5425
                        Fax: 756.3246

MEXICO – MEXIQUE
OECD Mexico Centre
Edificio INFOTEC
Av. San Fernando no. 37
Col. Toriello Guerra
Tlalpan C.P. 14050
Mexico D.F.   Tel. (525) 528.10.38
                        Fax: (525) 606.13.07
E-mail: ocde@rtn.net.mx

NETHERLANDS – PAYS-BAS
SDU Uitgeverij Plantijnstraat
Externe Fondsen
Postbus 20014
2500 EA's-Gravenhage   Tel. (070) 37.89.880
Voor bestellingen: Fax: (070) 34.75.778

Subscription Agency/   Agence d'abonnements :
SWETS & ZEITLINGER BV
Heereweg 347B
P.O. Box 830
2160 SZ Lisse   Tel. 252.435.111
                        Fax: 252.415.888

**NEW ZEALAND –
NOUVELLE-ZÉLANDE**
GPLegislation Services
P.O. Box 12418
Thorndon, Wellington   Tel. (04) 496.5655
                        Fax: (04) 496.5698

NORWAY – NORVÈGE
NIC INFO A/S
Ostensjoveien 18
P.O. Box 6512 Etterstad
0606 Oslo   Tel. (22) 97.45.00
                        Fax: (22) 97.45.45

PAKISTAN
Mirza Book Agency
65 Shahrah Quaid-E-Azam
Lahore 54000   Tel. (42) 735.36.01
                        Fax: (42) 576.37.14

PHILIPPINE – PHILIPPINES
International Booksource Center Inc.
Rm 179/920 Cityland 10 Condo Tower 2
HV dela Costa Ext cor Valero St.
Makati Metro Manila   Tel. (632) 817 9676
                        Fax: (632) 817 1741

POLAND – POLOGNE
Ars Polona
00-950 Warszawa
Krakowskie Prezdmiescie 7   Tel. (22) 264760
                            Fax: (22) 265334

PORTUGAL
Livraria Portugal
Rua do Carmo 70-74
Apart. 2681
1200 Lisboa   Tel. (01) 347.49.82/5
                        Fax: (01) 347.02.64

SINGAPORE – SINGAPOUR
Ashgate Publishing
Asia Pacific Pte. Ltd
Golden Wheel Building, 04-03
41, Kallang Pudding Road
Singapore 349316   Tel. 741.5166
                        Fax: 742.9356

SPAIN – ESPAGNE
Mundi-Prensa Libros S.A.
Castelló 37, Apartado 1223
Madrid 28001   Tel. (91) 431.33.99
                        Fax: (91) 575.39.98
E-mail: mundiprensa@tsai.es
Internet: http://www.mundiprensa.es

Mundi-Prensa Barcelona
Consell de Cent No. 391
08009 – Barcelona   Tel. (93) 488.34.92
                        Fax: (93) 487.76.59

Libreria de la Generalitat
Palau Moja
Rambla dels Estudis, 118
08002 – Barcelona
             (Suscripciones) Tel. (93) 318.80.12
             (Publicaciones) Tel. (93) 302.67.23
                        Fax: (93) 412.18.54

SRI LANKA
Centre for Policy Research
c/o Colombo Agencies Ltd.
No. 300-304, Galle Road
Colombo 3   Tel. (1) 574240, 573551-2
                        Fax: (1) 575394, 510711

SWEDEN – SUÈDE
CE Fritzes AB
S–106 47 Stockholm   Tel. (08) 690.90.90
                        Fax: (08) 20.50.21

For electronic publications only/
Publications électroniques seulement
STATISTICS SWEDEN
Informationsservice
S-115 81 Stockholm   Tel. 8 783 5066
                        Fax: 8 783 4045

Subscription Agency/Agence d'abonnements :
Wennergren-Williams Info AB
P.O. Box 1305
171 25 Solna   Tel. (08) 705.97.50
                        Fax: (08) 27.00.71

Liber distribution
Internatinal organizations
Fagerstagatan 21
S-163 52 Spanga

SWITZERLAND – SUISSE
Maditec S.A. (Books and Periodicals/Livres
et périodiques)
Chemin des Palettes 4
Case postale 266
1020 Renens VD 1   Tel. (021) 635.08.65
                        Fax: (021) 635.07.80

Librairie Payot S.A.
4, place Pépinet
CP 3212
1002 Lausanne   Tel. (021) 320.25.11
                        Fax: (021) 320.25.14

Librairie Unilivres
6, rue de Candolle
1205 Genève   Tel. (022) 320.26.23
                        Fax: (022) 329.73.18

Subscription Agency/Agence d'abonnements :
Dynapresse Marketing S.A.
38, avenue Vibert
1227 Carouge   Tel. (022) 308.08.70
                        Fax: (022) 308.07.99

See also – Voir aussi :
OECD Bonn Centre
August-Bebel-Allee 6
D-53175 Bonn (Germany)   Tel. (0228) 959.120
                        Fax: (0228) 959.12.17

THAILAND – THAÏLANDE
Suksit Siam Co. Ltd.
113, 115 Fuang Nakhon Rd.
Opp. Wat Rajbopith
Bangkok 10200   Tel. (662) 225.9531/2
                        Fax: (662) 222.5188

**TRINIDAD & TOBAGO, CARIBBEAN
TRINITÉ-ET-TOBAGO, CARAÏBES**
Systematics Studies Limited
9 Watts Street
Curepe
Trinidad & Tobago, W.I.   Tel. (1809) 645.3475
                          Fax: (1809) 662.5654
E-mail: tobe@trinidad.net

TUNISIA – TUNISIE
Grande Librairie Spécialisée
Fendri Ali
Avenue Haffouz Imm El-Intilaka
Bloc B 1 Sfax 3000   Tel. (216-4) 296 855
                        Fax: (216-4) 298.270

TURKEY – TURQUIE
Kültür Yayinlari Is-Türk Ltd.
Atatürk Bulvari No. 191/Kat 13
06684 Kavaklidere/Ankara
                  Tel. (312) 428.11.40 Ext. 2458
                        Fax : (312) 417.24.90
Dolmabahce Cad. No. 29
Besiktas/Istanbul   Tel. (212) 260 7188

UNITED KINGDOM – ROYAUME-UNI
The Stationery Office Ltd.
Postal orders only:
P.O. Box 276, London SW8 5DT
Gen. enquiries   Tel. (171) 873 0011
                        Fax: (171) 873 8463

The Stationery Office Ltd.
Postal orders only:
49 High Holborn, London WC1V 6HB
Branches at: Belfast, Birmingham, Bristol,
Edinburgh, Manchester

UNITED STATES – ÉTATS-UNIS
OECD Washington Center
2001 L Street N.W., Suite 650
Washington, D.C. 20036-4922 Tel. (202) 785.6323
                        Fax: (202) 785.0350
Internet: washcont@oecd.org

Subscriptions to OECD periodicals may also be
placed through main subscription agencies.

Les abonnements aux publications périodiques de
l'OCDE peuvent être souscrits auprès des
principales agences d'abonnement.

Orders and inquiries from countries where Distribu-
tors have not yet been appointed should be sent to:
OECD Publications, 2, rue André-Pascal, 75775
Paris Cedex 16, France.

Les commandes provenant de pays où l'OCDE n'a
pas encore désigné de distributeur peuvent être
adressées aux Éditions de l'OCDE, 2, rue André-
Pascal, 75775 Paris Cedex 16, France.

12-1996